関東学院大学経済学会叢書

Flying Smart with Low-Cost Carriers in Japan:
A Numerical Analysis of Innovative Business Strategies in the Aviation Industry

Sayaka SHIOTANI

塩谷さやか [著]

HAKUTO-SHOBO

東京 白桃書房 神田

Flying Smart with Low-Cost Carriers in Japan:
A Numerical Analysis of Innovative Business Strategies in the Aviation Industry

ISBN 978-4-561-76217-1

Published by Hakuto-Shobo Publishing Company, Japan
5-1-15, Sotokanda, Chiyoda-ku, Tokyo, Japan
Zip 101-0021
www.hakutou.co.jp

First Published in 2017

© Sayaka Shiotani 2017
All rights reserved
Printed in Japan

No part of this book may be reproduced, scanned, stored, or distributed in any printed, electronic form or by any means without prior written permission of both the copyright owner and the publisher of this book. Please do not participate or encourage piracy of copyrighted materials in violation of the author's rights. Purchase only authorized editions.

The greatest care has been taken in this book. However, no responsibility can be taken by the publisher or the author for the accuracy of the information presented.

Preface

The goal of this book is to define the requirements for establishing Low-Cost Carriers (LCCs) in Japan, both from management and aviation policy standpoints. This study discusses factors related to the success of LCCs outside of Japan, and analyzes characteristics regarding the stagnancy of LCCs in Japan. Analytical tools such as financial simulation for profitability analysis using the corporate model, and the Monte Carlo method for risk analysis are applied. Based on simulation results, successful establishment factors of LCCs in Japan from a management perspective, as well as proposals on reform related to aviation policies that are restricting management policies, will be presented.

The aviation industry has been experiencing harsh business circumstances provoked by intense competitive surroundings. This is a result of deregulation as well as external factors such as international terrorist atacks, steep rise in oil prices, and the epidemic. With the global deregulation movement in the airline industry since the 1980s, LCCs have established their businesses very rapidly. Following this global trend, the Legacy Carriers (LCs) are falling into financial difficulty, whilst LCCs are highly active and successful in markets of North America, Europe, and Asia except Japan.

Firstly, this book focuses on the analysis of critical successful factors in the foreign market. Then, it examines the conditions and business environmental issues that make the foreign LCC business model ineffective in the Japanese market. Moreover, a successful LCC business model is introduced and verified using a variety of simulations, including financial simulation using the corporate model, and risk analysis using the Monte Carlo method.

These two sets of analytical results are put together then applied to other areas such as policy making, regulations, and market structural changes. Furthermore, the book

Preface

comes up with six critical points for the management policies of new airline companies: (1) promotion of higher productivity and lower cost, (2) appropriate airfare and the fare structures, (3) appropriate route selections and the number of flights, (4) proactive utilization of secondary airports, (5) penetration of the air cargo market, and (6) availability of sufficient funds for supporting the preparation and establishment of a new entity. Both Skymark Airlines and Peach Aviation followed the points mentioned above except (5), and delivered different results, which will be further discussed in Chapter 6 and 8.

The government has always tightened the regulation of the Japanese aviation industry. In order to consider and unfold the LCC business establishment conditions, an analysis of the government policy is essential. By integrating the results of the policy analysis and simulation analysis, this research concludes that the following reforms are necessary from the perspectives of the aviation policy and the promotion of competition, in order to eliminate the regulatory and the market's structural factors that restrict the management freedom of the new airlines: (1) switch the market intervention method on market structural restrictions from proactive to reactive, (2) completely eliminate the government control over supply and demand adjustments in both domestic and international routes, and restriction on the foreign capital cabotage, and (3) establish new airport policies for promoting more active use of secondary airports. Particularly, (1) and (2) could also be applied to LCs, which is mentioned in Chapter 7. Moreover, the topic regarding (3), the privatization of airports and the effect on LCCs, are discussed in Chapter 5.

Although this may not be a subject of an empirical analysis, the new airlines have shown that the character of the top management plays a vital role. It is important that the top executive has passion, a cool-head, and a thorough analytical mindset to become an innovator himself or herself. By presenting the revitalization of the Japanese aviation market, and the innovations that are necessary for the LCCs in Japan through this book, it would be very fortunate, if the new airlines in Japan continue to create innovations through daring management methods and make great strides in the future.

Acknowledgement

When I was working as an international flight attendant on an Legacy-Carrier, before moving on to my academic career, I witnessed both the rise of LCCs and the fall of LCs in the international aviation market. It was not until the end of the 1990s that the two airlines entered the domestic aviation market in Japan. In contrast to LCCs abroad, LCCs in Japan were facing financial troubles. There were not many aviation companies entering the domestic market, which caused a negative effect. On the other hand, this was a beneficial situation for people, working at a major airline company, and therefore had less competition to worry about. As a result, this situation got me deeply fascinated in the stagnancy of Japanese LCCs when I began my career as an academic researcher, having been given the opportunity to study abroad and work at an airline company in New York. After leaving the airline company in 2006, I decided to further pursue my research on the stagnancy of LCCs at Waseda University. My interest in this field was further deepened by the financial engineering approach regarding the analysis of stagnancy causes of LCCs, which was introduced by an emeritus professor Masaki Ohta of Waseda University. He was an expert both in aeronautics and financial engineering. Ultimately, without this encounter, I would not have been able to complete my research for my doctoral thesis and deepen my knowledge on the subject.

In pursuit of my academic goal, however, I have become aware of the fact that businesses in the aviation industry can hardly solve their issues just by management policies, due to strict regulations. Furthermore, the issues which lie in the aviation policy must be incorporated. Whilst continuing with my research, I have began to acknowledge the importance of further focusing on this perspective. In this book I have, to the best of my abilities, conducted a comprehensive research, including proposals on the reform of aviation policies.

Acknowledgement

This book reflects my previous doctoral thesis explaining the current progression of LCCs overseas and Japan's relative stagnancy in LCCs. This thesis led to the publication of *Shinki kokugaisha jigyoseiritsu no kenkyu: Nippon ni okeru business model to koku seisaku no kakushin* [*Key factors for the success of a low-cost carriers in Japan: Innovation in business models & aviation policy*] (2008, Chuokeizai-sha, written in Japanese) which resulted in receiving my doctor's degree in 2008. This book also highlights the newly improved culmination of my research at Massachusetts Institute of Technology (MIT), whilst I was achieving the Master of Science in Management of Technology (MOT) degree of Massachusetts Institute of Technology Sloan School of Management Sloan Fellows Program in Innovation and Global Leadership. In this research, I have compensated the incomplete methods and upgraded their qualities. Finally, I have then collected my research into one and put it into writing.

In this new book, I have updated the latest financial issues and risk analysis, using financial simulation that is based on newly improved corporate models and the Monte Carlo method. This book reflects the current situation of LCCs, updates inputs for models, and incorporates competition status into the model. In addition, I have mentioned the necessary reforms that Japan must make when it comes to management regulations that are causing a strain on further aviation policies. The recent cases of Skymark Airlines, Japan Airlines, and Peach Aviation as well as the management of airports are used to explain and support the discussion of the need for such reforms. Moreover, although network expansion and capital cost of LCCs will grow over the years, it is vital to understand how LCCs can manage the never-ending decline in cost in response to major aviation companies.

The positive aspects of this research are: (1) it is the first academic research that focuses on LCCs in Japan by applying a management administration approach as an analytical tool, (2) it provides a business approach on the aviation industry that observes more degree of freedom in management by deregulation, and (3) it is the first research that applies financial simulations by incorporating financial simulation using the corporate model and risk analysis using the Monte Carlo method. Moreover, the analysis methods of this research are comprehensive in the way that it focuses on simulation analysis as a core aspect, along with other sources such as papers, articles, economic analyses, and interviews with various professionals, including

Acknowledgement

airline company personnel and policy makers in and outside of Japan.

Researches regarding foreign LCC markets exist, but not paticularly about the situation in Japan due to the short history of Japanese LCCs. Previously published literatures only include autobiographies written by managers and newspaper articles. This book examines LCCs from an academic, business, and economic point of view.

Needless to say, I could not have completed this book without support and guidance from everybody who has been involved in my pursuit of achieving my academic goals. When it came to publishing the book as well, the financial supporters of Kanto Gakuin University, and Eiichiro Oya, the CEO, of Hakuto-Shobo Publishing Company have helped me a great deal.

First and foremost, I would like to show my deepest appreciation to an emeritus professor Ohta, a financial engineering professor at Waseda University, who has been my advisor whilst studying for my master and doctoral programs. He has continuously enlightened me on the aviation industry from an econometric standpoint, even after retirement. His insights and inputs have helped me complete this book. I would also like to mention Hisashi Owada, an emeritus professor of Waseda University, for the tremendous help. He is an international law professor who has guided me with research when I was facing various obstacles. He also gave me useful comments and important advice on research while writing this book.

I am greatly indebted to J. F. Oberlin University for giving me the opportunity to study at the MIT Sloan Fellows Program in Innovation and Global Leadership for 18 months, and for providing me with such superb educational experience.

I would like to express my deepest gratitude to my thesis advisor, and statistics professor, Arnold I. Barnett of MIT Sloan School of Management. His encouraging support and wisdom has guided me to know exactly what I should be aiming for. He has broadened my perspective and expanded my network for future businesses in marketing. Moreover, I would like to give my appreciation to Ezra F. Vogel, an international politics professor at Harvard University. He has enlightened me with exceptional insights on exquisite Japanese craftsmanship. Both Barnett and Vogel have helped me greatly with this research, and hoping that I did them justice in reflecting upon their advice and suggestions regarding this book.

Moreover, I would like to say thank you to all my friends from my time at Boston, and colleagues of MIT Sloan School of Management, who have encouraged me, have given me the opportunity to tackle issues in life, and provided me with a bigger picture for the future. They have shared their expertise and helped me get through one of the toughest, but most fruitful times of my life. I was truly honored to have met them and have cherished every moment of our short time together. They are still my precious friends and always direct me in the right path.

I need to include a special note of thanks to Harvard University Asia Center. My experience as a visiting associate professor there, with all the scholars, helped me enrich my research on business in Asian countries and the aviation industry.

Furthermore, I am obliged to the professors at the College of Economics, from Kanto Gakuin University. They have provided me with certain opportunities and support in order to help me complete this book. I would particularly wish to thank the following people: Fumio Tanaka, the dean of the College of Economics, and Seiji Tsuji, the department chairperson of Business Administration. They have both given me practical advice and have encouraged me as I completed my work.

I cannot forget to appreciate the help I have received from the students and professors of Waseda University, especially those at the School of International Liberal Studies, where I have been lecturing part-time. They have been one of the most inspiring and supportive people, gracing me with important advice and helping me throughout my journey. I would not have been able to come this far if it was not for the experience of getting to know them all.

Additionally, I am fortunate to have had my business experience at Japan Airlines, Co. (JAL), Ltd., having worked there for more than 10 years. This company gave me the opportunity to go study abroad as an employee. It allowed me to build my business experience as a flight attendant, which has become the backbone for my area of research. I am sincerely thankful to them and hoping that my research outcome will both contribute to the vitalization of the Japanese aviation market and benefit my former supervisors and colleagues in JAL.

Finally, I would like to thank my family, who have supported me endlessly no matter what. I have gone through sleepless nights during my studies under the MIT Sloan Fellows Program, and whilst writing this book, my family has constantly thought about my health, and cared about my well-being throughout my toughest times. My mother Mitsuko, father Yasuichi, brother Eiji, and my late grandmother Hiroko have especially looked after me, encouraged me, and supported me in every way they could.

Every useful insight I have presented in this research is all thanks to the people above. Without their heartwarming support and acknowledgement, it would have been impossible for me to finish this book. I have mentioned them in this acknowledgement, as a token of my gratitude.

Sayaka SHIOTANI

塩谷 さやか

Feb 14, 2017

About the Author

Sayaka SHIOTANI, Ph.D.

Associate Professor of Economics at Kanto Gakuin University in Japan.

Dr. Shiotani is a recognized figure who researches Low-Cost Carrier businesses. After her career at Japan Airlines Co., Ltd. (JAL) whilst receiving a bachelor degree from Fordham University in New York with honors, as well as an MBA and a doctor's degree from Waseda University, she worked as an associate professor at J. F. Oberlin University and went on to pursue her academic goals at the Massachusetts Institute of Technology Sloan School of Management Sloan Fellows Program, Class of 2013. She has also been a visiting scholar at Harvard University Asia Center. She now teaches as a part-time lecturer at the School of International Liberal Studies, Waseda University.

Her first book, *Shinki kokugaisha jigyoseiritsu no kenkyu: Nippon ni okeru business model to koku seisaku no kakushin* [*Key factors for the success of a low-cost carriers in Japan: Innovation in business models & aviation policy*] (Chuokeizai-sha, 2008) won many awards: the Academic Award from the Japan Society of Logistics and Shipping Economics (2008), the Japan Society of Information and Management (2009), the Japan Society of Public Unity Economy (2009), and Sumita Award for Promoting Aviation Study from Transport Reseach Foundation (2009).

Dr. Shiotani analyzes LCCs and airport management through her academic viewpoint and her business experience as an international flight attendant at JAL, and presents policy proposals to revitalize the aviation industry. Her focus includes tourism, aviation, service management, and information and communication both from economic and management perspectives. Moreover, she has recently been spreading her knowledge regarding regional revitalization. She is also a certified hospitality advisor at many schools and companies. During her free time, she uses her expertise as a sommelier and enjoys wine.

Major works:
As a single author: *Shinki kokugaisha jigyoseiritsu no kenkyu: Nippon ni okeru business model to koku seisaku no kakushin* [*Key factors for the success of a low-cost carriers in Japan: Innovation in business models & aviation policy*] (Chuokeizai-sha, 2008). Fundamental challenges for inbound tourism promotion: Toward creating a more attractive country with more openness and through deregulation? *Journal of Japan Foundation for International Tourism*, *12*, (2005); Real option ho ni yoru shinki kokurosen kaisetsu koka no hyoka: Tei juyo, ko risk rosen kaisetsu model no kochiku [Evaluating an investment decision to expand new air routes for an airline company based on the real option approach]. *Journal of Public Utility Economics*, *56*(4), (2005); Mineika ni mukete no kuko kigyokachi suikei to kaikaku subeki seidoteki yoin: EV/EBITDA ho ni yoru shisan to kigyokachi jitsugenka no tameno gutaiteki joken [Methods for estimating the value of airports toward privatization and several aspects for structural reform: The assessment based on EV/EBITDA method and specific conditions for realizing the company value]. *Journal of Japan Society of Logistics and Shipping Economics*, *39*, (2005); Cable television jigyo ni okeru koikika / kibo kakudaisaku no jissho bunseki oyobi koutekishiensaku kaikaku no kihonteki hokosei: Seisan kansu ni yoru kibo no keizaisei no sokutei [An examination of the Area-Widening and expansion strategy of the cable television (CATV) industry based on a production functions analysis to estimate its economy of scale and a study of reform of public subsidy policies to the CATV industry]. *Journal of Public Utility Economics*, *58*(1), (2006); Corporate Model ni yoru shinki kamotsu kokugaisha no seiritsu yoken no kenkyu: Monte Carlo ho ni yoru risk bunseki wo fukumete [Feasibility study on a newly entrant freight airline by a corporate-model simulation: With its risk assessment based on the Monte Carlo approach]. *Journal of Japan Logistics Society*, *14*, (2006); Gekika suru kyosoka ni okeru kokugaisha no kokyaku (CS) senryaku: Japan Airlines no case [Airlines' customer satisfaction (CS) strategy in an increasingly competitive environment: The case of Japan Airlines]. *Hospitarity*, *17*, (2010); Koku yusojigyo no kikohendo taisaku to global sector approach: Post Kyoto giteisho he muketa jishuteki torikumi no kanosei [Air transportation industries' efforts to address climate change issues and the global sector approach: Possible voluntary measures toward a Post-Kyoto protocol era]. *Journal of Japan Foundation for International Tourism*, *18*, (2011); Nippon no kuko keiei ni okeru kokusaika, mineika no hitsuyosei [A comparison of Japanese airport management with global trends]. *Journal of Japan Foundation for International Tourism*, *21*, (2014); Lead user methodology for innovation : A case study of Nissin Foods' Cup Noodles. *International Journal of Japan Academic Society of Hospitality Management*, *3*(1), (2015); Sharing economy: Shinrai kankei ni yoru

atarashii platform no sokushin [Sharing economy: Platform advancement for trust systemization]. *Journal of Japan Foundation for International Tourism*, 24, (2017); Targeting high end clients in international business expansion: Hospitality management as a part of foreign private banking strategy in domestic markets. *International Journal of Japan Academic Society of Hospitality Management*, 4(1), (2017); Customized business model for regional revitalization support: Innovative banking strategy for sustainable entrepreneurship. *International Journal of Japan Academic Society of Hospitality Management*, 4(1), (2017).

As a joint author: *Gendai no koku yusojigyo* [*Contemporary air transportation business*] (Doyukan, 2007); *Kanko rikkoku wo sasaeru koku yusojigyo* [*The Air transportation business that supports the tourism nation industry*] (Doyukan, 2010); *Kuko keiei: Mineika to kokusaika* [*Managing airports: An international perspective*] (Translated into Japanese with a concise summary, additional personal reviews, and analysis inserted.) (Chuokeizai-sha, 2010).
Keiei kyoiku jiten [*Educational dictionary of business management*] (Gakubunsha, 2006); *Kankogaku dai jiten* [*Dictionary of tourism*] (Kirakusha, 2007); *Umi to sora no minato dai jiten* [*Dictionary of ports and airports*] (Seizando-shoten, 2011); *Kotsu keizai handbook* [*The handbook of transportation economics*] (Hakuto-shobo, 2011).
"Kanko rikkoku" heno gimon: Inbound kanko seisaku to kanren kotsu seisaku ni okeru open ka no hitsuyosei [Is the "Visit Japan" campaign relevant?: Openness and deregulation are needed to promote Japan's inbound tourism]. *The Japan Society of Transportation Economics*, 49, (2005); Kaimono rejibukuro no yusyo kisei seido no arikata [Evaluation of price-incentive mearures to reduce plastic shopping bags]. *Journal of Public Utility Economics*, 58(2), (2006).

In addition to the works above, she has also written a great number of articles.

CONTENTS

Preface

Acknowledgement

About the Author

CHAPTER 1
Objective and Contribution 1
1 Objective and Awareness of Issues 2
  1. Background: The Development of the Airline Industry and Emergence of Low-Cost Carriers (LCCs) 2
  2. Awareness of Issues 3
2 Existing Researches in the Area and Contributions of This Research 4
  1. Existing Researches 4
  2. Contributions of This Research 6

CHAPTER 2
Recent Low-Cost Carriers (LCCs) of the World and Growth Factor Analysis 9
Introduction 10
1 LCCs of the United States 13
  1. Development of LCCs in the American Aviation Market 13
  2. Major LCCs in the United States 17
2 European LCCs 30
  1. Development of LCCs in the European Aviation Market 30
  2. Major LCCs in Europe 31
3 Asian LCCs 37
  1. Development of LCCs in the Asian Aviation Market 37
  2. Major LCCs in Asia 38

3. Alliance of LCCs in Asia: Promoting Global Competition *44*
- **4 Characteristics of LCCs and Common Factors in the Market Worldwide** *47*
  1. Deregulation of the Industry *47*
  2. Common Factors of Business Models *49*
  3. Operational Resources and Availability of Funds *54*
- **Conclusion: Summary of Common Factors of Successful LCCs** *55*

CHAPTER 3
Current Japanese Low-Cost Carriers (LCCs) and Stagnancy Factor Analysis ... *57*

Introduction *58*

- **1 Current Status of LCCs in Japan** *59*
  1. History of LCCs Prior to New Entry *59*
  2. Current Status of LCCs *61*
  3. Summary of Study of Factors Hindering Development of LCCs *90*
- **2 Analysis of Problems of Management Policy** *91*
  1. Cost Structure Problem *92*
  2. Competition Problem Between LCCs and LCs *96*
  3. Problem of Unfocused Customer Target and Airfare Structure *98*
  4. Problem of Route Structure *100*
  5. Inconvenient Operations *100*
  6. Concentrated Use of Hub Airports *101*
  7. Lack of Business Policies and Corporate Identity (CI) *102*
  8. Dependence on Public Funds *103*
  9. Summary for Institutional Problem Studies *103*
- **3 Analysis of Problems of Aviation Policy** *104*
  1. History of Aviation Deregulation in Japan and Western Countries *105*
  2. Significance and Viability of Deregulation and Promotion for Competition *111*
  3. Contestability of the Air Transport Market and Fare Competition *114*
  4. Problems of Current Aviation Policy and Their Impacts on LCCs *118*
- **Conclusion: Summary for Simulation Analysis** *135*

CHAPTER 4
Identifying the Success Factors Through Simulations for New LCCs 139

Introduction   *140*

1   Assumption of the Business Model   *141*
  1. Hub Airports   *141*
  2. Route Selections   *142*
  3. Target Customers, Operations, and Aircraft Type   *143*
  4. Airfare   *144*
  5. Composition of Aircraft and Operation Rate   *145*
  6. Sales and In-Flight Service Cost   *145*
  7. Personnel and Maintenance Cost   *145*
  8. Operations Size at Launch and Financing   *146*
  9. The Requirements for the New LCC Business Model   *147*

2   Structuring of Corporate Model, Case of Simulation and Input Data   *148*
  1. Structure of Corporate Model, Calculation Process and Classification of Input Data   *148*
  2. Simulation Case and Input Data   *154*

3   Results of Financial Simulation by Using the Corporate Model   *170*
  1. Outline of Case Study and Cumulative Ordinary Profit   *170*
  2. Simulation Results of Financial Statement   *171*
  3. Simulation Results of Major Management Index   *178*

4   Risk Analysis by Monte Carlo Simulation   *184*
  1. Steps of Risk Analysis   *184*
  2. Preconditions of Monte Carlo Simulation   *186*
  3. Calculation Result of Monte Carlo Simulation   *188*
  4. Results of Risk Analysis by Setting Cut-off Rate   *195*

5   Comprehensive Consideration of Results of Simulation   *202*
  1. Examination of Each Simulation Case   *202*
  2. Consideration by Management Factor   *203*
  3. Desirable Management Policy of LCCs   *212*

Conclusion: Meanings Behind the Analysis Results and Future Challenges of Methods *213*
1. Suggestion for Successful Business Models *213*
2. Contribution of Analysis Methods and Future Challenges *215*

CHAPTER 5
Reforming Airport Management in Japan: Effective Methods and the Necessity of Privatization *217*

Introduction *218*

1 Pioneers of Airport Privatization *219*
1. Cases in the U.K. and Australia *219*
2. Possibilities of Privatization in Local Airports *220*

2 Merit of Airport Privatization *222*
1. Expected Benefits *222*
2. Airport Regulation Reform and Consistent Privatization *225*
3. Integration of Aviation and Non-Aviation Businesses *226*
4. Integrated Management of Commercial Facilities and Aviation Facilities *228*
5. Multiple Airports in the Same Metropolitan Area Should Compete with Each Other *229*
6. Prospective Development of the Aviation Service Industry in Airports *233*

3 Current Situation of Privatization in Japanese Airports *235*
1. Case of Privatization *235*
2. Future Issues Concerning the Method for Selecting Airport Concessions in Japan *238*
3. Initiatives to Link Infrastructure Privatization to Regional Revitalization *240*

Conclusion *241*
1. Privatization Is Liberalization for Business Management *242*
2. Privatization Without Regulations Is Impossible *243*

Contents

CHAPTER 6

Skymark Airlines' Bankruptcy and Recovery: The Achievements and Misdeeds of Authoritarian Management of an "Independent LCC" 245

Introduction *246*

1 The Pros and Cons of Authoritarian Management *247*
 1. Moving Forward with Motivated Employees *248*
 2. The Conflict Between ANAHD Affecting the Process of Civil Rehabilitation *250*

2 Series of Events that Led to the Bankruptcy of the Third-Force Airline *252*
 1. Financial Condition of Skymark Airlines Prior to the Bankruptcy *254*
 2. Cash on Hand Decreased Despite Good Business Results *255*

3 As a Result of the All-Out War After the Bankruptcy, "Skymark Airlines' Proposal" Passed *258*
 1. The Key to Business Reconstruction Is the Negotiation to Reduce the Debt *260*
 2. The Opportunity and Risk ANAHD Obtained in Exchange for Skymark Airlines *262*

4 Major Issues of the Aviation Policy Regarding Skymark Airlines' Rehabilitation *267*
 1. Fair Allocation Method for the Arrival and Departure Slots *267*
 2. Promoting the Market Competition Without the Government's Lead *270*
 3. Impact of Skymark Airlines' Bankruptcy on Regional Airports *271*

5 Start of a New Organization: Business Rehabilitation by the Three Forces *272*
 1. Multitude of Issues for the New Skymark Airlines' Independence *274*
 2. The Essence of the New Skymark Airlines' Support Is in Its Realization *275*
 3. Drastic Change of LCCs' Competitive Environment *276*

Conclusion *277*

CHAPTER 7

Japan Airlines: The Bankruptcy and Management Re-Establishment of a "Domesticated LC" 279

Introduction: From the Bankruptcy to the Public Relisting *280*

1 Overview of the Business Restructuring Plan of JAL *282*
 1. Evaluation of the Business Restructuring Plan *283*

2. Assessment of the Rehabilitation Method   *290*
2 **Protective Aviation Policies Indirectly Affecting Japanese Airlines**   *294*
   1. Consequences of Government and Citizens' Intervention   *295*
   2. Let JAL Keep Its Own Sovereignty   *298*
3 **Increasing the Effective Use of Assets and Breaking Through the "Slowdown"**   *299*
Conclusion: A New Era of Competition in the Global Aviation Market   *303*
   1. The Proper Form of Corporate Reorganization   *303*
   2. JAL's Future in the Aviation Market   *305*

CHAPTER 8
Peach Aviation: ANAHD's Successful Affiliated Japanized LCC *307*

Introduction   *308*
1 Overview of Peach Aviation   *308*
   1. Peach Aviation's Performance Review and Success Factors   *308*
   2. Sharp Route Expansion   *309*
   3. The Acquisition of Knowledgeable and Superior Employees   *310*
   4. Raising Funds for the Establishment   *314*
   5. Establishing and Spreading the Brand Concept of Peach Aviation   *315*
2 Development and Innovation of Peach Aviation   *319*
   1. Coexistence of Low-Cost and High-Quality   *320*
   2. Installation of the Terminal for the Exclusive Use of LCCs   *320*
   3. Aircraft Procurement Method and Establishment of Operation System   *321*
   4. Securing Punctuality and Safety with Innovative Technologies   *322*
3 Analyzing the Factors of Rapid Growth and Successful Performance   *323*
   1. Room for Improvement and Growth in the Mature Aviation Market   *324*
   2. Sustainable Growth and Evolution of Peach Aviation   *325*
Conclusion: The Succesful Japanization of an LCC   *327*

CHAPTER 9
Conclusion and Future Challenges 331

Introduction *332*

1 Conclusion of Management Policy *332*
  1. Building Low-Cost Structures *332*
  2. Setting up Appropriate Fare Levels and Fare Structures *334*
  3. Setting of Route Structure and Number of Flights *335*
  4. Proactive Use of Secondary Airports *336*
  5. Securing Sufficient Funds to Prepare for Launch and Early Stages of Operations *337*
  6. The Key Factors for a Successful LCC Management Policy *338*

2 The New LCC Business Model Suitable for LCCs' Endurance in Japan *339*
  1. Similarities and Differences in Strategy Between Skymark Airlines and the New LCC Business Model *339*
  2. The Comparison Between the Simulation and Skymark Airlines *341*

3 Conclusion of Aviation Policy *343*
  1. Abolishment of Restrictions on Market Structures and Measures to Be Taken *343*
  2. Complete Abolishment of Control over Supply and Demand Adjustment and Foreign Capital Restrictions *344*
  3. Promoting Proactive Use of Secondary Airports and Privatization of Airports *346*
  4. Significance of Skymark Airlines' Entry in the Market *347*
  5. The Requirements for a Suitable Aviation Policy for LCCs *349*

4 Recommendation for Future Challenges *350*

List of Abbreviation and Acronyms

The Structure of the Book and Relationship with Past Research

References

CHAPTER 1

Objective and Contribution

Chapter 1

✈ 1 Objective and Awareness of Issues

The goal of this book is to define the requirements for establishing Low-Cost Carriers (LCCs) in Japan. This study discusses factors related to the success of LCCs outside of Japan, and analyzes the stagnancy of LCCs in Japan. Analytical tools such as financial simulation for profitability analysis using the corporate model and Monte Carlo method for risk analysis are conducted to examine the successful establishment of Japanese LCCs. Based on the results of such simulations, this book explains an understanding of management issues related to LCCs. Moreover, institutional issues such as laws and regulations that restrict the management policies of LCCs are discussed, as suggestions are also made regarding their necessary reforms.

◊ 1. Background: The Development of the Airline Industry and Emergence of Low-Cost Carriers (LCCs)

For a long time, after the end of World War II (WWII), the airline industries worldwide were strictly regulated when it came to entries, prices, and competitions, and were put aside in order to protect the vested interests of large-sized Legacy Carriers (LCs). Since the late 1970s, however, the stream of deregulation, initiated in the U.S., soon spread to Europe and Asia. As clear competition surfaced amidst such situations, airline companies started deploying new business models, such as network expansion using hub and spoke systems, yield management, Computer Reservation Systems (CRS), and internet ticket sales.

Yet, the global aviation industry of the 21st century has faced a number of events that have shifted the management environment rapidly. Increased fear of air travel, an example initiated by the September 11 Attacks, augmented security measures for the boarding process, the rise of liability insurance costs, leisure and business air travel restrictions caused by epidemics such as SARS, the avian flu, and higher fuel costs. This resulted in the number of passengers to decrease due to the slow economy worldwide, and have caused a recession for the aviation industry. LCs, especially in the U.S., suffered a severe decline in their businesses.

While conventional larger airline companies were suffering from economic depression and other related issues, LCCs have noticeably started to get more successful, in contrast. Thus, many of them are now currently expanding their businesses worldwide.

LCCs have traits of combining high-frequency short and middle-distance markets, promoting simple yet effective operations, using a single type of aircraft, and initiating low prices to attract cost-conscious customers. In the U.S., Southwest Airlines, JetBlue Airways, and other LCCs are accounted for 30% of all domestic passengers. Between European countries, Ryanair and easyJet have grown to 200–400 routes each with the LCCs share within Europe reaching 30%. Starting with AirAsia from Malaysia, about 30 LCCs have entered the Asian market from 2000 and the number has steadily grown for more than 10 years.

2. Awareness of Issues

Such global movements shown above is also affecting Japan with gaps on timing and scale. The Japanese aviation industry has been protected under very strict, demanding adjustment regulations until the end of the 21st century. As a result, Japan Airlines (JAL), All Nippon Airways (ANA), and Japan Air System (JAS) have ruled the domestic market. However, as the global movement of deregulation reached Japan in the late 1990s, the new entry of airline companies was finally approved. In 1998, Skymark Airlines and Air Do entered the domestic scheduled airline market, the first time in 50 years.

Nonetheless, compared with LCCs in North America and Asia, Japanese LCCs have been sluggish and the entry rate has been very low despite new measures. That being the case, the question at hand is why are foreign LCCs succeeding, whilst Japanese counterparts are struggling.

This book, with such awareness of issues in mind, examines solutions, namely requirements and conditions that Japanese LCCs have to fulfill in order to have a successful establishment.

2 Existing Researches in the Area and Contributions of This Research

1. Existing Researches

Researches made prior to this book will be introduced again in later chapters. Studies explaining the overall significance of this research will be listed in this section.

Exemplary foreign prior researchs regarding LCCs from an economical perspective are roughly classified into two categories; one is deductive research, which deducts policy implication from abstract models, and the other is inductive research which induces conclusion from actual cases. The former example includes a study by Sinclair(1995), which discusses entries and exits of LCCs in the aviation market. The latter examples include a study by Windle & Dresner(1999) that analyzes the influence of new LCC entries over LC's fare pricing policy, another by Williams(2000) which discusses the deregulation of the aviation market and the LCCs' business development from an empirical point of view, Barzagan(2004) and Reynolds-Feighan(2001), which verifies the differences between LCCs' operations and scheduling, and finally Gudmundsson & Kranenburg(2002), which showcases an empirical analysis on how the entry of LCCs have impacted the airfare in deregulated markets.

The studies which focus on the influence of deregulation by picking up a specific airline is an example which Bennet & Craun(1993) presented. These analyzed factors of deregulation have brought about successful development for Southwest Airlines. Moreover, an example by Morrison(2001), which also discusses the impact of Southwest Airlines on the airline industry, has made a great impression.

In Japan, there are a number of literatures which discuss the LCCs in North American and European markets. Among them, the ones that are especially relevant to the subject taken up in Chapter 2 and 3 are, a research by Murakami(2005a) which examines how new entries of LCCs in the U.S. domestic market in 1998 have affected the LC's airfare policy and transportation capacity, and proved that they will be more beneficial for the society if LCCs differentiate themselves in service and pursue low-cost. Another by Fujimura (2005) which verifies the differences between both LCs and LCCs in terms of operations and pricing strategies.

While most literatures discuss LCCs in the U.S., Barrett (2001) analyzes the conditions of new LCCs entering the European aviation market. Prior researches that focus on Asian LCCs include Hanaoka (2004), which discusses how international and domestic deregulation in Southeast Asia, including Thailand, have made an impact on the new entries of LCCs, and the fact that LCCs in Thailand are accepted by customers for low fares and branding. Another research is presented by O'Connell & Williams (2005), which verifies the potential success of LCC business models of North America and Europe in Asia.

As shown above, most previous researches were analyzed from an economic point of view. There are only a limited number of literatures that focus on LCCs' management strategies from a business management perspective. For example, studies by Lawton (2002) and Freiberg & Freiberg (1998) discuss Southwest Airlines', business management in detail. Sawada (2005), who is the founder of Skymark Airlines, a leading LCC pioneer of Japan, also wrote about his company's business strategies. Moreover, there are a limited number of studies and essays which discuss the stagnancy factors associated with both the management policy and the aviation policy of individual LCCs. For example, Chujo (2005) are some of the only documents that can be read in terms of such contents.

Nevertheless, there is no available research that focuses on the successful establishment factors of an LCC, which examines the success factors of LCCs in North America and Europe, defines stagnancy factors of LCCs in Japan, and then based on such results, analyzes profitability of LCCs through corporate simulation models as well as risk analysis using the Monte Carlo method.

Although much existing researches have presented financial simulations based on corporate simulation models and risk analyses, none of them have been released to the public, as they are strictly for business uses only such as project evaluations and risk analyses.

Chapter 1

◘ 2. Contributions of This Research

The following showcases the book's novelty and characteristics, prior to studies introduced in the previous section.

(1) Research about foreign LCC markets exist, but does not focus mainly on situations in Japan since the history of Japanese LCCs is very short. This book examines LCCs from academic, business, and economic points of view, unlike previously published literatures which only include the managers' autobiography books and newspaper articles.

(2) Analyses using financial simulations consisting of corporate models have not been applied beyond business use. This research combines financial simulations and risk analyses using the Monte Carlo method. Additionally, for the first time, these types of analyses are academically used by the aviation industry.

(3) This research covers not only analysis results, but also detailed business policies, which are necessary for the establishment of profitable LCCs.

(4) Throughout the long history of heavily regulated transportation industries in Japan, the government has defined almost all management policies from pricing to investments. Therefore, there have been very limited roles for business entities to create business strategies. Thus, only a few business analysis tools have been applied. The course of deregulation and the promotion of a more competitive market, business strategies have been playing vital roles in running successful transportation-related businesses. This book presents new business analysis tools and promotes practical results for situations in the aviation industry.

(5) This book presents proposals both on management policies and institutional reform in the aviation market by extracting structural and institutional problems that are restricting implementation of the free management policy, and by analyzing these problems comprehensively from an economic perspective.

(6) The analysis methods of this research is comprehensively designed to focus mainly on simulation analysis, along with other sources such as papers, articles, economic analyses, and interviews with various professionals including airline company personnel and policy makers in and outside of Japan.

(7) This research makes an effort to deepen the depth in discussion regarding

themes relative to this book, by picking up individual case studies, and verifying the reliability of estimated results as well as the versatility of the model.

Finally, there are many questionable issues that should be further taken into account. Those include the constant review of marketing improvement measures and simulation rate, and the discussion of whether or not contestability and unfair regulations should be allowed in aviation markets. It has become important for me to deepen my knowledge and further pursue my research on such aspects.

Although there is room for additional research regarding future challenges presented in the final chapter, I believe this book is the first comprehensive study that discusses the successful establishment factors of LCCs in Japan. It is delivered through a wide scope of analyses, deep considerations of detailed elements, and diversified analytical tools.

CHAPTER 2
Recent Low-Cost Carriers (LCCs) of the World and Growth Factor Analysis

In this chapter, the current state of LCCs in Europe, Asia Pacific, and the U.S. will be described. After verifying each business model, common elements from progressive LCCs as well as the market environment surrounding LCCs are extracted. These will become key factors when analyzing the stagnancy of new Japanese LCCs in the following chapters. The purpose of this book, however, is not about a business analysis of foreign LCCs, but to indicate business and aviation policies essential for new Japanese LCCs' prosperity. Thereby, primary knowledge vital for details to be studied later on will be provided by defining the characteristics of foreign LCCs. This chapter contains revised contents from Shiotani(2008).

 Introduction

The airline industry has been experiencing severe business circumstances since the 1990s, affected by the global economic instability as well as unpredictable, threatening events including the September 11 Attacks, the Iraq War and the SARS epidemic. Due to such circumstances, the global aviation market is showing two major trends.

The first trend is the so-called "global alliance", a partnership between airline companies across borders. Currently, most of the established LCs providing services on international routes have joined the global alliance. In Europe, LCs joined one of the three major partnerships: "Star Alliance", led by Lufthansa, "Oneworld", led by British Airways, and "SkyTeam", led by Air France. These three top groups, through strong partnership, have joined hands with LCs in the U.S. for global network expansion. As for Japan, ANA joined Star Alliance, and JAL, which has not joined an alliance for a long time, finally joined Oneworld in 2007.

The second trend is the expansion of market shared by LCCs. With the development of global alliance, LCs are trying to survive the trend of global deregulation and intense competition, but are falling into financial troubles caused by unforeseen events described above. In contrast, LCCs, which are competing with low cost and fares, are expanding their market share without forming any alliances. LCCs such as Southwest Airlines and Ryanair are competing with LCs by enhancing their low-cost structure, and gaining success in North America, Europe, and Asia.

Nowadays, the development and overview of major LCCs worldwide are as listed in Figure 2-1. Among the LCCs, those such as Southwest Airlines and Ryanair have done better than some of the legacy carriers, in the number of passengers they carry, as shown in Table 2-1.

The purpose of this chapter is to outline the current status of LCCs in the U.S., Europe and Asia by studying their business models and market environment, obtaining common factors in LCCs that continue to grow. Such analysis will examine reasons behind the stagnancy of the new emerging airline companies in Japan, which will be discussed later.

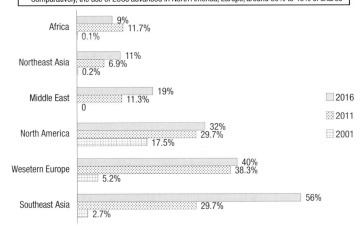

Figure 2-1 LCCs share of the world market

- In Northeast Asia including Japan, the LCC share is around 11%
- Comparatively, the use of LCCs advanced in North America, Europe; around 30% to 40% of shares

Note: Northeast Asia (Japan, South Korea, China, Taiwan, and Mongolia)
Source: Created by the author based on Centre for Aviation's (CAPA) website, June 2016

Table 2-1 Number of worldwide airline passengers

(passengers)

Rankings of Airlines 2015						
International			Domestic			
	Airline	Passenger (thousand)			Airline	Passenger (thousand)
1	Ryanair	86,370		1	Delta Air Lines	129,433
2	easyJet	56,312		2	Southwest Airlines	129,087
3	Lufthansa	48,244				
4	Emirates	47,278		3	China Southern Airlines	100,683
5	British Airways	35,364		4	United Airlines	90,439
6	Air France	31,682		5	American Airlines	87,830
7	Turkish Airlines	31,016				
8	KLM	27,740		6	China Eastern Airlines	66,174

Source: Created by the author based on each airline's website, June 2015

Chapter 2

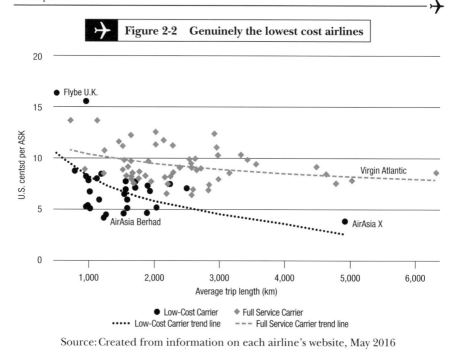

Figure 2-2 Genuinely the lowest cost airlines

Source: Created from information on each airline's website, May 2016

Although there are certainly disagreements over defining what an LCC is, the broad definition of an LCC given in this book is as follows: unconventional airlines that has a relatively short history regarding business models and has established a principle of offering low fares in comparison to LCs through the pursuit of cost reduction. It may be slightly misleading to define an airline corporation such as Southwest Airlines as "a new airline company" since it was established in 1971 and has grown to be the largest airline company in the U.S. This company, however, is still undoubtedly "unconventional", because of its business model, in contrast to other models adopted by LCs. Therefore, it can still be considered "a new corporation" in a relative and historical sense. The history and development of these LCCs will be explained in the following sections.

Chapter 2

1 LCCs of the United States

◇ 1. Development of LCCs in the American Aviation Market

The business models of LCCs in the U.S. have been developed as part of a deregulation process. By September 2006, the share of LCCs reached 30% of the American aviation market. Southwest Airlines, a renowned LCC, has now grown to match the scale of other LCs.

● 1.1 The American Aviation Market in the 1980s and New Entries

Since 1978, when the Airline Deregulation Act was established under Carter Administration, other regulations regarding price and new entries were abolished[1]. This political trend encouraged LCCs to join the market. The productivity of LCs has significantly decreased as a result of long-term protection under such regulations. The LCCs have therefore taken advantage of this situation and have entered the market with low personnel costs and fares, intensifying the competition against the overpriced fare of LCs. To retain the upper hand, LCs tried to expand their market share by creating mergers, activating the use of hub and spoke systems, implementing CRS-based yield management (pricing method that maximizes profits per flight), and attracting customers through Frequency Flyers Programs (FFPs).

From the 1980s to 1990s, many LCCs[2] (new airlines or cheap airlines, as they were called at that time) could not survive in the competitive market, confronted with new business strategies by LCs. Hence, most went bankrupt. People Express Airlines is an example of an LCC that went bankrupt as a result of losing its customers by frequent accidents and disruption of schedules, losing control over hub airports due to LCs' maximized use of hub and spoke systems, poor capital strength that failed

---

1 The Airline Deregulation Act is a 1978 United States federal law that deregulated the airline industry in the United States removing U.S. federal government control over such things as fares, routes and market entry of airlines, introducing a free market in the commercial airline industry under Carter Administration. This also was the beginning of the "Open Sky" policy.
2 However, at the time, it was referred to as New Airline or Cheap Airline.

Chapter 2

to cover the cost for introducing IT measures such as CRS, and the successful lock-in of customers by LCs through FFPs.

When LCCs enter routes shared by LCs, the LCs set their fare at the same or lower prices than that of the LCCs, staying competitive within the price line by covering deficits from the routes with surpluses of other routes. This resulted in shutting out the new entries.

In other words, People Express Airlines could not attract customers by the FFP, was unable to leverage networking, and was slow in applying the CRS. Promoting cheap fares was its only marketing strategy. As a result, it was confronted with low-price counterstrategy by LCs with insufficient initial funds. People Express Airlines could not compete and was pushed out of the market.

Throughout the competition, American Airlines, Delta Air Lines, Northwest Airlines, and United Airlines, the four major companies that were established through large-scale mergers, claimed 60% of the market share in the 1900s. The restructure of these companies was conducted in accordance with new strategies, which included the expansion of networks through hub and spoke systems, and focused on company location when it came to establishing hub airports and the number of gates it occupied[3]. Under such circumstances, most of the smaller LCCs could not survive except for a few, such as Southwest Airlines.

- **1.2 Development of American LCCs at the End of the 1990s**

Despite these business strategies, LCs began to become incompetent from the end of the 1990s. Most of them reported severe losses by the fourth quarter of 2000. The reasons are as described below:

(1) Demand for air travel declined due to the economic recession after the collapse of the dot-com bubble. The targeted business customers switched to choosing cheaper seats over the more expensive ones, due to cost saving measures implemented by

---

3 The beginning of the alliance due to the expansion of networks through code-sharing between other airlines and the U.S. followed by the screen display modification of the CRS.

the companies they worked for.

(2) During the competition over share expansion against their competitors, LCs excessively invested in cabin facilities, services, FFPs, yield management and systems for customer data management in order to maintain customer loyalty from their high-yielding customers. This caused the companies to lose their management power.

(3) LCs which had already been under pressure with high personnel cost of their workers whilst trying to keep their vested rights, had to suffer an even higher cost structure from further increase of salaries based on the labor-management agreement concluded in 1991 as well as high pension savings.

(4) Hub and spoke systems raised demand in the market, but also caused congestion and flight delays at the hub airports and inconvenience in connecting flights. These circumstances gradually dissatisfied the customers.

(5) Through IT development that simplified information gathering and transmission, customers were able to compare prices and services among airlines.

(6) Fuel became more expensive.

In addition to these factors, the September 11 Attacks, the Iraq War, the SARS epidemic, and the steep rise in jet fuel cost led to further financial damage to the LCs. As a result, United Airlines and US Airways went into bankruptcy in 2002. In 2005, Delta Air Lines, the third largest American airline, and Northwest Airlines, the fourth largest, both filed Chapter 11[4] (Table 2-2). As shown in the table below, 11 LCs went under Chapter 11 protection. In 2002, US Airways exited Chapter 11 by merging with an LCC, America West Airlines.

Whilst LCs was struggling, LCCs became gradually active again in the markets. The main active LCCs in the U.S. in the early 2007 were Southwest Airlines, America West Airlines, ATA Airlines, JetBlue Airways, AirTran Airways, Frontier Airlines, and Spirit Airlines. These LCCs, compared to those in the 1980s, competed with high

---

4   Chapter 11 is a chapter of Title 11 of the United States Bankruptcy Code, which permits reorganization under the bankruptcy laws of the U.S. Chapter 11 affords the debtor in possession a number of mechanisms to restructure its business. A debtor in possession can acquire financing and loans, reject and cancel contracts, void debt collection and so on. It is practically a national remedial action for private enterprises.

Chapter 2

 Table 2-2 Major LCs which filed Chapter 11 of the United States Bankrupty Code after 2000

	Year	Chapter 11
Pinnacle Airlines	2012	Filed
Ryan International Airlines	2012	Filed
American Airlines	2011	Filed
Delta Air Lines	2005	Filed
Northwest Airlines	2005	Filed
Aloha Airlines	2004	Filed
Hawaiian Airlines	2013	Filed
United Airlines	2002	Filed
US Airways	2002	Filed
Midway Airlines	2001	Filed
Trans World Airlines	2001	Filed

Source: Created by the author based on each airline's website, December 2016

costs and strong financial ground, and often sought to compete with the LCs on the same route. The market share occupied by LCCs reached 29.7% in 2011, and reached 32% in 2016, as shown in Figure 2-1.

Yet, it is necessary to note that some LCCs were facing financial troubles. For example, in 2005, ATA Airlines and Southwest Airlines received aid. In 2006, Independence Airlines, which was seeking capital investors or buyout under protection of Chapter 11, went into compulsory liquidation only 18 months after its business started.

In addition, LCCs established by LCs as their affiliates in order to compete with other LCCs were also facing financial troubles. For example, Song, an LCC established by Delta Air Lines, was reabsorbed by Delta Air Lines in May 2006 only 3 years after its own business had started. This was partly due to its failure to reduce personnel cost by using Delta Air Lines' flight crew for operations.

Below is the overview of the current status and strategies of Southwest Airlines and JetBlue Airways, both of which are demonstrating remarkable positive growth. In contrast to other low-performing businesses of air transport markets in the U.S., which are under intense competition and confronted with various external factors, they are producing good results.

2. Major LCCs in the United States

2.1 Southwest Airlines

Southwest Airlines is considered as a typical example of an LCC business model, well-known to be a representative of LCCs, established in Dallas, Texas, 7 years before domestic liberalization of aviation policies in the U.S. was initiated in 1971. It may be slightly misleading to define such an airline corporation as "a new airline company", in that sense. The company survived the market, while many other LCCs in the 1980s did not. Southwest Airlines grew to be the second largest airline company in the world for their number of domestic passengers in 2005.

The main characteristic of Southwest Airlines' business model is its execution of six strategies to differentiate itself from the LCs. These are as follows:

The first strategy consisted of highly frequent operations of direct and short-distance routes. In the 1980s, LCs attempted to penetrate the market by focusing on expanding their network through hub and spoke systems as a business strategy, reorganization of the industry by mergers and acquisitions, increase in distribution of aircraft and personnel, and the use of multiple types of aircraft. Southwest Airlines, on the other hand, used point-to-point strategy as its main method to differentiate itself from the LCs. The strategy refers to providing services with low fares, high-frequency, and direct short-distance routes using secondary airports in large cities, where LCs were rarely stationed. With this strategy, Southwest Airlines successfully concentrated its resources to enhance profitability rather than expanding its market shares, thus distinguishing itself from LCs. While many of the LCCs in the 1980s competed similarly and directly against LCs by entering major long distant routes, Southwest Airlines focused on short-distance domestic routes in certain areas, without having to specify its need for network expansion. Even at the beginning of the year 2006, both average flight distances and average flight distance lengths of Southwest Airlines were shorter compared to those of traditional LCs, and 80% of its flights were short-distance trips that frequently connected two cities directly. The company's highly frequent operation has been offering a sense of reassurance to customers, compared to that of other LCCs where operation schedules were frequently disrupted.

The second strategy was the incorporation of proactive use of secondary airports. Southwest Airlines began and developed services on routes from Dallas Love Field Airport, which is located close to the city, but not from Dallas/Fort Worth International Airport, which is the hub airport of the city. Therefore, the use of secondary airports instead of hub airports, which were preferred more by other airlines due to larger crowds, resulted in higher availability of arrival and departure slots, and lower airport facility usage fees. It also extended operation time by minimizing the time on the ground and increased the average number of operations per day, both of which contributed to cost reduction.

The third strategy was the pursuit of rationalization and cost reduction through the use of B737 aircraft, the only flight equipment on short-distance routes. The 513 aircraft owned by the company by December 2007 were all B737. The use of a solo type of aircraft saved costs for the training of crew members, required a single type of maintenance manual, reduced inventories of repair parts, and enhanced the efficiency in parts procurement. The company can also receive large discounts from aircraft and engine manufacturers by purchasing supplies from them in large quantities. No-frills service, which was made possible by short-distance flights, also contributes to cost reduction and provision of low fares. Another cost reduction effort was to apply a sales system that deals directly with passengers, and not via the CRS that are used by travel agents.

The fourth strategy was the establishment of a Corporate Identity (CI). Both associate and flight attendants on duty waited on customers wearing casual outfits with a friendly manner to achieve high satisfaction from customers. The company was also successful in distinguishing CI through a team establishment called "Southwest Spirit". Southwest employees had developed a sense of teamwork by working beyond the job description. It was mandatory for all types of employees including pilots, flight attendants, and mechanics to collaborate. Experiencing each other's responsibilities contributed not only to the development of profound understanding of teamwork but also to the achievement of cost reduction.

The fifth strategy was the building of employee loyalty towards the company through CI that was based on the concept of Southwest Spirit. Loyalty was also presented as one of the company's themes, which was described as "customer satisfaction comes from employee satisfaction." Southwest Airlines, ranked top of the "100 best companies to work for" by *Fortune*, and has been renowned as a company with high Employee Satisfaction (ES). The company announced that it would value its employees from the management policy point of view, such as providing higher salaries to acquire more qualified people. Based on its management policy, high ES is achieved by providing employees with an enjoyable working environment, in which the positive mood would eventually be passed on to the passengers, ultimately contributing to Customer Satisfaction (CS) and enhancing productivity. In order to promote such teamwork, the company's former chairman, Herb Kelleher, would sometimes protect his employees from unreasonable complaints from customers. This is described as Southwest Airlines' "employees first, customers second" rule. It may sound paradoxical to some due to the company's attempts of building customer satisfaction. Nevertheless, it is based on a concept that when a company cannot protect its employees from unreasonable behavior by customers, the employees will not feel comfortable in fulfilling their job responsibilities. This is a rational approach as ignorance of such complaints and behaviors from the management will eventually lead to lower customer satisfaction.

The sixth strategy, which is also related to the establishment of CI, was the expression of the company's social role to its employees. To begin with, Southwest Airlines promoted air transport. The company then made its position clear to its employees that popularization of air transport is part of the management policy and social role. As a result, true ES was developed through their understanding of the company's social role and the significance of their job to the society. This eventually led to CS.

This successful airline has been also impacted by the recent steep rise in oil prices. The company is rich in liquidity and in fuel hedging (approximately 80%) compared to other airliners, so the impact of the rise in oil prices should be relatively small to them. Nevertheless, the company is struggling to reflect the rise in cost on airfare. As a result, 3% of the flights were shifted from short-distance routes to long-distance routes. It also began implementing measures to increase profit such as charging for in-flight entertainment systems.

Chapter 2

The following are recent, remarkable facts about Southwest Airlines. In 2011, Southwest Airlines made a management plan that emphasized the following strategies: (1) AirTran Airways integration, (2) All-New Rapid Rewards frequency flyer program, (3) the increase in the number of B737, (4) fleet modernization, and (5) replacement of its reservation system. Southwest Airlines had said that taking these actions would drive more revenue, reduce unit costs, and improve its financial performance. Among these measures, however, the acquisition of AirTran Airways and the addition of new aircraft (including fleet modernization) are sources that may lead to challenges as follows.

AirTran Airways was acquired by Southwest Airlines in 2012, and the latter succeeded in extending its network. However, AirTran Airways mainly provided hub and spoke services rather than point-to-point services, and approximately half of AirTran Airways' operation route originated from Atlanta, Georgia. According to the management plan of Southwest Airlines, the company will maintain operating its point-to-point route service for the convenience of customers in terms of reducing the flight duration time. Therefore, I focused on how Southwest Airlines absorbs AirTran Airways' hub-and-spoke style network and merges it with its point-to-point style network.

Southwest Airlines, on the other hand, may develop a new style of service in the near future. Regarding the increment of aircraft, Southwest Airlines owned 694 aircraft in 2012 whereas it owned 537 aircraft in 2009 (including leased aircraft). For example, in 2012, the number of B717-200 was 88, B737-300 was 20, B737-500 was 128, B737-700 was 424, and B737-800 was 34. In contrast to 2009, it had only three aircraft models: 172 B737-300, 25 B737-500, and 340 B737-700. As you can see, Southwest Airlines utilizes only Boeing aircraft. However, it has added different types of aircraft such as the B717-200, by acquisition of AirTran Airways, and the B737-800. This may raise the maintenance costs. Thus, when a company expands its business, its network and asset including its flight equipment gets even more diversified and complicated, even though they had been striving to reduce the cost. This is an unavoidable issue if Southwest Airlines continues to seek expanding its business.

Southwest Airlines has been used as a great LCC business model example, and has been leading the LCC market. It provides low-priced airfare and reduces inflight duration cost by holding the basic strategy of LCCs such as unifying aircraft types, operating point-to-point routes by taking advantage of the secondary airports, and implementing no-frills service. As a result, it has improved the benefits to the customers and has expanded its business successfully. However, Southwest Airlines has now grown as sizable as other airline companies, and it may have to reconsider its business strategy accordingly.

For instance, Southwest Airlines introduced the FFP. This strategy was developed by major airlines, and does not work for LCCs. If the company uses this strategy in the wrong way, it may receive significant damage to its business, as Pan American World Airways and JAL did. The structure of the strategy is to categorize customers and manage each individual, increasing the cost. Therefore, it is rare for an LCC like Southwest Airlines to introduce the FFP, and this will remain as an attention grabber in the aviation industry and its related fields.

In addition, there is a limit to the point-to-point strategy efficiency. Point-to-point operation is useful for large-demand routes. In contrast, hub-and-spoke operation is beneficial to smaller demand routes. Accordingly, if Southwest Airlines continues to extend its operation routes by using the point-to-point strategy, it may reach a dead end at some point. Acquisition of AirTran Airways, for instance, seems like a case where its business strategy exceeds its limitation. It will be interesting to see how Southwest Airlines handles the point-to-point strategy even after such questionable integrations.

I have conducted a SWOT analysis of Southwest Airlines below. All the information comes from Southwest Airlines' website. It describes similar explanations discussed above.

Strengths
(1) Reasonable Valuation: The company carries a price to earnings ratio of only 14.10%, which is relatively cheap by market standard.
(2) Widespread Accessibility: At the end of 2011, the company offered service in 72 cities out of 37 states, promoting across the entire U.S., and the acquisition of AirTran

Airways now extends its accessibility internationally, mostly over Mexico and the Caribbean islands. The company operations are by no means concentrated in a specific region.

(3) Dividends: The company currently pays out quarterly dividends, which annualizes the company's dividend as yielding 0.44%. While this dividend may seem insignificant, it still covers six months of the Certificate of Deposition (CD) rate.

(4) Modest Sales Growth: The sales growth has doubled year-on-year. However, the company's growth is predicted to slow down to a modest, high single digit rate in the future.

(5) Established Brands: Much of an airline's success is due to its reputable brand, as fliers flock to more established and distinguished companies with track records of safety. Having an established brand is a major advantage.

Weaknesses

(1) Debt: The company is estimated to have 361 million USD of debt on its balance sheet, and until the company pays off these debts, they will continue to be a significant hindrance on their businesses.

(2) Mounting Operating Expenses: The average cost per gallon of fuel from 2002 to 2015 grew 180%. Consumers are constantly demanding added services and amenities to their flights, and the unions are viciously battling for more money for their members; at the end of the day the company is not left with much profit (net profit margin is 1.14%).

(3) Relatively Expensive Price of Product: While Southwest Airlines is known for offering great values, buying a plane ticket is still a very costly act, and in times of economic downturns, people simply do not have extra money.

Opportunities

(1) Company Expansion: Just in 2011, the company had added Charleston, South Carolina, Greenville-Spartanburg, South Carolina and Newark, New Jersey to the list of cities the company services. Further company expansion is probable.

(2) Gaining Market Share: Recently, American Airlines appeared on the news with a negative review due to loose seats and massive layoffs. As a result, Southwest Airlines has gained an opportunity to capture the business American Airlines once had.

(3) Acquisitions: On May 2nd, 2011, Southwest Airlines acquired AirTran Airways,

and further acquisitions are undeniable, especially with Southwest Airlines being a relatively large company.

Threats

(1) Weather Uncertainty: As we have seen with Hurricane Sandy, natural disasters can cause major losses for airline businesses, and since such phenomena can come as an uncertainty, it will certainly affect the company.
(2) Immense Competition: The airline industry is incredibly competitive, and the race to get consumer businesses often leads to margin contractions.
(3) Vulnerability to Rising Oil Prices: When jet fuel prices rise, airline companies are faced with the problem of possibly dissatisfying their customers and losing their businesses, or absorbing the costs themselves and ruining their margins.
(4) Exposure to the Unstable U.S. Economy: The company operates mainly in the U.S., and thus any economic slowdown that involves the American economy could drastically hurt its business, whilst other international companies weather the storm.

It is crucial to take a closer look at Southwest Airlines, especially from the year 2013. Since the company has increased its size drastically, businesses cannot sustain itself just by the traditional range of LCCs. The new business model is a hybrid form of LCs and LCCs, delicately executing the beneficial factors from each side while measuring out the risks that follow. From 2013–2016, Southwest Airlines began to offer and expand non-stop flight services gradually, partnering with other airports to create more destinations. Additionally, in order to systemize their training, they have launched a TOPS program called "The Airport Experience" to fulfill customers' needs. As a result, the revenue passenger miles in June 2015 have reached 10.8 billion. Even while maintaining its accomplishments by numerical figures, the company does not fail to keep up with its ethical service to the military personnel, its own employees, and the customers, constantly winning awards in different sectors in the past consecutive years. This company is a great example of LCCs due to its success stemming largely from its unique business model, used by many other LCCs as a reference. Its history is as shown in Table 2-3.

Chapter 2

Table 2-3 History of Southwest Airlines

	History
1971	Began service between Houston, Dallas, and San Antonio in Texas
1973	Reached early profit for the first time
1977	Southwest Airlines Company Common Stock listed in New York Stock Exchange
1979	Implemented self-check-in machines in 10 cities
	Began service to cities outside Texas(Dallas–New Orleans)
1980	Completely owned B737 aircraft for the first time
1982	Began service to San Francisco, Los Angeles, San Diego, Las Vegas, and Phoenix
1983	Reached 9.5 million passengers
1984	Selected as "No.1 Customer Satisfaction" for 4 consecutive years
1985	Aquired Muse Air as a wholly-owned subsidiary conducted a more convenient point-to-point service
1986	Opened its Training Center for Pilots and Flight Attendants to a host of cities
1987	Selected as "No.1 Customer Satisfaction" for 6 consecutive years
	Inaugurated Frequent Flyer Program
1988	Launched "New Friends" campaign(Partnered with Sea World in Texas, and manufactured aircraft painted with an orca motif)
	Achieved first triple crown in "On-Time", "Baggage Handling", and "Customer Complaints"
1989	Began new service to routes using Oakland International Airport as a base
	Marked earnings of 1 billion USD, and was acknowledged as a major airliner
1992	Achieved annual triple crown for the first time in the American airline industry
1994	Acquired Morris Air and implemented ticketless service
	Began service to 7 pacific northwestern cities(including Seattle, Spokane, Portland, and Boise)
1996	Started online ticketless service
1997	Began service to its 51st destination
1999	Began service to New York
2002	Implemented self-check-in system to approximately 250 airports
2003	Partnered with television network
	Selected as Airline of the Year by *Air Transport World* magazine
2004	Began online boarding ticket service
	Began service to its 60th destination(Philadelphia), resulting in 2,800 flights to the U.S. destinations
2005	Began code-sharing with ATA Airlines
2007	Remained in surplus for 34 consecutive years
2008	Won three 1st place Freddie Awards for its Award Redemption, Best Award, and Best Customer Communication
	37th Anniversary
2009	Ranked as No. 7 on its list of the World's Most Admired Companies in *Forbes* magazine
	Began the new nonstop service between Denver–Boston Logan, Denver–Spokane, and Denver–Reno/Tahoe
2010	Recognized as the top airline in the annual Air Cargo Excellence Survey conducted by *Air Cargo World* magazine
	Net income of 450 million USD–459 million USD excluding special items, 88,191,322 passengers carried, 1,114,451 trips flown
2011	Completed all aircraft inspections in accordance with the FAA Airworthiness Directive(AD)
	Acquisition of AirTran Holdings by Southwest Airlines confirmed by the shareholders
	Celebrates its 40th Anniversary
	Announced as one of the top 50 Best Places to Work in Glassdoor's annual Employees Choice Awards

2012	Received approval by the Federal Aviation Administration(FAA) for a Single Operating Certificate(SOC)
	Announced route authority approval from the U.S. Department of Transportation(DOT) to operate new international flight between Denver International Airport–Cancun International Airport
	Recognized by the Airforwarders Association as the "Domestic Carrier of the Year" for 3 consecutive years
2013	Launched low fare nonstop trips and flight schedule extension
	Built further relationships with flight companies, such as AirTran Airways
	Converted 3 of AirTran Airways' cities to its own stations
	Full year income reached 754 million USD
2014	Introduced "The Airport Experience", and TOPS(training and operational system)
	Expanded nonstop service to 17 U.S. cities and 6 new destinations in Latin America
2015	Linked 43 destinations to Dallas Love Field
	Flew 10.8 billion revenue passenger miles in June
2016	Nonstop service to 99th city served
	Designated as a Military Friendly employer for 8 consecutive years
	Began nonstop service to Republic of Cuba

Source: Created by the author based on Southwest Airlines' website, December 2016

● 2.2　JetBlue Airways

JetBlue Airways has continued to grow rapidly since its establishment in 2000. It has used several business strategies that are different from those of a typical LCC.

The company's first strategy is to target business passengers who normally use LCs. This is a different strategy from the Southwest Airlines' business model, which aims for cost reduction by no-frills service. With "Value for Money", as its catch phrase, the marketing strategy focuses on offering high-quality services(such as IT-based functions, leather seats, and satellite television for each passenger) with a relatively lower fee or "value price". The company also puts its attention in developing human resources for providing high-quality services under the "High Tech & High Touch" slogan.

The second strategy is the use of hub airports. Instead of using secondary airports and focusing on short-distance routes, which were done regularly by typical LCCs, the company has been based at JFK Airport, a hub airport in New York, since Southwest Airlines started its business. It has been focusing on high-demand and long-distance routes between New York and major cities of the west coast(Los Angeles, Seattle), and between New York and Florida. With this strategy, the company has been successful in establishing a system of securing stabilized revenue by attracting business passengers, who frequently use flights. This was made possible by its sufficient

Chapter 2

initial funds of 160 million USD, an inclusive funding from George Soros.

The third strategy is using an extensive IT system that is supported by the funding mentioned above. The company is implementing a wide range of IT measures, including a "paperless cockpit", in which both the pilot and co-pilot have laptop computers, and they access to the central computer system installed at the headquarters so that they can both establish the most efficient flight plans within a limited time. They input and calculate the weight and balance of the airplane. The company uses IT to minimize time and procedures for reservation processes, sales of tickets, check-in, and handling of baggage at a low cost. There are 600 virtual call center operators working from home, waiting on customers by Voice over-IP (VoIP) connection regarding ticket reservations by phone. The company also uses IT to shorten check-in waiting times and has established a baggage-tracking system by using electronic tags. Its intensive use of IT outlines the company's CI, and contributes to branding and differentiation. IT is also applied to enhancing security measures. This was promoted from the aftermath of the September 11 Attacks, when passengers became highly concerned about their security. Some examples are the installation of monitoring cameras in the cockpit, so that ground staff can monitor via satellites and from hidden cameras inside the cabin. What was more amazing was the introduction of biometrics applications (such as detection of fingerprints) at terminals.

The fourth and final strategy is the use of "cost per Available Seat Mile (ASM)" as an index for management efficiency, which contributes to reduction in operation cost. Currently, its cost is less than 7 US cents, which is approximately 25% lower than the average LCs.

JetBlue Airways also implements strategies commonly applied by other LCCs as seen in Southwest Airlines' business model. Some examples are the sole usage of A320 for reducing operation cost, the application of direct sales model for selling seats directly to clients and not through travel agents, and application of ticketless entries for all reservations.

On the other hand, some have shown criticisms regarding JetBlue Airways' management policy, which focuses on short-term efficiency without redundancy in cost. In the

Table 2-4 JetBlue Airways' capacity distribution by region

(ASM/%)

	2015	2014	2013
Caribbean & Latin America	30.2	31.4	28.1
Florida	29.2	29.3	30.9
Transcontinental	28.5	26.3	27.9
East	5.7	5.7	5.0
Central	3.8	4.7	5.2
West	2.6	2.6	2.9
Total	100.0	100.0	100.0

Source: Created by the author based on JetBlue Airways' *JetBlue's 2016 Annual Report*

winter of 2007, when a cold wave hit the East Coast including JFK Airport, where JetBlue Airways was based, the company revealed poor management skills, having been forced to cancel a large number of flights. However, this tactless behavior can be seen even in legacy carriers, so it might not be an issue limited to LCCs only.

According to the annual reports of JetBlue Airways, it sells vacation packages through JetBlue Getaways, a one-stop, value-priced vacation website and service designed to meet customers' demand for self-directed packaged travel planning. JetBlue Getaways packages offer competitive fares for air travel, along with a selection of JetBlue-recommended hotels and resorts, car rentals and attractions. It also offers à la carte hotel and car rental reservations through its website which generates ancillary service revenues. As you can see, JetBlue Airways focuses a lot on both business and vacation travelers. The historic distribution of its availability and capacity in seat miles by region is shown in Table 2-4. According to the table, it has had a large share of flights to leisure resort areas such as Florida and the Caribbean. Since JetBlue Airways has successfully been growing in size and business, according to its well-thought out and systematic strategies, the company has been on a steady rise and its business seemingly would not fail or decline in the following years.

● 2.3 Spirit Airlines: Ultra-Low-Cost Carrier

Spirit Airlines shows a very unorthodox business model that has been critically carved into cutting the cost and making a profit, even while being criticized by many customers and users. Its main tactic is its tightly aligned business and operating model. Although Spirit Airlines shows the lowest rating score for customer satisfaction and thousands of complaint cases, Ben Baldanza, Chief Exective Officer (CEO), simply counts this factor out of consideration.

With the company's model quote "Bare Fares", it will basically charge almost anything other than the customers themselves. However, customers are quickly drawn to its service, even with the discomfort of being overly charged due to the unbundled fares. Spirit Airlines offers fares at the lowest price, which in turn profits them more. Some of its chargeable factors are boarding pass printout, check-in, baggage claim, overhead counter use and even refreshments. Any service or weight offered by the company is subjected to extra payment. This is strictly an impersonal model, but if used in detail by the customers' own efforts, it can turn into the most cost-effective model. The targeted class of customers have complained, but complied with the rules of Spirit Airlines due to its affordability. This result showcases its marketing strategy from a purely valued perspective. As of May 2014, the all-in-fares of Spirit Airlines is approximately 40% less than those of other domestic airlines. In 2011, it has earned the top net profit in comparison to other well-known airlines.

After 2011, Spirit Airlines reached the highest operating margin of 17.1% in year 2013. It reached 26.9% in 2015. This shows that aside from the overall balance of factors that resides with the company, resulted in its growth as the low cost satisfied the basic needs of customers.

The model also meets the demand of the times. Apart from the cost, the infrastructure is relatively new compared to that of other airline companies, with less breakdowns and lower maintenance fees in case of a breakdown. This prompts Spirit Airlines to promote short turnaround intervals between flights. Cutting costs is the key to gaining attention, and Spirit Airlines focuses on attracting people with the same mind-set. This has worked successfully as the average percentage of plane occupancy is about 85% to 90%. Compromising the seat arrangement that makes customer's comfortable such as shortening the leg space, and cutting out the reclining function of the seat to offer more seats to increase the seat vacancy, never worked since most flights remained almost full.

The cost reduction does not apply only for customers, but also for internal operations

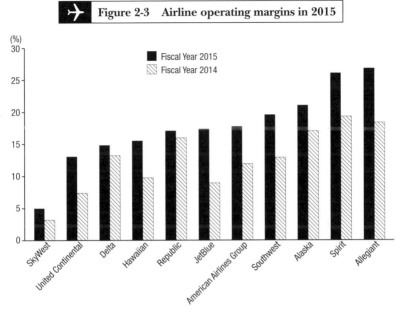

Figure 2-3　Airline operating margins in 2015

Source: Oliver Wyman n.d.

of Spirit Airlines' own employees. By operating only three aircraft types (A319, A320, and A321), employees may have easier interchanging shifts for the operation. Therefore, less complexity will remain throughout the crew members.

While this model may be questionable as to whether it can have a long-term stability, results show that the LCC business model with a specific target may lead to success, even without receiving accolades for all aspects of the airline. This is an interesting and attractive model and provides a good example for future LCCs.

● **2.4　Affiliate LCCs of LCs**

To compete against LCCs, LCs in the U.S. began to establish their own LCCs. However, they struggle with facing challenges in overall management of their LCCs. Affiliated LCCs are following the business strategies of Southwest Airlines that presents no-frills services, saves maintenance cost and training cost by using a single type of aircraft, and saves personnel cost by employing non-union workers. Despite such efforts, however, these measures did not have much effect, and are not impacting the cost reduction process. The existing labor contracts of the leading LCs cannot be altered even when the affiliates are created, so it simply cannot lead to personnel cost reduction. Another reason is that the management system of the affiliate is taking over the traditional system of its parent company.

2 European LCCs

1. Development of LCCs in the European Aviation Market

Most of the LCs in Europe grew by benefiting from protection and preferential treatments as National Corporations, under governmental law. However, deregulation has been gradually promoted since 1987, under the process of the EU integration. Accessibility of airfare and markets were liberalized in 1993.

In 1997, transportation between three countries in the EU including deregulation of cabotage (the right to operate in domestic routes) was permitted. With this complete liberalized policy, the European airline companies were able to operate freely within the EU. Due to this deregulation process, the aviation industry was restructured. Major airline companies were able to further expand services on routes by mainly using hub airports across borders. This move promoted the entry of LCCs.

An aviation agreement was reached internationally between the EU and the U.S., which promoted the "Open Sky" policy[5] (liberalization of international airlines). Partnership between European and the U.S. airline companies on Atlantic routes is being developed.

Furthermore, the European aviation industry has been seeing continual restructuring and consolidation due to the severe management environment since 2000. National and former national LCs based in countries with small domestic airline markets are seeking ways to partner with LCs such as Lufthansa, British Airways, and Air France.

---

5 It is a custom to conclude a civil aviation agreement and prescribe interests to acquire international air traffic rights. The EU, as one nation, concluded an agreement with the U.S. to liberalize the international aviation industry.

Chapter 2

One international management merger between airline companies was between Air France and KLM in 2004. Alitalia is also planning on joining "Air France = KLM". Swiss International Air Lines, which was previously with Swissair before its bankruptcy, has decided to partner with British Airways. This partnership movement between airline companies in Europe is linked to the worldwide alliance formation. In Europe, as previously described, all airlines have partnered with one of the three major alliances, embodied by Lufthansa, British Airways, and Air France respectively.

While these LCs are undergoing restructuring, LCCs are actively advancing into the market by taking advantage of the system that allows cabotage and transport between three countries. A large number of LCCs are now operating in the current European aviation market; Ryanair and easyJet, two of the major LCCs, provide service on high-frequency, short and middle-distance routes with low fares, and use secondary airports in the suburbs by following the business model of Southwest Airlines. Other LCCs include Air Berlin in Germany, Sterling Airlines in Scandinavia, and Bmibaby, a British traditional middle-ranked airline company and an affiliate company of British Midland Airways. LCCs accounted for 20% of the European airline market in early 2006, and 30% in 2007, producing a similar growth rate to the U.S. market. The share was expected to reach 50% in 2010. Ryanair and easyJet occupied a total of 42% of the entire airline passenger transport in 2004 on a certain route between Dublin and London. This threatened the market share of LCs. Competition among LCCs has intensified as well, and in 2005, Ryanair announced its service initiation in London Luton Airport, a hub airport for easyJet. Below is the overview of the business model of Ryanair and easyJet, the two major LCCs of Europe.

2. Major LCCs in Europe

2.1 Ryanair

The history of Ryanair is shown in Table 2-5. The core management policy of Ryanair is an intensified version of cost reduction measures in Southwest Airlines' business model. The company, which had been competing against Aer Lingus, was able to avoid bankruptcy with the support of the Irish Aviation Authority. Since then, the company has been steadily growing in scale and enhancing its profitability. It has also been taking advantage of the EU integration as an opportunity to expand its

Chapter 2

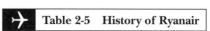 Table 2-5 History of Ryanair

	History
1985	Conducted inaugural flights between Waterford Airport and Gatwick Airport
1986	Began service between Dublin Airport and London Luton Airport at half the price of airfare of the LCs
1987	Leased jet airplane increased to 15 networks
1990	Became the first European LCC which followed and restructured the Southwest Airlines' low-fare model
1991	Moved base from London Luton Airport to Stansted Airport
	Achieved a profit of 293,000 pounds in spite of the impact from the Gulf War
1992	Reduced routes from 19 to 6
	Passed 100,000 monthly passengers for the first time in Ryanair's history
1993	Passed 1 million annual passengers
1994	Operated the first B737 aircraft
	Began service between Dublin Airport and Manchester Airport, Dublin Airport and Glasgow Prestwick Airport
1995	Achieved passenger transport performance between Dublin Airport and London that exceeded the performance of LCs
1996	Launched Leeds, Cardiff and Bournemouth routes
1997	Began service to Stockholm, Oslo, Dublin, Beauvais and Charleroi from London Stansted Airport
	Later in the year, began service to Dublin, London, and Paris from Glasgow Prestwick Airport
	The U.K. Civil Aviation Authority praised its on-time operations between Dublin Airport and London Luton Airport
1998	Selected as "Airline of the Year" and "Best Managed National Airline"
1999	Selected as "Best Value Airline" in the U.K.
2000	Implemented "Ryanair.com" an online reservation system
2001	Selected Brussel South Charleroi Airport as a base for European routes
	Passed 1 million monthly transport passengers
2002	Ranked top for customer service in Europe
2003	Acquired buzz for operation at half price
	Exceeded British Airways in the airline market in the number of monthly transport passengers
2004	Ranked as the top airline in a Google web poll
2005	Ranked as the third airline, following AF/KLM and Lufthansa in the number of passengers in international routes
2006	Carried a record of 42.5 million passengers in the year they accepted delivery of Ryanair's 100th B737
	Launched the web check-in service to check-in online across entire route networks
2007	Opened 201 new routes and 3 new U.K. bases(Bournemouth, Birmingham, Belfast)
2008	Opened 223 new routes and 4 new bases(Alghero, Bologna, Cagliari, Edinburgh)
2009	Opened 8 new bases in Bari, Brindisi, Faro, Leeds Bradford, Oslo Rygge, Pescara, Porto, and Trapani
2010	Took delivery of additional 40 new aircraft as Ryanair's fleet rose to 272 B737
2011	Opened 6 new bases in Baden, Billund, Budapest, Paphos, Palma de Mallorca, and Wroclaw, as network grew to 50 bases with over 1,500 routes
2012	Traffic grew by 5% to 79.3 million passengers with an average fare of 48 EUR without any fuel surcharges
	Opened 7 new bases in Chania, Eindhoven, Fez, Krakow, Maastricht, Marrakech and Zadar
	Grew to 57 bases with over 1,600 routes
2013	Traffic grew by 3% to 81.7 million customers with an average fare of 46 EUR without any fuel surcharges
	Opened 4 new bases in Athens, Brussels, Lisbon and Rome, and announced 3 new bases for winter 2014 in Cologne, Gdansk, and Warsaw
	Grew to 68 bases with over 1,600 routes

Chapter 2

2014	Traffic grew by 11% to 90.6 million customers with an average fare of 47 EUR without any fuel surcharges
	Placed orders for 183 B737-800s and 200 B737 Max 200s(including 100 options)
	Opened new bases in Bratislava, Cologne, Gdansk, Glasgow and Warsaw
2015	Announced full year net profit of 1.24 billion EUR, the first airline to carry 100 million passengers in a year(an increase of 43% on the previous year)

Source: Created by the author based on Ryanair's website, December 2016

services in the entire European market.

The company is focusing on the cost strategies of Southwest Airlines that include saving in landing fees by using secondary airports in the suburbs, minimizing in-flight service, charging for food, drinks and newspapers, and directly selling to customers and not through travel agents. It is also focusing on ticket sales via the Internet and requesting discounts from manufacturers by ordering a large number of single type aircraft in bulk.

In addition, the company is implementing more radical cost reduction measures unseen in Southwest Airlines, such as employees paying for their own uniforms and training costs, and the selling of non-refundable tickets. In recent years, the company abolished blinds and reclining seats to shorten the preparation time for takeoffs, and secured the revenue from baggage fees by increasing the baggage weight limit. The company is also considering charges for in-flight entertainment and gambling to increase revenue.

The strategy of LCCs is using the secondary airports in the suburbs and attracting passengers from other areas as well. This has also contributed to the development of the areas surrounding the airport. The operating entities of the secondary airports and adjacent cities have provided subsidies to invite LCCs. For example, Charleroi Airport in Belgium, which has been used by Ryanair as a secondary airport, appraised Ryanair's achievement of providing services to 1 million passengers, and allocated a subsidy of 3.4 million EUR.

In 2005, the EU committee decided on banning local subsidies as shown in the case above about Charleroi Airport. This company based its fundamental policy on minimizing government intervention in the market. The measures, which have been working in favor of LCCs to survive the competition against the LCs, are now geared in the opposite direction as the share of LCCs in the market have expanded. This situation indicates the growth of European LCCs, but also the concerns for future LCCs.

Ryanair has been anticipating the European tourism boom mostly from Chinese tourists, and is seeking for an opportunity to partner with Air Macau to enter the Chinese market. If Ryanair begins the service between Europe and China, the company is going to have to modify its business model of short, middle-distance and high-frequency flights. This is considered to be one of the measures to be taken by LCCs that can no longer anticipate rapid growth.

The financial report of Ryanair in 2012 has mentioned its achievement of a 25% increase to 503 million EUR, an annual profit that they have received by the end of the year. Revenue increased by 19% to 4,325 million EUR as traffic grew by 5% and average fare rose by 16%. Unit costs rose by 13% due to a 30% increase in fuel costs and a 6% increase in sector length. Besides fuel, however, adjusted sector length unit costs were flat. At the end of 2012, Ryanair achieved a profit growth of 25% to 503 million EUR and the traffic grew by 5% to 76 million. It has obtained 294 aircraft and over 1,500 operation routes.

Due to the rise of oil prices and the recession in the EU, some airlines such as Malev, Spanair, and Cimber Sterling have closed down their operations. Despite such conditions, Ryanair have expanded its business operation by opening a new base in Budapest. In addition, they are planning to increase their range to Spain, Scandinavia, and provincial U.K. in order to benefit their local consumers.

Overall, Ryanair has succeeded and grown significantly due to the LCC model. It has always been a reliable, dominant international airline, having constantly maintained a high ranking for their customer satisfaction. Ryanair has followed the trending LCC model with low risks, and have expanded their company to new destinations. As shown in Table 2-5, the company is subjected to constant positive growth.

● 2.2　easyJet

easyJet entered the market in 1996 by providing high-frequency, short and middle-distance services from London Luton Airport, a secondary airport, and in Liverpool, Aberdeen, Nice and Barcelona. In its early days, the company targeted tourists from London. easyJet, in principal, currently follows the low-fare, high-frequency point-to-point operation and no-frills strategy, same as Southwest Airlines and Ryanair. The characteristics of the company are listed below.

The first characteristic is its rapid business operation expansion strategy. easyJet ordered 12 B737-300 in 1997 as a part of its business expansion strategy. In 2001, the company began services from Amsterdam to Belfast, Edinburgh, Gatwick, and Nice, and used Amsterdam as its hub. Then, in 2002, the company acquired GO, an LCC affiliate company of British Airways, to expand its routes. It established a high-density network in the entire Europe area and attracted business customers. The company is shifting its gears from approaching the niche market of tourists to targeting business passengers.

The second characteristic is its diverse business operation. In 2004, easyJet partnered with Hotelopia to enter the hotel business market. It also partnered with a rental car company, and is currently expanding into other businesses closely related to the aviation market.

Moreover, easyJet emphasizes its no-frills characteristic by a "not-so-sophisticated" advertising method, as shown on its aircraft (The painting of the reservation phone number and company logo in big letters rather than a classy, IT influenced image like JetBlue Airways, etc.).

easyJet operates over 600 routes across 30 countries with a fleet of over 200 aircraft. It employs over 8,000 people, including 2,000 pilots and 4,500 flight attendants members. In 2012, easyJet flew over 59 million passengers. The combination of airports and the range of destinations show easyJet's broad networking across different geographies and customer types. As a matter of fact, over half of its sales now originates from outside the U.K. Getting passengers to their destinations on time is the key focus for easyJet. Every three months, easyJet updates its web page with its

Chapter 2

most recent performance numbers. Other facts about easyJet are shown in Table 2-6.

Table 2-6 History of easyJet

	History
1996	Began service between London Luton Airport–Aberdeen International Airport
	Began service between London Luton Airport–Nice, and between London Luton Airport–Barcelona El Prat Airport
1997	Opened a website "easyJet.com" which provides flight information, etc.
	Ordered B737-300 aircraft
1998	Began online reservation service at "easyJet.com"
1999	TEA changed its name to easyJet Switzerland, and located headquarters to Geneva
	Selected as "Best Low-Cost Airline" in a readers' poll by a business magazine
2000	John Quelch, president of London Business School, became part-time director
	Launched website section in Spanish
2001	Began service from Amsterdam Airport Schiphol–Belfast International Airport, Edinburgh Airport–Nice Côte d'Azur Airport
	Began service between Geneva Airport–Barcelona El Prat Airport
	Began service between Amsterdam Airport–Gatwick Airport
	Achieved online sales of a total of 10 million seats
	Began service from Gatwick–Barcelona El Prat Airport, Edinburgh Airport, Malaga Costa del Sol Airport, Palma de Mallorca Airport and Zurich Airport
2002	Began service between Paris Charles de Gaulle Airport, Liverpool John Lennon Airport, London Gatwick Airport–Nice Côte d'Azur Airport
	Began service between London Gatwick Airport–Athens International Airport
	Announced acquisition of GO
2003	Began service between Paris Charles de Gaulle Airport–Barcelona El Prat Airport, Marseille Provence Airport, Milan Malpensa Airport, Nice Côte d'Azur Airport–Toulouse Blagnac Airport
	Began service of confirmation and change of reservation on the website
2004	Began service between New Berlin Schönefeld Airport, Liverpool John Lennon–London Gatwick Airport
	Began service between Bristol Airport–Valencia Airport
	Expanded routes to Italy
	Began hotel business operations through partnership with Hotelopia
2005	Ranked 6th in the number of passengers among international airlines
2006	Introduced Speedy Boarding, giving passengers better choices over their seating arrangements
2007	Completed acquisition of GB Airways, a London Gatwick-based airline operating to destinations across Southern Europe and North Africa
2008	Opened its 19th base at Paris Charles de Gaulle
2009	Operated over 400 routes with over 175 aircraft in 27 countries
2010	Reached 500 routes and had the highest number of passengers flown for the second year in a row. Voted best low-fares airline for 10th consecutive years
2011	Confirmed orders for 15 additional A320 planes
2012	Have proudly announced a 3 year plan for the European commitment to raise funds for UNICEF
2013	Exceeded 60 million passengers within a 12 month period for the first time
2014	Announced plans to apply new technologies to aircraft, to be more efficient, and reduce delays while maintaining industry-leading punctuality and safety records
	Promoting deals to buy the new generation A320 neo aircraft starting in 2017

Source: Created by the author based on easyJet's website, December 2016

As you can see, easyJet is another well-established LCC approved by its competitors in the industry. As the new plan for A320 foreshadows a massive expansion in size of the carrier and the industry itself, 2017 seems to be a huge step for easyJet to bring about a new perspective into the LCC market.

3 Asian LCCs

1. Development of LCCs in the Asian Aviation Market

The Asian aviation market is characterized by its rapidly rising market scale in conjunction with the growth of upper class and middle class, fostered by the economic growth in Asia. The market in China and India, where large amounts of middle class people exist, is expected to grow to a huge extent.

Many of the Asian airline companies in Europe were under governmental regulations and protections as national corporations. The aviation markets of Asia other than the Japanese ones are small, especially in Southeast Asia. The share of international aviation markets in the country is larger. However, the international aviation market is under governmental law. Route entries have been determined by bilateral aviation agreement, and vested rights of existing national flag carriers have been protected for a long period. Moreover, there are a very limited number of secondary airports in larger cities, which are normally used by the LCCs in North America and Europe as a platform for development.

Yet, under the stream of recent global deregulation, Asian airline companies, especially in Southeast Asian countries like Malaysia, Singapore and Thailand, have been placed in a predicament due to its competitive environment. The Open Sky movement under bilateral aviation agreement, and deregulation of foreign airline companies' entry, are especially stimulating opportunities for LCCs, which present low fares as their selling point.

AirAsia's rapid growth in Malaysia, due to low fare services, has proven that the market can promote the use of air transport to passengers from an economic segment who have never been aboard on an aircraft before. This success has influenced the neighboring countries of Malaysia, and brought about Asian LCCs' dramatic growth. The company is providing services both on domestic routes in Malaysia and between three other countries by using affiliate companies that were established in its base country. The company continues to grow as an LCC not only in Malaysia, but also throughout the entire Southeast Asia region.

The reason for this is because LCCs in Southeast Asia are forced to advance into the international route market due to the small domestic airline markets in the area. In this sense, the Open Sky Agreement reached by governments of Southeast Asian countries as described above expanded the LCCs' opportunity to enter the market.

Governmental policies and infrastructure plans supporting the development of LCCs are also playing a critical role in the expansion of LCCs in the market. For example, exclusive LCC terminals are under construction at major international airports in Singapore and Malaysia. Thailand as well, with a construction of a new airport, is considering the possibility of converting Don Mueang Airport into an exclusive LCC airport.

In 2007, LCCs in Asia held approximately 10% of the market share. With governmental support, as mentioned above, a study forecasted that the share would reach 20% or more by 2010.

A detailed analysis of the strategy of AirAsia, the major leading LCC in Asia, will be discussed next. The current status of Singapore, Thailand, Indonesia, India and China will be reviewed as well.

2. Major LCCs in Asia

2.1 AirAsia: Malaysian LCC

AirAsia Malaysia, which began service in December 2001, initiated the LCC boom in the Asian market, and grew to become the largest LCC in Asia.

AirAsia began its service based on an LCC business model, similar to that of Ryanair and Southwest Airlines, including low-fees, no-frills services, charging for in-flight food and drink services, and internet reservations. The company, with remarkable growth, expanded its services to 57 routes as of November 2005. The total number of passengers reached 1.1 million in November 2005, 4 years after its business foundation. While other airlines fell into financial difficulties, the company continued to grow by double digits, both in sales and profits.

The five strategies of AirAsia are striking up potential demand, rapid expansion of international routes by establishment of affiliate companies in other countries, full-scale cost reduction measures, brand differentiation, and hands-on policy. All are explained below in detail.

2.1.1 Promoting Potential Demands From Customers

One goal of AirAsia is to initiate demand from a group of potential customers. The company provides airline services with low fares, even lower than long-distance bus fares, to passengers of a certain economic segment, who cannot afford, and therefore have never used air transportation.

The domestic routes of AirAsia directly compete with Malaysia Airlines. Instead of competing directly against the major airliners and stealing their customers, the company aims to differentiate itself from Malaysian Airlines by creating a new niche market through providing potential customers, who had been disregarded by Malaysia Airlines, with low-fare tickets, and expanding its scale in the aviation market. Its logo, "Now Everyone Can Fly", clearly explains the strategy. The fact that the number of domestic airline passengers in Malaysia increased from 9 million to 13 million in December 2001, when AirAsia began its service, demonstrates the expansion of the Malaysian aviation market brought about by its management strategy.

2.1.2 Rapid Expansion of International Routes by Establishment of Affiliate Companies in Other Countries

AirAsia initially operated only on domestic routes, but has recently expanded its network to international routes. In January 2006, the company started international services to Thailand, Indonesia, Macau, Singapore, China, the Philippines and Cambodia. Considering the small scale of domestic Malaysian aviation market, the

Chapter 2

company has focused primarily to expand its services through international routes.

In 2004, AirAsia established Thai AirAsia in Thailand as its affiliate company with Shin Corporations, which holds 49% of shares of AirAsia. AirAsia of Thailand started services both on domestic and international routes to and from Bangkok and Phuket. This affiliate company has achieved high load factor (76%) in a short period of time, and recorded surpluses by November 2005.

In 2005, AirAsia also acquired AW Air International, an Indonesian commercial airline, and established PT Indonesia AirAsia with 49% of shares. The associate carrier provides services to Indonesian domestic and international routes. It expanded its operation scale, having focused on a route to and from Bali, which was of high-demand.

In the same year, AirAsia signed a memorandum with Phu Yen Province Committee in Vietnam to agree on both international and domestic flights from Tuy Hoa Airport as a base for advancing into the Vietnamese market. The company, however, announced that it would not start operations on the route between Singapore and Kuala Lumpur. This was because Indonesia AirAsia was not able to obtain authorization for the Jakarta Soekarno-Hatta International Airport–Singapore Changi Airport route from the Civil Aviation Authority of Singapore (CAAS).

In late 2008, AirAsia established "AirAsia X" as a sister company for long-distance routes. With its logo, "everyone can fly Xtra long", the company aims to develop routes to countries of East Asia, Australia, Middle East and Europe. AirAsia X once connected a route to Japan but had previously abolished it. Now, in 2016, it is planning to revive the route for the future. These days, AirAsia operates on 165 routes over 25 countries and has built daily and weekly flights, such as the one between Manila and Taipei. AirAsia X has also expanded their routes, having recently been approved by the FAA to acquire the U.S. region to its list in 2017.

AirAsia uses both Kuala Lumpur International Airport (KLIA) and Johor Bahru Airport as hub airports. It uses Don Mueang Airport in Bangkok, its affiliate AirAsia in Thailand, as a base for expansion on international routes. Johor Bahru Airport,

Chapter 2

adjacent to Singapore, is regarded as a secondary airport of Singapore Changi Airport.

2.1.3 Cost Reduction Measures

Cost of AirAsia per Available Seat Kilometer (ASK) is 2.41 US cents, which is the lowest among the airline companies worldwide. Cost per ASK excluding fuel accounts for 1.4 US cents, demonstrating a staggering cost structure (Both data were announced by the company in November 2005). This means that the cost per flight is as low as 150 million JPY if a B737 aircraft from AirAsia flew the distance between Tokyo and Osaka at a load factor of 80%. The reasoning behind these low-cost achievements will be studied here based on a limited amount of published material.

(1) Operation Cost (Fuel Cost, Pilot Personnel Cost)
Operation cost accounts for the largest cost structure of an airline company. AirAsia is reducing operation costs through the following methods:

The first measure is the avoidance of fuel price risks through the procurement of fuel cost hedging transaction, and turning off the air conditioners during landing. Fuel cost was hedged in 2005 by 50% and by 100% in 2006. This measure worked effectively against the steep rise of fuel cost.

The second measure is the use of the paperless cockpit, a method used by JetBlue Airways. Under this system, the pilot inputs data on a load sheet and the computer calculates its cost.

The third measure is the effective use of aircraft through various procedures, including strict punctuality of check-in and boarding times, improvement of punctual timing by minimizing boarding times and non-reserved seats, shortening of grounding time, and use of galley space as seats enabled by no provision of food.

The fourth measure is the use of a single type of aircraft, which saves cost for aircraft purchasing and maintenance, general maintenance cost, and training for crew members as seen in Southwest Airlines and Ryanair. The company initially used a 149-seat B737-300. It is now planning on purchasing a 180-seat, fuel-efficient

A320 in large quantities. In 2005, the company ordered 100 A320 (40 of them are optional) from Airbus, and some of them have already been used for operation. The Boeings are expected to be replaced to Airbuses.

(2) Maintenance Cost (Maintenance, Mechanic Personnel Cost)
Outsourcing is considered to be an effective measure for reducing maintenance cost, and so on. (However, new Japanese airlines increased their cost by outsourcing aircraft maintenance). AirAsia is promoting cost reduction by either outsourcing or in-housing, depending on the aspects of its business. Engine maintenance and repair, as well as its circulation parts, are outsourced. The successful development of AirAsia largely relies on the fact that an independent aircraft maintenance company is located in the area. AirAsia is now providing airport-handling services not through outsourcing, but through in-housing, which would result in an 82% cost reduction compared to its previous fiscal year.

(3) Passenger Services (In-Flight Service, Flight Attendant Personnel Cost)
AirAsia does not provide food or drink services. Malaysian domestic routes do not see the need of in-flight services because their routes are short or middle-distant. Limiting in-flight services is a cost reduction measure, which highly affects customers. The satisfaction of passengers after a flight should be equally proportional to their expectations before the flight. This highly noticeable cost reduction is part of Ryanair's business model. Passengers would be satisfied if they received generally expected services to some extent, but did not expect much from in-flight services during pre-boarding. Therefore, AirAsia uses flight attendants effectively by simplifying in-flight services; the company reduced the number of flight attendants from six to three. When DRB-HICOM was its parent company, the number of flight attendants per flight was six. Simplification of in-flight services cut back the workload of flight attendants. As a result, flight attendants are working six flights per day, and can focus on in-flight sales, etc.

(4) Airfare Structure and Ticket Sales Expense
AirAsia sells one-way tickets only to simplify the business. Airfares, depending on how early the ticket is purchased, consists of eight different types. Moreover, similar to the LCCs in North America and Europe, the company saves the fees paid to travel

agents by using the internet effectively. Although it is common in North America and Europe, payments by credit card or internet reservations are rarely seen in Malaysia. Therefore, some think that this factor hinders new LCCs from entering the market. However, AirAsia was successful in having processed 45% of its reservations via the Internet, when only 18% of Malaysians regularly use the Internet. This is because various incentives are provided to customers using the Internet, and many younger passengers access and retrieve information from the Internet on a regular basis. Therefore, the key for an airline company with IT functionalities is to encourage its target customers to use the Internet, regardless of how much it is used in the domestic markets. This is heavily considered from a strategic business and management effort point of view.

2.1.4 Brand Differentiation

Along with the low-fare strategy is branding strategy regarding design and style. This emphasizes originality from other Malaysia Airlines, hence its quote, "Cheap, but also young and stylish". To emphasize "youth", AirAsia uses red as their image color. Flight attendants wear bright red uniforms, for example, while Malaysia Airlines attendants wear the country's national colors. In 2005, the company signed an exclusive contract with Manchester United F.C., a British football team, in demonstrating a "stylish" airline, one that is up to date and not simply a low-fare airline.

Moreover, by maximizing exposure of the company's CEO, Tony Fernandez, to the media and consciously overlapping his image with that of Richard Branson, chairman of Virgin Atlantic Airways, the company has created an image of "young, active, and free" AirAsia in comparison to Malaysia Airlines, which remains in its traditional roots. AirAsia focuses on altering itself to be "young" and "high-tech", setting its targets on young students as potential customers.

2.1.5 Hands-On Policy

AirAsia, in order to emphasize its commitment to the company's "hands-on policy", has built its head office within KLIA. This has provided easier accessibility for contacts between the employees and the management, and developed unity within the company. This effort does not directly lead to cost reduction, but aims to develop a wide team effort in working on issues such as punctual flight schedule operation and directly handling passengers who complain about flight delays. This effort is also considered to raise a company-wide awareness of "cost and culture".

● 2.2 Government Preferential Treatment

AirAsia grew rapidly not just by its corporate effort but also by low personnel costs, and benefits from the government's policies on regarding development of LCCs and aviation infrastructure.

The Malaysian government is currently conducting repair work on runways at KLIA so that it can be compatible with the A380 aircraft. In addition, the largest terminal for the exclusive use of LCCs in Southeast Asia is under construction (predicted to be five times larger than that of the LCC terminal at Changi Airport in Singapore), with some exemption from facility fees. AirAsia has been receiving various government preferential tax treatments. The company was given an exemption from capital investment tax, which is 70% the amount of taxable revenue from the Malaysian government for 5 years from 2004. In conclusion, the Malaysian market shows remarkable measures in both the LCs as well as the promotion of LCCs' development that have been implemented.

◘ 3. Alliance of LCCs in Asia: Promoting Global Competition

Most successful LCCs that have excelled and flourished have all sought business on a worldwide scale. Successful LCCs such as AirAsia and Jetstar Airways (Australia) have made their subsidiaries internationally to pursue convenience and network expansion while maintaining their scale at large. However, the remainder of smaller LCCs with little history has felt the struggle of such network expansion. Thus, they have decided to create several partnerships to stay in the competition of the LCCs.

On May 16th of 2016, eight middle and small sized LCCs, including Scoot, Vanilla Air, and Jeju Air, formed "Value Alliance". Until now, each LCC focused on saving costs and maintaining low fees, but did not create partnerships and rather increased their range of routes individually. However, since most of the LCCs did not have much popularity independently, they have formed an alliance that offers multiple routes combined. These LCCs would promote brand name value of their airlines and would try to stay in competition even with the dominant LCCs, such as AirAsia or Jetstar Airways.

In the process of forming such an alliance, Air Black Box developed a system that would link reservation systems of all eight airlines so it would be easier to manage transfer systems. This will make transitions between airlines smoother and new routes would be offered to the customers. For example, if customers try to take the first section of a consecutive flight with Vanilla Air, they could choose their destinations, such as Hong Kong or Taipei, which may not be offered within Vanilla Air itself, but are within the airlines of the same alliance to efficiently plan their trips. Flight delay issues can also be resolved quickly, and payment would not be a problem. The customers would be allowed to substitute their flights with other airlines within the alliance for free. This shows that non-direct LCC flights would be able to offer customers to visit cities for a cheaper price, and offer trips within all the routes of the alliance group.

Out of the alliance members, Vanilla Air, Scoot, Cebu Pacific Air, and Jeju Air have direct routes to and from Japan. The customers can easily fly to cities, such as Taipei, Bangkok, Manila, and Singapore, and transfer to flights like "Nok Air", which does not have a direct route to Japan. Thus, interconnecting satellite airports to one another can expand the routes of the alliance. Vanilla Air alone had only covered six cities including both domestic and international, but after joining Value Alliance, it can now dominate over 160 different cities. The flight tickets can be automatically sold through other airlines which ultimately creates a win-win situation between many aviation companies.

Moreover, major LC airline alliances such as Star Alliance have mutual partnership services for thorough check-in, code-sharing, and mileage point systems. Value alliance, however, does not offer such services, because it would cause an increase in airfare. LCCs have also planned to increase their values without having to spend much expenses, initiating interconnecting transfer services from fall 2016. Meanwhile, the top two LCCs of Asia Pacific region, AirAsia Group and Jetstar Airways Group, have already established a firm network. The AirAsia Group includes

AirAsia Japan, which prepares to fly on domestic routes only based in Chubu Centrair International Airport, and consists of nine subsidiaries in six countries. Using the A330 aircraft, Tokyo International Airport–Kuala Lumpur International Airport, and Narita International Airport–Bangkok International Airport are operating routes that require more than four hours, and from those routes, there are strong networks that connect to Southeast Asian countries. AirAsia's launching services, such as check-in and mileage point systems similar to the alliance system of major airline companies, will also be promotional factors for the aviation industry.

The Jetstar Airways Group consists of four subsidiaries over five countries (Australia, New Zealand, Singapore, Vietnam, and Japan). The greatest advantage for Japanese customers of this factor is the 11 domestic routes that Jetstar Japan established. Jetstar Japan has been expanding its domestic lines for 4 years by adding aircraft. Since it entered the international route in 2015, the next step would be to establish the hub airports in the three cities of Tokyo, Osaka, and Nagoya, which would connect to the Pacific Rim. It would not be possible to use the thorough check-in system from regional airports transferring to Narita International Airport's international flights, but it would be possible to transfer in a case of a delay, if conditions for the flight ticket are met. While the networks of the two major LCCs are stable, it will be necessary for Value Alliance to attract more LCCs into the alliance.

Intense competition within the countries of Asia seems to take a similar form to the situation in Europe. Even AirAsia in Malaysia, an airline that brought huge changes in Southeast Asia, has recently been struggling due to the rise of Lion Air in Indonesia. Although it has gained some profit, the group itself as a whole within other subsidiaries suffered much loss.

On the other hand, Ryanair in Europe in March 2016 gained 1.24 billion EUR of net income to net sales of 19%. The reason for this rise is the competitive environment situation. In Europe, the competition among the European LCCs has died out and stabilized, as there were once 50 LCCs that have now been reduced to 30 surviving. Barely any changes were made thereafter. On the other hand, Asia is currently in the spotlight for LCC development as it only began its expansion about 20 years after those in the U.S., and 15 years after those in Europe. However, with such huge market expansion opportunities, it has only been recent that the LCCs began to enter Northeast Asia, including Japan. While Southeast Asia comes up to the LCC market share of 60%, Japan only has 10%.

Japan's LCCs were presumed to have the most success, as they had the "golden route", to their advantage for a sweet spot location. However, in just a year, this went out of hand. Aside from Japanese LCCs, six LCCs, such as Tigerair in Taiwan, have increased their passenger seats by 42% in the route between Japan and Taiwan. Moreover, the LCC market in Asia is also expected to head into intense competition by retracing the Western history of LCCs. It is important for Japanese LCCs to improve and come up with practical solutions to stay competitive and thrive in the market. Much attention will be drawn to the LCC alliance's trend from now on.

4 Characteristics of LCCs and Common Factors in the Market Worldwide

Thus far, the development and successful factors of LCCs in North America, Europe and Asia (other than Japan) have been viewed and analyzed. The analysis shows major LCCs such as Southwest Airlines and Ryanair in North America and Europe, and AirAsia in Asia that share a large number of common factors in terms of their business models and market environment.

1. Deregulation of the Industry

The first common element is the cost competitiveness of the LCCs over the LCs. While deregulation was in process, and the airline industries were growing, the past protectionism was regarded as harmful to the productivity of the LCs. Many Asian countries are behind European and North American countries when it comes to deregulation in the aviation market. Moreover, the existence of the national flag carrier, as part of government measures, places LCCs in a disadvantageous competition environment.

Since Asian countries are lagging behind European and North American countries in the markets, the recent line of deregulation in the aviation industry, has spread to Asia, which promoted the LCCs' growth in the market. There is now a growing recognition in Asian countries that liberalizing the aviation policies rather than protecting the national flag carriers, contributes to further economic developments in Asia.

In Malaysia, for example, former Prime Minister Mahathir positioned the aviation industry as the key industry for the nation's development. Under the vision of promoting the development of Malaysian economy by positioning KLIA as a future hub in Asia, the government implemented an expansion plan for airport facilities to a scale that significantly exceeds its current domestic air transport demand. At the same time, the plan also includes proactive LCC promotion measures, such as LCC terminal construction and capital investment tax exemption for AirAsia.

In addition, the existence of national flag carriers highlights the reason behind the existence of LCCs. Major airline companies of Southeast Asia are renowned to be low in cost, but the standard of cost is subjected to only wealthier countries. Within the domestic market, they are still considered high in cost.

As for international routes in Asia, it is shown that "the framework of the aviation market is not based on Open Sky Policy, but on bilateral aviation agreements between Asian countries. Therefore, provision service of LCCs on international routes cannot enter the Asian market"[6]. In reality, the Open Sky Policy is being applied in Southeast Asian countries within the frameworks of bilateral agreements. LCCs such as AirAsia and its affiliates acquired international routes based on these bilateral agreements.

The Asian airline industry has experienced the same process that airlines in North America and Europe have gone through. In this process, the cost-incurring nature of LCs, which had been nurtured by protectionism, encouraged the appearance of LCCs along with deregulation. Yet, the speed of the process was different in Asia compared to North American and European countries.

---

6 Williams (2000), p.172.

The difference, as demonstrated by the LCC promotion measures by Mahathir described above, is that government policies strongly support LCCs in Asia (other than Japan), compared to North American and European countries. AirAsia, for example, started its business after it acquired Tune Air, a government-affiliated company. The company is said to have acquired Tune Air with the amount of 160 million JPY approximately out of Tune Air's debts of 4.3 billion JPY. If this is true, it can be said that AirAsia was established with strong government support. Moreover, one cannot overlook the fact that these LCC promotion policies have largely contributed to AirAsia's rapid growth. Recent construction of terminals for the exclusive use of LCCs in Asian countries can be regarded as part of LCC promotion measures provided by the government.

To sum up, the market in Asian countries (other than Japan) is placed at a slightly more disadvantageous situation than those in North America and Europe. However, LCCs have developed to the same extent as those in North America and Europe through governmental promotion measures.

2. Common Factors of Business Models

The second common factor is business models and market environments (except deregulation) that enhance the competitiveness of LCCs. This factor consists of competitiveness of cost elements and differentiation elements. Competitive elements include low-cost measures such as full-scale, no-frills services, with the use of a single type of aircraft, and high accessibility to operational resources. Differentiation elements include establishment of CI, fare structure according to market needs, and proactive use of secondary airports. Some elements such as the use of secondary airports are attributable to both elements.

2.1 Cost Reduction Measures

The common factor of such successful LCCs is cost reduction through high-frequency flights by using a single type of aircraft on specific routes. This helps save usage fees of airports and other fees by the utilization of secondary airports, the no-frills in-flight service, and the use of IT to reduce operation and sales cost. The gap difference between LCCs and LCs in personnel costs is getting smaller in the U.S. by the productivity enhancement effort made by the LCs. Competitiveness of the LCs over LCCs in this sense is in decline. The gap in personnel costs in Europe and Asia, on the other hand, still contributes to LCC's low-cost structure. Another productivity enhancement measure implemented in many LCCs is the involvement of pilot and flight attendant in cleaning and sales.

LCCs must enter the route with high-demand if they wish to increase the profit ratio by improving efficiency through the effective use of aircraft on short and middle-distant routes with high-density. In other words, the common LCC factor is to enter a profitable route. This goal was simply achieved by the act of liberalization. In this regard, LCCs in Europe with small domestic markets and in Asian countries (other than Japan) with underdeveloped markets tend to seek international, high-density routes instead of domestic ones. Therefore, global aviation liberalization will be the key factor in their growth and expansion.

● 2.2 Factors Contributing to Low-Fares

The common differentiating factor between LCCs and LCs in its services is the low fares resulting from low cost. Some other factors include competition level in the entire market and customers with low-fare preference. These factors are discussed, although they are not directly related to the discussion of business models.

2.2.1 Market Competition Level

When the competition level is below average in a market, LCs can go against LCCs when it comes to going through the same routes with a less costly fare. They have done this by taking advantage of their effective and large networks as well as their monopoly-oriented influences on other routes. Furthermore, the disappearance of many LCCs in the U.S. in the 1980s was due to LCs having enhanced their productivity under the protection of Chapter 11. Ultimately, LCCs could no longer compete with a low-fare policy, which reflected only the difference in personnel costs. LCs were successful in competing with counteractive fares against LCCs. In contrast, LCCs have been active again since the late 1990s despite the measures implemented by the LCs to enhance productivity. The competition in the entire market, including the competition between the LCs, has become far more intense.

In a sense, the competition level that the deregulation progress brings to the market will become important for a fair competition. In Europe, liberalization policies within the EU are encouraging competition within the area, though not as intense as in the U.S. In Asian countries, liberalization within the frameworks of bilateral agreements is raising the competition level. Some countries in Asia (including Japan), however, are still under heavy protectionism. Therefore, liberalization in these countries has not progressed as far as it did in Europe.

2.2.2 Low-Fare Market

Moreover, we can expect that low-fare offers from LCCs will further generate new demand, but it is important to promote same efforts within all airlines. In Malaysia, AirAsia acquired passengers who used to travel on long-distance buses and automobiles by offering drastic discounts on its airfare. The company successfully obtained its own niche market as a result. In Thailand, the passengers of LCCs were found to have lower incomes than the passengers who travel on major airlines. This means that cheaper airlines can establish their domestic operation even in small regions where the demand for air transportation is limited due to the relatively short distances between major cities—only if substitutions for existing transportation are offered at a reasonable cost. This means that the LCC model is viable, depending on the price and availability of the mode of transport. This is the case even in the domestic airline market with low air transport demand due to short distances between cities.

The above is also applicable in developed countries. The airline industry has the option of acquiring passengers from low-cost and long-distance buses. Ryanair and easyJet are obviously targeting these low-income passengers who usually prefer bus travel. In the U.S., Europe, and Asia (except for Japan), people use roadways rather than railways as their major means of transportation, and LCCs can expect a shift in those areas. In Japan, where citizens use trains a lot, different tactics are being used to attract such customers. However, like some Skymark Airlines' passengers who switched from long-distance buses, it is still reasonable to expect people switching from roadway and railway transportation as well.

Chapter 2

● 2.3   Differentiation by Using Secondary Airports

As proven by many of the cheap airlines in the U.S. that have sprung up and then disappeared during the 1980s, it has become difficult for LCCs to survive in the industry, those that only operate by offering low fares. It has become necessary for them to differentiate themselves in factors other than airfares.

Some of the most conspicuous instances are those of Ryanair, easyJet, and Southwest Airlines, which successfully differentiated themselves from legacy airlines by using secondary airports. They adopted secondary airports to express originality corresponding to differences in territorial spheres. It was also adopted to target those passengers who complained about overcrowded hub airports and loss of time due to congestion. The use of secondary airports also leads to cost reduction by promoting competition between airports and area development surrounding the airports. Moreover, secondary airports could be seen as no-frills airports, different from those of legacy airlines equipped with superabundant features (for those passengers who expect low-cost travels), which again will lead to cost reduction as well as being distinct.

In Asian countries, the use of secondary airports is cumbersome and LCCs face disadvantages due to this, in comparison to those in Europe and in North America. However, in the case of AirAsia, it has used Johor Bahru Airport in Malaysia as its secondary airport next to Changi Airport in Singapore. Many new airports are being constructed in Asia and there are possibilities that some older airports, such as Gimpo Airport in Korea, could be used as secondary airports to new ones, such as Incheon International Airport. Having witnessed the remarkable development of LCCs, major terminals (not only in Asia) are planning to construct no-frills terminals exclusively for LCCs, and this overall trend is expected to be favorable for them.

● 2.4   Establishing CI

Successful LCCs, therefore, have been making efforts at differentiating themselves not only from LCs, but also from other LCCs. Southwest Airlines, for example, has established its corporate image as "a corporation friendly both to the customers and the employees", while AirAsia adopted IT and uniform designs that are nouveau and stylish. As shown in the advertisements of Virgin Atlantic Airways and AirAsia, whose core operations are on par with their charismatic chairmen, Sir Richard Charles Nicholas Branson and CEO Fernandez, we cannot overlook LCCs that have established their brand images and CI during the earliest stages of their businesses by conveying explicit messages of their own definition and model to the passengers.

On the other hand, some LCCs like JetBlue Airways, offer high-quality "frilled" flights (IT-equipped cabins, genuine leather seats, and individual satellite TVs, etc.) for relatively low fares as a part of their promotion tactics, while many LCCs commonly offer "no-frills" flights. This contributes to differentiation from the other LCCs. Moreover, this is a positive attraction amongst LCs that do not offer pillow and blanket services and even charge crew meals. The image of "LCC = Cheap Airline" now has a negative image.

● 2.5　Expansion of Service to Long-Distance Routes

LCCs are recently advancing into the long-distance market, which has not been their main focus for almost 20 years, with the exception of Virgin Atlantic Airways. The four companies in North America and Europe including Astraeus Airlines began services to North Atlantic regions. AirAsia established its affiliate company to service long-distance routes. Oasis Hong Kong Airlines began service between London and Hong Kong. This trend does not apply to the conventional LCC business model of short and middle-distance routes using small-sized aircraft.

The four companies in North America and Europe set all seats of their 220-seat B757 or B767 aircraft as business class, and have secured an exclusive terminal or lounge in order to differentiate themselves from conventional LCCs. Furthermore, they offer low fares (30% to 60%) that can compete with the fares of LCs' business class by reducing the cost. As the Silverjet's website says, this is because no assistance is required for competitive and cheap economy class. This is a new low-cost strategy and a differentiation strategy. The four companies are mainly using secondary airports. This means that they are still applying part of the conventional LCC business model.

Chapter 2

◊ 3. Operational Resources and Availability of Funds

In regard to LCCs in North America and Europe, the case of access to operational resources is not different from that of new enterprises in other industries. The technical challenges of launching an LCC are not so different from the efforts of establishing a new bus or truck company. Entrepreneurs in Europe and the U.S. can easily access operational resources in neighboring countries if they cannot access the domestic resources.

It is likely that the above situation was created in these regions because the aviation industry in these regions have developed not only the operations of regular flights, but also in the areas of general aviation (geometrical surveys and photographing) and in a variety of transportation businesses, including chartered flights and air taxis under deregulation, proving itself over 30 years of history, having made the competition in the industry a normal affair.

In Asia, the situation is different from that of North America and Europe. Some claim that the hard aspects of the market, which support new entries into airline transportation, such as the number of independent maintenance companies, are not matured in Asia. It is undeniable that the industry in Asia lags behind those in Europe and North America in this respect, however, some independent maintenance companies do exist in some places in Asia, and have been partly supported by governments with the aim of protecting the industry. AirAsia, for example, is outsourcing its maintenance to companies abroad. The company compensates for the insufficiency in the domestic and independent maintenance facilities through international co-operations. It is fortunate for those Southeast Asian countries (Malaysia, Indonesia, Singapore and Thailand) that are geographically close to each other.

In Europe, North America, and in Asia (except for Japan), an LCC is considered to be a lucrative business if it is successful as exemplified by JetBlue Airways, a corporation that entered the industry with abundant capital. In addition, there is an avid desire for investment in new enterprises in Asia, where rapid economic growth has recently taken place. In some Asian countries, the government is actively supporting the growth of LCCs, and its stance is making it much easier for entrepreneurs in the airline industry to obtain funds to launch businesses.

Conclusion: Summary of Common Factors of Successful LCCs

In this chapter, the development process of LCCs in the U.S., Europe, and Asia (other than Japan) was outlined and analyzed. As a result, the following common factors were found in LCCs that continue to grow in the LCC markets:
(1) Removal of institutional barrier by deregulation
(2) Cost advantage in labor productivity over LCs
(3) Cost advantage through a management strategy focusing on limited routes using the same aircraft
(4) Low-cost measures through no-frills service and IT
(5) Low airfare resulting from the above (2) to (4)
(6) Differentiation from LCs using secondary airports in the same city
(7) Marketing strategy according to targeted group of customers
(8) Avoid creation of "LCC = Cheap Airline" image
(9) Establishment of Corporation Identity (CI) from an early stage
(10) High availability of management resources and funds

The above factors differ to some extent in the U.S., Europe, and Asia, and are not shared by all LCCs. It can be said, however, that these are the factors that apply to many regardless of where they are based. In the next chapter, the reasons for the stagnancy of new Japanese airline companies will be studied by comparing these successful factors of foreign LCCs. In this chapter, the success factors of LCCs in the world are analyzed only from the result of observations of foreign LCCs. Neither detailed analysis of financial statements nor analysis from the viewpoint of business leader's qualities or management organization has been conducted. The purpose of this book is to analyze the management of LCCs in the world by presenting both management policies and aviation policies critical to the development of new Japanese airline companies. The purpose of this chapter was to outline the characteristics of LCCs worldwide to obtain major findings required for the study to be conducted later.

CHAPTER 3
Current Japanese Low-Cost Carriers(LCCs) and Stagnancy Factor Analysis

In this chapter, the current condition of the new Japanese airlines will be outlined. The reason behind the sluggishness of Japanese LCCs will then be examined from a business perspective by comparing with foreign LCCs and their success factors. Subsequently, negative factors of the Japanese aviation policy will be exhibited as a background of these managerial circumstances. As a result, it has arrived to the conclusion that if certain requirements are met such as(1)a certain size of business,(2)high productivity to allow low fares,(3)active use of secondary airports,(4)free setting of number of flights and route alignment including the advance in international air routes,(5)preparation of sufficient amount of funds, and(6)differentiation through marketing scheme, the potential expansion of LCCs as can be seen in the U.S. and Asia would be possible in Japan as well.

This chapter refers to the contents from Shiotani(2008).

Chapter 3

✈ Introduction

In Japan, nine LCCs (Skymark Airlines, Air Do, Solaseed Air, Star Flyer, Peach Aviation, Vanilla Air, Fuji Dream Airlines, Spring Airlines Japan, and Jetstar Japan) have entered the aviation market since 1998. On the other hand, the oligopoly structure of the three Japanese LCs that were consolidated later into two, still remains. JAL Group and ANA Group, the two remaining major LCs, have held 33.4% and 40% each of market shares of domestic passengers in 2015, respectively. While the two LCs hold the majority of the shares, Skymark Airlines, Jetstar Japan, and Peach Aviation cover 6.3%, 5.1%, and 3.3% each. Adding up the remainder LCCs altogether would still only constitute 11.9%.

In this chapter, an overview of the current status of Japanese LCCs will first be presented. Furthermore, the reasons behind their stagnancy in Japan will be analyzed from a management policy perspective, including a comparison with successful factors of LCCs outside of Japan. The problems of the LCCs are determined as follows: (1) high cost structure due to small business size and lack of resource procurement ability, (2) intense airfare competition against LCs by depending only on lowering fares, (3) obscure customer target, (4) inappropriate route setting, (5) concentration of hub airport usage, (6) inconvenient operations, (7) lack of management policies and corporate identity (CI), and (8) dependency on public funds.

Moreover, negative structural and institutional factors that caused management problems will be presented. These restrictions are being eased, compared to the 1990s, when the first LCCs entered the market. There is a huge difference in labor costs compared to LCs. Therefore, my hypothesis of this book is that there is room for development for LCCs even in the Japanese market, if certain conditions including the following are met: clear scale of business size, high productivity that leads to low airfares, proactive use of secondary airports, free setting of routes and number of flights including expansion of services to international routes, procurement of sufficient funds and differentiation through unique marketing. This will be the basis for the business model, which will be presented in the next chapter.

Chapter 3

The significance of discussion within this chapter is that even though it is based on existing studies in several related fields as well as interviews with Skymark Airlines and Administrative Reform Committee personnel, the problems from the management policy and aviation policy point of view are discussed in a comprehensive manner.

1　Current Status of LCCs in Japan

1.　History of LCCs Prior to New Entry

Before discussing the current status of Japanese LCCs, it is necessary to understand the Japanese market, especially the changes made in its legal system. Studies on the Japanese deregulation process and its problems in comparison with those of Europe and the U.S. will be discussed in detail later. Here, a brief explanation of the beginning of the LCCs will be presented.

In Japan, based on the concept in which the aviation industry must be developed under the protection and support of the national government, measures to protect scheduled airline companies was implemented for a long period after the end of WWII, and prohibited new entries. According to the Civil Aeronautics Act(CAA), which specifies that "aviation capacity must not significantly exceed demand for air transport volume due to launch of business,"[1] entry of an airline company involved supply and demand adjustment for the start of business, setting routes and numbers of flights, and distribution of arrival and departure slots at the airport. Domestic airfares were to be authorized by Ministry of Land, Infrastructure, Transport and Tourism(MLIT), and its standard was for guaranteeing profits and not for causing price competition. Until the so-called "45/47 Structure"[2] was abolished in 1986, the market was compartmentalized with JAL on international routes, and ANA and JAS on domestic routes under this regulatory philosophy. The airlines maintained high profitability due to high price settings without any problems.

1　Chapter 101.2 in CAA before amendments in 2000.
2　"45/47 Structure"designated by the government, specified business rules for the operating airlines up until its abolishment in 1986.

Even after the abolishment of the "45/47 Structure" in 1986 and the so-called "New Aviation Policy"[3] coming into effect, market adjustments were mitigated between the two LCs, and other new entries. "The fare authorization system"[4] remained effective. The standard cost system introduced in 1990 enhanced artful regulation of airfares. In 1995, a system was established in which airlines reported discounted fares up to 50% as well as special discount fares for flights with low utilization factors. In 1997, the scope of the fare system, which liberalized regular fares within a 25% range of standard cost, was implemented. However, there were few opportunities for the airlines to use the system until new entries were approved.

Given the global deregulation trend, the Deregulation Subcommittee of the Administrative Reform Committee advised the abolishment of supply and demand adjustments. With this advice and from the fact that LCCs entered the market with half-priced airfares, drawing attention of the entire society, LCCs were allowed to enter the market 50 years after the war. In September 1998, Skymark Airlines began service between Tokyo International Airport and Fukuoka Airport, and Air Do began service between Tokyo International Airport and New Chitose Airport in December of the same year. As for airfares, after tenacious negotiations by Skymark Airlines, introduction of half-priced fares was approved. Amendments made to the CAA in

---

3 "New Aviation Policy" is based on a report submitted by Transportation Policy Council to MLIT in 1986 on "Future Operation Structure of Airline Companies". The contents included:
(1) Approved entry of multiple companies for operating international scheduled flights. Abolishment of the "45/47 Structure", which allowed JAL's exclusive operation of international scheduled flights.
(2) Set licensing criteria for domestic routes, which approves entry of the second company to the route with an annual demand of more than 700,000 passengers (Double track) or entry of a third company to the route with an annual demand of more than 1 million passengers (Triple track). This prevents excessive competition in the major domestic routes, which have been exclusively operated by JAL and ANA, by operating flights more than the users' demand. Competition will be promoted within the above framework, and was still not allowed.
(3) Privatize JAL, and abolish protection from the government. In 1992, the criteria above were changed to annual demand of 400,000 passengers for double track and annual demand of 700,000 passengers for triple track (500,000 and 800,000 respectively for routes with airport restrictions). The criteria were abolished for existing domestic routes.

4 A policy to make the airline companies comply with the airfare that MLIT has set for both high-demand routes and regional routes.

Chapter 3

2000 changed the pricing system from "authorization" to "report in advance". Airline companies could then determine airfares on their own.

2. Current Status of LCCs

The Table 3-1 below is the current status of LCCs in Japan. Examples of the history and management policy of each LCC in Japan will be presented.

2.1 Skymark Airlines

2.1.1 Beginning of Business and Inaugural Flight

Skymark Airlines was established in 1996 with a large amount of capital from HIS, a discount travel operator. In 1998, after 2 years of preparation, the company had started its service between Tokyo International Airport and Fukuoka Airport. By then, the company's capital totaled up to 2,575 million JPY as a result of several allocations of new shares. Initially, the company had only three arrival and departure slots at Tokyo International Airport, and it operated three round-trips with just one aircraft. Above all, it acquired a large number of passengers by offering an airfare

Table 3-1 LCCs operating domestic routes in Japan

	Hub Airports	Aircraft	First Operation
Vanilla Air	Narita International Airport	A320	December, 2013
Jetstar Japan	Narita International Airport Kansai International Airport	A320	July, 2012
Peach Aviation	Kansai International Airport Naha Airport Narita International Airport	A320	March, 2012
Fuji Dream Airlines	Sizuoka Airport Komaki Airport	ERJ175 ERJ170	September, 2009
Star Flyer	Kitakyushu Airport	A320	March, 2006
Solaseed Air	Tokyo International Airport Naha Airport	B737	August, 2002
Air Do	Tokyo International Airport New Chitose Airport	B767 B737	December, 1998
Skymark Airlines	Tokyo International Airport Kobe Airport	B737	September, 1998
AirAsia Japan	Chubu Centrair International Airport	A320	Postponed indefinitely
Spring Airlines Japan	Narita International Airport	B737	Postponed indefinitely

Source: Created by the author based on annual reports of each airline

of 13,700 JPY, which was cheaper than that of LCs. The company saw remarkable seat occupancy of 86% by February 1999.

2.1.2 From Start of Business to Record of Surplus

Six months later, despite its successful start, it suffered from deficit. The main factors for the company's financial difficulties included high outsourcing costs of maintenance at the initial stage, restrictions on arrival and departure slots, and the fact that the two LCs had set the same discounted fare as Skymark Airlines. Nevertheless, cost reduction measures such as self-management of maintenance, ticketing, and pilot training became effective, and the company recorded surplus both in business profitability and profits in 2004 and 2005, respectively.

Skymark Airlines expanded its service on routes from Tokyo International Airport to major cities in other regions. As a result of trial and error attempts to enter new routes in addition to the former Tokyo International Airport–Fukuoka Airport route, it has eventually expanded operations, and as of 2007, it had operated routes to Fukuoka Airport, Kobe Airport and New Chitose Airport.

In 2007, Skymark Airlines used six B767 and two B737. The company initially applied European and US business models to reduce the costs for training and maintenance by using a single type of aircraft. These days, types of aircraft are selected according to the demand of the route. The company had a strong relationship with ANA at the beginning of their business, but now has a better partnership with JAL, and is under code-share agreements with the company.

Skymark Airlines had been in a close relationship with HIS, a bucket shop. However, it has also aimed to become an airline company that appeals to business passengers since most people used the Tokyo International Airport–Fukuoka Airport route for business reasons. As a result, they did not follow the no-frills service policy, but instead offered free towels, drinks and snacks, and "super seats" for business passengers as part of their in-flight service. Their unique services also provided a seating section exclusively for women, which was unseen in foreign airlines. Since 2007, they have continued to offer services including responses to flight cancellation and in-flight drink services.

2.1.3 Radical Change in Route Structure

Skymark Airlines started to exploit international charter routes in 2002. It had operated two flights every weekend between Tokyo International Airport–Incheon International Airport, but cancelled the route because of poor convenience and load factor. The company was planning on operating Tokyo International Airport–Incheon International Airport flights, under the condition that they would be assigned an arrival and departure slot for short-distance international routes after the completion of the airport. It would have been the first LCC in Japan to launch scheduled international flights if the plan had succeeded (Table 3-2).

In November 2005, in conjunction with route restriction starting in February 2006, Skymark Airlines undertook a significant change in its fare system. Various new prices under this system were created including sizable discounts in normal fares and limited time discounts of 5,000 JPY. Their management policy is to emphasize advantages and differences in airfares to compete with LCs.

In the spring of 2006, Skymark Airlines focused on routes with high passenger demand. The company increased the number of flights for its major route between Fukuoka Airport–Tokyo International Airport and further began service between New Chitose Airport–Kobe Airport, Tokyo International Airport–Kobe Airport / New Chitose Airport. Kobe Airport opened in February 2006, and Air Do announced a counteractive reduced airfare for the Tokyo International Airport–New Chitose Airport route. The competition between LCCs is expected to become more intense. On the other hand, the company discontinued operations between Tokyo International Airport–Osaka International Airport / Tokushima Airport / Kagoshima Airport. The company used its arrival and departure slots in Tokyo International Airport for a new route instead. Such drastic route structure reform may be regarded as a "secondary foundation" since it is clearly focusing on promoting major routes. Operating performance of its Kobe Airport–Tokyo International Airport route is underway mostly because the number of flights of the two leading companies is low. This proves that entry to the Kobe Airport–Tokyo International Airport route will play a key role in the simulation results presented in Chapter 4.

Chapter 3

✈ Table 3-2 History of Skymark Airlines

Year	History
1996	Established with capital of 150 million JPY
1998	Began service between Tokyo International Airport–Fukuoka Airport
1999	Began service between Fukuoka Airport–Osaka International Airport, Osaka International Airport–New Chitose Airport
	Capital of 3.589 billion JPY as a result of allocation of new shares to a third party
2000	Listed at Tosho Mothers stock exchange. Capital of 3.839 billion JPY
	Reached a total of 1 million passengers in March
	Discontinued operations between Fukuoka Airport–Osaka International Airport, Osaka International Airport–New Chitose Airport
	Began service of 12 flights between Tokyo International Airport–Fukuoka Airport
2002	Began service between Tokyo International Airport and Kagoshima Airport
	Started charter flights to Tokyo International Airport–Incheon International Airport
2003	Began service between Tokyo International Airport–Aomori Airport, Tokyo International Airport–Tokushima Airport
	Discontinued between Tokyo International Airport–Aomori Airport
2004	Merged with Zero Group
2005	Began service between Tokyo International Airport–Kansai International Airport
	Started 10 seasonal flights per week between Tokyo International Airport–Naha Airport
	Capital of 3.663 billion JPY as a result of allocation of new shares to a third party
	Discontinued between Tokyo International Airport–Naha Airport
2006	Began service of 14 flights between Tokyo International Airport–Kobe Airport
	Discontinued operations between Tokyo International Airport–Kansai International Airport, Tokyo International Airport–Tokushima Airport, and Tokyo International Airport–Kagoshima Airport
	Began service of 20 flights between Tokyo International Airport–New Chitose Airport
	Changed business name to Skymark Airlines Inc.
2007	Began to issue inflight magazine "SKYMARK"
2008	Began service of 6 flights between Tokyo International Airport–Asahikawa Airport
	Capital of 4.777 billion JPY because of allocation of new shares to a third party
	Moved main office to Tokyo International Airport
	Began seasonal service between Fukuoka Airport–Naha Airport
2009	Began regular service of 4 flights between Fukuoka Airport–Naha Airport
	Began self-training by a full flight simulator equipped at headquarters
2010	Began regular service of 4 flights between Kobe Airport–Fukuoka Airport
2011	Concluded purchase agreement of A380 with Airbus
	Opened Kobe office at Kobe Airport
2012	Began service of 4 flights between Narita International Airport–Fukuoka Airport
	Began service of 4 flights between Tokyo International Airport–Kobe Airport
	Closed service between Kitakyushu Airport–Naha Airport, Tokyo International Airport–Kitakyushu Airport
2013	Closed Kobe Airport office
	Stopped regular service between 4 different routes
	Began regular service between 9 different routes
	Started recruitment of crew members and their job training
	Listed on the First Section of the Tokyo Stock Exchange

2014	The arrival of A330	
	Began service of A330 between Tokyo International Airport–Fukuoka Airport	
	Stopped regular service between 11 different routes	
	Began regular service between 5 different routes	
	Restarted service between Ibaraki Airport–Chubu Centrair International Airport	
2015	Delisted from the First Section of Tokyo Stock Exchange	
	Stopped service of 10 different routes	
	Began seasonal service between New Chitose Airport–Naha Airport	
	Initiated the Civil Rehabilitation Act	
	The rehabilitation plan approved	
	Reduced all capital stock and increased recycling worth to 18 billion JPY	
	Started restructure and received capital injection from ANAHD and Integral Corporation	
2016	The termination of the Civil Rehabilitation Act	

Source: Created by the author according to Skymark Airlines' website, December 2016

Table 3-3　Revenue operating profit margin of major airlines (FY2015)

(%)

Skymark Airlines	0
Peach Aviation	12.9
AirAsia	32.24
Ryanair	18
Southwest Airlines	20.77
JAL	15.7

Source: Created by the author based on each airline's annual report, December 2016

In 2004, Skymark Airlines merged with a system development department named Zero Group, an Internet service provider. This was to proactively promote IT for the purpose of cost reduction and improvement of customer convenience. This reform will also include the improvement of the in-house system environment, such as the ticketing system.

Skymark Airlines had initially planned to introduce A330, and apply it to major domestic routes such as Kobe Airport–Tokyo International Airport. With regard to expanding new operational routes, it planned to operate a route to Sendai Airport in July 2012. However, it has been suspended due to rapid extension of new operational routes from Narita International Airport and Kansai International Airport by newcomers (LCCs). The company therefore attempted to open new routes to

Chapter 3

Matsuyama Airport because of its middle term management plan. In addition, the company also planned to increase the number of flights on the Tokyo International Airport–Naha Airport route if the operation hours were extended, and introduce A380.

Skymark Airlines was the price leader in the domestic aviation market before it was directly influenced by the emergence of other new LCCs. For instance, the company had offered tickets for the Tokyo International Airport–New Chitose Airport route at 16,000 JPY, whereas JAL and ANA offered at standard price of 34,000 JPY. However, due to the emergence of other LCCs in 2012, the company's high annual average of load factor rapidly decreased to 80%, and Skymark Airlines had run a deficit in the first quarter of 2012 (Table 3-2).

In addition, at that time, Skymark Airlines was facing another challenge. There were no increase in the number of arrival and departure slots at Tokyo International Airport. The arrival and departure slots at Tokyo International Airport are often referred as essential facilities, indicating that there is a huge competition by airlines over these slots. Tokyo International Airport routes led to Skymark Airlines' growth which peaked in the domestic market at the time, and allowed the company to have a clear advantage over other LCCs. However, there was an increase in the number of domestic arrival and departure slots in association with the construction of the fourth runway, which resulted in the extinction of Skymark Airline's advantage.

As a countermeasure against this situation, Skymark Airlines planned to introduce A330 and apply it to the main domestic routes such as Kobe Airport–Tokyo International Airport. By replacing with larger A330 aircraft with two class seating, the company could enhance its capacity.

Sources have also stated that Skymark Airlines was originally planning to operate a new international route between Kobe Airport and an airport in New York using A380. Although this aircraft provides seating for 550 people in a typical three class (first, business, and economy) configuration, Skymark Airlines planned to provide only for 380 people, total of both business and premium economy class, and none for the economy class.

Chapter 3

The aviation industry scrutinized this strategy because it was a unique business model, which had not been successful in the entire aviation history. Originally, LCCs including Skymark Airlines were only good at operating short-distance routes, and although some LCCs tried to operate an Atlantic Ocean route in the past, almost all of them failed. The reasons behind such failure were due to (1) operations by used aircraft, (2) high-cost structure due to small-sized business equipped with four to five aircraft, (3) no back-up plans since they were operating the Atlantic Ocean route. Considering the mistakes mentioned above, Skymark Airlines had started implementing the following strategies:A380, a brand new, supersized and fuel-efficient aircraft, was introduced to reduce cost per seat. It is said that the cost per flight between Narita International Airport–John F. Kennedy International Airport is 25 million JPY, which means that some profit is obtained if a company can operate at a load factor of 60% at a price of 120,000 JPY one way. Skymark Airlines plans to provide for the premium economy class at a price of 240,000 JPY and over, and business class at a price level of 300,000 JPY. Considering that JAL and ANA provide business classes at a price between 500,000 JPY and 1 million JPY with a load factor of 80% in the same route, there is a chance for customers to create a high-demand for Skymark Airlines. Skymark Airlines seemed to attract customers away from the major airlines.

In conclusion, based on the concept of LCCs, Skymark Airlines changed its original business model of using a single type of aircraft, taking short-distance routes, having only a single class, and succeeded in attempting new challenges in Japan. Skymark Airlines succeeded in trying new strategies, which none of the other LCCs had ever done. Even though it was said that the alternative LCC brought competition to the Japanese aviation market, Skymark Airlines faced difficulties after a while.

I would like to describe the difficulties it faced, the success and failure of management strategies, and the perspectives that was concluded from the management of the entire corporation in detail. This is analyzed and properly clarified in Chapter 6.

Chapter 3

● 2.2　Air Do

2.2.1　Beginning of Business and Inaugural Flight

Air Do began service in December 1998, following Skymark Airlines, in the Tokyo International Airport–New Chitose Airport route, which was one of the most high-demanded routes operated by the LCs. This route has the highest passenger traffic in the country, recording 9 million annual passengers per year (Table 3-4).

By the time the company launched its inaugural flight, its capital had increased to 3.58 billion JPY. Air Do initially listed a large number of corporations and individuals in Hokkaido as shareholders. This was based on the concept, "Wings for Hokkaido", describing an airline company with close connections to Hokkaido and

Table 3-4　History of Air Do

	History
1996	Established with a capital of 14 million JPY
1998	Began service between Tokyo International Airport–New Chitose Airport with 3 round-trips daily
2000	Started service between Tokyo International Airport–New Chitose Airport by 2 aircraft with 6 round-trip flights daily
	Exceeded 1 million passengers in December
2002	Exceeded 2 million passengers in March
	Filed civil rehabilitation proceedings at Tokyo District Court and submitted rehabilitation plan
	According to the rehabilitation plan, capital was reduced by 100% Capital was increased to 2 billion JPY as a primary rehabilitation process
	Closed outsourcing contract with ANA on operation as well as agreement for joint operation of domestic routes
2003	Started first domestic code-sharing with ANA between Tokyo International Airport–New Chitose Airport
	Began service of 3 aircraft between Tokyo International Airport–Asahikawa Airport
	Exceeded 3 million passengers in August
2005	Began service of 4 aircraft between Tokyo International Airport–Hakodate Airport
2006	Began service of 5 aircraft between Tokyo International Airport–Memanbetsu Airport
2008	Reached 10 million passengers flown
	Began service of 7 aircraft between New Chitose Airport–Sendai Airport
2009	Began service of 8 aircraft between New Chitose Airport–Niigata Airport
	Began service of 9 aircraft between New Chitose Airport–Fukushima Airport, Toyama Airport, Komatsu Airport
2011	Began service of 10 aircraft between Tokachi-Obihiro Airport–Tokyo International Airport
2012	Introduced reserve aircraft and held 12 aircraft in total
2013	Began service between Kushiro Airport–Tokyo International Airport, New Chitose Airport–Okayama Airport, New Chitose Airport–Kobe Airport
	Holds 13 aircraft in total
2014	Achieved 20 million passengers
	The first international charter flight operated
2015	Planning to abolish 4 routes to Niigata Airport, Fukushima Airport, Toyama Airport, and Komatsu Airport

Source: Created by the author according to Air Do's website, December 2016

using this as a boost for Hokkaido's economic revitalization. Initially, Air Do was given only three arrival and departure slots, same as Skymark Airlines, and started operations between Tokyo International Airport and New Chitose Airport with only one aircraft for three round-trip flights daily. The fare was 16,000 JPY while the LCs' were 25,000 JPY. This low-cost fare drew attention, and a load factor of 90% was initially achieved.

However, the company's limited scale of flight operations and low convenience did not attract business passengers, as for the case of Skymark Airlines. Moreover, several accidents showcased the inexperienced environment of the airline industry; for example, its initiation of the inaugural flight right after it closed a lease contract for its first aircraft, when the company still had to pay a monthly aircraft lease fee of 100 million JPY for the first six months. In addition to poor management problems, Air Do suffered from both counteractive airfares and distribution of management resources concentrated on LCs, as Skymark Airlines did. In 1999, LCs set a "specially discounted" airfare for flights that were operating at similar hours to Air Do's ones. In addition, JAL raised its aircraft maintenance fee by slightly over 10%. Air Do was outsourcing its aircraft maintenance to JAL at that time. As a result, Air Do faced counteractive airfares presented by LCs, and cost increased dramatically losing its management vitality.

Additionally, Air Do attempted to increase the load factor by reinforcing the partnership with sales agents. However, the attempt backfired, with the agency commission oppressing the management. The airfare was raised to make up for the kickback, but resulted in the superiority of the customers to fall, falling into a vicious spiral.

Another negative aspect of Air Do was its poor financial base. Though its capital at the beginning of service was larger than that of Skymark Airlines, the financial ground had been apparently weak, and the company tended to depend on public subsidies and loans. For example, when it started business in 1998, a loan of approximately 1 billion JPY was issued by the Prefectural Office of Hokkaido as a deposit on its aircraft lease and 300 million JPY by the City of Sapporo. In December 2001, when the company faced a financial crisis, Air Do also received loans of 1.7

Chapter 3

Table 3-5 Air Do's management index

(million JPY)

Fiscal year	6th March, 2002	7th March, 2003	8th March, 2004	9th March, 2005	10th March, 2006
Operating revenue	11,973	11,356	18,544	22,252	29,553
Current profits	▲2,918	▲1,635	1,476	1,678	2,173
Current net earnings	▲824	1,251	430	1,801	2,255
	11th March, 2007	12th March, 2008	13th March, 2009	14th March, 2010	15th March, 2011
	29,920	29,563	32,149	34,962	38,219
	▲344	462	841	512	1,740
	▲741	719	334	595	1,086
	16th March, 2012	17th March, 2013	18th March, 2014	19th March, 2015	
	43,172	42,236	49,498	49,087	
	3,588	1,806	363	1,845	
	2,171	640	123	640	

Source: Created by the author based on information on Air Do's website, December 2016

billion JPY and 500 million JPY, respectively, from the Prefectural Office and the City of Sapporo. It also received an additional 2 billion JPY of subsidies, but its cumulative deficit reached 7.53 billion JPY due to the steep rise of aviation insurance costs in the aftermath of the September 11 Attacks. This resulted in the company seeking for court protection under the Civil Rehabilitation Act in June 2002. Its capital that had been increased to 7.2 billion JPY was reduced by 100%, and 90% of the creditors' claim was cut.

However, we cannot simply conclude that Air Do failed just because the customers left. The average load factor from the inaugural flight to its bankruptcy accounted for 71.6%, a relatively high level for an airline company. Sales at the closing of fiscal year 2000, at the time of bankruptcy (11.97 billion JPY), showed an increase of 23% compared to the previous quarter. Operational cost (14.53 billion JPY) also showed an increase of 14%, resulting in a current, account deficit of 2.9 billion JPY (Table 3-5). This demonstrates that Air Do was operating under a high cost structure with 2.9 billion JPY of deficit despite the fact that it demonstrated a 70% load factor. Its cost structure was built upon the outsourcing maintenance fee, which accounted for one quarter of the sales (3 billion JPY annually) and the aircraft lease fees, as well as its dependence on public loans and subsidies, which eventually led to the lack of management efforts.

2.2.2 After Bankruptcy

Air Do received full support from ANA for rehabilitation after it went bankrupt. After the merger of JAL and JAS, the number of flights between Tokyo International Airport and New Chitose Airport reached 25 combined. ANA gained an advantage in partnering up with Air Do since they would be able to provide a total of nineteen flight services all together. As of 2007, with ANA's assistance, Air Do was able to operate three routes to New Chitose Airport, Asahikawa Airport (since July 2003) and Hakodate Airport (since March 2005) from Tokyo International Airport. It had started operations in February 2006 between Tokyo International Airport and Memanbetsu Airport. All flights were code-shared with ANA. In March 2007, the company had operated with three B767-300 and two B737-400.

As for in-flight services, the company offers "partial" no-frills service, targeting business passengers. A limited choice of services including drinks are offered for cost reduction purposes. However, due to its small-scaled operation, the costs are high and inefficient. It has also become highly inflexible because of its philosophy "Wing of Hokkaido", with the routes limited to those flying to and from Hokkaido. Therefore, there is a limit on the management's flexibility, since route expansion can only be conducted under ANA's support.

Air Do, after seeking court assistance under the Civil Rehabilitation Act, received an allocation of invested share funds established by the Development Bank of Japan. With business alliance with ANA, acts such as temporary staffing service and the purchasing of 50% of seats has allowed the company to gain profit both in fiscal year 2004 and 2005.

In January 2013, Air Do announced its management plan through 2013–2015 called "Mid-term Management Plan: Rolling Plan", in order to improve revenue. According to the plan, Air Do will hold a total of 14 aircraft (four B767-300, five B737-700 and five B737-500) by the end of 2013. Air Do plans to open new three operational routes (Tokyo International Airport–Kushiro Airport, New Chitose Airport–Okayama Airport and New Chitose Airport–Kobe Airport), and increase the number of flights for an operation route (New Chitose Airport–Sendai Airport) in 2013. Thus, Air Do will enhance its operation network and convenience for its customers. Additionally, it will expand its operation network by introducing a new B737 aircraft. Air Do is also aiming to raise its load factor through stronger partnership with sales agents, but commission charges to the agents have pressed management. Air Do has fallen into a vicious cycle by raising the airfare to make up for the loss, and as a result, have lost passengers.

• 2.3 Star Flyer

Star Flyer was established on November 17th, the day the Wright brothers first flew. In March 2006, it launched the operation of 24 daily flights between Tokyo International Airport and Kitakyushu Airport that same month. In November, they discontinued operations of two round-trip flights, one leaving Tokyo International Airport early in the morning and the other arriving at midnight, because of the decrease in the utilization factor due to problems such as poor accessibility to the airport. Thus, they operated 22 round-trip flights per day. They were the first to enter the market since Skynet Asia Airways, and the capital was approximately 3.9 billion JPY. Considering high business passenger needs in Kitakyushu, they targeted business passengers using four A320, and applied the marketing strategy of JetBlue Airways by applying leather seats, and expanded space between seats. They operated on a 24 hour schedule starting early in the morning, leaving at 05:30 a.m. and arriving at 07:05 a.m., and leaving at midnight and arriving at 01:35 a.m. However, this schedule was not appreciated as expected due to the low access of Kitakyushu Airport at midnight and early in the morning, as well as the dislikes of one-day business trips by business passengers of Kyushu. The airfare for adults was set at approximately 25,000 JPY, compared to 30,000 JPY by leading airlines.

In June 2007, Star Flyer, based in Fukuoka Airport, started a joint operation with ANA between the Tokyo International Airport–Kitakyushu Airport routes. At the time, Star Flyer was struggling from cash flow that consisted of lease payments and maintenance expenses, thereby the partnership with ANA really helped. By 2012, ANA itself became the largest shareholder with a share of 17.96%.

Henceforth, Star Flyer began expanding its business by operating international flights (between Kitakyushu Airport–Gimpo International Airport), but resulted in an operation loss in 2013 due to the depreciation of JPY. The increase of fuel cost and equipment leasing expenses as well as intense competition among LCCs were the main cause for the loss. In 2014, Star Flyer appointed people from ANAHD to the highly important jobs such as the presidency position, and many personnel were allocated to departments such as finance and planning.

The new management team reinforced the joint operations and withdrew from the routes that were considered unprofitable. As a result, after a steep fall and rise, the performance of Star Flyer has recovered with an operating surplus in 2014. Although the investment ratio was small, the success factor of ANAHD's rescue plan was sending in its own people to reliably improve the management.

● 2.4 Solaseed Air (Former Skynet Asia Airways)

Solaseed Air is an LCC based in Miyazaki Airport, and formerly was Skynet Asia Airways until November 30th, 2015. The company started to operate the Tokyo International Airport–Miyazaki Airport route in August 2002 following Skymark Airlines and Air Do, providing low airfares, spacious seating arrangements, and in-flight drink services with products of Miyazaki. Moreover, from February 2009, the company also opened the Naha Airport–Kagoshima Airport route, the Naha Airport–Nagasaki Airport route, and from August 2003, launched the Tokyo International Airport–Kumamoto Airport route.

In November 2004, Solaseed Air announced "NEXTSNA" and discontinued in-flight magazines, newspapers, beverages, and dropped the fare accordingly. However, advertisements, and code-sharing with other airlines were not successful since these methods failed to differentiate the company from other LCCs. Inadequate investment in aircraft maintenance led to frequent malfunctions which caused flight cancellations. As a result, the number of passengers decreased and the business did not improve due to a poor estimation of the expected number of customers.

In June 2004, with the management support of the Industrial Revitalization Corporation (IRC) of Japan, ANA became the second largest shareholder and formed a business alliance with Skynet Asia Airways for its restructuring. The company introduced a new CRS same as ANA, and began operations on the Tokyo International Airport–Nagasaki Airport route since August 2005. By specializing in the route between Tokyo and Kyushu, Skynet Asia Airways aimed to further attract customers by expanding publicity in the Kyushu district, and improving the convenience for business passengers and tourists visiting the Kyushu district. However, as a result of the code-share operation with Skynet Asia Airways, ANA automatically obtained half of the prioritized arrival and departure slots, which was originally meant to help LCCs' business. Skymark Airlines, the biggest LCC at the time, insisted that it was unfair to give the same number of priority slots for LCCs to Skynet Asia Airways, which is practically a subsidiary of ANA.

In March 2013, net income was the highest out of all the business results in the past (about twice the amount from the previous year) totaling of 1,101 million JPY, and a surplus of 6 consecutive fiscal years was recorded. As a result, deficits that were accumulated since the beginning of the project have been eliminated. Operating profit tripled to 1,945 million JPY from the previous year, due to cost savings by the introduction of new models and the increase in the number of passengers and passenger load factor. From March 29th, 2015, Skynet Asia Airways started their service to Chubu Centrair International Airport and operated the Naha Airport route with one round-trip flight daily. In addition, the company also started promoting low cost by renewing their aircraft. For such reasons, Solaseed Air replaced the used aircraft with new B737-800 even if it meant to pay the cancellation fee in the middle of leasing. This was because the fuel consumption and maintenance cost would be reduced each by 20% and 30% by using the new aircraft.

Since Solaseed Air does not have a high-demand main route, the company has difficulty in achieving a 70% passenger load factor. Thus, Solaseed Air needs to change its profit structure to make a profit out of a load factor of 60%. Their unit cost has been decreasing from 9.46 JPY to 8.95 JPY in a year from 2012. In 2017, they plan to aim for the 7-JPY range.

Still, it is not easy for a small prefecture in the south of Japan to attract people from the entire country. In order to attract visitors from the metropolitan area, Miyazaki planned a two-day invitation trip for payers of Hometown Tax of 10,000 JPY or more, in cooperation with the local municipalities. The trip was planned with original services such as the increased number of free check-in baggage. Due to these efforts, the seats were full on these flights. The cooperation between the airline and municipalities resulted in a great success. With these unique strategies, the airline continues to differentiate itself from other LCCs.

● 2.5　Vanilla Air

Vanilla Air took over AirAsia Japan under the investment of ANAHD, after the termination of the partnership between ANAHD and AirAsia Japan. The company made inclusive tickets, which freed the fees for checked baggage, rescheduling, and refund. Moreover, Vanilla Air began to deliver innovative services such as Vanilla Air Insurance which covers transportation and accommodation expenses when there is a delay of four hours or more or cancellation of flights. Vanilla Air is certainly focusing on the quality of the service, providing Japanese-style customer service unlike any other LCCs, and is moving forward utilizing the lessons learned from AirAsia Japan's failure. Although Vanilla Air is still based in Narita International Airport, as AirAsia Japan did, its strategy differs significantly, considering the fact that the previous company set the priority on price over quality. I would like to analyze the strategies of Vanilla Air and how they will utilize what they have learned from their failure as AirAsia Japan.

The lesson they have learned from the failure of AirAsia Japan was the pros and cons of expanding its size in such a short period. In 2013, Vanilla Air insisted that the company would be specialized in flights to resort and leisure destinations, and to put a greater weight on international routes. In addition, the company increased the number of aircraft, from eight in 2014 to ten in 2015, which also increased the number of destinations accordingly, from the previous five domestic routes to five international routes. Vanilla Air is planning additional destinations such as Micronesia (including Guam and Saipan) and Southeast Asia. The company will be prioritizing these international routes from Narita International Airport, and is even considering to start middle-distance flights, such as Hawaii. Although it is natural for a Narita-based airline to have more flights to leisure and tourist destinations that are low in business user demand. Vanilla Air still holds routes to New Chitose Airport and Naha Airport, which are also business destinations. The reason to keep these two destinations was its potential as a touristic destination and the willingness of the local people to attract tourists. Even though the standard business model of LCCs is to rely on short-distance flights, it is inevitable for an airline company with international routes to focus on middle-distance flights. However, the company has to consider introducing new aircraft other than A320 to fly the middle-distance routes.

The company puts an emphasis on time management, aiming for delay rates to be less than 15% and cancellation rates to be less than 1%. Vanilla Air had introduced a new aircraft with low-maintenance, which allows the work process between flights to be shortened creating a buffer in the turn-around time in case of a delay to absorb the delay time and make adjustments possible, which eliminates the necessity of a spare aircraft. Equally important is the policy of focusing on the quality, which is based on the lesson from AirAsia Japan's failure. Though Vanilla Air has a simple customer service strategy, they are working on the quality and customer satisfaction to change the reputation of LCCs. In achieving such, the company is cogitating to lower the price while maintaining its quality. Moreover, Vanilla Air is currently trying to find alternative sources of income, for instance, coming up with an idea different from other airlines to increase the utilization of the airplanes.

Furthermore, Vanilla Air conceives that the role model of LCCs has changed in recent years. For example, Scoot under Singapore Airlines and AirAsia X have been successful with their middle-distance flights, hence indicating that the typical strategies used by LCCs are not the only way to succeed, and to similarly operate like LCs does not mean a failure. In accordance to the transition in the market and the customer's mindsets, the management of airlines are also changing. It is important for Japanese airports to change their cost structure correspondingly with the changing business model of LCCs. In addition, Vanilla Air also joined Value Alliance that benefits customers on a connecting flight. For example, when a customer uses Vanilla Air for the first flight leg, the customer can also purchase a connecting flight ticket to destinations where Vanilla Air does not provide service.

ANAHD is taking over the management of Peach Aviation and Vanilla Air to some extent, due to the investment the company made to these two airlines. These two

Chapter 3

airlines are leading the market as the airlines specialize in middle-distance flights to leisure destinations. Consequently, I have analyzed that ANAHD does not eliminate the possibility of merging the two companies in a long-term strategy. Vanilla Air's creative strategy to manage the low airfares is praiseworthy.

● **2.6 Fuji Dream Airlines (FDA)**

FDA, which has been connecting local Japanese airports since 2009, is performing well, as a nonconformist of the aviation industry. The greatest feature of this company is that it is not like either an LC or an LCC, having accumulated 25 billion JPY worth of initial funds, therefore was not seen as a competitor in both markets. Moreover, the cost is low, but the overall price is not reasonable, so the company is gaining profit. In addition, it also achieves CI as a regional airline company linking different regions together. It continues to enter regional routes one after another, collaborating with the local governments as a local company, and contributing to regional revitalization. There are four unique aspects in its management strategy that goes against the common sense of the aviation industry. FDA executes a notable business model, an airline that succeeded by only servicing regional routes connecting regional locations to other regional locations. Since it is not a high-demand route compared to other Japanese LCCs, I would like to analyze it in detail.

Shizuoka Airport, which is said to be the last regional airport in Japan, opened in 2009, and a local company there established FDA to support the revitalization of the region. As other LCCs faced business difficulties, FDA continued to perform well and have now grown to operate 15 routes nationally to 14 cities based in two hub airports: Komaki Airport and Shizuoka Airport.

The FDA, which started service just from three routes, revived JAL's withdrawn routes one after another, and has now grown to operate on 16 routes with 68 flights. In 2015, it achieved a surplus and increased the initial number of aircraft from two to eleven. Independent LCCs in the domestic aviation industry are facing difficulties to continue operating alone; Skymark Airlines, Air Do and other companies have been supported by ANAHD and are restructuring their businesses. Most of the other LCCs are also in the ANA group. Amongst such circumstances, the FDA continues to scale up.

Chapter 3

2.6.1 The Biggest Success Factor is Selection of its Most Suitable Aircraft

FDA still owns the whole capital of the local company that has been established, and is operating joint flights with JAL on some routes. However, this has been characterized as not being dependent. Ten routes out of 16 are operated by the solo service of FDA and are responsible for connecting local airports that other companies are not interested in. They are trying to avoid the "high-demand routes" which originate from Tokyo International Airport. Such a strategy became possible by regional jet equipment of the small Embraer(Brazil), which FDA first introduced in Japan at the time of entry. It is the third most popular model in the world after Boeing(USA) and Airbus(Europe). The mainstream style of a domestic aviation industry is using the aircraft of Boeing or Airbus with 170 to 180 seats, but the 80-seat Embraer is the perfect size for FDA's region-to-region route service.

Moreover, the operating costs of flight equipment maintenance and airport rental fee, whether it has 80 seats or 180 seats, will remain almost unchanged. In other words, it does not mean that a smaller aircraft is easier to make profits. It is common sense in the airline industry to combine "high-demand routes" and "180 seats". However, FDA can remain independent and maintain its growth even by using local routes using 80-seat planes, if these four unique strategies have been conducted.

2.6.2 Cost Reduction: Developing an In-House Training System at an Early Stage

Having a full training facility within a company not only secures safety, but also allows people, especially employees, to respond to sudden demand such as increase of passengers and take-off and landing at previously unvisited local airports. A flight simulator generally takes about 2 billion JPY of initial investment alone, so for new-coming LCCs that want to use flight simulators, it is normal to provide training in an overseas airline company or rent from domestic LCs such as JAL or ANAHD. Skymark Airlines and Star Flyer currently have their own flight simulator, but initially they rented the flight equipment from other companies.

However, FDA which started out with two Embraer machines for approximately 3 billion JPY, decided to introduce the aircraft from the very beginning. In the aviation business, ten aircraft make up for one unit, and the early decision-making with the future in mind resulted in the success of FDA. In addition, when JAL went bankrupt

Chapter 3

in 2010 and withdrew from Komaki Airport, the immediate decision to use Komaki Airport and Shizuoka Airport as two hub airports, also allowed them an upper hand in expanding its number of routes. Consequently, it enabled the company to increase their number of pilots from 15 to more than 90, since the training could be done in-house with their own flight simulators. This saved time and the cost to go abroad and train, working to the advantage of the management strategy.

The flight simulator also contributes to safe operation when there is an accident. Following an airplane accident in July 2015, FDA was able to immediately and faithfully reproduce the emergency-landing situation with a simulator under the presence of MLIT. The aircraft was able to return to normal operation in just three days. In addition, since the simulator of Embraer was not owned by other domestic airlines, this brought unexpected value of hundreds of million JPY by renting it to other Japanese airline companies. This is a good example of an initial investment through quick decision-making that led to the success of a management strategy.

2.6.3 Improve Profitability by Developing Unique Sales System

The "self-sufficiency" of FDA includes many different things. The company's policy is to own things that other companies usually outsource. By developing and operating the CRS within the company, it has become possible to not only save the cost on the system usage fee, but also to introduce a new fee structure instantly without letting the major airlines know about their customer information. This increased the level of freedom significantly for the business operation.

The sales system of managing seats and routes on its own is said to be the core of airline operations. However, other LCCs will have no choice but to rent ANAHD's CRS. FDA has created its own CRS based on a software package for regional airlines, gaining an advantage over other LCCs. The most effective use of this system was when it improved profitability in September 2009, by introducing a fare that responds to unique fluctuations in demand, unlike the fare structure of domestic routes thus far. As a result of this principle of self-sufficiency in infrastructure, the boarding rate, which was 49% in the first year, had grown to 62.4% by 2015 despite being focused on the regional routes, approaching the boarding rate of 64.1% of LCs. In addition to this principle of self-sufficiency in infrastructure, FDA has launched its own strategy

Chapter 3

to further differentiate itself from other major competitors.

2.6.4 Raise Latent Demand by Close Collaboration with Local Governments

By focusing on local routes that other airlines do not operate on, the local governments will cooperate in digging up passenger demands, and also get support for campaigns and charter flight tours.

The relationship between the local governments, with regional airports that have few passengers, and the airlines, is far from fair; the airlines always had an upper hand. Especially for existing major airlines, it is the management's decision to withdraw from local routes that is not profitable, and the local governments that are frightened of the withdrawal, often issued subsidies. However, FDA has approached the local governments on an equal level and developed the demand together earning their trust. This approach is not limited to regular flight services.

2.6.5 Develop New Markets with "Charter Flight"

FDA has pioneered a new market for charter flight tours that connect regional airports together. By allocating two aircraft for charter flights at all times, and connecting them directly to regional airports with extra arrival and departure slots, FDA is currently developing a new tour with travel agencies for a brand new market.

JAL and ANAHD also fly charter flights, but many of them are for high-demand routes such as Tokyo International Airport–Naha Airport, and they are limited to only a few tens of flights per year. In contrast, FDA dispatched about 900 charter flights in 2015, exceeding over 2,000 cumulative flights as of June 2016, and reached a total number of 53 airport destinations nationwide.

This has been made possible since there were common elements such as the fact that two FDA aircraft have the equivalent number of seats to two sightseeing tour buses, and that even if it was the first regional airport to fly to, the pilots were able to train using the flight simulator at any time. The rapid expansion of the charter business continues, and is supported by the local travel agencies resulting in a virtuous cycle.

The cooperation with the region is an indispensable element in this charter project. Moreover, FDA is receiving assistance from municipalities in certain areas, such as for promotional expenses and securing hotel reservations. It is important to further accelerate the development of a new market by collaborating together with the airlines, local governments, and travel agencies.

2.6.6 Focus on Non-Financial Value

Local companies do not pursue short-term earnings, but place more importance on other values such as the employment of the locals and the regional symbiosis. Although cost may increase in the short term, such actions, on a long-term basis, would return to help to increase the permanence of the enterprise and the local area. FDA describes its aspiration as, "although currently there is an unexpected development where the number of inbound tourists visiting Japan has increased suddenly, at the time of our establishment, we thought that it would be a great asset to the people living in Shizuoka Prefecture to develop a plan looking far ahead into the future and that is why we supported it", and "the biggest problem for the regions is the lack of cultural education; it is necessary to promote human exchange in order to solve the issue. As a result, it will lead to the independence of Shizuoka." Fundamentally, there is a spirit of symbiosis in the aviation industry as well, and the actions and the ideas of FDA seem entirely like those of the local government responsible for the regional revitalization.

2.6.7 Future Management Strategy of FDA

FDA plans to operate international routes with charter flights, in accordance with major events scheduled inside and outside of the country. It is steadily procuring flight equipment to increase from the current 11 aircraft to 22–23 aircraft, and is considering to further cooperate with LCs.

FDA plans to play the role of a "spoke" airline company, which connects a "hub airport" such as Narita International Airport and Tokyo International Airport used by the major domestic and international airlines, by jointly operated flights.

This method is not possible with the current system because it does not directly connect with the LC's sales system. In order to make this possible, improvements of

Chapter 3

the passenger system is needed urgently, and the project is initiated with a future goal of operation in 2 years. The new system will allow seats to be managed mutually from both parties in real time.

The unique strategy of FDA to go against the common sense, such as the timing of the introduction of Embraer aircraft and taking advantage of JAL's poor management to capture the change in flow of the aviation business resulted in a rapid growth for FDA. Its future progress will most likely continue.

● **2.7 Spring Airlines Japan**

The routes of Spring Airlines Japan, which was first initiated by the Spring Airlines group of China, had begun operations at Narita International Airport from June 27th, 2014. This airline played the role of transporting Chinese passengers domestically around Japan. The Wuhan Tianhe International Airport–Narita International Airport route began regular international flights on February 13th, 2016, and the Chongqing Jiangbei International Airport–Narita International Airport route on February 14th, 2016. JTB, the largest travel agency in Japan, has also invested in Spring Airlines Japan, and is considering to expand the travel business to and from China with the international travel agency of Spring Airlines, the parent company of Spring Airlines Japan. Overall, Spring Airlines Japan would be able to stand out from domestic Japanese LCCs and hope to see new demand contributing to the revitalization of regional economies, with the aim of improving the convenience for users.

● **2.8 The New AirAsia Japan**

2.8.1 Re-Entry to the Japanese Market

Although the new AirAsia Japan is aiming to re-entry into the Japanese aviation market, chances are becoming very small due to repetitive service plan postponements through trial and error.

AirAsia Japan is an LCC jointly established by AirAsia Malaysia led by CEO Tony Fernandez, and ANA in August 2011. Although the airline started its service in August 2012, the business performance was poor; the first president was replaced after only five months and the new president was assigned from ANA. However, in less than half a year later, ANA and AirAsia Japan withdrew from their partnership. In contrast to the liberal management style of ANA, the management style of AirAsia Japan was to seek results as soon as possible, and the opposite cultures of each company clashed. ANA refused Tony's offer to buy its shares, but instead bought all the shares and acquired the airline as a fully owned subsidiary, changed the airline's name to Vanilla Air, and started a whole new company.

At that time, it was unexpected for ANA group that the president of AirAsia Japan left without going back to ANA. The reason was because it was decided that Vanilla Air was to restart with a new management team and the former president, an excellent personnel, was to return to ANA. Later, it was said that he had been cooperating with Tony working on establishing a new airline company in Japan.

In July 2014, Tony established the brand new AirAsia Japan with Rakuten as a new partner and made the former president of AirAsia Japan the new CEO. About a year later in the fall of 2015, the company acquired AOC (management permission for air transportation business), and started preparing for service. However, in November 2015, since the preparation of the new AirAsia Japan had been facing a lot of trouble with little progress made, Tony suddenly decided to dismiss the president of the new AirAsia Japan, according to the advice from his surroundings who were dissatisfied with the president. MLIT had been skeptical with AirAsia Japan, which withdrew in just a year from the start of service. The reason why the new AirAsia Japan, beginning from such a negative reputation, was able to acquire AOC from MLIT was due to the credibility of the former president of AirAsia Japan.

Nevertheless, it was ANAHD that accepted the former president of AirAsia Japan back. The reason why ANAHD accepted him was due to his high abilities and the high utility value of "hybrid talent"—his learning of the LCC business under Tony and the accumulation of knowledge on the Southeast Asian market. ANAHD is considering to launch an airline company in Myanmar, and the company found him suitable as a management staff.

In exchange of the former president of AirAsia Japan, Tony restarted the new AirAsia Japan with the former management team of Skymark Airlines. In fact, Skymark

Chapter 3

Airlines was the only growing airline that belonged to neither JAL nor ANAHD, but went bankrupt in January 2015. With the injection of capital from ANAHD, the management team of Skymark Airlines was dismissed. In order to launch a third force, the mutual feeling of grudge against ANAHD united the team. This change occurred suddenly and surprisingly in early January 2016. Immediately after the management team of AirAsia Japan greatly changed, the former executives of Skymark Airlines decided to talk with Tony, and convinced him to operate in line with Japanese aerial law and customs. The executives explained that to expand the markets in Japan, it is important to understand the aviation regulations and the way business is run in the country. At AirAsia headquarters, there are many staffs that are confident in their companies successful experiences, and thus did not agree to the conservative Japanese aviation policy.

2.8.2 The New AirAsia Japan's Ambition and the Reality

The scheduled flights for the new AirAsia Japan were postponed to April 2016 since they were not able to acquire the AOC until October 2015. The launch still has not been initiated as of today in 2017. There are three business regulations that require approval, after acquiring the AOC from MLIT, which they applied by June 2016, but has not yet been approved. After the former president of AirAsia Japan left, the schedule of flight services has been repeatedly delayed since the new management team took over.

Even in such a situation, Tony stuck to the Japanese market since the airfares in Japan were high from a global standpoint. Tony himself loves Japan a lot and named the airline AirAsia X, servicing the middle-distance routes, named after the Japanese band called X-Japan that he likes. Furthermore, in Southeast Asia, there is still a deeply rooted admiration towards Japan, with the belief that success in Japan contributes to the AirAsia Japan brand.

However, in reality, the situation is severe due to the continuous postponement of new flight services. The new AirAsia Japan has already used up 5 billion JPY out of the total capital of 7 billion JPY. Moreover, expenditures of 300 million JPY is required each month, and eventually the capital would all be exhausted. Even if flight services were able to restart in 2017, the company would be late 5 years in comparison to

Chapter 3

Peach Aviation or Jetstar Japan, which already had been established as LCCs, and at which time it would have missed out on the opportunity to initiate its services at the main airports such as Narita International Airport and Kansai International Airport, which have no arrival and departure slots left now. There is no other choice but to use Chubu Centrair International Airport as a base. However, the size of the demand of the aviation market is half of that in the Kansai region, and quarter of that in the Chubu region. It is not going to be easy regaining a lag of 5 years in service, and the new AirAsia Japan is facing a tough time.

2.9 Affiliate LCCs of LCs

2.9.1 The Existing Japanese Regulations that Affect Affiliate LCCs

The airline babies, LCC subsidiaries owned by LCs, have been operating only a few routes so far. Their business has been stable, but it takes several years to become as developed as the LCCs in the U.S. The airfare is almost the same as the LC's special fare and its early reservation discount fare, if all of them are under the same situation, whereas it may be less than half of the LC's special or early reservation fare comparing them under the no-frills condition.

Since the end of the 1990s, when the LCCs appeared globally, many LCs have established airline babies, however, most of them have gone out of business. One of the reasons could have been the difficulty in carrying out business following the customs of their parent companies, such as employment environment with the budgets as little as those of independent LCCs.

If an airline baby is still able to continue its business, it might be using completely different routes from the parent company. The parent company itself is remarkably productive, and its finance and human resource management is highly independent. If the airline babies continue to be dependent on their parent companies, they will not succeed in the business.

Customers might not regard an airline baby as an LCC as long as they see its parent's brand in it. This means that the consumers may not use the baby airline for cheaper airfare. In contrast, such low cost affiliates may have the risk of ruining the prestigious brand name of their parents. If so, the parent company must place its baby airline abroad to not reflect the color of the company. The parent ought not to be involved in framing the marketing plan for the subsidiary company. It is questionable whether or not there is a benefit for the baby airline being subsidized.

Furthermore, the parent company ought to have a baby airline abroad because of the regulations in Japan. Due to the laws on foreign capital (which must not exceed one-third of the capital) and cabotage restriction in Japan, a foreign based affiliate cannot operate domestic routes in Japan. Foreign capital companies are also prohibited in running domestic routes. Even if these regulations were to be abolished, restrictions by the Labor Law must be loosened so that foreign employees are allowed to work in Japan. On the other hand, the problem of hiring foreign employees for the operation of domestic routes still remains. Furthermore, if the capital power of Japanese parent companies does not affect their affiliates, then it is questionable whether it is even worth establishing an affiliate. It may be less harmful for parent LCs to keep as little control over the LCC market as possible by providing some capital.

This method of partially coping with existing regulations might in turn have made these laws lose their significance. The most ideal situation for the aviation industry is a world in which anyone can establish a company freely, and one can choose to work for an airline company the one likes.

It takes time in changing the investors' non-risk taking attitude, which had been cultivated by the Japanese social climate and delays in deregulations. In order to improve the market effect and increase social surplus, it is better to let investors enter Japan and its market, instead of making them question their actions.

The major institutional factors indicated above which prevent the establishment of airline company with efficiency are: restrictions on foreign capital and cabotage. In modern times, when investments in LCCs are active, there is easing of the regulation on foreign capital investment for the airline companies, including Asian capital, which is showing a rapid growth, so that the airline companies can procure funds from across the world.

Moreover, the reasons behind the abolishment of regulations on foreign capital and cabotage are to improve consumer interests, to see if these measures are necessary and effective for the LCs to proactively use LCCs, and to offer the Japanese airline companies a broader range of choices for revitalization. It would be important and effective for the advancement of LCCs to abolish the regulation on foreign capital rather than implementing policies on promoting LCCs. In addition, it is necessary to abolish the regulation on restricting the LC's affiliate's usage of particular airports and allow them to use the airports freely so that they can demonstrate their maximum efficiency.

This section has simplified the negative factors of the aviation policy regarding the procurement of capital, which is affecting the affiliate LCC business, in order to make the following section clearly understandable.

2.9.2 Comparison of Parent LCs' Dedication

Jetstar Japan established by both JAL and Jetstar, and Peach Aviation established by ANA started to operate in 2012. They limited the percentage of foreign capital to one-third, which met the capital requirements of a Japanese airline company under Japanese regulations mentioned above. I would like to explain the current situation through my perspective and ideas regarding the topic.

Even though Peach Aviation and Jetstar Japan started at the same time, they delivered different results due to the support provided by the parent LCs. The difference mainly in the support and commitment of ANAHD and JAL, the respective investors of each company, led to this difference in the results. When the year ended in March 2016, Peach Aviation eliminated its cumulative losses in just 4 years since its establishment. It had an operating profit of 6.2 billion JPY, and a profit margin of 12.9%. Its successful business stood out achieving the performance equal to other major airline companies.

However, other airlines thought that the superb performance by Peach Aviation was due to the parent company, ANAHD, bearing the costs such as maintenance and so forth. Nevertheless, that does not accurately analyze the management of Peach Aviation, and as long as they think those factors are the reasons for its success, other

Chapter 3

airlines will never catch up to Peach Aviation. It was however true that ANA helped establish such successful Peach Aviation in February 2011. This all began in 2008 when the president of ANA ordered the president-to-be of Peach Aviation to complete the research on LCCs, and establish an LCC business within 3 years. The research included: reading extensively on documents regarding LCCs, flying on LCC flights, and visiting LCC companies.

In addition, the president of Peach Aviation had also asked Patrick Murphy, a legend in the LCC industry, to help the company out as an advisor. He is one of the founders of Ryanair, the largest LCC in the European market. One of the most important factors for LCCs that he believed was cost reduction in all of the business processes. Peach Aviation tried to lower costs as Murphy had said, but could not keep fixed indirect cost to 5%. In the end, however, Peach Aviation succeeded in lowering the total cost by raising the utilization rate of the aircraft instead.

From there, Peach Aviation paid full attention to improving the utilization rate of the aircraft by themselves. Not a single aircraft was allocated as a spare out of the entire 17 aircraft; the equipment was all in full operation without any time to waste. Currently, the operation time for each of the 18 aircraft exceeds 10 hours each. Researching the LCC thoroughly led to its success, resulting in the management strategy that positioned the base in Kansai International Airport operating 24 hours a day and quickly launched the international routes.

Another success factor is the partner selection. ANA has chosen First Eastern, a Hong Kong fund as a co-investor so they can monitor their management situation constantly. Their demand for return on investment is severe, and the chairman always participates in the board of directors meeting, looking over the details very carefully with a professional eye.

Moreover, by partnering up with the leading LC, the company is able to reach the goal of becoming a successful domestic LCC. This is done by incorporating smooth efficiency by using know-hows of its partner's management. This method will make sure that the strong capital power of the LCs will not have a negative impact on them. The success of Peach Aviation, which led the domestic LCC business earlier, was able to move forward through the management efforts of ANAHD, breaking the jinx that an LCC can not succeed in Japan. This successful case study will be further discussed in Chapter 8.

Meanwhile, Jetstar Japan, which was established mainly by JAL in 2012, continuously suffered from a huge deficit, with a cumulative loss of over 30 billion JPY. In the earlier days, Jetstar Japan executed "First Mover Advantage" and designated the seizing of the market as its top priority. In just 2 years from its launch, a high-speed business expansion to 24 aircraft (now 20 aircraft) was pushed forward. However, the maintenance system failed to catch up with the expansion of the scale, with the aircraft arriving one after another, resulting in a situation in which five aircraft had been stalled in Narita International Airport. The lease fee and parking fee resulted in a cost increase of 35,000 USD–45,000 USD per aircraft per month. As a result, Jetstar Japan had repeatedly asked the shareholders, Qantas Airways of Australia and JAL, to increase the capital in exchange for an investment, which led to an investment amount of 19.5 billion JPY by JAL through a total of four capital increases. However, JAL has left the management to Qantas Airways since there were not many cases of LCs successfully managing an LCC in the world, and decided to only make the investment.

In terms of human resources, ANAHD transferred highly experienced and intelligent staff with an one-way ticket to major working sections within Peach Aviation, such as the president position and management executive. The relation between ANAHD and Peach Aviation is well known, and their success will be a matter of how each keeps its originality and independence. On the other hand, JAL had sent only one person with a two-way ticket to Jetstar Japan in order for the person to work in the maintenance section. Furthermore, JAL's lack of effort and motivation could not prevent the uncontrollable expansion policy of Qantas Airways, resulting in poor performance. Nevertheless, the company managed to make a profit by June 2016. With the establishment of base in Narita International Airport and the launch of international flights, the operation time of 18 aircraft has exceeded 10 hours, along with the average boarding rate having improved by 9% in a year due to review of routes. Moreover, the cash flow stabilized, and from August 2015, money did not become a problem anymore.

Chapter 3

While Peach Aviation wished to draw an expansion strategy of creating a 30-aircraft system by the 2020 Tokyo Olympics, Jetstar Japan became conservative and tried to top off the plan with a 21-aircraft structure by 2017, saying that it is undecided after that. Peach Aviation has overtaken Jetstar Japan with respect to the management of scale that Jetstar was so particular about. ANAHD seriously committed to the LCC business head on whilst JAL was indecisive. This is a clear example that showcases the division between success and failure in LCC businesses, according to differences in motivation between two parent companies.

As mentioned in the beginning of this chapter, the domestic competition will be among the nine LCCs for the time being, but is unlikely that the domestic demand will continue to rise. It is necessary to raise new demands and attract the repeaters. Moreover, it is expected that there will be an increase in the number of foreign LCCs, mostly from Asia, that will extend their services to Japan. Therefore, it has and will become the most important topic for Japanese LCCs to find ways to capture the demand of the inbound foreigners visiting Japan. On the whole, it is essential for the airline to contribute to the benefit of the customers.

3. Summary of Study of Factors Hindering Development of LCCs

As can be seen above, legal factors inhibiting the entry into the market by LCCs have already been eliminated. However, current developments of Japanese LCCs is quite slow, compared to those in Europe, Asia and the U.S.

Before verifying the factors and measures to be taken in detail in Chapter 9, a list of factors inhibiting the development of the LCCs that can be derived from each company's history and current status will be presented here as a summary for further discussion.

(1) In the Japanese aviation market, there is a high concentration of passengers on the routes from Tokyo International Airport and Osaka International Airport. However, the scale of the airports in the Tokyo Metropolitan area is quite small (total of five runways in Narita International Airport and Tokyo International Airport). Moreover, the arrival and departure slots are full both in Tokyo International Airport

Chapter 3

and Narita International Airport.[5] LCs mostly occupy these arrival and departure slots. Under such circumstances, it is difficult for LCCs to increase the number of flights, even though they have increased potential demand by lowering fares. Therefore, they are in a disadvantageous position in the competition.

(2) LCs have an advantage compared to other airline companies. Therefore, they temporarily lower fares to match the fares of the LCCs or to an even lower level (predatory price) for the purpose of shutting out LCCs.

(3) Due to the concentration of management resources within LCs, the LCCs may be at a disadvantage in outsourcing their aircraft maintenance and training crew members.

(4) There are only a few number of airports both in the Tokyo Metropolitan area and the provincials, that can be utilized as secondary airports. Therefore, it may be difficult for LCCs to reduce costs or to differentiate oneself as like it is a general practice in Europe and the U.S. These factors will be examined in detail later.

2 Analysis of Problems of Management Policy

Approximately 20 years have passed since LCCs entered the aviation market in Japan. However, the market has yet to see a rapid expansion of shares as was seen in the European and U.S. markets. The reason for this is often described as the Japanese institutional issues, which will be studied in Section 3.

Problems in the management policy of the Japanese LCCs, however, have also contributed to their sluggishness. By reviewing the current status of the Japanese LCCs as previously discussed, the management policy issues derived from lengthy deficit operations of LCCs will be analyzed and studied. This study will demonstrate how these management problems have been derived from the aviation policy issues

---

5 Utilization factor of Tokyo International Airport of all domestic passengers is approximately 60%. The factor will reach 80% if the factors of Osaka International Airport and Kasai International Airport are added to it. Moreover, one of the two runways of Narita International Airport is 2,180 meters long. Cities with much less population than Tokyo have airport capacity as follows: three airports and ten runways in Washington D.C, three airports and nine runways in New York, five airports and eight runways in London, and two airports and six runways in Paris.

Chapter 3

as well.

1. Cost Structure Problem

1.1 Problems due to Minimum Scale Operation

The forecast and actual data of Skymark Airlines' revenue and cost, before and after flight operations are as follows. The company forecasted the load factor to be 60%, but it actually was 57.7%. With the difference of only 2.3%, its forecast was quite accurate. In contrast, the difference between the forecasted and the actual cost is large, accounting for 5 billion JPY. This may be due to the cost structure that is typical of an airline company.

The costs of airline companies consist of fixed and variable costs. Fixed costs include office and branch rental charges and general administrative expenses. Some variable costs are completely proportional to production volume, while some are not. Examples of those include fuel costs, airport usage fees (such as landing fee and aeronautical navigation aid usage fee). Examples of those that are not, at least for a short period, include depreciation costs, lease expenses, maintenance costs, advertising expenses, and rental charge of airport facilities and ground handling costs. Fixed costs and common expenses such as variable costs that are not proportional to production volume become an obvious factor that elevates cost per unit of Japanese LCCs, which started operations using one aircraft. Moreover, price per aircraft can be lower if purchased in quantity. Lease expense per aircraft can also be lowered, if leased in quantity.

The same can be said for maintenance costs. Skymark Airlines initially outsourced the aircraft maintenance to ANA, and had been paying an outsourcing fee of more than 3 billion JPY annually. As the company started in-house maintenance in 2002, maintenance cost per aircraft was reduced. However, such cost reduction has not contributed to the company's efficiency, compared to that of the leading companies, since it possessed only a few aircraft. Therefore, its maintenance cost per aircraft remains high.

This situation can bring out a presumption that, although Skymark Airlines was initially planning on initiating operations with three to four aircraft, it was unable to increase the number of aircraft since it could not obtain sufficient amount of funds as well as arrival and departure slots. As a result, it had started operations with an average cost that ended up much higher than expected.

Skymark Airlines' ground handling cost and usage fee for airport ground facilities are also significantly higher than those of the three leading companies. Skymark Airlines initially operated three round-trip flights per day, which meant that it used the airport counter only three times a day. This, unsurprisingly, highly elevated its cost per passenger. If CRS is to be implemented, its cost will rise since the components of CRS must be bulk purchased, thus increasing the cost per passenger if the company cannot secure a large number of passengers. The LCs, on the other hand, only need one computer system to manage a large scale of operations because they handle a large number of flights.

It is generally viewed that the aviation market has less to no economies of scale. However, as described above, economies of scale works effectively from the time when an LCC enters the market until it grows to a certain minimum scale. Therefore, based on the aspects taken from the situation regarding Skymark Airlines, which started operations with only one single aircraft, the simulation model in Chapter 4 will study the viability of establishment of LCCs by using a corporate model, which conducts operations with 15 aircraft from the beginning of business, one of the factors that yield a positive result.

● 1.2 Lack of Resource Procurement Ability at New Entry

LCCs in North America and Europe have lowered their costs by outsourcing parts of their business operations such as the aircraft maintenance. What is unique about the Japanese LCCs, as Skymark Airlines admits, is that they can reduce costs by self-managing the training for crew members and maintenance.

In the Japanese aviation market, management resources are dominated and distributed by the LCs. Therefore, an LCC, due to lack of negotiation power and limited options of outsourcing companies, must outsource its production facilities including the aircraft maintenance to an LC, which results in high outsourcing costs. This is a circumstance specific to Japan. In order to avoid high outsourcing costs, LCCs need to establish an in-house system even though its cost will still be higher than that of LCCs in North America and Europe. It requires a certain amount of time until such system is established, therefore an LCC, meanwhile, needs to continue paying outsourcing fees.

When looking at the procurement cost, which is essential for the business operation of airline companies, Air Do procured B767-300ER through a lease. This fee was 100 million JPY per month, which was double the amount compare to leading airline companies that were paying for leasing. The company had to sign the lease contract at such a high cost since the number of aircraft to be leased was small. This refers to the problem of management of scale as described above. Additional reasons include a lack of past performances and low credibility. These elements were unavoidable in the early stages of new entry.

As for the maintenance cost, all LCCs outsourced parts of their business operations to LCs. As a result, the maintenance cost per unit became extremely high. Air Do paid JAL 3 billion JPY as an outsourcing fee, and Skymark Airlines also paid ANA 3 to 4 billion JPY annually. Skymark Airlines reduced costs, as a result of the implementation of in-house aircraft maintenance system, which started in 2002. This measure reduced the maintenance cost, but has not yet reached the standard level of the leading companies. With the preparation of establishing a Maintenance Repare and Overhaul facility (MRO) currently in progress, there will be a day when LCCs can outsource reasonably to corporations specifically for maintenance in the near future.

The reason for sizable disparity in ground handling costs and ground facilities usage fees between LCCs and the two LCs is due to the management of scale and weak negotiation power of LCCs. By taking the example of Skynet Asia Airways, which entered the market in the summer of 2002, the company had to pay JAL's affiliate company 5 million JPY as a monthly check-in baggage fee at Miyazaki Airport. If it could handle this procedure in-house, it could reduce the cost to 2.6 million JPY, which accounts for one-tenth of its outsourcing fee. However, its only choice was to outsource the procedure to JAL because it owned the baggage belt conveyors at the airport.

Air Do did not implement a reservation/sales operation system because it simply was not able to afford it. This situation required a significant amount of time in notifying the airfare pricing and schedule to sales agents. Moreover, it would be difficult to study the utilization characteristics of the customers.

As seen in the example of ramp buses operated at Tokyo International Airport, the differences between the newcomers and leading companies will be less if businesses became fully independent from the two leading companies. This independence should exist in every business field including maintenance and ground service operations at airports.

● 1.3 Inconsistent Management Effort of Cost Reduction

Another reason for the high cost is LCCs' lack of management efforts, compared to those in North America and Europe, as explained below.

1.3.1 Non-Use of Single Type of Aircraft

It is essential from a managerial point of view for airline companies, especially for LCCs, to use only a single type of aircraft for the purpose of saving costs on pilot training and maintenance, etc. This is clearly described in the examples of LCCs in North America and Europe. On the other hand, as previously seen in the example of Air Do, LCCs in Japan procured aircraft of different types through lease as a result of not using a single type of aircraft. Other LCCs including Skymark Airlines used the same type of aircraft.

1.3.2 Inconsistent Provision of No-frills Service

In-flight services play an essential part in cost reduction too. Many LCCs in North America, Europe and Asia provide no-frills service as an unique business feature. Ryanair is known to have pervaded the LCC's low-cost concept to passengers in Europe through its consistent no-frills service.

On the other hand, Japanese LCCs such as Skymark Airlines and Air Do seem to have a non-exhaustive policy on no-frills services. They provide a limited choice of services including food and drinks. The main reason for this is because Japanese customers are not used to no-frills services. Another factor can be, since they treat both tourists and business passengers equally, their target customers are not clear.

1.3.3 Problems of Sales System

LCCs in North America, Europe, and Asia, for the purpose of simplifying selling costs and reducing other costs, focus on building their online sales network. On the other hand, Japanese LCCs do not possess their own IT-based sales network. For example, Skymark Airlines depends on HIS, a travel agency, due to their close mutual relationship. Air Do and Skynet Asia Airways depend on ANA's sales system due to their close relationships with ANA. Recently, the number of LCCs to develop and own their original CRS, in order to simplify and reduce costs as FDA did, has been increasing.

2. Competition Problem Between LCCs and LCs

Skymark Airlines' initiation of the Tokyo International Airport–Fukuoka Airport route caused an intensive airfare competition between the newcomers and the three LCs. When Skymark Airlines entered the market, its normal fare was set to 13,700 JPY for three of its round-trip flights. The fare was approximately half the airfare of the three LCs, which was 27,400 JPY. Air Do began service between Tokyo International Airport and New Chitose Airport with an airfare that was 40% lower than that of the three leading companies. This indicates that the LCC played a role as a price leader. As for the issues of the aviation and competition policies will be discussed in detail later. A study from a corporate management perspective will be examined here, including the history of competition between Skymark Airlines and the three leading companies. Moreover, airfare levels will be mentioned, and the airfare structure will be discussed later on.

The leading companies competed against the LCCs by lowering their fares to that of LCCs. (Both Skymark Airlines and Air Do entered the market in September and December 1998 with 50% to 60% of the airfare of major LCs.) The leading companies were taking a firm stand at first, but the total seat occupancy of the two LCCs exceeded 70%, whilst that of the LCs was less than 60%. As explained before, JAL launched

Chapter 3

an adjacent route to LCCs with the airfare half the price in March 1999. Of course, the airfare introduced by JAL was not a ordinary priced fare, but a discount fare with restricted use. Such restrictions were not actually applied, but a substantial fare reduction for six JAL flights were executed.

The media criticized JAL's strategy of "lowering the airfare for flights that fly closely was carried out to LCCs" as a "bullying act". However, since the other two leading companies followed JAL's strategy, JAL had to continue lowering its airfares for flights flying adjacent routes to those of Skymark Airlines, and Air Do as well as the other leading companies. Since the other two followed JAL's footsteps, the reciprocal action resulted in three-quarters of all the airline companies' airfare to level with LCCs. The discounted fare of LCs was set in 1996 for the Tokyo International Airport–New Chitose Airport and Tokyo International Airport–Fukuoka Airport route, both having operated a large number of flights. Discounted rates from normal airfares differed by period, route, and time zone, and were set considering factors such as competitive relationships with other companies, and demand for each route and flight. The three leading airline companies, before the entry of Skymark Airlines and Air Do, applied the discounted fare only to flights with low demand such as those early in the morning or late at night.

Skymark Airlines lost its passengers by increasing the number of flights with special discount fares. Facing financial difficulties due to the decrease in number of passengers, the company had no choice but to lower its airfare. In July 2000, its normal fare was lowered to 16,000 JPY. A special discount fare was set for all flights between Tokyo International Airport and Fukuoka Airport. Skymark Airlines, with insufficient number of flights and name recognition, began to lose passengers it once took away from the leading companies.

Skymark Airlines worked on several measures for its fare setting such as round-trip air flight settings and Sky Value airfare. However, the three leading companies followed in each case. The repetitive cycle of counteractive airfare pricing by the three leading companies, loss of passengers, decrease in revenue, and rise in airfares were the major factors that forced Skymark Airlines to face financial difficulties. Air Do suffered similarly from such strategies by the three leading companies.

Chapter 3

In conclusion, the history of airfare competition signifies foremost, in terms of airfare level, how LCCs can be competitive against leading companies, if their airfare is discounted to approximately 40% when other conditions are favorable. The individual cost (cost which is not accrued unless a particular flight was operated) of an LC's route from Tokyo International Airport accounts for 60% to 65% of their normal fare. Therefore, it is not easy for them to further reduce their airfare. Accordingly, it is important for LCCs to maintain an airfare level of 60% that of leading companies.

It also signifies how difficult it is for an LCC to compete only with low fares if it can not deal with elements other than airfare levels. Key elements include conditions that hinder LCCs from increasing their number of flights due to restrictions on arrival and departure slots, measures for airfare structure as discussed below, and differentiation by factors other than airfares.

The final problem is market contestability, which will be discussed later in detail. If the market is contestable, and competition progresses to a certain extent in other markets, LCs cannot set predatory airfare lower than the level described above. Competition in the domestic market, at the time of new entry, had not progressed yet. Therefore, LCs had more opportunity to gain excess profit from the routes that were not selected by Skymark Airlines and Air Do. This put both companies in a disadvantageous situation.

3. Problem of Unfocused Customer Target and Airfare Structure

The problem in the business strategy of Japanese LCCs is that they are not focused on any customer segmentation. LCCs in other countries focus on their own selected targets. For example, Southwest Airlines focuses on a class of passengers who are sensitive to airfare levels. JetBlue Airways focuses on business passengers. Additionally, AirAsia focuses on middle to low income passengers who do not regularly travel by air.

In contrast, Japanese LCCs such as Skymark Airlines and Air Do, despite their low airfares, tried to deal with all types of customers including tourists, travelers, and business passengers without selecting any specific targets, and competing solely with low fares. Japanese LCCs, similar to cheap airlines in the U.S. in the 1980s, did not target any particular customers, and had no special selling points except for providing low fares. Therefore, they could not keep their customers satisfied once reasonable airfares lost its credibility.

A remarkable example is Star Flyer, which began service in 2006, launching a management policy targeted specifically at business passengers for Kitakyushu Airport–Tokyo International Airport round-trip flights. It applied the marketing strategy of JetBlue Airways by selecting routes set at early in the morning and midnight that allowed passengers to use their time effectively, providing leather seats equipped with TV.

This indicates that if LCCs cannot offer services at a low cost constantly, or if they cannot provide special discount fares, they must start targeting specific customers with little price elasticity to differentiate. Differentiation by focusing on a certain group of customers, and according to price elasticity of demand is effective in aviation services.

Another factor is the constant rivalry with other transportation systems. Japan has a highly developed railroad network including the Shinkansen. Railroad services became another major competitor in addition to LCs. Airline companies are especially exposed to intense competition against the Shinkansen regarding short-distance routes with high-demand in fare and time. Moreover, competition against road transportation is unavoidable with the development of the highway network. Examples include Peach Aviation and Skymark Airlines, which attracted customers away from long-distance bus markets when it first entered the aviation market.

While the main competitors of LCCs in North America and Europe is road transportation, Japanese LCCs need to offer cheaper fares compared to high speed buses and Shinkansen fares for adjacent routes, considering the competition they have with road transportation and the Shinkansen, in order to increase demand.

◘ 4. Problem of Route Structure

The route structure of Japanese LCCs, soon after they entered the market, was unfairly assigned. The Tokyo International Airport–New Chitose Airport and Tokyo International Airport–Fukuoka Airport routes were not an issue. The second Skymark Airlines aircraft was assigned to the Osaka International Airport–New Chitose Airport and Osaka International Airport–Fukuoka Airport routes which had low demand. Such route structure prevented airlines from operating aircraft efficiently. Moreover, resources could not be focused on a particular station, which resulted in the cost to increase due to the unnecessary rise in the number of stations.

On the other hand, LCCs in North America and Europe can focus on specific routes and conduct operations with high frequency. The difference in cost and ability to attract customers is clear between Japanese and the Western airliners.

Such poor route structure has also hindered new entries. This is not a problem regarding the management policy, but an institutional issue such as the arrival and departure slots. Japanese LCCs do not make a foray into international markets to seek routes that work to their advantage, as European and Asian LCCs do. This is, however, an exception for Skymark Airlines, which finally expanded itself to the charter market as the first LCC to ever do so. This was concluded as an institutional problem, reflected by the protectionist characteristics of the Japanese international aviation policy.

◘ 5. Inconvenient Operations

It is understandable that both Skymark Airlines and Air Do could not attract passengers since they had to start operations at low frequencies of three round-trip flights with only one aircraft. This indicates that a company would be placed in a disadvantageous position both cost-wise and revenue-wise, as previously mentioned, unless it begins with a certain scale. Needless to say, this was due to the restrictions on arrival and departure slots at Tokyo International Airport, which resulted into an institutional problem. Lesson learned: Skynet Asia Airways operated six daily round-trip flights

Chapter 3

on the Tokyo International Airport–Miyazaki Airport route with two aircraft.

The company eventually had to seek assistance from the Industrial Revitalization Corporation (IRC), but the problem did not lie in the operation strategy itself. IRC stated that, "Skynet Asia Airways' provision of low fares and convenient airline passenger services from Tokyo International Airport to an long-distance airport is appropriate for a fundamental business operation strategy," and it implies that the direction of the strategy itself was not wrong. Skynet Asia Airways' bankruptcy was due to its problem in cash management, the steep rise of insurance cost in the aftermath of the September 11 Attacks, the decrease in demand, and its initiation in 2002, when the aviation industry was under harsh circumstances.

6. Concentrated Use of Hub Airports

One unique characteristic of Japanese LCCs is that their initial route originates from Tokyo International Airport, which is an existing hub airport. Examples of this include the Tokyo International Airport–Fukuoka Airport route by Skymark Airlines and the Tokyo International Airport–New Chitose Airport route by Air Do.

In contrast, one of the success factors of leading LCCs in North America and Europe such as Ryanair and Southwest Airlines is the use of secondary airports. The reasons for this, which are especially true for larger cities, are listed as follows:
(1) Demand for secondary airports is superior to that of hub airports used by LCs due to easier accessibility.
(2) Management entities of secondary airports are proactively working on marketing to airlines for the purpose of competing against hub airports through implementation of measures such as reducing usage fees. In addition, facilities of secondary airport can reach out to LCCs without having to provide services that apply to all customer segments as it is done by hub airports. Cost reduction through this strategy will lead to a decrease in airport usage fees for LCCs.
(3) LCCs will not be directly compared with the luxurious facilities and large-sized aircraft of LCs.
(4) Secondary airports are not crowded, which attracts passengers and airline companies.

Needless to say, the above factors do not deny the use of hub airports. However, as the use of secondary airports will contribute to differentiation and cost reduction, LCCs must investigate the proactive use of secondary airports. It is also necessary, on the other hand, to study institutional problems in the Japanese market, those that restrict the use of secondary airports. The use of secondary airports is limited in Japan because there is only a small number of them, and their use is prohibited for institutional reasons.

◘ 7. Lack of Business Policies and Corporate Identity(CI)

Similar to other business operations, both visionary business leaders with expertise as well as a clear management policy and CI play an important role in the management of airline companies. From such perspective, Japanese LCCs lack in the establishment of CI. In other words, airlines such as Skymark Airlines, Air Do, and Skynet Asia Airways are associated only with cheap fares. In the past, such airlines existed even in the U.S. such as People Express, in which the CI was expressed as "low fare". Airline companies with such philosophy were not able to keep attracting passengers. Presenting cost reduction as the company's main business objective developed images of concern over safety, restructuring, and cutbacks in personnel. Moreover, it resulted in worsening the corporate image exerting negative influence on the employee's morale.

On the other hand, it is widely known that Southwest Airlines became successful not only because of cheap airfares, but also because of its family-oriented and humorous services. AirAsia, with the motto of "Now Everyone Can Fly", is successful in cost reduction in various aspects, while presenting a image and brand that is "young and energetic" and "high tech". It is important for a company to conduct cost reduction, whilst establishing a goal with social value, and to differentiate oneself from other brands.

Partnerships between LCCs and LCs are getting stronger. Examples include the partnership between ANA and Air Do, which target revitalization with ANA's support. In addition to, the partnership between Skynet Asia Airways with ANA, and Skymark Airlines and JAL that are code-sharing since 2005. However, this trend may play a negative role in LCCs' business strategy in terms of originality and differentiation.

8. Dependence on Public Funds

Another characteristic of Japanese LCCs, except Skymark Airlines, is the public assistance from local public authorities. Examples include the support by the Prefectural Office of Hokkaido for Air Do, and by the Prefectural Office of Miyazaki for Skynet Asia Airways. Local public authorities deliver subsidies to LCCs and support them directly through measures such as low interest loans. Air Do received financial aid and representation at the Prefectural Office of Hokkaido as a member of directors. However, injection of public funds without the clarification of the management responsibility can cause lack of management efforts.

The bankruptcy of Air Do, in spite of spending over 5 billion JPY of public funds, is a typical example of this. It is not by chance that Skymark Airlines was the only company out of all new Japanese airliners that circumvent bankruptcy and recorded surplus in recent years. This problem, however, shows that fund procurement is a challenge in the new Japanese air transport market, as shown in the example of Skynet Asia Airways. One of the reasons behind its bankruptcy was poor procurement of funds. Effective measures for this issue will be mentioned later.

9. Summary for Institutional Problem Studies

The study here has demonstrated that the reasons for the sluggishness of Japanese LCCs are (1) high-cost structure, (2) intense airfare competition against LCs depending only on lowering fares, (3) unclear customer target, (4) inappropriate route settings, (5) restriction of use of hub airports, (6) inconvenient operations, (7) lack of management policies and corporate identity (CI), and (8) dependence on public funds.

As for the high-cost structure, the problem lies also in the lack of effort by LCCs to reduce costs. Therefore, companies must make substantial efforts on implementing cost reduction measures. It is important to note, however, that an institutional problem also contributes to such structures. As for the airfare competition, counteractive airfare reductions by LCs is a threat. This indicates the need for examining the competition level of the entire market. Settings of route structure and number of flights are categorized as an institutional problem due to the restriction of arrival and departure slots.

Unspecified customer targets, the use of hub airports instead of secondary airports, lack of management policy and CI, and dependence on public funds are categorized as management policy issues, and they must be dealt by LCCs themselves. Out of all these problems, the non-use of secondary airports is due to institutional and physical factors. Dependence on public funds is derived from Japanese managerial characteristics. These institutional problems will be discussed later on.

3 Analysis of Problems of Aviation Policy

In the previous section, the reason for the sluggishness of new Japanese LCCs compared to European LCCs was discussed from a strategic business perspective.

The problems of management policy, however, are also influenced by institutional restrictions. For example, it is best from a business perspective, to lower the price of a commodity. However, if its price is fixed due to a pricing regulation system, lowering the price is not an option. Moreover, even if there is no pricing regulation, some systems and market structures in the past have had an impact on pricing. Therefore, it is necessary to discuss not only managerial improvements, but also whether management decision-making is hindered by governmental policies or systems, and if so, whether such policies and systems are viable or not, and how they should be reformed.

The Japanese aviation market was under strict governmental policies, in terms of entry and pricing for a long period after the end of WWII. Finally, in 2000, supply-and-demand regulation was abolished because the CAA was amended. In other words, the number of flights and airfare are now liberalized, to enter into the market. However, system wise, regulation policies that lasted for half a century with the oligopoly structure of the market shaped by these regulation policies are continuing

Chapter 3

to influence the current market. In my opinion, this has significantly restricted the development of Japanese LCCs.

The main focus of this section is to analyze the aviation policy issues from the viewpoint mentioned above that are essential in order to discuss the factors for development of new LCCs. Prior to that, for readers who are not familiar with the aviation policy, the discussion below will explain why such system restrictions did not become a barrier in the development of the European and U.S. LCCs, but did in Japan, by comparing the history of Western and Japanese deregulation measures. Furthermore, the validity of deregulation and competition promotion measures will be discussed; feasibility of contestability will then be examined. Finally, the aviation policy issues will be covered.

1. History of Aviation Deregulation in Japan and Western Countries

1.1 United States

Deregulation of the aviation market began in the U.K. and the U.S., and spread to a global scale. While it has been promoted gradually since the 1970s within its regulation system, deregulation in the U.S. was implemented at once by the change in the system according to the law in 1978. In the U.S., however, the State of California had experienced liberalization at a state level before it was implemented on the federal level. Moreover, whether to have regulations on air transport or not had already been discussed since the 1970s.

Full-scale development of worldwide commercial airline companies has not been seen until the end of WWII. In the U.S. and Europe, between the end of WWII up until the 1970s, the fact that the aviation business could benefit from governmental protection measures was derived from the theory of infant-industry protection, as well as the notion that receiving governmental restriction as aid service was taken granted, as can be seen from the railway business that was historically under strict regulation despite its recognition as the representative of means of transportation. Therefore, new entrants suffered strict laws taken for safety and technical aspects, including strict regulation economically regarding new entry and pricing. In the U.S., such regulations also controlled the number of flights and services. The Civil

Chapter 3

Table 3-6 Domestic deregulation process in the U.S.

	Events
1978	Airline Deregulation Act was enacted
1981	Liberalization of entering/exiting the market
1983	Fare liberalization
1985	Civil Aeronautics Board was dissolved

Source: Created by the author based on Sheehan (2013)

Aeronautics Board was established as an independent board for monitoring such economic regulations (Table 3-6).

However, since the beginning of the second-half of the 1960s, this situation started receiving increasingly harsher criticism and disputes regarding inefficiency caused by demands against intense regulations. This was due to the control of supply and demand, including the significance of the existence of Civil Aeronautics Board. By that time, the airline industry had shown a steady growth from its establishment. Consumer oriented dogma and movements as well as criticism against anti-competitive control over supply and demand increased. A contestable market theory was developed for introducing competition policy into the aviation market within the state, where liberalization had already been implemented, presenting finer performances.

The Airline Deregulation Act was enacted in October 1978, followed by the abolition of control over charter planes. With the Deregulation Act, several deregulation measures were implemented. The Act ordered, except for safety regulations, the complete liberalization of new entries and pricing in a phased manner. In 1985, the deregulation process led to the dissolution of Civil Aeronautics Board as a full-scale reform in deregulation. It is clear to see that "abolition of regulations" rather than "easing of regulations" had occurred in the U.S.

With this liberation policy, the first generation of LCCs were established. They took advantage of the gap in productivity between the major airline companies of high cost structure as a result of being protected by regulations for a long period. The LCCs entered the market with low fares as a result of cost differences, and stimulated the airline industry to a large extent.

Since then, there has not been a significant change in the deregulation policy in the U.S. As a result, only competitive airlines remain in business, like so in any industry. The LCs have survived by applying various management measures, including survival by going bankrupt and by utilization of FFP or CRS taking advantage of its strong networks. Confronted with such productivity improvement measures implemented by major airline companies, many of the so-called "cheap airline companies", which were oriented with low fares, went out of business. In fact, as was analyzed in Chapter 2, the only remaining LCC among those that entered the market in the 1970s and 1980s was Southwest Airlines.

Therefore, the U.S. aviation market can be featured as a market with a continuous wave of new entries. In the U.S. aviation market with less supply and demand adjustment controls, entering and exiting the market is liberalized. Pricing was completely free, and there was no administrative intervention by the government. With strict antitrust laws, newly entered companies have been under open competition with LCs. Some companies withdrew, and new companies would enter the market. These trends, which have been repeated since the beginning of liberalization of the aviation market, have promoted the development of both LCs and LCCs, vitalizing the market.

- **1.2 Europe**

In Europe, deregulation was promoted by the U.K. and the Netherlands. Since domestic airline markets are small, the pressure was applied on deregulation and liberalization targeted at the international airline transportation within the European continent, and such bilateral airline transportation agreements concluded between the U.K. and the Netherlands, and between the U.K. and Belgium, opened the new era of freedom. New entries could now begin operating, and this movement spread to the other countries in Europe. Thereafter, the EU led the deregulation of the airline industry, since this was regarded as one of the most important steps toward the integration of Europe.

As a result, a common aviation policy was adopted for the interest of the airline industry before the beginning of the 1980s in the U.K., the Netherlands, and Belgium and in other countries that were ahead in deregulation. Other countries in the EU also took the same stance by the beginning of the 1990s, though the deregulation of the entire airline industry was achieved as late as 1997. By that year, the European airline industry had exceeded success as further as that of Japan, giving LCCs such as easyJet and Ryanair a chance to participate in the industry. This further created a huge potential demand for the European industry. In the region, however, the power of the LCs was strong compared to the U.S., since LCCs were concentrated in the routes and areas in the U.K. where liberalization was promoted. On the other hand, differences in productivity between the LCs remain significant compared to those between the leading companies and LCCs in the U.S. This means that there is still room for development for LCCs in the market.

● **1.3 Japan**

Despite being known as a developed nation, Japan is considered an exception in Asia. While the history of its airline industry is similar to those in the U.S. and Europe, in the 1970s, Japan alone failed to follow the global trend towards deregulation

Table 3-7 Domestic deregulation process in Japan

	Events
1951	JAL founded
1952	CAA enacted and ANA founded
1953	JAL started international flights
1970~	Business scope defined: JAL to operate international / domestic high-demand routes, ANA to operate domestic high-demand routes regional routes, etc. "45/47 Structure" established
1978	Air liberalization began in the U.S.
1986	ANA entered the international market
	"45/47 Structure" abolished
	Control over supply and demand adjustment continued
1990	Fare liberalization began
1995	Scope of fare system implemented
1997	Complete elimination of new entry regulations
1998	Skymark Airlines and Air Do entered the market
2000	CAA amended, control over supply and demand adjustment, fare authorization system abolished
2002	Skynet Asia Airways entered the market
	Air Do applied for the Civil Rehabilitation Act and ANA began supporting reconstruction
2004	Skynet Asia Airways accepted management support of Industrial Revitalization Organization
	Capital and business alliance with ANA
2006	Star Flyer entered the market
2007	Partial Open Sky realized in "Asia Pacific Gateway Initiative"
2012	Star Flyer restructured with capital increase and so on with ANA as stockholder
2015	Skymark Airlines applied for the Civil Rehabilitation Act

Source: Created by the author based on the website of MLIT, December 2016

Chapter 3

(Table 3-7). While the U.S. and the U.K. had already gradually begun working on deregulation in the 1970s, Japan had to protect its aviation industry through complete market compartmentalization in the field of scheduled aviation services under the so-called "45/47 Structure".

As explained previously, the "45/47 Structure" was a protective governmental policy that prohibited mutual entries of airline companies. It is true that this protective policy played an important role in the development of Japanese airline companies, which had been small on a global level. The problem, however, was the control over supply and demand adjustments that remained the same, whilst the aviation industry was seeing significant developments. This resulted in a delay in implementing a deregulation policy, compared to Europe and the U.S.

Upon receiving the report of the Council for Transport Policy in 1986, the "45/47 Structure" was finally abolished. Nevertheless, strict control over supply and demand adjustments continued to be effective in Japan, in contrast with deregulation trends in the U.S. and Europe. As for domestic routes, airline companies could then apply double/triple track, a governmental policy to rescue airline companies (i.e., JAS), which were forced to operate flights under the "45/47 Structure". However, they still could not determine the number of flights and fares on their own. All companies had to apply the same fare standard for the same route, and competition over the number of flights was not allowed either.

In 1994, a registration system for a part of the discounted fares was established. Moreover, a scope of the fare system for regular fares was established in 1996, and this led to deregulation to some extent. Both MLIT and the LCs, however, had a negative attitude toward the possibility of accepting new entries since they needed to address the restriction of arrival and departure slots at crowded airports.

Japan finally showed a movement towards deregulation, marked by the enactment of the revisions made to the Aviation Act in 2000. This change was realized by the support of the administration reform committee as well as pressure from the public opinion, and from two new corporations that were ready to participate in the industry. With the revisions made regarding the Aviation Act, the control over supply and

Chapter 3

demand was abolished in principle, and pricing by airlines no longer required governmental permission. The only mandatory act was the report of prices to the authorities. The deregulation of the airline industry in Japan lagged more than 20 years behind that of the U.S., where the regulations were abolished in 1978. The revisions made to the Aviation Act in 2000 are:

(1) The change in the fare pricing system so that airline companies may report fares in advance. The authorities may order changes of fares only when it is too expensive or is aimed only for the purpose of shutting out competitors.
(2) The abolishment of supply and demand adjustments of routes. Airline companies may now set routes or increase/decrease the number of flights just by reporting this to the authorities.
(3) The abolishment of the licensing system for each route and the adoption of a system that assesses business management capabilities.
(4) The abolishment of captain license that was conducted for each route.

With these changes, airline companies can now determine routes, number of flights, and fares by themselves, in principle at least. From a legal perspective, liberalization was achieved at the same level as in the U.S. The chronological events regarding deregulation of control over supply and demand adjustments and pricing regulation are as listed in Table 3-7.

● 1.4 Difference Between Western Countries and Japan in Deregulation

As discussed above, deregulation in Japan was delayed compared to those of Europe and the U.S. As a result, while LCCs in Europe and the U.S. have developed the know-how through experience that has been accumulated from their history of liberalization for over 20 years, the two LCCs in Japan have entered the market with almost no management experiences. This trend is still reflected in the management policy of Japanese airline companies, and welcoming LCCs to the market has been a new experience for both regulatory authorities and LCs. They have dealt with new entries with no experience whilst designing a market system to effectively manage competition.

Another major difference between Japanese and the Western deregulation policies is the implementation of low-leveled Japanese policy that was delayed. Controls over

Chapter 3

supply and demand were indeed abolished, but the current Japanese deregulation policy that still allows regulatory authorities to control airline companies must have played a negative role in the development of airline companies new to the Japanese market.

◆ 2. Significance and Viability of Deregulation and Promotion for Competition

● 2.1 Reason for Control over Supply and Demand in the Past

Control over supply and demand adjustments is also called quantitative business regulation. This refers to the regulation that controls the number of suppliers and quantity of supplies. As mentioned earlier, after the end of WWII before deregulation was introduced, the aviation market was under the control of supply and demand adjustments for a long time. The reasons for such control over supply and demand adjustments were as follows:

(1) To develop and protect infant industries
(2) To avoid destructive competition in the industry with a large scaled industry
(3) To secure resources that internally subsidize underperforming routes, which are considered to be necessary from the standpoint of social needs

Moreover, various economic regulations were implemented in conjunction with control over supply and demand adjustments since, because prices might be determined in a monopolistic manner and the quality of service might be degraded. In addition, businesses tend to perform non-pricing competitions under price regulations. In order to prevent this, several service regulations were implemented. As a result, the aviation industry was not considered appropriate for such competition and control over supply and demand adjustments, pricing regulations, and qualitative regulations have hampered not only new entries, but also competition between LCs.

Chapter 3

● 2.2 Problem of Control over the Supply and Demand

2.2.1 Protection of Infant Industry

"Infant industry" refers to an industry in its developmental stage that has many uncertainties. Such an industry is considered to have potential social effectiveness, but its future is questionable. Therefore, there may be no proactive investor if the industry has to go through market mechanism. In some cases, such an industry will be protected by public subsidies or competition inhibited policies.

At early development stages, the aviation industry needed a significant amount of funds and knowledge. With uncertainties with investment in the industry, the number of investors were limited, and thus there was significance to the protection and development of the aviation industry led by the government. Protection and development measures have been implemented in several countries as a way of inhibiting competition or capitalizing participation of the government for airline companies. As the aviation industry grew, however, the idea of protecting it and inhibiting competition became inappropriate. It became unrealistic to regard a modern aviation industry as an infant industry.

2.2.2 Economies of Scale

The airline industry had traditionally been regarded as having economies of scale. This perspective has also played a role in implementing competitive inhibition through control over supply and demand adjustments.

In the aviation industry, however, there is a difference from the railway transportation such as the lower cost for fixed plants, since they are not managed by airline companies. Therefore, the cost ratio of stationary facilities is low, and most existing studies point out that revenue stream is almost consistent, or even slightly higher, with economies of scale.

Moreover, as previously mentioned, at an early stage of the aviation industry, the cost for aircraft and the capitalization rate had been relatively high. As the industry grew, it became more common to utilize used or leased aircraft, so the fixed cost ratio and sunk cost was lowered. This enabled airline companies to easily enter and

Chapter 3

exit the market, which led the industry to be more adaptable for competition. The level of sunk cost due to destructive competition has thus become lower.

Needless to say, this does not deny the fact that running a business by operating with a certain number of aircraft is effective from a management point of view. The reason for this is that, in addition to economies of scale, both economic efficiency of transport density and network are functional in the pure sense. What needs to be discussed here is whether economies of scale is large enough to justify control over supply and demand adjustments. An enormous amount of social loss is expected when a free market competition results in destructive competition under the control of supply and demand adjustments, and leads to a sunk cost of a bankrupt company resulting in a large social loss. In this regard, a corporation can remain competitive in the market as a result of making products with scale merits. In the case of the aviation industry, the scale of economy is not large enough to justify regulations of new entries, because scale merits can be small enough to be written off by productivity. This method may be regarded as one of the management tools.

If a route with small demand does not result in entries of multiple airline companies due to the requirement of a certain scale of business management, control over supply and demand adjustments for regulating entries does not need to be implemented. Instead, if we left it to the market, an effective corporation will survive. A corporation that does not survive will have sunk cost that is about the same level as that of any other industry, as discussed earlier. Moreover, even with no new actual entries, a potential threat of new entries will prevent LCs from setting monopolistic fares. The study on the contestability of the entire market in this regard will be presented later.

2.2.3 Maintaining Underperforming Routes by Internal Subsidies due to Social Needs

Similar to other public utility industries, aviation companies have to subsidize the cost for underperforming routes to remote islands or rural areas using the excess profits from the profitable departments of the company. One of the reasons for implementing control over supply and demand adjustments was to make LCs cover the deficit of such underperforming services.

The continuous operation of underperforming routes must be promoted as a means of income redistribution. The effectiveness of subsidies coming from particular resources, however, is low compared to general assignment of income between regions. Furthermore, the use of internal subsidies can have an adverse impact on income distribution unless the users of performing routes have constantly higher income than those of underperforming routes. Therefore, it is inefficient to distribute income using particular resources by internal subsidies.

Moreover, under the supply and demand adjustments, the productivity decreases since the competition becomes inactive. On the other hand, with intense competition, efficient airline companies such as LCCs or commuter airline companies will enter the market, and LCs will then improve productivity under competitive pressure. As a result, an underperforming route may well be converted into a performing one.

2.2.4 Advantages of a Competitive Market

As discussed above, there is no longer a reason to implement a competitive-inhibition policy by the control over supply and demand adjustment as in the past. In addition, it is important to promote competition in the Japanese aviation market from the governmental policy point of view, because the productivity of airline companies has significantly deteriorated due to a long-term competitive-inhibition policy. This has resulted in high airfares and inflexible services.

There is no room for discussing general advantages of deregulation. To give a specific example, the Economic Planning Agency estimated the annual average user profit ratio of two routes of Skymark Airlines and Air Do to be 2.36 billion JPY. If we add the profits derived from lowering the airfares of the leading airlines, which operate at 10 times the size of LCCs, to the two companies' profits, customer benefits would more than double. This must be the result of control over supply and demand adjustments due to long-term protective measures for the industry that disregarded the consumer benefits.

3. Contestability of the Air Transport Market and Fare Competition

As mentioned above, the air transport market is in theory adaptable for competition.

Nevertheless, the share ratio of LCCs in the Japanese domestic air transport market is not as high as it is supposed to be. This could be partly due to poor management and institutional issues of the LCCs. Before studying its institutional problems (or parts of its institutional problems), we need to study if the market itself is contestable. I mentioned previously that economies of scale is not large in the airline industry. If a market with economies of scale is contestable, no particular market regulation policy will be necessary.

Below is an analysis of the competition status of the Japanese aviation market with new entries, focusing on the competitive relationship between the LCs and the LCCs, and studying whether the Japanese market is contestable or not. This will be a prerequisite for discussing the competition policy.

● 3.1 Contestable Market Theory

A contestable market can be defined as a market that allows easy and free entry as well as easy exit with low sunk cost, because fixed cost can be recovered. A contestable market allows effective competition between new entries and LCs. With that being said, compared to the traditional market model, market competition can be explained as follows. The resistance reaction of LCs towards the newcomers is a precondition. Market price goes down with new entries. As a result, the price and production volume will change. On the other hand, with contestable theory, market competition is studied by considering both actual and potential entry.

To explain, potential new entries have the same competitiveness as that of the LCs in the market. If the entry and exit are liberalized, the market is maintained at an ideal state even without an actual entry. Even though the market is monopolistic due to economies of scale, monopolistic prices cannot be set because of the threat of potential entry through "hit-and-run strategies". Whether or not the entry/exit cost is high depends concretely on the amount of sunk cost. Even if the fixed cost was high at the time of entry, it could have been lowered if value remained high. This stimulates the willingness of LCCs to enter the market. Moreover, in a contestable market, the Bertrand-Nash hypothesis is applied. Under this hypothesis, LCs cannot immediately lower prices, therefore the time for taking such a countermeasure is delayed.

According to these hypotheses, the seven conditions for establishing a complete contestable market are as follows (according to Murakami et al., 2006):

(1) Both LCCs and LCs produce similar resources, and the consumers can purchase whichever one of their resources.
(2) Production cost of LCCs and LCs is the same.
(3) Companies are ready to enter price competition.
(4) No cost will be accrued for switching to another competitor.
(5) Entry/exit is free, and no sunk cost will generate.
(6) There is a time lag in setting prices by LCs.
(7) No excess demand or supply will occur in the industry.

From this, can we surely assume the Japanese aviation market to be contestable? Each aspect will be studied with the actual cases in Japan to find out.

● 3.2 Study of the Domestic Aviation Market

3.2.1 Similar Resources

The quality of the LCCs and the LCs, including in-flight services, is approximately the same. There was a huge difference in the number of flights and availability of airport facilities between new entries at the initial stage and LCs for institutional reasons, but this problem has been solved recently. As a result, there is no such difference anymore. Therefore, we can say that conditions of (1) have been met.

3.2.2 Similar Cost Function

As noted previously, there is a huge cost difference among LCCs and the leading companies. Condition (2) has not been met.

3.2.3 Price Competition

As mentioned previously, both LCCs and LCs can set prices on their own. As competition over fares is intense, airfare is obviously a key competition parameter. Therefore, Condition (3) is met. It is necessary to note, however, that there is a huge difference in the number of flights for LCCs at an initial stage for institutional reasons. Moreover, this competition was under special circumstances in which new entries were not allowed to increase their transportation capacity.

3.2.4 Consumers Restricted in Company Selection

Even in the case of discounted fares under certain conditions, such as for selected flights only or with advance purchasing options, customers can choose another airline next time. No passenger will be restrained by any airline. Therefore, Condition (4) is generally met. However, development of the FFP is questionable under this condition.

3.2.5 Sunk Cost

Discussion of sunk cost is rather complicated. In the aviation business, a large amount of resources including aircraft can be outsourced, therefore the cost is low. Needless to say, leasing cost can also be a sunk cost. Initial expenditures adding up to 5 billion JPY cannot be ignored by new entries of smaller scale. High-cost outsourcing can be reduced by self-management training of crew members and maintenance, but the cost in this case will be categorized as sunk cost. Moreover, after the control over supply and demand adjustments were abolished, certain routes could not be discontinued due to protests by the local residents. This can delay an LCC from discontinuing service on such a route because services depend on public funds. In conclusion, sunk cost is not necessarily high from a technical perspective. The problem lies in the market environment in which management resources are concentrated in the LCs. Furthermore, sunk cost becomes high due to the issue of capital procurement market, in which companies depend on public funds.

3.2.6 Time Lag of Airfare Change by LCs

As mentioned previously, the LCs changed fares on the same day as Skymark Airlines and Air Do did. Condition (6) has not been met.

3.2.7 Excess Demand and Excess Supply

Many of the routes entered by the LCCs are bound for Tokyo International Airport. It depends on the time and season, but such routes had experienced excess demand by the time Skymark Airlines and Air Do entered the market. This is more of a problem that has to do with airport capacity and airport policies, however. Moreover, with the recent expansion of airport capacity, excess demand on domestic routes is being eased.

● 3.3 What the Study Results Signify

The study above shows that the Japanese domestic aviation market is not completely contestable. This does not, however, deny promotion of competition or suggestion of re-regulation. The reason for this is that of Condition (2) and (6). Condition (2) is the result of an institutional restriction. Therefore, an institutional reform for solving this problem is required. Condition (2) also results from the lack of efforts by new companies to reduce costs. These management and institutional problems can be solved if worked on at the same time. After institutional reforms, the companies should basically let the market forces play out, implementing desirable after-the-fact regulation.

It is too early, however, to conclude if the aviation market really is contestable since there are some factors (such as impacts of strategies through FFP, CRS, hub and spoke systems developed by LCs) that must be discussed at another opportunity. With such aspects and gray zones shown, it is risky to simply regard a market as completely contestable. After-the-fact regulation must be definitely conducted in principle, but it is necessary to provide some sort of asymmetric regulation that supports new entries.

Below is a study on how the long-term competitive-inhibition policy weakened the contestability of the Japanese domestic aviation market and hindered the development of airline companies.

◘ 4. Problems of Current Aviation Policy and Their Impacts on LCCs

As discussed earlier, in the Japanese aviation market, amendments made to the CAA in 2000 abolished the control over supply and demand adjustments system. The impact of such long-term regulation policy, however, was effective when the LCCs entered the market, and still remains to some extent. There are two reasons for this. Firstly, this was due to the delay in deregulation compared to the worldwide trend, the spirit of liberalization that has not yet infiltrated neither the authorities nor the industry. Secondly, as one of the reasons why deregulation was delayed, authorities that were in charge of deregulation were not in favor of it. Deregulation was implemented by pressure only from outside of the ministry. Therefore, pro-regulation ideas may still exist amongst authorities and within the industry. This book will study the impact of such ideas regarding LCCs.

● 4.1 Delays in Deregulation

The fact that ideas of pro-regulation still remain strongly among the authorities and within the industry, can be seen through the process of initiating services conducted by Skymark Airlines and Air Do, the latest LCCs. Until the fall of 1996, when Skymark Airlines and Air Do declared entry into the market, MLIT was not willing to promote airfare deregulation. Their attitude, however, is said to have changed when the new entry of Skymark Airlines and Air Do became public. The mass media covered this story on a daily basis, and confronted with the public opinion, MLIT became more serious in discussing the authorization of new entries. They decided that it was not in their best interest to be against the public opinion, in the long run. This must have resulted in working on the entry of Skymark Airlines and Air Do proactively. However, the trend of promoting new entries and encouraging competition was only supported by the public opinion.

MLIT officials may not necessarily welcome liberalization. If they lose a wide range of their privileges to regulate pricing and entries, this will mean that the existence of the Japan Civil Aviation Bureau (CAB) in MLIT will be questioned. On the surface, system reform was implemented for orienting deregulation, and amendments made to the CAA in 2000 abolished supply and demand adjustment provisions, but many of the privileges of the authorities remained.

This caused both a direct and indirect impact on the development of Japanese LCCs. The authorities have put all sorts of pressure on the LCC's initiation of their license application stage. Moreover, indirect and various competitive-inhibition policies shown as an issue of arrival and departure slots and maintenance ability were seen as disadvantages to the LCCs (Indirect institutional impact will be discussed later). Negative attitudes toward deregulation by the authorities are indeed a burden to LCCs.

It is not fair, however, to only introduce the new entry side of opinions. It is necessary to listen to the opinions of the regulation authority side as well. In fact, when an

Chapter 3

LC, which once accepted outsourcing of the maintenance of an LCC, and later refused it, MLIT issued a statement forcing the leading company to accept. When Skynet Asia Airways entered the market, the authorities issued an order prohibiting lowering of fares by leading companies. The authorities, thus, have demonstrated their stance in favor of the LCCs.

Therefore, I would like to simply state here that, in any market, a new entrant must be a challenger, and must deal with non-cooperative governmental services. It is hard, but not impossible. Both Skymark Airlines, and Air Do procured licenses with the spirit essential to new entrants, and obtained approval from MLIT regarding half-priced or nearly half-priced fares, which resulted in the abolishment of the lower limit regulation. It is too early to conclude that the development of LCCs in the market is denied only due to the attitude of authorities.

As mentioned above, the passive attitude of the regulatory authorities, which might be the legacy of competitive-inhibition policy, can be a secondary problem, even though it is challenging for LCCs. On the other hand, the market's institutional and structural restrictions are more challenging for LCCs. Verification of the problems regarding the Japanese aviation market confronted by LCCs is shown below.

- ## 4.2 Limited Airport Capacity

4.2.1 Importance of Capacity of Airports in Tokyo Metropolitan Area

Two-thirds of the Japanese domestic aviation volume is supported by the demand in Tokyo Metropolitan area and Tokyo International Airport. With only a few exceptions, Tokyo International Airport is substantially the only airport out of all in Tokyo Metropolitan area, which allows operation on domestic routes. Therefore, for LCCs, the key to their operation is whether or not they can operate routes in and out of Tokyo International Airport, and secure the same number of flights as the LCs. Tokyo International Airport, however, is a very busy airport with insufficient capacity. Moreover, the LCs have already occupied the existing arrival and departure slots. Most of the increased slots by Tokyo International Airport's offshore expansion work have already been assigned to the LCs. As a result, when Skymark Airlines and Air Do entered the market, they only obtained three flights each.

Chapter 3

Below is the study on the kind of management problem caused by distribution of arrival and departure slots at Tokyo International Airport as essential facility to LCCs. This will be followed by a study of ideal distribution. The following explains the negative impacts on LCCs including lower airport capacity caused by delay in the development of secondary airports.

4.2.2 The Arrival and Departure Slots of Tokyo International Airport as an Essential Facility

Essential facility refers to essential productive factors and facilities in the industry. If a particular company monopolizes such facilities, competition will be restrained, and LCCs would struggle to enter the market.

In an industry with a long-term regulation policy, LCs that have been allowed to monopolize under a regulation system, often occupy essential facility. In the field of telecommunications, the former Nippon Telegraph and Telephone Public Corporation monopolized telephone wire rights. In the field of electric power, a local monopolistic electric power company monopolized transmission and distribution facilities.

Ultimately, even after deregulation, past privileges remain active, and major facilities go under a particular former monopolistic company. In such cases, entry of a company is approved by the abolishment of control over supply and demand adjustments. A new entrant is restricted from using facilities and from actual entry itself unless a new system with access rights for the essential facility is designed. In the case of the aviation market, protective policies over the LCs have been maintained for a long time, and a number of human and material management resources have been unevenly allocated to the LCs. This is becoming a huge barrier to new entrants. The most important resources that can be described as part of the essential facility problem are the arrival and departure slots at Tokyo International Airport, which accounts for two-thirds of the Japanese domestic aviation volume. Vested rights were granted to LCs to occupy arrival and departure slots on a first-come-first-serve basis. Without redistribution of arrival and departure slots, the entry of LCCs can be difficult as well as competition with LCs will be impeded.

As mentioned previously, Skymark Airlines and Air Do, the first two companies that entered the market as new firms in 1998, were initially given only three routes each, to and from Tokyo International Airport. Therefore, they could not expand their operation size. The LCs were operating ten flights each from Tokyo International Airport to Fukuoka Airport and from Tokyo International Airport to New Chitose Airport, thus LCCs with restricted numbers of arrival and departure slots could not compete with LCs by increasing the number of flights, since the system did not allow them to do so.

Under such circumstances, both Skymark Airlines and Air Do decided to compete with lower airfares, 50% by Skymark Airlines and 50% to 60% by Air Do. They demonstrated a load factor of more than 80% in the first six months when the fare level of LCs remained steady before the company entered the market. After March 1999, however, when JAL, followed by the other two LCs, lowered their fares, the new entrants suffered financial difficulties.

The issue of arrival and departure slots led Skymark Airlines to inefficiently use its second aircraft, and increased the company's deficit. Based on proper management policy, its second aircraft should have been flying between Tokyo International Airport–Fukuoka Airport, but this was impossible. Thus, the company was forced to choose the Osaka International Airport–New Chitose Airport and Osaka International Airport–Fukuoka Airport routes, which were minimally profitable.

Moreover, the company had to compete with the Shinkansen on its Osaka International Airport–Fukuoka Airport route. As the route is shorter, their aircraft were used as an alternative transport option to ferries. The yield of the route between Osaka International Airport and New Chitose Airport is low, since it is built for tourists. In addition, it could not become competitive since it was the only flight the company had. Moreover, the fact that the company had to open two stations (Tokyo International Airport and Fukuoka Airport) and two additional stations (Osaka International Airport and New Chitose Airport) within a short period of time had become a burden.

In 1998, when Skymark Airlines and Air Do entered the market, the distribution of arrival and departure slots were quite disadvantageous for the LCCs. As previously mentioned in this chapter, economies of scale does not function in the aviation market, but a constant scale of operation is necessary. It is known from experience that a business with a number that exceeds the flight ratio is at a disadvantage in being selected by consumers. Moreover, the management wished to increase the number of flights, but it is clear that restrictions on arrival and departure slots impeded it to do so.

The LCCs were later given prioritized slots, but the barrier caused by the lack of arrival and departure slots at their initial stage, not only weakened Skymark Airlines and Air Do financially, but also created the sentiment that the LCCs would not survive, and discouraged investors' motivations. These aspects caused a negative impact on the development of Japanese LCCs.

4.2.3 Problem of Distribution Method of Arrival and Departure Slots

The deregulation subcommittee of the Administrative Reform Committee pointed out that the arrival and departure slots at Tokyo International Airport would be the key to achieving effective competition between Japanese domestic airlines, including LCCs. At the end of 1996, before the entry of Skymark Airlines and Air Do, the same committee made a recommendation on the issue of arrival and departure slots. They suggested that the distribution method, which was on a "first-come-first-serve" basis, must be abolished and that slots be redistributed. The distribution method recommended was to promote competition under airport capacity restrictions and to select "competition tendering or an arrival and departure slot distribution method that is unbiased and highly transparent as its alternative"[6] in order to stimulate airline companies to improve productivity. This eliminates arbitrary and discrete arrival and departure slot allocations, and allows for implementation of free management policy with unlimited regulatory control by authorities that distribute arrival and departure slots.

To cope with this advisory, MLIT also began a study of a new distribution method, which will be explained further in Chapter 6. In March 2000, slots were reallocated according to this method and MLIT selected a point rating method, by which the ministry assigns slots based on evaluation items predetermined by the ministry.

---

6 Administrative Reform Committee (1997), p.484.

Redistribution conducted in March 2000 can be appraised from the fact that the increase in the number of slots was approved for LCCs. Later, prioritized slots were assigned to new entries. Both Skynet Asia Airways and Star Flyer can now set their desired number of flights. Currently, LCCs do not have to encounter the adverse circumstances that Skymark Airlines and Air Do initially did.

The fact that the ministry selected a point rating method means that free setting of the number of flights may become difficult. In a point rating method, the responsible authority, which is the evaluator, can rate the airlines arbitrarily by placing the desired emphasis on the desired evaluation items. This also means that the responsible authorities can still control airline companies through distribution privileges. In this way, supply and demand adjustments have not yet completely been abolished. Therefore, free setting of routes and number of flights has not fully been materialized.

4.2.4 Passive Attitude Toward Development of Secondary Airport

In order to expand airport capacity for a short term, it is essential to maximize utilization of the existing facilities. One of the policies is to use secondary airports in Tokyo Metropolitan area, namely, share military airports and utilize small airports located in various districts of this large urban area. The sequence of developments of the leading European and U.S. LCCs such as Ryanair and Southwest Airlines shows how proactive the use of secondary airports play an important role in the management strategy of the LCCs. On the contrary, secondary airports have been seldom used in Japan. This is one of the negative factors in the development of LCCs.

The first reason for this is that there is not much difference between primary and secondary airports. The second is that the Japanese aviation policy is focused more on the development of scheduled flights and protective measures. There is no governmental policy for general aviation as seen in Europe and the U.S. Therefore, Japan has never developed a plan for using secondary airports, and as a result, there are only a few secondary airports that are small in scale compared to those in Europe and the U.S. This becomes a serious bottleneck in promoting competition in the aviation market.

Nevertheless, new construction of airports such as Kobe Airport as a secondary airport of Osaka International Airport and Kansai International Airport, domestic hubs in the Kansai area, which is considered second to Tokyo metropolitan area in terms of size, as well as Kitakyushu Airport as a secondary airport of Fukuoka Prefecture, Japan's third hub, will contribute to the development of LCCs.

It is highly possible that new airports will be constructed in large urban areas and that the existing secondary airports will be utilized. Government policies determine the roles of airports in Sapporo Okadama Airport, Komaki Airport, and Hiroshimanishi Aiport regarding new airports in the respective areas. Commuters are only allowed to use the airports, but people can still potentially use small middle-sized jet airplanes.

Moreover, there is potential use of airports including Okegawa Airfield with airport facilities that are not accepting scheduled flights, or military airports such as Yokota Airbase, Naval Air Facility Atsugi, Iruma Airport, and Ibaraki Airport, which are not currently accepting commercial flights. These airports may be used as long as there are no system changes. New secondary airports may be built even within Tokyo Metropolitan area, based on the example of the airport built in London Docklands. It is essential to use secondary airports in order to solve the problems of preferential treatment of LCs, the aviation policy's overemphasis on scheduled flights, and unfair government airport policies. This could lead to the development of LCCs.

It is also to be noted that participation of the local community, where the airport is based, is an important factor in the use of secondary airports. For example, the development of Ryanair was boosted by the support of secondary airports used by the company as well as by the local government.

The EU Committee is questioning such support from the perspective that subsidies given to a particular airline company may lead to unfair competition. In Japan, different from Europe, where secondary airports have been proactively utilized since WWII, the use of secondary airports has been limited as part of the governmental policy. When considering the historical background, special measures such as subsidies from the local community for the time being may be an option. The reconsideration of management and privatization of existing airports might enable the utilization

Chapter 3

of secondary airports, which will be precisely explained in Chapter 5.

● 4.3 Problem of Uneven Distribution of Operational Resources

4.3.1 Uneven Distribution of Operational Resources and Limited Choice of Self-Management

As mentioned above, the most important resources considered as an essential facility in the case of air transport are the arrival and departure slots at the airports. They are not the only resources that are unevenly allocated; uneven distribution of maintenance capabilities and facilities also cannot be neglected.

As it was analyzed in Chapter 2, the European and U.S. aviation markets have a number of airline companies and have recognized developments of the aviation industry (non-scheduled flights or general aviation) in fields other than scheduled flights. On the other hand, the Japanese commercial airline market has kept governmental policy prioritized in scheduled flights for a long time. Therefore, the development of the aviation industry outside of scheduled flights has been delayed.

Moreover, even in the scheduled flight transport market, various management resources including facilities, labor, and know-hows are unevenly allocated to LCs. New entries in Europe and the U.S. have a larger selection in procuring management resources, except for the resources possessed by public institutions such as the arrival and departure slots from bankrupted airlines to non-scheduled airlines and general airlines. Japan is in a totally different environment since more choices and mutual competition will be promoted and price will be optimized. Uneven distribution of management resources is disadvantageous to new entrants and resources such as airport arrival and departure slots, irrigation facilities, airport counters, and labor resources including crew members, flight attendants, mechanics and ground staff are unevenly allocated. As a result, management know-how, including the use of buses within the airport area, is also unevenly allocated to LCs.

These problems, including the attitude of MLIT as previously mentioned, can be true for new entries in any industry to some extent. Skymark Airlines could deal with the problem of buses or gates by itself. Uneven distribution of management resources is a fate for new entrants, therefore, it is required to develop a management strategy to overcome such problems, as a challenger.

4.3.2 Issues in Maintenance Capability

Companies can deal with inadequacies in areas such as human resources and aircraft to some extent, but they cannot deal with maintenance facilities and capability alone. When Skymark Airlines and Air Do entered the domestic market, maintenance services were only available for LCs. As a result, LCCs were not able to enter the market if they could not outsource maintenance services to the leading companies.

One possible option for this problem was to outsource the maintenance services externally such as to Hong Kong or Singapore, which have excellent maintenance facilities, and airline companies with maintenance capabilities. This is technically viable, but for LCCs with only a few aircraft, it was unrealistic to leave the aircraft non-operated for a long period, and to send them outside of Japan spending extra fuel costs. In addition, the businesses outside of Japan might have not been serious about signing a maintenance contract with an unknown new Japanese airline company. Therefore, under these uniquely Japanese circumstances, measures such as "warning", which was undertaken by Japan Fair Trade Commission in order to protect new entrants at the initial stage, are needed.

Such "warning", however, must be limited to within the initial period of LCCs, based on the fact that Skymark Airlines, which entered the market a few years ago, has grown to have its own maintenance capability. After the first stage, it is desirable to monitor actions taken by LCs that accept maintenance to judge if such action were to be regarded as unfair competition and to implement countermeasures as necessary.

● 4.4 Problem of Predatory Pricing

4.4.1 Uncertain Predatory Pricing with Fair Price Competition

Inhibition policy of traditional companies still remains and impedes the development of LCCs. Predatory pricing by the LCs is a problem that needs to be addressed as one of the most important examination subjects.

It is sometimes said that LCCs in Japan are struggling to develop mainly because

LCs are trying to shut them out by setting equal low fares. JAL was criticized for this reason when it reduced its fare on a similar route to an LCC six months after it entered the market. Japan Fair Trade Commission made a statement that the commission would watch the market carefully.

The media had news coverage when Air Do became affiliated with ANA due to financial trouble. It reported that Air Do went out of business due to either the reduction of fares by leading airlines or bullying by leading companies. If an LCC exits the market without any problems whatsoever, then it is considered to be a normal consequence. It simply shows that an inefficient supplier had exited the market.

If leading companies control a non-competitive market and compete only against new companies by setting a differential fare lower than theirs in the market, then the fare is regarded as a so-called predatory pricing, and will cause unfair competition and inappropriate resource distribution.[7] It is unavoidable for an LCC to exit the market under such competition. On the other hand, if the LCC exits the market due to predatory pricing by a leading company, this will have a negative impact on public welfare. It is essential to assess if the price set by an LC is predatory.

4.4.2 History of Initial Fare Competition Between LCCs and LCs

If an LC, with its monopolistic power as a background, can set a predatory price in contrast to new companies, it means that LCCs do not have to expand their production volume, moreover, the existing businesses have monopolistic power except in markets where LCCs have entered. In the U.S., where domestic routes are completely liberalized, competition exists in markets other than those with new entries. Therefore, if an LC, which sets a predatory price in a particular market, cannot make up the deficit resulting from the particular market in another market, resulting in strangling their own necks. Moreover, in the U.S., if airline companies can determine the entry

---

7 Predatory pricing refers to the price system in which one uses its superiority in the market structure (such as monopolistic position) by setting a high price in a market advantageous to one and a price lower than the cost in a competitive market for the purpose of shutting out competitors. It is considered to be a kind of "dumping" by the Anti-Trust Law and it is prohibited.

and the number of flights on their own, new entrants can increase production volume to survive with their current routes, and by also adding other routes.

In contrast, at the time when Skymark Airlines and Air Do entered the market in Japan, those with no new entries were under the supply and demand adjustment regulation. Price competition barely existed. In addition, the LCCs only had three arrival and departure slots each, so they could not expand their supplies by increasing the number of flights. In addition, they did not have room to lower their fares. This led the LCs to set predatory prices.

The details of price competition are as previously described. To summarize and highlight the problems, Skymark Airlines entered the market in September and Air Do in December 1998 with fares that were 50% to 60% of those of LCs. JAL first counter-responded in March 1999 by reducing fares of similar routes to half. The mass media strongly criticized this action. The two other leading companies, however, immediately followed suit. As a result of such mutual reactions, approximately three-quarters of flight fares of all companies, including routes similar to those of Skymark Airlines and Air Do, were lowered to the same level. Under such circumstances, JAL's strategy of reducing airfare to a flight level similar to LCCs could no longer be regarded as predatory pricing. In fact, Japan Fair Trade Commission stated that a warning would be necessary for JAL when it announced the reduced fare because it had the potential to be an unfair competition, but the commission ended up with only observing the situation.

4.4.3 Definition of Predatory Pricing

Given the background mentioned, it will remain unrealistic to set a predatory price by reducing the fare for a particular flight for the purpose of shutting out new entrants. An LC, however, can still set a predatory price as a result of setting the same low fare for the same route as the LCC's, and increasing the fares of other routes. Therefore, predatory pricing will be defined before forecasting future circumstances. Generally speaking, predatory pricing can be defined when the following conditions are both met:

(1) when differences between the price in a particular market with competitors and the price in other markets are large

(2) when a monopolistic price can be set in another market

Regarding Condition (1), from an economic point of view, predatory price can be defined on the basis of whether the unjustifiable difference in price is lower than the individual cost (or average variable cost) or not in the market.[8] If the fare for a particular route exceeds the individual cost of the route, the price can be justified from both the management and resource distribution perspective. Needless to say, airline companies set the prevailing fare at a level that exceeds individual costs, and the price of the fare of the LCs are set to approximately 60% of the normal fare. On the other hand, their prevailing price of the fare between Tokyo International Airport and Fukuoka Airport at the time, when Skymark Airlines entered, was said to be set to the minimum level at which individual costs could be recovered. Therefore, a price of a particular route cannot be defined as predatory unless it becomes less than half.

As for Condition (2), predatory price is determined according to the level of price competition between the LCs on a route with no new entries.

4.4.4 Future Fare Competition and Possibility of Predatory Pricing

JAL's strategy for reducing the airfare for flights similar to those of LCCs previously mentioned, motivated ANA to become involved in fare competition, and as a result, promoted competition among the two leading companies. Competition on routes with no new entries progressed and discounted fares were applied to other routes. The trend to lessen discounted fares in dominant routes is still present, but Japan Fair Trade Commission (2001) presented slow expansion of application of discounted fares. Therefore, it is now difficult to set a cheap fare for a route with new entries, and to make up the deficit by monopolistic excess profit from a route with no new entries. Considering the above, it is not easy for an LC to set a price for a monopolistic

---

8   This is known as the AT rule in the U.S. Individual cost refers to additional cost or avoidable cost incurred only with particular services. Individual cost for a particular route in air transport is not incurred unless this particular flight is being operated. Individual costs include fuel cost, airport fee, aeronautical navigation aid usage fee, and cost related to in-flight services. On the other hand, common expenses include expenses incurred even without operating a flight such as company expenses, interests or depreciation cost. In the case of an LC such as JAL, personnel cutback cannot be performed easily. Personnel cost is included in common expenses because crew members do not always fly the same route.

route at more than double the fare of a competitive route when it comes to Condition (1) for predatory pricing.

In addition, it is important to note that current restrictions on the arrival and departure slots, and the number of flights are eased compared to the time when Skymark Airlines and Air Do entered the market. Therefore, if the competition between LCs continues at the same standard, the survival of LCCs might not become a serious problem from the predatory pricing point of view, as seen at the time when Skymark Airlines and Air Do entered the market. This is the idea presented by Chujo (2005). According to Chujo, it cannot be said that the fares set by the leading companies were predatory. Therefore, in a competitive aviation market, the possibility of predatory pricing is much lower, and thus before-the-fact regulation must not be implemented.

It is certainly unrealistic to assert that the bankruptcy of Air Do was caused by bullying of the leading companies, as reported by the mass media. If lowered fares set by LCs cannot be determined as predatory, financial trouble by Air Do must simply be a result of competition, and should not be described as an elimination process due to "bullying". Study of the current status of the aviation market reveals that the problem of predatory pricing must be dealt with by after-the-fact regulation. Implementing asymmetrical regulation by before-the-fact regulation could lead LCCs to depend more on public aid. Therefore, I agree with the idea of dealing with the problem not by before-the-fact but after-the-fact regulation.

I do not agree with Chujo (2005), however, on the following point. Although the monopolizing powers of LCs are on the wane, there are still considerable numbers of monopolized routes. In addition, there is a sizable disparity in the financial strength needed to survive price competition between LCCs and LCs. Moreover, as was covered in this chapter, Japanese LCCs struggle until they grow to a certain size. They are also weak in securing funds. It would incur a loss in the market in the long run if some LCCs quit before constructing their operational ground. Moreover, as mentioned previously, the fact that the aviation market is not necessarily contestable must be taken into consideration.

Chapter 3

In conclusion, I support Japan Fair Trade Commission in prohibiting the leading companies to match fares (LC's action to lower fares to match LCCs) as before-the-fact regulation, especially when Skynet Asia Airways entered the market. However, these cases would traditionally not be utilized by before-the-fact regulations but by after-the-fact regulations, such as the case of predatory pricing in the previous paragraph. The effects of long-term competition must be appreciated by restricting the setting of counteractive fares only until a small LCC with little funds develops.

• 4.5 Capital Market Problems and Dependency of LCCs

The above analysis shows how the situation of LCCs is significantly improving compared to the situation when Skymark Airlines and Air Do entered the market. From such perspective, the reason for Skynet Asia Airways' failure, which entered the market later on, will be discussed here.

4.5.1 Importance of Initial Capitals

Skynet Asia Airways was not exposed to restrictions of arrival and departure slots, unlike Skymark Airlines and Air Do. Therefore, there were more number of flights in the Tokyo International Airport–Miyazaki Airport route than those of the two leading companies. Moreover, the company was not exposed to the threat of predatory pricing thanks to the intervention of Japan Fair Trade Commission, which prohibited fare matching by the LCs.

Needless to say, the company could have improved its management performance if it could have reduced costs by using secondary airports or by self-managing its maintenance. These were, however, not the factors that led the company to go bankrupt. The main reasons for its bankruptcy were lack of management ability, high dependence on local government, and lack of funds that could have enabled it to survive its initial investment cost and deficit for a certain period of time after the foundation of business.

When Skynet Asia Airways entered the market, the predecessor of Air Do had gone bankrupt, and Skymark Airlines had not recorded a surplus. It was then difficult for the company to appeal the advantages of the new industry and its investment grade to motivate investment to investors. Skynet Asia Airways could have avoided filing a reorganization plan of bankruptcy, if it had attracted more investors who could take on the risk. This example indicates that a new entrant needs high fund procurement ability to survive competition for a certain period of time until it settles down in the market. This is more of a problem regarding the management policy of the company, which could not attract investors, as previously mentioned.

In contrast, in some Asian countries, risky LCCs are starting businesses with sufficient funds. It is typical in Japan that the required amount of funds cannot be procured from general investors. Investors tend to be reluctant to invest in businesses with no past performances. The social economic background of Japan regarding public funds that will be discussed later on, or foreign capital restrictions that restrict investment from outside of Japan that is typical in the aviation market, may also contribute to this circumstance.

From a legal perspective, airline companies are allowed to use one-third of foreign capital. However, this does not appeal to foreign capital investors with no management rights and no controlling interest in the company. Improvements in the Japanese social economic characteristics counteracting with venture capital, and abolishment of foreign capital restrictions will lead to improvements in capital procurement restrictions to a large extent.

4.5.2 Dependence of LCCs on Public Funds

Some point out that the behaviors of Japanese investors, which are strict towards new ventures, and the behaviors of new entrants relying on public resources without taking risk themselves, comes from social economic characteristics of Japan. It is true that Skymark Airlines survived the market with its uninterrupted business attitude, but Air Do and Skynet Asia Airways, which depended on public subsidies, were not successful. One of the reasons for that is the company's dependence on public assistance derived from social economic characteristics as well as the attitude of the public sector, which offered them help.

Air Do was a company in Hokkaido, which was supported by local, non-public and powerful human resources. However, after the sudden death of its first president, it lost power and became dependent on the Prefectural office of Hokkaido. It could even be called a publicly owned airline. Prefectural subsidies and remedies for Skynet Asia Airways might have caused a negative impact on the company's competitive spirit.

It is true that Japanese LCCs need public support to some extent, and have to survive to be competitive for a long period. Otherwise, the oligopoly by JAL and ANAHD will continue, and it is not the role of this book to discuss this matter in detail. Hereafter, I would like to simply conclude that companies must be warned with full attention so that they will not be highly dependent on public aid.

- ### 4.6 Necessity of Global Airline Industry Liberalization

LCCs in Europe, the U.S. and Asia (other than Japan) tend to exploit the international market when they do not find sufficient demand in their domestic markets. In Japan, the advancement of LCCs in the international market is limited to charter flights. The reason can be attributed to its inappropriate route structure, and also partially depends on management decisions, and in the difference between the degree of freedom in Japan and foreign countries. In addition, not only LCCs but also LCs are demanding the partial liberalization of the market. This topic will also be mentioned in Chapter 7.

The Japanese international aviation policy still has some protectionist aspects,[9] while international aviation has a global and the "Open Skies" trend. The international aviation framework is basically established by bilateral agreements, and between Japan and foreign countries, is based on protectionism, except for the one with the U.S. This is true not only for Japan; foreign airline companies cannot commercially operate on domestic routes in another countries (prohibition of cabotage). Foreign capital must not exceed one-third of the entire capital.

In the past, when the aviation industry was under slow development both on a domestic and worldwide scale, the fact that an aviation company in one's country was competing in the international market was significant in many aspects such as

---

9   Under bilateral aviation agreements between Japan and another country, in general, the number of routes, flights, and airline companies must be the same between the two countries. Airfares need authorization from both countries.

Chapter 3

national prestige, foreign currency acquisition, and national defense. However, these aspects can now be seen in fields other than aviation. National defense has, in some aspect, lost its importance, and hence is desirable to promote and expand competition for improving consumers' profit and for recovering competitiveness in the Japanese aviation industry by placing it in the global competitive environment.

In such sense, current bilateral agreements must be oriented for liberalization. The opportunity of entry into the market must be given to foreign capital airlines, and reform must include no restrictions in the number of entries or flights with free fare settings. In the long run, such measures must lead to agreements between multiple countries. This is a measure to be taken by Japan to follow the global Open Sky trend.

In addition, restrictions on foreign capital and cabotage to foreign companies must be abolished so that they can enter the Japanese domestic market. In an era when entering into almost any field including the manufacturing industry and service industry to the markets between multiple countries is possible, there is no reason for the aviation market to have exceptions in order to protect competition.

Abolishment of foreign capital restrictions, and liberalization of international air transport will allow a wider choice of routes by LCCs. The degree of freedom will be increased in business fields such as fund procurement in conjunction with the abolishment of foreign capital restrictions. In fact, the result of the simulation analysis in Chapter 4 demonstrates that expansion of services to international routes by LCCs is a reasonable option.

Conclusion: Summary for Simulation Analysis

In this chapter, the situation of LCCs in Japan was overviewed. The reasons for their sluggishness were analyzed by exploring the following issues: (1) high-cost structure due to small business size and lack of resource procurement ability, (2) intense airfare competition against LCs depending only on lowering of fares, (3) unclear customer target, (4) inappropriate route settings, (5) concentration of use of hub

Chapter 3

airports, (6) inconvenient operations, (7) lack of management policies and corporate identity (CI), and (8) dependence on public funds.

As most of the problems mentioned above exist with the management of LCCs, LCCs can solve these problems if they make efforts to the extent of those made by the LCCs in Europe and in North America.

However, institutional and market structural factors hinder the development of airline companies, and thus corporate efforts alone might not be able to overcome the problems listed above. The institutional and/or market restrictions that may be inhibiting the development of LCCs that were studied compared to the situation in Japan with those in Europe and in North America. Studies have shown that, at the time when LCCs started operations, the institutional factors shown below existed as the remnants of policies that had protected some airline companies for a long time.

(1) The human and material resources for aviation have been unevenly allocated to LCs, which raised the cost of acquiring resources for LCCs compared to that for LCCs in Europe and North America. In particular, the number of arrival and departure slots at hub airports, and the accessibility to the maintenance facilities set strict restrictions for LCCs at the time of entry.
(2) It is difficult to use secondary airports in major cities.
(3) Although LCs did not set fares to prevent new entries, LCCs are still likely to face disadvantages in price competitions against LCs, since domestic competition has not been as active compared to European and North American markets.
(4) The availability of funds is limited.
(5) Entry to international routes has not been liberalized.

The restrictions mentioned above, however, have been mitigated to a large extent since the time when LCCs first entered the market.

As for the number of arrival and departure slots, LCCs are now given some prioritized slots, although problems remain in terms of resource distribution in the aviation market. As for the maintenance of airplanes, some LCCs have begun self-management

Chapter 3

maintenances. Moreover, for predatory pricing, it will not impede the development of LCCs to a large extent, if at all. Problems with other resources are to be solved through the efforts of LCCs, although some issues are still under the influence of the aviation policies from the past.

We cannot forget, however, that the development of LCCs may be hindered by the fact that the use of secondary airports, selection of routes (including international routes), and procurement of funds are limited. As for the predatory pricing, after-the-fact regulation must be applied, but consideration for counteractive fares is necessary.

In conclusion, to compare and summarize the component factor of competitiveness between foreign and Japanese LCCs, it is estimated that LCCs can develop in Japan and expand to LCCs in Europe, North America, and Asia (except for Japan) under the following conditions: (1) size of operation above a certain level, (2) high productivities that enable low fares, (3) proactive use of secondary airports, (4) choice in the number of flights and routes (including international routes), (5) availability of sufficient funds, and (6) differentiation through marketing realization, and if no market or institutional regulations prohibit the realization of these elements.

Additionaly, a simulation will be performed in Chapter 4 for the viability of business establishment of the LCCs by using concrete samples of the airlines that meet the above conditions. What is implied in the simulation result will be compared with the result in Chapter 3 that leads to the final conclusion.

CHAPTER 4
Identifying the Success Factors Through Simulations for New LCCs

Up until previous chapters, it has arrived to the conclusion that the potential expansion of LCCs as can be seen in the U.S. and Asia(except Japan) is conceivable in Japan if certain requirements are fulfilled. In this chapter, this observation will be reexamined from a empirical point of view. Firstly, a specific business model will be constructed on the assumption that the new airline company holds success factors presented in the previous chapter. Subsequently, the validity of the business model will be verified by applying the corporate simulation model. Finally, the examination results will be concluded from both the business model and the simulation to clarify the prerequisites that have to be met for a successful LCC business launch. The significance of this simulation using the corporate model is its execution of both profitability analysis and risk analysis using the Monte Carlo method. It should be emphasized that the model created for this book is not only an examination of profitability and risk analysis, but also a model that can incorporate verified factors and be extensively used.

The simulation methods utilized in this chapter is based on Shiotani(2008), whereas the preconditions, the results, and the interpretations are largely updated.

Chapter 4

✈ Introduction

Japanese LCCs are not yet successful compared to North American and European LCCs. In this chapter, factors that hinder the healthy growth of Japanese LCCs are identified and analyzed by using successful factors of foreign LCC models as references. As a result, if certain conditions are fulfilled, a successful establishment is feasible within Japanese LCCs, as seen in those of North America, Europe, and other Asian countries.

In this chapter, observations are further examined from an empirical perspective. Firstly, an LCC business model is constructed using the success factors and criteria that are identified in the previous chapter. Secondly, the model is verified with corporate simulation models for its validity. And finally, investigation results from both the business model and simulations are combined and examined as successful establishment factors.

One significant value of this research is that the aviation business was analyzed by using a business analytical tool. Another value is adding risk analysis to the financial simulations of the corporate model. Most previous studies only focus on fixed data, however, new aviation companies now such as LCCs have higher risks and revenue compared to existing businesses. Therefore, not only profitability, but uncertainty has to be verified with appropriate methods. In this chapter, the Monte Carlo simulation is applied for the risk analysis, including sensitivity analysis for critical indices of business balances, in order to investigate the possibility of new business conditions from multiple perspectives. The third value is the implementation of the comprehensive empirical corporate model simulation, after considering the outcomes of the business model based on the analysis results in the previous chapter. The fourth is the corporate model itself. The model includes the following features:
(1) Many variables that have significant effects on the results of the management of aviation and transportation industry, (2) the ability to calculate the variable in the financial sheets and management indices to consider the risk analysis and profitability, and (3) the construction of the model enables it to assume the results easily since it is corresponding to the variable. The model is very versatile with it being flexible to

Chapter 4

make changes, and be translated easily for external use.

1 Assumption of the Business Model

Prior to simulation, this section revisits the strategies of successful overseas LCCs, and further discusses what kind of business model is used to make the assumption of the LCC.

1. Hub Airports

Most Japanese LCCs use Tokyo International Airport as their starting base for deploying routes. In other words, the airport can be described as their "hub". However, Tokyo International Airport has very strict arrival and departure slots and will not increase the number of slots dramatically, even after its offshore expansion work has completed. In contrast, as described earlier, Ryanair and easyJet avoid using crowded Heathrow Airport in London, and instead utilizes secondary airports such as London Stansted Airport and London Luton Airport as main hubs. This business model enabled their growth in Europe.

Potential airports that can take over the role of alternate secondary airports to Tokyo International Airport in the Tokyo Metropolitan area are the U.S. military airports such as Yokota Air Base and Naval Air Facility Atsugi. However, using these airports as a alternative for Tokyo International Airport is unrealistic. Hyakuri Airbase (Ibaraki Airport), a Japanese Self-Defense Force airport, will be converted into a military-civilian airport in the near future even if it is far from Tokyo. Considering such conditions, this research assumes the location of the LCC's hub airport to be Kobe Airport. Kobe Airport, established in 2006, is located in the second largest metropolitan area in Japan after Tokyo, Osaka. Kobe Airport has already proven its high route demands in the market.

With a 2,500-meter runway, Kobe Airport can accommodate middle-distance international flights, including core routes in Asia. Unlike Kansai International Airport, Kobe Airport has much better access to the Kansai area; it is only 8 kilometers

Chapter 4

away from Sannomiya Station, a railway station located in the district of Kobe Airport, one of the major cities in the area. Due to the airport's high accessibility to downtown, Kobe Airport is attractive to passengers from the western and central parts of Kansai area. This new airport does not have any vested interests from existing LCs, has no constraints on available slots, and no operating hour regulations for both passenger and cargo operations. Furthermore, the landing fees of Kobe Airport are much lower than those at Osaka International Airport and Kansai International Airport. The airport usage fee is lower, since Kobe Airport is an airport managed by local governments in Japan, which is a municipal airport in which the usage fees and other rules can be settled individually. These conditions make Kobe Airport very attractive and competitive for LCC businesses. By collaborating with airport operators, LCCs may be able to negotiate and settle cheaper airport usage fees with the airport operators, and contribute in the further airport development.

Based on these advantages, this study assumes Kobe Airport to be the secondary airport. In the verification process of using the corporate model in later sections, these are the advantages of Kobe Airport: cheaper airport usage fees than a hub airport such as Kansai International Airport, and settling the number of flights more freely and flexibly than Osaka International Airport. In addition, LCs have already established their bases and facilities at Kansai International Airport and Osaka International Airport. They do not have any plans or vision to expand their facilities into Kobe Airport due to operational and financial issues. In fact, JAL group has already withdrawn their business from Kobe Airport. These factors make Kobe Airport more attractive for LCCs to use as a hub.

2. Route Selections

For route selections, a typical LCC model operates short and middle-distance routes from a hub airport using small aircraft, and increases the frequency of its operations.

From Kobe Airport, the LCC can choose two different strategies for route deployments. The first is by introducing routes of lower demand and then switching them to routes of higher demand. The second strategy is by competing against LCs in high-demand routes at the initial stage. However, the selection of high or low-demand is starting to become a relative issue. For LCCs, it is critical to operate in high-demand routes at higher frequencies. If the hub airport is located in the Tokyo Metropolitan area, the low-demand routes are going to become relatively higher in Kobe Airport, and choosing such routes may adopt the two strategies above. However, in the case of Kobe Airport as a hub, the size of demand in the Kansai area is dramatically smaller than in the Tokyo Metropolitan area, and it is difficult to secure earnings from choosing relatively smaller routes from Kobe Airport.

In conclusion, the new LCC would only have a choice of selecting higher demand routes, if Kobe Airport is chosen as its hub for route deployment. If appropriate high-demand routes are not found in the domestic market, LCCs need to expand its vision to international routes as well. Traditionally, the routes of Japanese LCCs have been limited to the domestic market, however many LCCs in North America, Europe, and Asia have expanded their routes internationally. A new business model based on the assumption of active deployment of the international expansion strategy may become critical, if that is more effective. Due to such predictions, simulations in later sections show the combined results of domestic and international cases.

Additionally, route selection is structured with direct routes (point-to-point) only and excludes connecting routes, in order to save marketing and station costs. Skymark Airlines, as described in earlier analysis, suffered from inefficiency of expensive marketing and station costs at the time of its foundation. This occurred due to restrictions that forced the company to have multiple stations despite its small operations. From the above, the new LCC in this study limits its route selection to direct flights only.

◘ 3. Target Customers, Operations, and Aircraft Type

When considering high-demand routes from Kobe Airport, short and middle-distance routes become the root of the whole foundation. Moreover, a customer strategy focusing on business passengers as the main target should be developed. As such, two specific conditions need to be considered. Firstly, the critical decision factor for business customers who use short and middle-distance flights is the highly frequent operations. Secondly, as described in the chapters 1 and 2, a large number of

Chapter 4

successful LCCs operate smaller aircraft with high frequency than larger aircraft with low frequency. Adding the estimated demand size of relatively high-demand flight routes from Kobe Airport on the above, deploying 100 to 150-seat aircraft with high frequency operations would be the appropriate selection. A 150-seat B737-800 aircraft has been selected for the business model after deliberation of such strategies.

◘ 4. Airfare

Most LCCs in North America and Europe offer low airfares by taking advantage of cheap operation costs. In this study, the new LCCs target business customers who travel frequently and offer low airfare based on the low-cost operations. Based on the analysis results of the previous chapter, it is better for LCCs to set the airfare to around 60% of LCs' normal fare. If the airfare goes below 60%, the fare will clearly go below the profitable level. This is applicable for both LC and LCC cases. As for new entries into the market, the goal is to go under 60% of the normal fare and strive to save costs. Compared to the less competitive local routes, LCCs intend to maintain the airfare at the level of 50%. In addition, these high-demand major routes tend to have lower unit costs compared to those of local routes.

To set up an appropriate international airfare, a new Japanese LCC has to consider not only domestic LCs as its competitor, but also foreign carriers. Pricing is a key element for the business model to be set up at the same level: the so-called "cheap airfare" is 40% to 50% discount of LC's usual airfare, in order to maintain a profit at a feasible level. With such assumptions, this is the basic strategy that LCCs use for an approximately 40% discount for small-demand and 50% discount for high-demand, feasible routes. This study showcases the LCCs' airfare discount rate at 50%, and 38% for the LCs' normal fare. The 50% rate is chosen to almost match the LCs' online discount sales, while travel agencies offer cheaper airfare package rates for consumers, even if the LCCs are able to offer a maximum 50% of the LCs' airfare. Furthermore, offering the same rate makes LCCs' rate structure clearer and more attractive. This approach makes their flights mostly packed from their launch and continues to help maintain a consistent demand curve.

Chapter 4

◇ 5. Composition of Aircraft and Operation Rate

Low-cost must be achieved if cheap airfare is to be a competitive element while maintaining high-frequency operations with smaller aircraft. The LCC in this model utilizes the measures below for the realization of low-cost.

Firstly, it is common sense in the aviation industry that using a single type of aircraft directly affects cost reduction. Successful LCCs imply such cost reduction thoroughly. Since this concept is a common factor of successful LCCs, adopting the "use of single type of aircraft" for saving training and maintenance costs is an essential part of the business model. As long as night-shift operations are restricted in local airports in Japan, the aircraft operation rate cannot be higher than that of European and North American LCCs. The operation rate for Japanese LCCs is not practically higher than that of LCs, and therefore is proper to set eight hours of operation per day, which is slightly longer operation hours than those of LCs'.

◇ 6. Sales and In-Flight Service Cost

Adopting sales methods used by successful LCCs, such as Southwest Airlines mentioned in Chapter 1, increased its emphasis on the use of IT-based ticket sales. In applying this, the handling fee may be 5% of its passenger sales, which is lower than that of LCs. In regard to in-flight services, traditional LCCs offer no-frills service, and relatively short-distance flights from Kobe Airport do not need to offer high value-added services. Thus, the new LCC introduces simple and inexpensive no-frills service at a cost of 100 JPY per passenger.

◇ 7. Personnel and Maintenance Cost

Furthermore, it is a critical challenge for LCCs to increase the productivity of pilots and flight attendants, while reducing personnel costs. As described earlier, studies have shown that the aircraft operation rate cannot be kept high, and thus personnel operation rate remains restricted in Japan. Meanwhile, labor productivity and personnel cost are interdependent, so it is easier to calculate a number if the other one is fixed.

Accordingly, in this business model, productivity is fixed at the same level as LCs, while the personnel cost is set at a similar degree of existing LCCs (15 million JPY for pilots and 3.5 million JPY for flight attendants), which is much lower compare to LCs. As for the training of pilots and maintenance capabilities are unevenly distributed within LCs. This is the main factor that Japanese LCCs, Skymark Airlines, and Air Do have struggled within their business management.

Considering the factors above, for long-term cost savings, pilot training ought to be implemented within its own company. Hiring retired and experienced pilots as well as foreign pilots who do not require basic training is certainly necessary for learning methods and developing the company's own training system. However, house-trained personnel data are used in the simulation to avoid confusion. With the limited number of aircraft types and route selections, the internal training cost is considered much lower compared to those of LCs. The training cost for an LCC pilot for this simulation is set to 50 million JPY, using data extracted from existing temp services and other LCCs.

Prior analyses used such assumptions on maintenance cost from data of large-sized LCs such as JAL and ANA's maintenance expenses. However, the actual cost of LCCs is much higher than that of LCs, since LCCs are outsourcing maintenance services to LCs' facilities with special prices. This exceeds the ideas of the past financial simulations.

Meanwhile, Maintenance Repair and Overhaul facilities (MRO) have become popular in Asian countries, thus lowering the overall maintenance cost. This co-founded outsource concept is predicted to be adopted by Japanese LCCs in the future. This simulation uses the same cost level as the maintenance cost of LCs.

◘ 8.   Operations Size at Launch and Financing

Both Air Do and Skymark Airlines started their businesses with just one aircraft. However, as analyzed in Chapter 3, an airline may continue growing its business until the newcomer in the aviation industry reaches a certain size in operations. Therefore, it is desirable to start with relatively larger-sized operations that cover the scope of demands. It is also difficult to prepare a large number of aircraft from the beginning of operation. With funds of 9.5 billion JPY available as a realistic restriction, 15 aircraft is the maximum size to begin with.

For this simulation, the number mentioned above is realistically applied to the business model: a fund worth 9.5 billion JPY with 15 aircraft. Furthermore, a certain number of passengers have to be obtained to maintain such operation size. This means that LCCs have to deploy operations on a certain number of routes. With 15 aircraft fleet, the LCC needs to operate 14 routes at once to fulfill this requirement. Even at the initial preparation stage of the simulation, provisional calculation clearly shows that operating on only a couple of routes would not help reach its profitable goals.

On the other hand, even if the LCC begins with a small fleet of 4–5 aircraft, a large amount of funding is required at its launch. JetBlue Airways started with 160 million USD of initial funding and succeeded, while companies such as Skynet Asia Airways struggled with fund shortages. Therefore, one key success factor for an LCC is obtaining adequate amount of funds at the foundation of business.

In this study, the simulation indicates the required cost of launching the new LCC as approximately 9.5 billion JPY. As analyzed in Chapters 2 and 3, this is the minimum amount for running a business; both Skymark Airlines and Air Do started out with initial funding of 3 to 3.5 billion JPY, but struggled with financial management thereafter.

◘ 9. The Requirements for the New LCC Business Model

To summarize the LCC business model mentioned above, requirements include securing sufficient initial funds, utilizing Kobe Airport, obtaining a secondary airport in the metropolitan area as a hub, deploying middle-distance point-to-point services radially from the hub airport, and focusing on no-frills services on smaller aircraft with high frequency, as an airline company of high productivity and low-cost. In addition, this LCC has an innovative vision to expand its business internationally with freer and more flexible air cargo segments and route selections.

Chapter 4

The following section displays the successful establishment condition of new LCCs based on the example business model above. Furthermore, the hypothesis will be analyzed by simulation analysis using the corporate model, rating the numbers and substituting the cases with more realistic input values that are applied to the corporate model.

Nowadays, a number of restrictions and regulations still exist in the Japanese aviation industry. In order to optimize the simulation results, some conditions are reflected, such as the replacement of the highly regulated and crowded Tokyo International Airport to Kobe Airport.

However, within the restrictions on policies and market structures, LCs' aggressive discount rate is not included in the condition. This is based on the analysis results in Chapter 3 that LCCs can survive with offerings at a level around 60% of LCs' usual airfare. In contrast, the assumption of such aggressive price offering from LCs is not realistic. Regarding bilateral agreements on international flights from Kobe Airport and the difficulty of raising funds, Open Sky is increased and the simulation of such conditions will be improved. The issues related to the market structure and aviation policies are discussed after the simulation results are drawn.

✈ 2 Structuring of Corporate Model, Case of Simulation and Input Data

In Section 1, a corporate model is structured in line with the business model from the previous section. The structure of the corporate model, the calculation process, and classification of input data and factors are explained. In Section 2, details of input data and factors are described.

◘ 1. Structure of Corporate Model, Calculation Process and Classification of Input Data

● 1.1 Structure of Model

A calculation flow chart of the corporate model is shown in Figure 4-1. Moreover,

Chapter 4

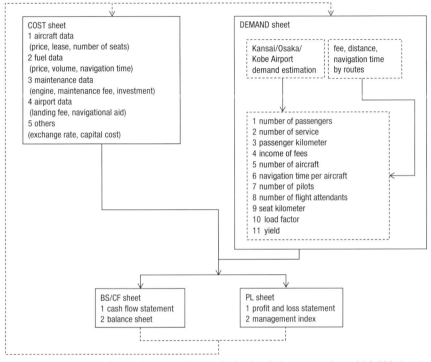

Figure 4-1 Structure of the corporate model and calculation process

Note: In the case of risk analysis, the Monte Carlo simulation is conducted 10,000 times.

main input data, calculation formula, and calculation results are indicated in the following three categorized sheets of Excel.

(1) COST sheet

Fundamental data, such as the exchange rate, are shown in this sheet. Cost related calculations have been conducted and results are indicated.

(2) DEMAND sheet

Routes are described by the airfare, distance of routes, aircraft operation hours and demand (number of passengers). The income by routes, the required number of aircraft and cabin crew, load factor and yield, and the calculation for demand can be done based on data related to demands, such as the number of passengers by

Chapter 4

routes, the number of service by routes, Revenue Passenger Kilometer (RPK) by routes, and Available Seat Kilometer (ASK) by routes, etc.

(3) BS / CF and PL sheet
Based on the calculation results of COST and DEMAND sheets, Balance Sheet (BS), Cash Flow Statement (CF), and Profit and Loss Statement (PL) are calculated. Moreover, primary management index is calculated and indicated in this sheet.

When one of the variables for input conditions is altered, data related to the financial statement and/or management index is changed accordingly.

● 1.2 Categorization of Input Data and Definition of "Base Value"[1]

A list of input data is shown in Table 4-1. Detailed explanation of the data will be discussed in the following subsection. In this subsubsection, a general categorization of data and "base value" are explained. "Base value" is provided for an efficient simulation and the input data for the first stage of calculation is summarized in the following three categories.

(1) Fixed input data
1) The value of data is fixed exogenously and unambiguously (ex. costs related to aircraft, maintenance fees, etc.).
2) The executives are given the option, but the value of data is fixed unambiguously and completely based on results of the study of the business model in the previous section. No other choices are taken into consideration (ex. airport and aircraft in use).

The reasoning behind the fixation of input data value is described in the explanation of the business model in Section 1 and the following subsection. In addition, a part of the fixed input data shown above will be treated as random variables for calculation in Section 3, though these are still fixed data for the risk analysis calculation in Section 4. The types of data that are used as random variables will be described in Section 4.

---

1 "Base value" is the initial input data.

Chapter 4

 Table 4-1 List of input data

Table 4-1-1 Data related to aircraft

Price (USD)	Maximum takeoff weight (t)	Number of seats (seat)	Property tax rate (%)
Insurance (%)	Lease cost (JPY/month/unit)		

Table 4-1-2 Data related to fuel

Unit price (USD/gallon)	Fuel consumption per flight hour (kl/hour)	Fuel tax (JPY/kl)	Unit price of oil (JPY/kl)
Oil consumption per flight time (kl/hour)			

Table 4-1-3 Data related to maintenance

Maintenance cost per navigation time (JPY/hour)	Periodical inspection cost (JPY/year/aircraft)	Investment in maintenance facility (JPY)	Cost of component (JPY/year/aircraft)

Table 4-1-4 Data related to airport

Landing cost for domestic airport (JPY/time)	Exceptional landing cost for Okinawa Airport (JPY/time)	Landing cost for Taiwan Taoyuan International Airport (TWD/time)	Landing cost for Incheon International Airport (KRW/time)
Landing cost for Gimhae International Airport (KRW/time)	Landing cost for Hong Kong International Airport (HKD/time)	Landing cost for Chinese Airports (USD/time)	Control tower cost for Chinese Airports (USD/time)
Domestic aviation support facilities (JPY/time)	Control tower cost for Japanese Airports (JPY/time)	Control tower cost for Korean Airports (KRW/time)	Control tower cost for Taiwan Airports (TWD/time)
Domestic airfield parking costs (JPY/day/plane)	Outsourcing cost of Kobe Airport (JPY/month)	Outsourcing cost for other airports (JPY/month)	Hong Kong airfield parking costs (HKD/time)
Ground rent of Kobe Airport (JPY/month)	Ground rent of other airports (JPY/month)	Number of staff for Kobe Airport (person)	Number of staff for other airports (person)

Table 4-1-5 Data related to personnel cost (Except pilots and flight attendants)

Number of employees (person)	Personnel cost for officers (JPY/year)	Personnel cost for general staffs (JPY/year)

Chapter 4

Table 4-1-6 Data related to operation

Normal passenger airfare of major airline company by routes (JPY)	Distance by routes (kilometer)	Operation duration time by routes (minute)	Aircraft operation hour (hour/day/plane)
Periodic training cost for pilot (JPY/person)			

Table 4-1-7 Others

Rate of administration cost (%)	Rate of sales charge (%)	Owned capital cost (%)	Initial investment cost (JPY)

Table 4-1-8 Exchange rate

China (JPY/USD)	Korea (JPY/KRW)	Taiwan (JPY/TWD)	Hong Kong (JPY/HKD)
United States (JPY/USD)			

Table 4-1-9 Variable and decidable input data for management

Authorized capital (JPY)	Discount rate of domestic airfare (%)	Discount rate of international airfare (%)	Initial training cost for pilot (JPY/person)
Personnel cost for pilot (JPY/year/person)	Personnel cost for flight attendant (JPY/year/person)	In-flight service cost (JPY/person)	Airfare receiving rate (%)

(2) Variable and decidable input data for management

1) Data (ex. capital amount, receiving rate)

It is easy to estimate the level of data determined by the minimum conditions leading a company to be in the black, and by common and reasonable judgements according to results of the study of the business model in the previous section. However, as a confirmation, an alternative case and simulation are conducted.

2) Data (ex. operation routes, level of airfare, operation with or without cargo)

Even though the level of data is determined by such minimum conditions and judgements according to the results of the study of the business model examined in the previous section, it is still important to compare the data to a certain extent. Some data patterns are prepared as input data.

According to the data categorized as (2) mentioned above, a large number of calculation combinations have been conducted by assuming various values and patterns including the cases of preparation level and calculations from the initial stages. However, if the overall results are mentioned here in this book, it may be very complicated and difficult to comprehend the indication. Therefore, the demand of passengers and the discount rate of airfares will be the focus of the next step.

In the following subsection, the definition of conditions for input variables, the calculation process and results based on such calculations will be described.

In this simulation, the discount rate of both domestic and international airfares indicated above are considered as variables for the case study.

(3) Output data as calculation results

Table 4-1-10 shows a part of the output data (data related to flight operation) from a calculation that utilized a corporate model. Among various types of data, total yield by year, and ASK are the most important indices to manage in the airline business. Moreover, 90 items of the calculation results are indicated on the Excel sheet, including the data shown in Table 4-1-10. Calculation items and results of financial terms are described in detail in Section 3.

In addition to the above, a corporate model can provide output data of financial statements and principal management indices.

Table 4-1-10 Output data of calculation

Passenger kilometer by routes and by year (passenger kilometer)	Number of flights by routes and by year (round-trip/day)	Number of aircraft by year (plane)	Flight duration by routes and by year (hour)
Annual number of pilots needed (person)	Annual number of flight attendants needed (person)	Passenger airfare income by routes and by year (JPY)	The number of seats provided by routes and by year (seat)
Domestic yield by year (JPY)	International yield by year (JPY)	Total yield by year (JPY)	Available seat kilometer (JPY)
Cost per passenger kilometer (JPY)	The number of staffs by year (person)	Sales charge (JPY)	

2. Simulation Case and Input Data

In this subsection, the simulation case and the input data using the corporate model are discussed. It should be noted that the input data used for the simulations are based on actual data and Shiotani(2008).

2.1 Operation Route

Kobe Airport is selected as a hub airport as mentioned earlier. Route structure is the radiating networks from Kobe Airport, and both domestic and international flights are operated simultaneously. When Kobe Airport was considered as a hub airport, a large demand, which can be the customers of the new LCCs, came to each route from Kobe Airport. For the demand of international routes, the LCCs do not particularly promote their sales and marketing like major LCs. There is more space for LCCs to gain profit by promoting their businesses and cultivating customers via a web-based online sales system.

Nowadays, although other countries request Japan to increase the number of flights, the Japanese companies cannot comply with the request, according to the results of the bilateral aviation agreements. Therefore, a chronic situation of excessive demand continues, and Japanese airline companies are allowed to sell their air tickets at a high price. If the operation network of LCCs is only constructed inside Japan, they do not compete with major airline companies since they may be able to issue a large number of cheap airline tickets. On the other hand, by constructing both domestic and international flights, the gateway function of Kobe Airport can be enhanced, and foreign passengers can reach final destinations via Kobe Airport. Considering the trend by passengers from Korea, Taiwan, and China, it can be expected that the number of customers and aircraft at Kobe Airport, which is said to be more convenient in travelling compared to other airports(Narita International Airport or Kansai International Airport), will increase if the airline provides more appropriate information on its website.

As a result, LCCs attract customers away from major airline companies. Operation routes are selected based on the large number of passengers. Table 4-2 shows the number of passengers in the current aviation market. Furthermore, operation routes

Chapter 4

 Table 4-2 The number of passengers by major operation route

(passenger)

Route	The number of passengers
Tokyo International Airport(Tokyo area–3 airports in Kansai area)	6,818,000
New Chitose Airport(Sapporo area–3 airports in Kansai area)	2,041,000
Fukuoka Airport(Fukuoka area–2 airports in Kansai area)	920,000
Naha Airport(Naha area–2 airports in Kansai area)	1,559,000
Kagoshima Airport(Kagoshima Airport–Osaka International Airport)	891,000
Miyazaki Airport(Miyazaki Airport–Osaka International Airport)	551,000
Kumamoto Airport(Kumamoto Airport–Osaka International Airport)	524,000
Sendai International Airport(Sendai International Airport–Osaka International Airport)	921,000
Nagasaki Airport(Nagasaki Airport–Osaka International Airport)	368,000

Table 4-3 List of considered operation routes

Domestic			
Kobe Airport– Tokyo International Airport	Kobe Airport– New Chitose Airport	Kobe Airport– Sendai International Airport	Kobe Airport– Fukuoka Airport
Kobe Airport–Naha Airport	Kobe Airport– Kagoshima Airport	Kobe Airport– Miyazaki Airport	Kobe Airport– Kumamoto Airport
International			
Kobe Airport– Incheon International Airport	Kobe Airport– Shanghai Hongqiao International Airport	Kobe Airport– Beijing Capital International Airport	Kobe Airport– Hong Kong International Airport
Kobe Airport– Taiwan Taoyuan International Airport	Kobe Airport– Gimhae International Airport		

selected for this study are as shown in Table 4-3.

In this study, as explained above, the reason behind the new LCCs' operation of both domestic and international routes is because it is necessary to have a business of a certain size (at least three or four routes). A provisional simulation analysis indicates that utilizing just one route is inadequate for the operation of a new LCC. Furthermore, the discussion about the number of aircraft presented in a later subsection, also shows that one to two route operations is insufficient to stabilize its business.

2.2 Cost-Related Figures

(1) Aircraft cost

In this study, B737-800 is to be introduced to the new LCC's business model. LCCs use A320 in many cases since it has the same specification of the cockpit and other common parts. In Japan, however, many airline companies have introduced Boeing, in accordance with a plan of the Ministry of Economy, Trade and Industry (METI).

In this study, LCCs do not provide cargo services since existing major airline companies have already provided the services without any complications. Since cargo handling is unnecessary, it is better to introduce the B737-800 aircraft without utilizing Unit Load Device (ULD). Consequently, in terms of efficiency of the maintenance service, it is advantageous and rational to introduce B737-800.

The estimated price and main specifications of B737-800 are shown in Table 4-4. In case of the procurement of an aircraft, assumption is set at the straight-line method of 17 years and 10% of residual value regarding the depreciation of the aircraft. The annual property tax rate is assumed as 1.4% of the procurement price. In the case of leasing an aircraft, it can be assumed that the leasing cost (operational lease) per month is 0.9% of the price of procurement.

(2) Fuel cost

According to various reports regarding fuel consumption of B737-800, it is assumed that the average fuel consumption per hour is 2.31 kilometers. Fuel price is 94 USD per barrel. The fuel cost is calculated by the following equation:

Fuel cost = operation hour × fuel consumption rate × fuel price

Moreover, a tax of 26,000 JPY for domestic flights is imposed on fuel costs. Data on fuel and oil estimated from the average price of recent years are listed in Table 4-5.

The fuel cost of an aircraft has commonly been estimated by referring to the data of major airline companies (i.e., JAL and ANA). However, in the cases of LCCs, many tend to spend a tremendous amount of money on fuel, which is comparatively higher than the estimation. It could be said that this huge aircraft fuel cost is an obstacle for many LCCs to sustain their businesses. Thus, one factor for LCCs' sustainable

Chapter 4

Table 4-4 Cost data of the B737-800 aircraft

Price of aircraft(million USD)	43
Price of aircraft by JPY(million JPY)	3,780
Maximum take-off weight(t)	63
The number of seats(seat)	150
Annual lease cost(million JPY)	408
Annual depreciation cost(million JPY)	200
Aircraft property tax rate(%)	1.4
Aircraft insurance rate(%)	1.14

Table 4-5 Data of fuel and oil costs

1 barrel = 42 gallon(USD)	94
1 barrel = 42 gallon(JPY)	8,460
Fuel price(JPY/kl)	53,200
Oil price(JPY/kl)	3,000
Fuel tax(JPY/kl)	26,000
Consumption of fuel(kl/hour/plane)	2.31
Consumption of oil(kl/hour/engine)	0.5
Consumption of oil(kl/hour/plane)	1.0
Fuel and oil cost for domestic flight(JPY/hour)	189,898
Fuel and oil cost for international flight(JPY/hour)	122,908

development is to reduce fuel costs.

(3) Maintenance cost

There is a recent growth movement to establish MRO service organizations in Japan. It will be a significant reduction of aircraft maintenance costs for all airline companies, and a chance for middle and small class companies to offer more jobs in Japan as well. It is assumed that the maintenance cost will be reduced by outsourcing the maintenance service to MRO anywhere in Japan since:

– The maintenance procedure will be simplified, by using only a single type of

Chapter 4

 Table 4-6   Estimated maintenance cost

Power plant overhaul cost(JPY/hour)	18,571
Air frame overhaul cost(JPY/hour)	8,333
Duration inspection maintenance cost(JPY/hour)	10,000
Periodic inspection cost(million JPY/year/aircraft)	10
Cost of components(million JPY/year/aircraft)	20

Table 4-7   Airport landing cost and parking cost for B737-800

(JPY/flight)

Japan	Domestic Naha Airport	78,866
	Domestic others	94,640
	International	83,000
	Parking cost for Kobe Airport(JPY/day)	5,040
Korea	Incheon International Airport	36,900
	Gimhae International Airport	21,482
Taiwan	Taiwan Taoyuan International Airport	28,099
China	Hong Kong International Airport	56,762
	International	60,750

aircraft, and standard parts can be procured in bulk. It will be possible to obtain Parts Manufacturer Approval (PMA) parts at bargain prices.
– Personnel cost for MRO service companies will be more competitive than those of major airline companies.
– MRO service companies can provide onboard maintenance, which is not yet provided by major airline companies.

Estimated maintenance cost per aircraft is shown in Table 4-6.

(4) Airport cost

Landing costs and airfield parking costs for B737-800, based on maximum take-off gross weight shown in Table 4-7, are estimated considering the inclination of recent years. The cost of the aviation support facility is shown in Table 4-8.

Chapter 4

Table 4-8 Cost for aviation support facility

(JPY/flight)

Japan	Kobe Airport–New Chitose Airport	105,210
	Kobe Airport–Naha Airport	26,302
	Kobe Airport–Other Airport	74,340
	International	180,000
Other routes		74,340

Regarding other costs, rental cost for Kobe Airport is 10 million JPY per month supposedly, and for other airports it is set to be 2 million JPY.

(5) Selling cost and in-flight service cost

Selling costs including agency commission and call centers related expenses are assumed to be 5% of passenger revenue. In-flight service cost means cost of beverages, newspapers, and magazines. Moreover, considering how traditional LCCs offer no-frills services, in-flight service cost is assumed to be 100 JPY per passenger in this study.

(6) Personnel cost

Personnel cost by occupation is assumed as follows:

(million JPY / person / year)

Board member	20
Ground worker	5
Pilot	15
Flight attendant	3.5
Training cost for pilot	50

(7) Capital

According to previous failures of LCC businesses in the past, it is desirable to start an LCC business with sufficient funds. The LCC will then be established with 9.5 billion JPY in capital.

Chapter 4

(8) Other conditions

Other input conditions are set as follows:

Dividend rate(%)	10
Corporate tax rate(%)	35
Initial expenses(billion JPY)	2

The exchange rate estimated from the average of recent years is shown in Table 4-9. Although USD currently has a low exchange rate to JPY, the value shown below is the average from past years.

Table 4-9 Estimated exchange rate

(JPY/each currency)

USD	90	HKD	16.68
RMB	16.52	KRW	0.10
TWD	3.69		

● **2.3 Demand-Related Data**

(1) Airfare receiving rate, passenger airfare level, discount rate of airfare

It is possible to obtain data related to existing operation routes from the Kansai area (Osaka International Airport and Kansai International Airport). Based on such data, candidates have been selected for the operation routes, and have estimated the number of passengers for them, then calculated the shares of new LCCs.

Firstly, the number of passengers for each route from Kansai area (Osaka International Airport and Kansai International Airport) was researched based on the information from MLIT. Selected routes have chosen areas in Kansai, which consist of around 700,000 people and 500 kilometer route distance as candidates.

Moreover, based on empirical assumptions, the number of domestic passengers for each zone is strongly correlated with the zone of each population and the amount of wholesale sales. The number of domestic passengers is estimated by the following equation indicated below. Thereafter, the number of domestic passengers from Kobe Airport including the numbers by each route is determined.

Chapter 4

The Kansai area consists of six prefectures (Shiga, Kyoto, Osaka, Nara, Wakayama and Hyogo) and is distributed into the zone by each city as a basic unit. The area of influence of Kobe Airport is the entire Hyogo Prefecture, excluding Itami City, Amagasaki City, and Takarazuka City.

The number of domestic passengers is calculated by the following equation:

$$Yi = 0.5 Pi + 0.5 Wi$$

i: zone (i =1 to n) (n is the number of zones for whole Kansai area)
Yi: the number of passengers of arrival and departure in zone of i
Pi: the population percentage in zone of i
Wi: sales rate of the wholesale in zone of i

As a result, the share of domestic routes of Kobe Airport is estimated to be 35% of the Kansai area.[2]

Finally, the market share of the new LCC will be discussed. As defined in the previous section, the airfare of the new LCC is on a lower level compared to other major airline companies and LCCs such as Skymark Airlines. It is difficult for major airlines to follow the low price of LCCs due to intense scrutiny from Japan Fair Trade Commission as well as progressive competition in the domestic aviation market.

Therefore, the new LCC can be estimated to occupy one-third of demands even if other two major airline companies have entered the market. According to the above, it is estimated that the share of major routes is 30%, and the share of local routes is 40%, since it is difficult for major airline companies to enter the local routes. The share rate of the Tokyo International Airport route is estimated to be 10%.

On the other hand, the international routes are selected in accordance with the following process. Since there is no public information related to the number of passengers of Kansai International Airport by route, focusing on airline companies which operate five flights per day to nearby Asian cities, and estimates the number of available seats based on the number of flights and aircraft types. Subsequently,

---

[2] According to Ohta(1981), the demand rate is strongly related with the wholesales rate and population rate. Then, the average of both factors are taken in this case.

Chapter 4

Table 4-10 Distance, duration and airfare for domestic flights

Route	Distance (km)	Duration (minute)	Basic airfare (JPY)
Kobe Airport–Tokyo International Airport	514	65	16,200
Kobe Airport–New Chitose Airport	1,235	105	30,500
Kobe Airport–Fukuoka Airport	535	70	15,850
Kobe Airport–Naha Airport	1,370	125	24,800
Kobe Airport–Kagoshima Airport	613	70	19,650
Kobe Airport–Miyazaki Airport	544	65	17,400
Kobe Airport–Kumamoto Airport	540	60	17,400
Kobe Airport–Sendai International Airport	716	55	14,400

Table 4-11 Distance, duration and airfare for international flights

Route	Distance (km)	Duration (minute)	Basic airfare (JPY)
Kobe Airport–Incheon International Airport	979	115	52,000
Kobe Airport–Shanghai Hongqiao International Airport	1,600	150	78,000
Kobe Airport–Beijing Capital International Airport	2,027	210	106,000
Kobe Airport–Hong Kong International Airport	2,868	255	91,000
Kobe Airport–Taiwan Taoyuan International Airport	1,968	180	87,000
Kobe Airport–Gimhae International Airport	657	95	46,000

the number of passengers have been estimated, as well as candidate operation routes (i.e., the route to Pusan becomes a candidate because many Korean residents live in the Kansai area.) After the estimation of the share of the new LCC routes that can be expected to achieve more than 55% of load factor even if it is only one flight per day, were selected. Furthermore, 40% of the shares of Kobe Airport is estimated on the condition of sharing routes with Kansai International Airport, and 35% of the shares of domestic routes. Finally, estimation of the share of the new LCC has been calculated. As discussed in the previous section, the new LCC's international airfare is expected to be at a competitive level against other foreign airline companies and discounted tickets. Considering the entry of foreign companies and the two additional Japanese major airline companies, it is expected that the new LCC can gain 20% of its share at least. Taking the discussion above into consideration, data is summarized in Table 4-10 and 4-11.

This study also focused on the discount rate of airfares and two case studies have been conducted as shown in Table 4-12.

Table 4-12   Discount rates

Case No.	Routes composition	Discount rate of airfare(%)
1	Domestic and international	38.3
2	Domestic and international	50.0

(2) The number of passengers by route

In Japan, the number of passengers is assumed unchangeable and this phenomenon is based on special domestic conditions. One of the major reasons is that there are no extra arrival and departure slots at major airports, such as Tokyo International Airport, Narita International Airport, Osaka International Airport, Fukuoka Airport, New Chitose Airport, Naha Airport, and Kobe Airport. In addition, in Kobe Airport, the number of arrival and departure slots per day is limited to 60, due to the correlation with the surrounding airports. Therefore, the service volume cannot be increased. Moreover, the current situation has hardly ever changed due to the high load factor generated by LCCs' popularity among individual customers. Thus, in this simulation study, the uncertainties such as events and annual climate conditions are included, and have carried out simulations without considering the growth rate.[3]

Taking the above landing records into account, the new LCC will most likely find enough demand at Kobe Airport after starting its operation. Therefore, in this analysis, after planning the number of flights by routes, the demand of passengers is estimated by a calculation formula. The load factor and operation rate are estimated as 76% and 98%, respectively. The number of passenger demand is calculated by the following equation:

no. of flights per day $\times$ no. of seat $\times$ load factor $\times$ 365 $\times$ operation rate

---

[3] In this simulation, the growth rate is based on a verifiable level, since the demand is expected to descend as the population decreases hereafter.

Chapter 4

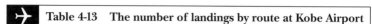 Table 4-13 The number of landings by route at Kobe Airport

	ANA	SNJ	ADO	SKY
Tokyo International Airport	2	-	-	7
Ibaraki Airport	-	-	-	3
New Chitose Airport	1	-	2	3
Naha Airport	-	3	-	2
Nagasaki Airport	-	-	-	4
Kagoshima Airport	-	-	-	2

Table 4-14 The calculated passenger demand

The number of flights a day	The number of passengers a year
2	83,000
4	166,000
6	249,000
8	332,000
10	415,000
12	498,000
14	581,000
16	664,000
18	747,000

Therefore, the planned number of passengers becomes as follows with the number of flights per day. It is a marketing strategy specific to LCCs only to secure the number of customers corresponding to the number of flights and seats supplied for each route. An LCC itself tends to conduct the service like this proactively. According to the above formula, the estimated results of passenger demand in both domestic and international routes were selected for this simulation as shown in Table 4-15.

Based on the above formula and Table 4-14, the estimated passenger demand, which should be acquired, is calculated in Table 4-15. The actual data of Fukuoka Airport, Miyazaki Airport and Kumamoto Airport are acquired from Osaka International Airport's, since the routes from Kobe Airport are not operated at the moment. The

Chapter 4

 Table 4-15 Estimated passenger demand by domestic routes

Route	Flight per day (flight)	Passenger demand (passenger)
Kobe Airport–Tokyo International Airport	18	747,000
Kobe Airport–New Chitose Airport	8	332,000
Kobe Airport–Fukuoka Airport	6	249,000
Kobe Airport–Naha Airport	6	249,000
Kobe Airport–Kagoshima Airport	4	166,000
Kobe Airport–Miyazaki Airport	4	166,000
Kobe Airport–Kumamoto Airport	4	166,000
Kobe Airport–Sendai International Airport	6	249,000

domestic route of Kobe Airport–Tokyo International Airport is the largest compared with other routes, and supposes that the passenger demand is 747,000 passengers. The passenger demand for each route is similar to the current situation.

In the same way, Table 4-16 shows the estimated passenger demand for each international route which is calculated by the formula described above. The data themselves are acquired from Kansai International Airport, since international routes from Kobe Airport have not begun yet. The fare collection rate, the ratio of passengers paid for the basic airfare, considered in the estimation both above and below, while it is not applied in the actual data. For example, if the number of flights of the Kobe Airport–Incheon International Airport route is set to six flights per day, the number of passenger demand is calculated by the formula as 249,000 passengers.

The former LCCs sought a scheme to establish a network and increase flights if demand increased. At the stage of holding smaller number of aircraft, if an LCC added one aircraft in its operation, it needed to increase five round-trip flights. It tended to be an excessive investment since there was no heavy demand.

In this analysis, the new LCC does not apply the strategy of increasing flights following the flexibility of demands, since an LCC operates only on routes with high demands. There is no surplus of slots in the airports, and it is not realistic to increase the

Chapter 4

Table 4-16 Estimated passenger demand by international routes

Route	Flight per day (flight)	Passenger demand (passenger)
Kobe Airport–Incheon International Airport	6	249,000
Kobe Airport–Shanghai Hongqiao International Airport	4	166,000
Kobe Airport–Beijing Capital International Airport	4	166,000
Kobe Airport–Hong Kong International Airport	4	166,000
Kobe Airport–Taiwan Taoyuan International Airport	4	166,000
Kobe Airport–Gimhae International Airport	2	83,000

Note: Kobe Airport, currently does not operate in international routes, however, if LCCs use Kobe Airport as its base in the future, it is conceivable that demand in international routes would arise.

number of flights if CAB does not instruct a reallocation of slots. Moreover, in slightly higher demand routes, attribution of passengers whom LCCs ought to acquire is limited, and is impossible to change the competitive situation with existing airline companies.

Travelers in Japan, in general, are not good at planning trips and reserving air tickets and accommodation. Most of them are more likely to participate in packaged tours called "Inclusive Tour Charter (ITC)" conducted by travel agencies or group tours created by organizations or associations. If the new LCC desires to acquire these passengers, it is critical to own larger aircraft and have a stronger sales structure.

The basic strategy of LCCs is to support individual travelers, and not only focus on a group of passengers. They need to be cautious in expanding flights. According to the results of a financial simulation, ordinary cumulative profit of 10 years is a useful index to make a decision on expansion of new routes and increase the number of flights. It is appropriate to make a decision when the LCCs are sufficiently funded. If the new LCC increases the number of flights or expands its business to a new route, it is necessary to introduce a new aircraft, train additional employees including pilots, co-pilots, maintenance engineers, ground staff, and introduce Grand Support Equipment (GSE), etc., in addition to considering whether the cost could be supplemented by initial reserves in order to make a decision.

Chapter 4

(3) The number of flights and passenger kilometer by routes

Each route already shows the size of demand in the number of flights, and the LCC could lead its number of flights aiming to gain about 10% to 50% of the route. The number of passengers per LCC depends simultaneously on the number of flights. This condition works only for the following situation: all the customers of LCCs are able to plan their own excursions and book air tickets and accommodation by themselves. However, LCCs can gain demand for all routes, and this is because most Japanese passengers are not able to organize tour plans and make reservations by themselves, thus usually choosing package tours. It can be concluded by analyzing the demographics of passengers that the number of passengers increases due to the number of flights.

LCCs originally gain profits from specific types of passengers. Therefore, the size of market as the denominator must be large. To achieve this goal, LCCs operate their flights on high-demand routes between large cities or on routes around the cities as a secondary option. In this analysis, the routes, which meet the following conditions, were selected: (1) those with large number of passengers from the Kansai area, and (2) those that LCCs can earn profits if it has taken part of the demand. Therefore, LCCs determine the number of flights not by the basic passenger demand but by the flexible availability of aircraft, rather than by the size of passenger demand to achieve maximum efficiency.

If an LCC decides to set two round-trips per day, there already exists a certain amount of demand. In this case, most load factors are fixed. Additionally, LCCs need to make an effort in selling tickets, and collaborating with the local communities to gain support from them, which will be explained in Section 5. Thus, the demand of route is determined by the number of flights, then leads to the number of passengers by assuming the accurate load factors. The demand of passengers is slightly and annually changing by various natural phenomena, such as typhoon, earthquake, and commercial events. In this simulation, these phenomena are expressed by probability distribution.

According to the discussion above, passenger kilometer is calculated by multiplying the number of passengers by distance. Seat kilometer is also calculated by multiplying

Chapter 4

 Table 4-17 Estimated passenger kilometer and seat kilometer by domestic routes

(million)

Route	Passenger kilometer	Seat kilometer
Kobe Airport–Tokyo International Airport	383	506
Kobe Airport–New Chitose Airport	410	540
Kobe Airport–Fukuoka Airport	133	175
Kobe Airport–Naha Airport	341	450
Kobe Airport–Kagoshima Airport	101	134
Kobe Airport–Miyazaki Airport	90	238
Kobe Airport–Kumamoto Airport	89	118
Kobe Airport–Sendai International Airport	178	235

 Table 4-18 Estimated passenger kilometer and seat kilometer by international routes

(million)

Route	Passenger kilometer	Seat kilometer
Kobe Airport–Incheon International Airport	243	321
Kobe Airport–Shanghai Hongqiao International Airport	265	350
Kobe Airport–Beijing Capital International Airport	336	443
Kobe Airport–Hong Kong International Airport	476	628
Kobe Airport–Taiwan Taoyuan International Airport	326	430
Kobe Airport–Gimhae International Airport	54	71

the number of flights by distance and the number of seats of an aircraft. Table 4-17 and Table 4-18 show the estimated results of passenger kilometer and seat kilometer by domestic and international routes, respectively.

● **2.4 The Number of Aircraft Required and Crews**

(1) Aircraft required

Operation hours of each airport, which are discussed in this study, are summarized in Table 4-19.

Major Japanese airports (Tokyo International Airport, New Chitose Airport, Fukuoka Airport and Naha Airport) and foreign airports, which are connected to Japanese

Chapter 4

Table 4-19 Operation hours by airport

Airport	Open	Close	Operating hours
Kobe	7:00	22:00	15:00
Tokyo International	-	-	24:00
New Chitose	-	-	24:00
Sendai International	7:30	21:30	14:00
Fukuoka	-	-	24:00
Naha	-	-	24:00
Kagoshima	7:30	21:30	14:00
Miyazaki	7:30	21:30	14:00
Kumamoto	7:30	21:30	14:00

airports, operate 24 hours by constructing a network around Kobe Airport. Additionally, no airline companies can divert to airports operating around Kansai International Airport, and is therefore expected for Kobe Airport to be open 24 hours, and for passengers to have access to it all day and night. In terms of alternative airports, Naha Airport and New Chitose Airport are assigned as the international routes of Kansai International Airport. Thus, if Kansai International Airport recovers enough capacity for the aircraft, it would repeatedly arrive from these alternative airports.

For all of these reasons, it is likely that the network around Kobe Airport expands the operation hours of aircraft. In terms of human resources, current operation introduces a 2-shift system, and even a 3-shift system in some workplaces, including outsourcing in order to materialize 24 hour operations. As a result, it is likely to take 3,900 operation hours of aircraft from 3,500 operation hours.

Therefore, the number of aircraft required is calculated by the following equation:

number of aircraft required =

$$\frac{\text{total flight hours of all routes} + \text{turnaround hours}}{\text{average of operating hours where average of operating hours is} (10.5 \text{ hours})}$$

Based on the discussion above, the number of aircraft required for domestic routes is eight and that for international routes is seven. Table 4-20 shows the number of aircraft required and flight hours per aircraft.

Chapter 4

 Table 4-20 The number of aircraft required and flight hours per aircraft

	Year1	Year2	Year3	Year4	Year5	Year6	Year7	Year8	Year9	Year10
Aircraft required	15	15	15	15	15	15	15	15	15	15
Aircraft held	0	0	1	1	1	2	2	3	4	5
Increase	0	0	1	0	0	1	0	1	1	1
Lease	15	15	14	14	14	13	13	12	11	10
Flight hour per aircraft	3,491	3,596	3,516	3,516	3,516	3,516	3,516	3,516	3,516	3,516

(2) The number of pilots and flight attendants

When aircraft flight hours are calculated, the number of pilots and flight attendants can be calculated also. According to the discussion of Subsection 2 with the experimental data of existing airline companies, the number of pilots and flight attendants for one aircraft are two and three, respectively. It is assumed that monthly operation hours per flight attendant is 70 hours with 10% of allowance ratio. In this study, the number of pilots is 148, and the number of flight attendants is 205. Since the number of aircraft has not changed for the past 10 years, the number of pilots and flight attendants have not either.

3 Results of Financial Simulation by Using the Corporate Model

1. Outline of Case Study and Cumulative Ordinary Profit

Following the calculation on Figure 4-1, financial simulation by means of the corporate model is presented on the Excel sheet by requisite parameters in Section 2.

In this section, the financial statement and calculated results of principal management index are shown and analyzed. In this subsection, the cumulated ordinary profit is analyzed in order to consider the results of financial simulation and mention the methods of calculation and analysis.

In this study, two cases of simulation are examined as shown in Table 4-21.

Chapter 4

Table 4-21 Outline of case study

Case No.	Routes composition	Discount rate of airfare (%)
1	Domestic and international	38.3
2	Domestic and international	50.0

Note: A projected result of cumulated ordinary profit is shown in Table 4-22.

Table 4-22 Discount rates of airfare and cumulative ordinary profit

Case	Discount rate (%)		Cumulative ordinary profit (million JPY)
	Domestic	International	
Case 1	38.3	38.3	96,137
Case 2	50.0	50.0	22,157

As for the business models, presented in Table 4-22, the 40% to 50% discount rate of both domestic and international routes are indicated inevitably to compete with airfares of foreign airlines. In both cases, the cumulative ordinary profits are positive. The cumulative ordinary profit of Case 1 is 96,137 million JPY and that of Case 2 is 22,157 million JPY.

Comparing Case 1 with Case 2, the cumulative ordinary profit of Case 1 is naturally better than that of Case 2. The cumulative ordinary output of Case 1 is more than four times larger than that of Case 2. This result comes from better revenue of passenger airfare against the same cost structure of operation. Case 2, of course, is still a positive value. This means that an LCC can run its business properly if the level of 50% discount rate is maintained.

2. Simulation Results of Financial Statement

The financial statements of Case 1 and 2 are indicated in Table 4-23 and 4-24, respectively.

Chapter 4

Table 4-23 Financial statement for the new LCC (Case 1)

Table 4-23-1 Profit and Loss Statement for Case 1 (million JPY)

	Year0 (PRE)	Year1	Year2	Year3	Year4	Year5	Year6	Year7	Year8	Year9	Year10
Domestic passenger traffic income	0	22,201	22,201	22,201	22,201	22,201	22,201	22,201	22,201	22,201	22,201
International passenger traffic income	0	18,966	18,966	18,966	18,966	18,966	18,966	18,966	18,966	18,966	18,966
Cargo service income	0	0	0	0	0	0	0	0	0	0	0
Operating income	0	41,167	41,167	41,167	41,167	41,167	41,167	41,167	41,167	41,167	41,167
Navigation expense											
Cockpit	0	2,205	2,220	2,220	2,220	2,220	2,220	2,220	2,220	2,220	2,220
Pilot training	1,500	5,850	50	0	0	0	0	0	0	0	0
Fuel	0	8,291	8,360	8,360	8,360	8,360	8,360	8,360	8,360	8,360	8,360
Maintenance	0	2,082	2,140	2,096	2,096	2,096	2,096	2,096	2,096	2,096	2,096
Aircraft depreciation	0	0	0	200	200	200	400	400	600	800	1,000
Aircraft lease	0	6,120	6,120	5,712	5,712	5,712	5,304	5,304	4,896	4,488	4,080
Aircraft property tax	0	0	0	0	47	41	36	77	66	102	133
Landing fee	0	2,617	2,617	2,617	2,617	2,617	2,617	2,617	2,617	2,617	2,617
Aviation support facility fee	0	2,387	2,387	2,387	2,387	2,387	2,387	2,387	2,387	2,387	2,387
Airfield parking fee	0	16	16	16	16	16	16	16	16	16	16
Depreciation	0	270	270	270	270	270	270	270	270	270	270
Aviation insurance	0	650	650	650	650	650	650	650	650	650	650
Airport support fee	0	576	576	576	576	576	576	576	576	576	576
Flight attendant fee	0	714	717	717	717	717	717	717	717	717	717
Other service fee	0	332	332	332	332	332	332	332	332	332	332
Depreciation of initial expense	0	400	400	400	400	400	0	0	0	0	0

Chapter 4

Selling and administration cost											
Sales charge	0	2,058	2,058	2,058	2,058	2,058	2,058	2,058	2,058	2,058	2,058
Officer's salaries	100	100	100	100	100	100	100	100	100	100	100
General clerk salaries	200	1,910	1,910	1,910	1,910	1,910	1,910	1,910	1,910	1,910	1,910
Kobe Airport rental charge	0	120	120	120	120	120	120	120	120	120	120
Domestic airport rental charge	0	96	96	96	96	96	96	96	96	96	96
Oversea airport rental charge	0	72	72	72	72	72	72	72	72	72	72
Others	0	217	217	217	217	217	217	217	217	217	217
Operating expenses	1,800	37,083	31,428	31,126	31,173	31,167	30,554	30,595	30,376	30,204	30,027
Operating profit	▲1,800	4,084	9,739	10,041	9,994	10,000	10,613	10,572	10,791	10,963	11,140
Non-operating expenses	0	0	0	0	0	0	0	0	0	0	0
Total expenses	1,800	37,083	31,428	31,126	31,173	31,167	30,554	30,595	30,376	30,204	30,027
Ordinary profit	▲1,800	4,084	9,739	10,041	9,994	10,000	10,613	10,572	10,791	10,963	11,140
Corporation tax	0	0	3,408	3,514	3,497	3,500	3,714	3,700	3,776	3,837	3,899
Profit after tax	▲1,800	4,084	6,331	6,527	6,497	6,500	6,899	6,872	7,015	7,126	7,241
Dividend	0	0	950	950	950	950	950	950	950	950	950
Undivided profit	▲1,800	4,084	5,381	5,577	5,547	5,550	5,949	5,922	6,065	6,176	6,291
Cumulative profit	▲1,800	2,284	7,665	13,242	18,789	24,339	30,288	36,210	42,275	48,451	54,742

Table 4-23-2 Balance Sheet for Case 1 (million JPY)

	Year0 (PRE)	Year1	Year2	Year3	Year4	Year5	Year6	Year7	Year8	Year9	Year10
Assets											
Liquid assets	2,700	7,454	13,505	16,372	22,989	29,609	32,848	39,840	43,595	47,861	52,642
Aircraft	0	0	0	3,380	2,980	2,580	5,560	4,760	7,340	9,520	11,300
Other properties	3,000	2,730	2,460	2,190	1,920	1,650	1,380	1,110	840	570	300
Total properties	3,000	2,730	2,460	5,570	4,900	4,230	6,940	5,870	8,180	10,090	11,600
Deferred assets	2,000	1,600	1,200	800	400	0	0	0	0	0	0
Total assets	7,700	11,784	17,165	22,742	28,289	33,839	39,788	45,710	51,775	57,951	64,242
Capital liabilities											
Debt balance	0	0	0	0	0	0	0	0	0	0	0

	Year0 (PRE)	Year1	Year2	Year3	Year4	Year5	Year6	Year7	Year8	Year9	Year10
Capital	9,500	9,500	9,500	9,500	9,500	9,500	9,500	9,500	9,500	9,500	9,500
Legal capital surplus	0	0	0	0	0	0	0	0	0	0	0
Surplus	▲1,800	2,284	7,665	13,242	18,789	24,339	30,288	36,210	42,275	48,451	54,742
Total capital	7,700	11,784	17,165	22,742	28,289	33,839	39,788	45,710	51,775	57,951	64,242
Capital and liabilities	7,700	11,784	17,165	22,742	28,289	33,839	39,788	45,710	51,775	57,951	64,242

Table 4-23-3   Cash Flow Statement for Case 1 (million JPY)

	Year0 (PRE)	Year1	Year2	Year3	Year4	Year5	Year6	Year7	Year8	Year9	Year10
Financing											
Brought forward	0	2,700	7,454	13,505	16,372	22,989	29,609	32,848	39,840	43,595	47,861
Capital	9,500	0	0	0	0	0	0	0	0	0	0
Gain listed	0	0	0	0	0	0	0	0	0	0	0
Undivided profit	▲1,800	4,084	5,381	5,577	5,547	5,550	5,949	5,922	6,065	6,176	6,291
Aircraft depreciation	0	0	0	400	400	400	800	800	1,200	1,600	2,000
Initial expense depreciation	0	400	400	400	400	400	0	0	0	0	0
Other depreciation	0	270	270	270	270	270	270	270	270	270	270
Total financing	7,700	7,454	13,505	20,152	22,989	29,609	36,628	39,840	47,375	51,641	56,422
Initial expenses	2,000										
Investment in aircraft	0	0	0	3,780	0	0	3,780	0	3,780	3,780	3,780
Investment in others	3,000	0	0	0	0	0	0	0	0	0	0
Repayment	0	0	0	0	0	0	0	0	0	0	0
Purpose of funds	5,000	0	0	3,780	0	0	3,780	0	3,780	3,780	3,780
Excess and deficiency	2,700	7,454	13,505	16,372	22,989	29,609	32,848	39,840	43,595	47,861	52,642
Debt	0	0	0	0	0	0	0	0	0	0	0
Carried forward	2,700	7,454	13,505	16,372	22,989	29,609	32,848	39,840	43,595	47,861	52,642

Chapter 4

 Table 4-24 Financial statement for the new LCC (Case 2)

Table 4-24-1 Profit and Loss Statement for Case 2   (million JPY)

	Year0 (PRE)	Year1	Year2	Year3	Year4	Year5	Year6	Year7	Year8	Year9	Year10
Domestic passenger traffic income	0	17,990	17,990	17,990	17,990	17,990	17,990	17,990	17,990	17,990	17,990
International passenger traffic income	0	15,369	15,369	15,369	15,369	15,369	15,369	15,369	15,369	15,369	15,369
Cargo service income	0	0	0	0	0	0	0	0	0	0	0
Operating income	0	33,359	33,359	33,359	33,359	33,359	33,359	33,359	33,359	33,359	33,359
Navigation expense											
Cockpit	0	2,205	2,220	2,220	2,220	2,220	2,220	2,220	2,220	2,220	2,220
Pilot training	1,500	5,850	50	0	0	0	0	0	0	0	0
Fuel	0	8,291	8,360	8,360	8,360	8,360	8,360	8,360	8,360	8,360	8,360
Maintenance	0	2,082	2,140	2,096	2,096	2,096	2,096	2,096	2,096	2,096	2,096
Aircraft depreciation	0	0	0	200	200	200	400	400	600	800	1,000
Aircraft lease	0	6,120	6,120	5,712	5,712	5,712	5,304	5,304	4,896	4,488	4,080
Aircraft property tax	0	0	0	0	47	41	36	77	66	102	133
Landing fee	0	2,617	2,617	2,617	2,617	2,617	2,617	2,617	2,617	2,617	2,617
Aviation support facility fee	0	2,387	2,387	2,387	2,387	2,387	2,387	2,387	2,387	2,387	2,387
Airfield parking fee	0	16	16	16	16	16	16	16	16	16	16
Depreciation	0	270	270	270	270	270	270	270	270	270	270
Aviation insurance	0	650	650	650	650	650	650	650	650	650	650
Airport support fee	0	576	576	576	576	576	576	576	576	576	576
Flight attendant fee	0	714	717	717	717	717	717	717	717	717	717
Other service fee	0	332	332	332	332	332	332	332	332	332	332
Depreciation of initial expense	0	400	400	400	400	400	0	0	0	0	0

Chapter 4

Selling and administration cost											
Sales charge	0	1,667	1,667	1,667	1,667	1,667	1,667	1,667	1,667	1,667	1,667
Officer's salaries	100	100	100	100	100	100	100	100	100	100	100
General clerk salaries	200	1,910	1,910	1,910	1,910	1,910	1,910	1,910	1,910	1,910	1,910
Kobe Airport rental charge	0	120	120	120	120	120	120	120	120	120	120
Domestic airport rental charge	0	96	96	96	96	96	96	96	96	96	96
Oversea airport rental charge	0	72	72	72	72	72	72	72	72	72	72
Others	0	198	198	198	198	198	198	198	198	198	198
Operating expenses	1,800	36,673	31,018	30,716	30,763	30,757	30,144	30,185	29,966	29,794	29,617
Operating profit	▲1,800	▲3,314	2,341	2,643	2,596	2,602	3,215	3,174	3,393	3,565	3,742
Non-operating expenses	0	0	0	0	0	0	0	0	0	0	0
Total expenses	1,800	36,673	31,018	30,716	30,763	30,757	30,144	30,185	29,966	29,794	29,617
Ordinary profit	▲1,800	▲3,314	2,341	2,643	2,596	2,602	3,215	3,174	3,393	3,565	3,742
Corporation tax	0	0	0	0	0	910	1,125	1,110	1,187	1,247	1,309
Profit after tax	▲1,800	▲3,314	2,341	2,643	2,596	1,692	2,090	2,064	2,206	2,318	2,433
Dividend	0	0	0	0	0	950	950	950	950	950	950
Undivided profit	▲1,800	▲3,314	2,341	2,643	2,596	742	1,140	1,114	1,256	1,368	1,483
Cumulative profit	▲1,800	▲5,114	▲2,773	▲130	2,466	3,208	4,348	5,462	6,718	8,086	9,569

Table 4-24-2 Balance Sheet for Case 2 (million JPY)

	Year0 (PRE)	Year1	Year2	Year3	Year4	Year5	Year6	Year7	Year8	Year9	Year10
Assets											
Liquid assets	2,700	56	3,067	3,000	6,666	8,478	6,908	9,092	8,038	7,496	7,469
Aircraft	0	0	0	3,380	2,980	2,580	5,560	4,760	7,340	9,520	11,300
Other properties	3,000	2,730	2,460	2,190	1,920	1,650	1,380	1,110	840	570	300
Total properties	3,000	2,730	2,460	5,570	4,900	4,230	6,940	5,870	8,180	10,090	11,600
Deferred assets	2,000	1,600	1,200	800	400	0	0	0	0	0	0
Total assets	7,700	4,386	6,727	9,370	11,966	12,708	13,848	14,962	16,218	17,586	19,069
Capital liabilities											

Chapter 4

Debt balance	0	0	0	0	0	0	0	0	0	0	0
Capital	9,500	9,500	9,500	9,500	9,500	9,500	9,500	9,500	9,500	9,500	9,500
Legal capital surplus	0	0	0	0	0	0	0	0	0	0	0
Surplus	▲1,800	▲5,114	▲2,773	▲130	2,466	3,208	4,348	5,462	6,718	8,086	9,569
Total capital	7,700	4,386	6,727	9,370	11,966	12,708	13,848	14,962	16,218	17,586	19,069
Capital and liabilities	7,700	4,386	6,727	9,370	11,966	12,708	13,848	14,962	16,218	17,586	19,069

Table 4-24-3 Cash Flow Statement for Case 2 (million JPY)

	Year0 (PRE)	Year1	Year2	Year3	Year4	Year5	Year6	Year7	Year8	Year9	Year10
Financing											
Brought forward	0	2,700	56	3,067	3,000	6,666	8,478	6,908	9,092	8,038	7,496
Capital	9,500	0	0	0	0	0	0	0	0	0	0
Gain listed	0	0	0	0	0	0	0	0	0	0	0
Undivided profit	▲1,800	▲3,314	▲2,341	2,643	2,596	742	1,140	1,114	1,256	1,368	1,483
Aircraft depreciation	0	0	0	400	400	400	800	800	1,200	1,600	2,000
Initial expense depreciation	0	400	400	400	400	400	0	0	0	0	0
Other depreciation	0	270	270	270	270	270	270	270	270	270	270
Total financing	7,700	56	3,067	6,780	6,666	8,478	10,688	9,092	11,818	11,276	11,249
Initial expenses	2,000										
Investment in aircraft	0	0	0	3,780	0	0	3,780	0	3,780	3,780	3,780
Investment in others	3,000	0	0	0	0	0	0	0	0	0	0
Repayment	0	0	0	0	0	0	0	0	0	0	0
Purpose of funds	5,000	0	0	3,780	0	0	3,780	0	3,780	3,780	3,780
Excess and deficiency	2,700	56	3,067	3,000	6,666	8,478	6,908	9,092	8,038	7,496	7,469
Debt	0	0	0	0	0	0	0	0	0	0	0
Carried forward	2,700	56	3,067	3,000	6,666	8,478	6,908	9,092	8,038	7,496	7,469

Chapter 4

Table 4-25 Case comparison by each management index (Case 1 and Case 2)

Principal Management Index	Case 1	Case 2
NPV(million JPY)	55,930	10,471
Cumulative EVA(million JPY)	54,742	9,569
Cumulative Ordinary Profit(million JPY)	96,137	22,157
Revenue Operating Profit Margin(%, average of 10 years)	23.35	6.64
ROA(%, average of 10 years)	21.2	9.1
ROE(%, average of 10 years)	21.2	9.1
Average Capital Ratio	1.00	1.00
Domestic Flight Yield(JPY/km)	12.9	10.4
International Flight Yield(JPY/km)	11.2	9.0
Domestic Flight Load Factor(%, average of 10 years)	76.0	76.0
International Flight Load Factor(%, average of 10 years)	76.8	76.8
Cost per Passenger Kilometer(JPY/km)	9.21	9.09
Cost per Seat Kilometer(JPY/km)	6.80	6.71
Single Year Deficit Cancellation Point(Year)	Year1	Year2
Cumulative Years Deficit Cancellation Point(Year)	Year1	Year4

◘ 3. Simulation Results of Major Management Index

In the following analysis, major economic figures, yield, Available Seat Kilometer (ASK) and cost per passenger kilometer will be discussed.

(1) NPV

Net Present Value (NPV) means Present Value (discounted net cash flow) that is expectedly generated by a company divided by Weighted Average Cost of Capital (WACC). NPV is calculated by the following equation:

$$NPV = \frac{CF_1}{(1+WACC)} + \frac{CF_2}{(1+WACC)^2} + \cdots + \frac{CF_n}{(1+WACC)^n}$$

CF_t: Net cash flow in year t
WACC: Weighted average cost of capital

n: Period of project (the last year includes terminal value)

The final year of discounted net cash flow includes terminal value deducted by WACC. A company can gain more cash flow if the value of NPV is large. NPV>0 means that a project is feasible.

In this simulation, the equity of the shareholder is assumed to be 9.5 billion JPY. The condition of NPV<0 is not insolvent unless it generates a loss of 9.5 billion JPY in present value. Both Case 1 and 2 are positive in NPV. From Year 1 to Year 10, the cash flow figure indicates that free cash flow tends to increase. NPV in Case 1 will eventually be 55,930 million JPY which is five times larger than the size of the equity, and NPV in Case 2 will be 10,471 million JPY, almost the same size as the equity capital. The company can purchase aircraft without debt loans in Year 3, Year 6, Year 8, and Year 9, Year 10 due to this sufficient free cash flow.

Prior to this study, I have examined many cases, which include various cases of the capital structure consisting of capital and liability. Its results showed that a large fund size is required even when starting a small-fleet LCC with several aircraft. Therefore, in this simulation, the case is examined under the condition of preparation of the initial fund of 9.5 billion JPY without a debt loan. Nevertheless, it is necessary to acknowledge case studies with debt finance.

(2) EVA

Stern Stewart defines Economic Value Added (EVA). It indicates management index of returns to shareholders. The value is generated when ordinary profits exceed the capital costs. Executives and shareholders consider EVA as a valuable index, since Return On Equity (ROE) which has been considered as a valuable index is not enough in order to demonstrate intrinsic corporate value. EVA is calculated by the following equation:

 EVA = EBIT (Earnings before Interests and Taxes) − Capital costs
 (capital costs are calculated by weighted average of shareholder's equity costs and borrowing costs.)

Figure 4-2 shows both EVA of Case 1 and Case 2. In Case 1, EVA becomes positive

Chapter 4

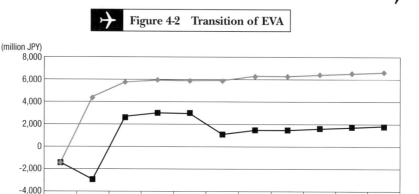

Figure 4-2 Transition of EVA

	Year0	Year1	Year2	Year3	Year4	Year5	Year6	Year7	Year8	Year9	Year10
Case 1	▲1,800	4,084	5,381	5,577	5,547	5,550	5,949	5,922	6,065	6,176	6,291
Case 2	▲1,800	▲3,314	2,341	2,643	2,596	742	1,140	1,114	1,256	1,368	1,483

from Year 1, and in Case 2, it becomes positive from Year 2. The absolute value of Case 1 becomes larger than Case 2 due to the good receiving rate[4] of airfare. EVA of Case 2 is temporally decreasing in Year 5, since the payment of corporate tax begins from this point.

From the first year, the value of EVA in Case 1 is positive. This means that the new LCC business became more valuable than what the shareholders had expected. The value amount is accumulated as surplus. In further studies, there are case analyses in which such surplus is reinvested for business expansion.

During the 10 years of business operation in this research, it may occur that aircraft need to have heavy maintenance. Simultaneously, the new LCC ought to have several reserved aircraft, a surplus of aircraft to be used in case of immediate needs for active aircraft. A fleet of the aircraft in its initial period is introduced for operations at the same time, so the timing for maintenance will be the same. Thus, having reserved aircraft is effective. The new LCC will shortly have to consider the operation of reserved aircraft and rational composition of aviation network, when it comes to making decisions about increasing the number of aircraft.

---

4 The receiving rate is related the ratio of the actual earnings of the seat sold to the normal airfare.

(3) Ordinary Profit

The transition of ordinary profit in each case is shown in Figure 4-3.

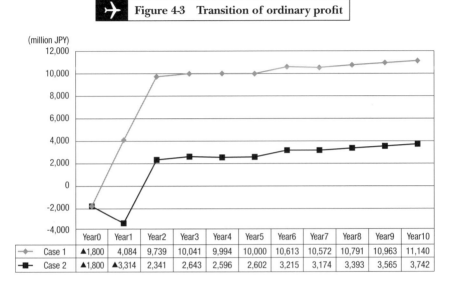

Figure 4-3 Transition of ordinary profit

	Year0	Year1	Year2	Year3	Year4	Year5	Year6	Year7	Year8	Year9	Year10
Case 1	▲1,800	4,084	9,739	10,041	9,994	10,000	10,613	10,572	10,791	10,963	11,140
Case 2	▲1,800	▲3,314	2,341	2,643	2,596	2,602	3,215	3,174	3,393	3,565	3,742

In Case 1, the ordinary profit will be positive from Year 1. Case 2 will be temporally negative in Year 1 since an initial training cost has generated in Year 1 transiently. In both cases the ordinary profit continues to be stable after Year 2, and in this study the revenue stays constant throughout Year 1 to Year 8. Therefore, the ordinary profit is influenced by the cost greatly. Fuel cost becomes the largest expense among the compositions of cost after Year 2. Fuel cost is influenced by the price of fuel per barrel and the currency exchange rate. It is important to pay attention to these two external factors. The second largest expense is the lease cost, and depending on the number of leased aircraft the company has, it can be reduced.

Generally, financial institutions such as banks tend to strongly pay attention to the ordinary profits since it expresses the results of ordinary activity of its businesses without extraordinary profit or loss. In Case 1 and 2, the ordinary profit transits to a sufficient level and has slightly increased after Year 2. As a result, this will become a decision-making factor when the new LCC negotiates a bank loan.

Chapter 4

(4) Revenue Operating Profit Margin

In each case, the transition of revenue operating profit margin is shown in Figure 4-4.

In Case 1, revenue ordinary profit margin has become positive since the first year and has kept at the level of approximately 25%. On the other hand, in Case 2, revenue operating profit margin has become positive in Year 2, but stayed at a low level of almost 10%. In both cases, the values of revenue operating profit margin increased slightly from Year 5 to Year 6 since depreciation of initial expense is completed in Year 5.

The research of the Japanese aviation industry[5] shows that the average revenue operating profit margin is 5%. Comparing such values with those of Case 1 and 2, the values for both Case 1 and Case 2 are higher than average. This is due to the new business that was able to establish a highly profitable route structure without

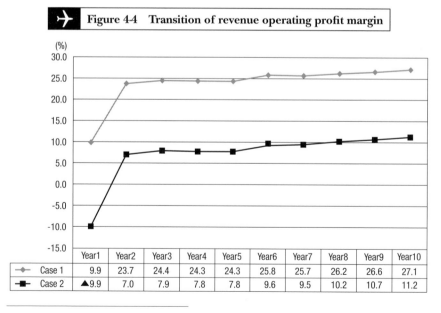

Figure 4-4 Transition of revenue operating profit margin

	Year1	Year2	Year3	Year4	Year5	Year6	Year7	Year8	Year9	Year10
Case 1	9.9	23.7	24.4	24.3	24.3	25.8	25.7	26.2	26.6	27.1
Case 2	▲9.9	7.0	7.9	7.8	7.8	9.6	9.5	10.2	10.7	11.2

---

5 The information on the general Japanese airline industry is based on the author's previous work.

investing a great expense. Regarding the maintenance cost, the new LCC can outsource the maintenance service in order to reduce their cost and cut down 2 billion JPY annually. Furthermore, the new LCC can select an appropriate route structure with a high demand of passengers in order to lower ASK to 6.8 JPY. By adopting such strategies, the new LCC can run a profitable business, and as a result, build revenue operating profit margin five times larger than that of the average aviation industry in Case 1, and twice as larger as the average in Case 2.

(5) ROA

Return On Assets (ROA) is an indicator of how profitable and relative a company is to its total assets. It gives an idea of how efficient the management is at using its assets to generate earnings. It is also an index to analyze how efficiently managers utilize capital from creditors and shareholders. ROA is calculated by the following equation:

$$ROA = \frac{\text{net income}}{\text{net assets}}$$

(Net assets are the general average of capitals between the previous and current year. However, in this simulation, year-end capital of each year is used.)

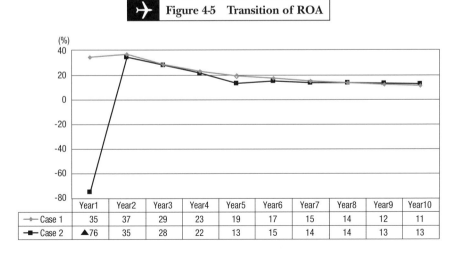

Figure 4-5   Transition of ROA

	Year1	Year2	Year3	Year4	Year5	Year6	Year7	Year8	Year9	Year10
Case 1	35	37	29	23	19	17	15	14	12	11
Case 2	▲76	35	28	22	13	15	14	14	13	13

Chapter 4

According to Figure 4-5, the average ROA over 10 years in Case 1 and Case 2 are 21.2% and 9.1%, respectively.

In Case 2, from Year 1 and Year 2, the value of ROA goes from negative to positive. This is why the operating profit is negative in the Year 1, but becomes positive in Year 2. Therefore, the value of ROA becomes positive in Year 2.

The ROA of a typical Japanese airline company is almost 4% to 5% and comparing this with the simulation results, the values of both Case 1 and 2 sufficiently exceed such percentages. On the other hand, in this study, ROA functions as a standard of returns to investors since it is equal to ROE. 10% of capital cost as a precondition has been set, and the values of ROA in Case 1 exceeded 10% during the entire period. Moreover, in Case 2, values exceeded most of the period besides Year 1. In conclusion, it can be said that the new business can reach a sufficiently acceptable level in terms of ROA analysis.

4 Risk Analysis by Monte Carlo Simulation

1. Steps of Risk Analysis

In Section 2 and 3, the profitability of new LCCs was analyzed and compared to the management indices in each simulation cases based on the corporate model. However, uncertainty is accompanied due to the future management environment. In addition to the profitability, the analysis of risks is essential to evaluate project value of new LCCs.

In this section, main variables, which are fixed in the simulation of the previous sections, are put into the corporate model as random variables. Monte Carlo simulation is then executed in order to analyze risks.

Risk analysis by Monte Carlo simulation is based on Value at Risk (VaR)[6] in financial

---

6 According to Beder (1995), Value at Risk (VaR) is a statistical technique used to measure

Chapter 4

engineering. VaR is used to calculate the probability of the amount of losses that are expected statistically, under the situation of the assets having some risks. For instance, "99% VaR" indicates that the probability of losses is 99% in cases when it is under a specific level, such as 1 million JPY. In other words, the probability that the losses will be more than 1 million JPY is less than 1%.

Firstly, in the simulation of risk analysis, input data (i.e., demands on individual routes, currency exchange rate) that impact the principal management indices, such as NPV, EVA, revenue operating profit margin, etc., are put in as random variables on the corporate model, which was created in Section 2. Secondly, Monte Carlo simulation is executed about 10,000 times and finally, the variables, which accompany random variables on major management indices, are calculated.

In the simulation of Section 3, the input data mentioned above are fixed. If input data are entered as random variables, then the output data and management indices which are calculated at the last stage, also become random variables. For example, when the currency exchange rate is entered as a random variable in the simulation models, variables such as the prices of aircraft, cost of fuel, and airport fees in foreign countries can have probability distributions. Total costs and various management indices can also be random variables.

In the next step, the cut-off rate is set on individual principal management indices, and a risk probability less than the cut-off rate is generated from the results of the Monte Carlo simulation. Corporate executives can determine whether specific projects should be implemented, by analyzing the risk probability that is less than the cut-off rate due to principal management indices.

Throughout the risk analysis, it is possible to identify whether the project has high or low risk, and high or low return. In other words, corporate executives can make

---

and quantify the level of financial risk. VaR modeling determines the potential for loss in the entity being assessed, as well as the probability of occurrence for the defined loss (cut-off rate). VaR is measured by assessing the amount of potential loss, the probability of occurrence for the amount of loss and the time frame. In this book VaR is referred to the definition mentioned above.

Chapter 4

decisions on investments by considering both the results of profitability and the results of risk analysis (the probability that major management indices become less than the cut-off rate).

◻ 2. Preconditions of Monte Carlo Simulation

In the Monte Carlo simulation, the variables in Table 4-26 to 4-28, which is fixed in the simulation of Section 3, are entered as random variables.

Table 4-26　Probability distribution of exchange rate

Value Driver	Distribution Model	Minimum	Mode	Maximum
Currency Exchange Rate (JPY/USD)	Triangular	85	90	95

These quantities are assumed to be random variables. First of all, these variables are indices that significantly influence management issues. Secondly, they are fundamental but uncertain indices to the management of airline companies. Moreover, variables, which are calculated from hereafter, are random variables. The variables in Table 4-26 follow triangular distribution, which is usually introduced in order to calculate changes of these types of variables. Referring to the current data sets the mode, the minimum, and the maximum in the triangular distribution. In terms of mode, the mean of the past six months is used, and the difference between actual maximum and actual minimum of the past six months is used to calculated the minimum (MIN) and the maximum (MAX). The MIN and MAX values here have been calculated as follows: the difference between the actual MIN value of the index data for the past six months and average was calculated. Then, the difference between the actual MAX value of the same index and the average was calculated. The greater value of the two was deducted from the average, labeling this to be MIN value. The greater value of the two was added to the average and this will be the MAX value. This shows that the difference between the mode and the MAX value is equal to the difference between the mode and the MIN value. This is due to the uncertainty of direction. These indices are likely to be plus or minus.

Chapter 4

On the other hand, LCCs have to take the marketing strategy of increasing the number of individual passengers for customer acquisition. Due to this strategy, possible load factor is fluctuated in the simulation.

Probability distribution (triangular distribution) of demand of domestic routes and international routes are indicated in Table 4-27 and 4-28, respectively. Among the factors related to demand, there are many uncertain factors influencing performance of the management. The factors of demand, rather than the factors of costs, have influence on the performance of the management. External factors, including, terrorism such as the September 11 Attacks, and aircraft accidents decreased demand significantly, and the worldwide events such as the Olympics have, in contrast, increased demand. Therefore, the annual demand on individual routes (the number of passengers) is calculated with the probability distribution in the simulation of Section 4 to analyze risks. Demand on domestic and international routes follows triangular distribution in each year.

This study adopts triangular distribution as explained in the previous section. In this study, considering the probability distribution of passenger demand, the minimum value is set based on the load factor of 67%, and the maximum value is set based on the load factor of 87% in each route.

Table 4-27 shows the probability distribution of passenger demand by domestic

Table 4-27 Probability distribution of passenger demand by domestic route

(thousand passenger)

Route	Distribution Model	Minimum	Mode	Maximum
Kobe Airport–Tokyo International Airport	Triangular	648	747	837
Kobe Airport–New Chitose Airport	Triangular	288	332	372
Kobe Airport–Fukuoka Airport	Triangular	216	249	279
Kobe Airport–Naha Airport	Triangular	216	249	279
Kobe Airport–Kagoshima Airport	Triangular	144	166	186
Kobe Airport–Miyazaki Airport	Triangular	144	166	186
Kobe Airport–Kumamoto Airport	Triangular	144	166	186
Kobe Airport–Sendai International Airport	Triangular	216	249	279

Chapter 4

 Table 4-28   Probability distribution of passenger demand by international route

(thousand passenger)

Route	Distribution Model	Minimum	Mode	Maximum
Kobe Airport–Incheon International Airport	Triangular	216	249	279
Kobe Airport–Shanghai Hongqiao International Airport	Triangular	144	166	186
Kobe Airport–Beijing Capital International Airport	Triangular	144	166	186
Kobe Airport–Hong Kong International Airport	Triangular	144	166	186
Kobe Airport–Taiwan Taoyuan International Airport	Triangular	144	166	186
Kobe Airport–Gimhae International Airport	Triangular	72	83	93

routes. Only large-demand routes from areas in Kansai of more than 700,000 people and routes of more than 500 kilometers are chosen to conduct the simulation, as mentioned in Section 1. In the same method, the distribution model for international routes is set as in Table 4-28.

3. Calculation Results of Monte Carlo Simulation

The following principal management indices are calculated as variables of probability distribution by Monte Carlo simulation: (1) NPV, (2) Cumulative EVA, (3) Cumulative Ordinary Profit, (4) Revenue Operating Profit Margin, and (5) ROA.

These indices of both Case 1 and Case 2 from the Monte Carlo simulation are indicated from Figure 4-6 to 4-25. The average, the standard deviation, the range of 99.99% (= 3.9σ), and the range of 95% (= 1.96σ) are indicated under each figure. The range of 99.99% is calculated by the average ±3.9 × standard deviation. The range of 95% is calculated by the average ±1.96 × standard deviation.

The reason for the indication of both the range of 99.99% and of 95% is because the automatic output data of the "Crystal Ball" simulation tool indicates the range of 99.99%, whilst generally the range of 95% is commonly used. However, both of them are indicated for investors who prefer risks or for executives to provide information. The range of 99.99% means almost 100% secure for investors. For example, in the financial industry, the range of 99.99% is introduced to thoroughly calculate the estimated value of VaR. Thus, the range of 99.99% is perhaps useful

Chapter 4

for Japanese financial institutions, which are interested in new LCC businesses. On the other hand, the range of 95% is useful for risk-taking investors and executives.

For instance, there are management indices, which have differences between the range of 99.99% and of 95%. In Case 1, the minimum value of cumulative ordinary profit for probability of 99.99% is 83,888 million JPY, whereas that for 95% probability is 88,085 million JPY. There is a difference of 4,197 million JPY, as a minimum range. As a result, risk-taking investors may be interested in this investment within the range of 95% even if critical Japanese investors do not make a decision to invest within the range of 99.99%. This claim leads to the statement of the last chapter of this book; a company should ask foreign investors to invest, and to enable them to do so, regulations to restrict the foreign investors should be removed.

(1) NPV
Figure 4-6 to 4-9 show probability distributions of NPV of both Case 1 and Case 2.

NPV must be a positive number as discussed in the previous section. According to the results of the simulation, the NPV of both Case 1 and Case 2 indicate a positive number. Even in Case 2, the lower limit(range of the 99.99%) is 3,158 million JPY. There is almost the same value of standard deviation between Case 1 and 2, whereas there is a large difference in each value of the average, 55,930 million JPY and 9,750 million JPY, respectively. This implies that Case 2 has a more significant risk than Case 1. In other words, a 38.3% discount rate of the airfare is set as a main strategy, but the discount rate can be increased up to a level of 50%, depending on circumstances such as the activities of competitors.

(2) Cumulative EVA
Figure 4-10 to 4-13 show probability distributions of cumulative EVA in Case 1 and Case 2.

In Figure 4-10 to 4-13, the same inclinations as those of NPV are indicated. In Case 1, the cumulative average of EVA is 54,742 million JPY and its standard deviation is 2,393 million JPY. This indicates the lower limit of probability of cumulative EVA to be 46,222 million JPY(range of 99.99%). On the other hand, in Case 2, the average

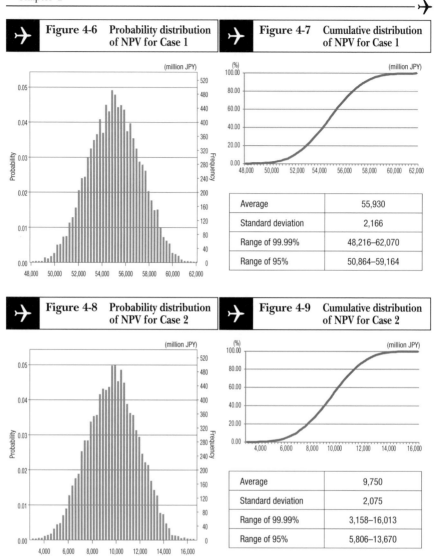

Figure 4-6 Probability distribution of NPV for Case 1

Figure 4-7 Cumulative distribution of NPV for Case 1

Average	55,930
Standard deviation	2,166
Range of 99.99%	48,216–62,070
Range of 95%	50,864–59,164

Figure 4-8 Probability distribution of NPV for Case 2

Figure 4-9 Cumulative distribution of NPV for Case 2

Average	9,750
Standard deviation	2,075
Range of 99.99%	3,158–16,013
Range of 95%	5,806–13,670

is 8,175 million JPY and the standard deviation is 1,837 million JPY. In a way, Case 2 is recognized as a risk scenario case, but the lower limit (range of 99.99%) is 2,749 million JPY, which is still positive.

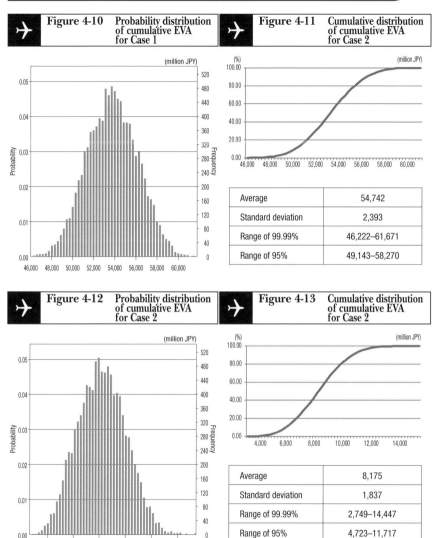

Figure 4-10 Probability distribution of cumulative EVA for Case 1

Figure 4-11 Cumulative distribution of cumulative EVA for Case 2

Average	54,742
Standard deviation	2,393
Range of 99.99%	46,222–61,671
Range of 95%	49,143–58,270

Figure 4-12 Probability distribution of cumulative EVA for Case 2

Figure 4-13 Cumulative distribution of cumulative EVA for Case 2

Average	8,175
Standard deviation	1,837
Range of 99.99%	2,749–14,447
Range of 95%	4,723–11,717

(3) Cumulative Ordinary Profit

Figure 4-14 to 4-17 show probability distributions of cumulative ordinary profit in Case 1 and Case 2, respectively.

Chapter 4

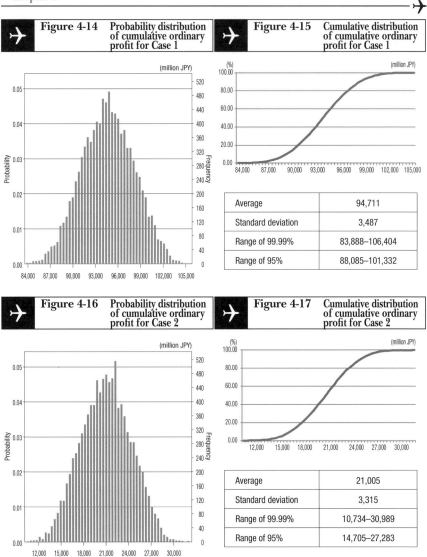

Figure 4-14 Probability distribution of cumulative ordinary profit for Case 1

Figure 4-15 Cumulative distribution of cumulative ordinary profit for Case 1

Average	94,711
Standard deviation	3,487
Range of 99.99%	83,888–106,404
Range of 95%	88,085–101,332

Figure 4-16 Probability distribution of cumulative ordinary profit for Case 2

Figure 4-17 Cumulative distribution of cumulative ordinary profit for Case 2

Average	21,005
Standard deviation	3,315
Range of 99.99%	10,734–30,989
Range of 95%	14,705–27,283

According to Figure 4-14, the average is 94,711 million JPY and the standard deviation is 3,487 million JPY. By comparing Case 1 with Case 2, it is indicated that Case 2 has a relatively larger range due to the significant difference in average.

(4) Revenue Operating Profit Margin

Figure 4-18 to 4-21 show probability distributions of revenue operating profit margin in Case 1 and Case 2, respectively.

In Case 1, the lower limit of the range of 95% is 21.58% and that of the range of

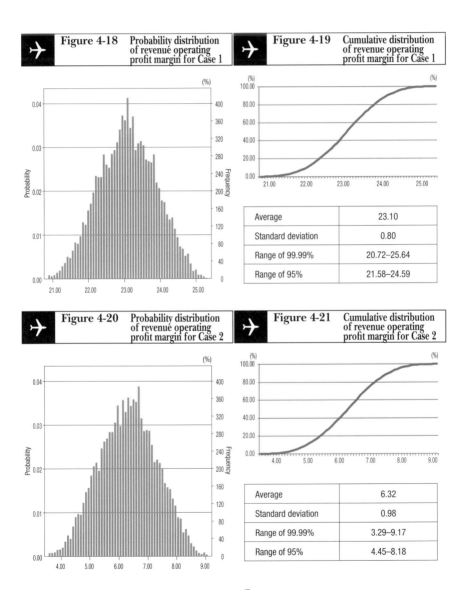

99.99% is still 20.72%. It could be said that the LCC can operate its business steadily with high performance in Case 1. On the other hand, in Case 2, the lower limit is 4.45% for the 95% range and 3.29% for the 99.99% range. In this case, whether these values are regarded as sufficiently satisfying or not for stakeholders including executives and shareholders is debatable.

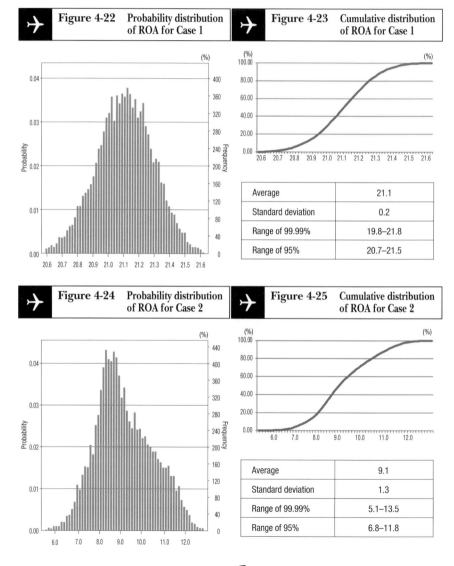

Figure 4-22 Probability distribution of ROA for Case 1

Figure 4-23 Cumulative distribution of ROA for Case 1

Average	21.1
Standard deviation	0.2
Range of 99.99%	19.8–21.8
Range of 95%	20.7–21.5

Figure 4-24 Probability distribution of ROA for Case 2

Figure 4-25 Cumulative distribution of ROA for Case 2

Average	9.1
Standard deviation	1.3
Range of 99.99%	5.1–13.5
Range of 95%	6.8–11.8

(5) ROA

Figure 4-22 to 4-25 show probability distributions of ROA in Case 1 and Case 2, respectively.

According to Figure 4-22 to 4-25, the standard deviation of Case 2 is 1.3% whereas that of Case 1 is 0.2%. This means that Case 2 showcases a slightly more uncertain situation relatively compared to Case 1. In other words, ROA is expressed as the following equation:

$$\text{ROA} = \text{profit margin on sales} \times \text{turnover of total capital}$$

That is, if ROA indicates good figures, either profit margin on sales or turnover of total capital, or both factors will be good figures. In contrast, if ROA performs below expectations, either one of these two or both of them must be worse. Considering the results of this simulation, in Case 1, ROA (as average) is 21.1% and revenue operating profit margin (as average) is 23.1%. Therefore, turnover profit can be calculated roughly as 0.9, which is almost the same level as the average of the aviation industry. Similarly, in Case 2, given that the average of ROA is 9.1% and average of revenue operating profit margin is 6.32%, turnover profit is estimated roughly at 1.43. Therefore, especially in Case 1, if profits are reinvested to expand businesses such as increasing operation routes, turnover profits may be able to improve.

4. Results of Risk Analysis by Setting Cut-off Rate

In this part, five indices are chosen as the evaluation factors for risk analysis on investment decision. Probability to be less than that of the cut-off rate is then calculated by setting the rate to each index. The following is information of risk investment analysis.

4.1 Risk Analysis of Management Index

The cut-off rate is set as shown in Table 4-29. Although it is a determinant of the level of cut-off rate, it is an absolute condition for cumulative ordinary profit and NPV becomes positive in terms of investment, and the condition that cumulative EVA becomes positive is an essential condition for investors. However, NPV is most likely to be positive in a short-term simulation, like this 10-year project. Thus, NPV

Chapter 4

Table 4-29 Cut-off rate of management index

Decision Index	Cut-off Rate
NPV(million JPY)	0
Cumulative EVA(million JPY)	0
Cumulative Ordinary Profit(million JPY)	0
Revenue Operating Profit Margin(%, average of 10 years)	4
ROA(%, average of 10 years)	3

could be an unrealistic choice for this analysis. It can also be said that cumulative EVA is most suitable for investors, since cumulative EVA indicates that the company is being more profitable than expected.

Considering management indices, such as revenue ordinary profit margin and ROA, the level of the cut-off rate is different from the intensions of executives and the business environment. Additionally, profitability varies depending on different industries. In this case, the average value of the receiving rate of major airlines(listed companies only) over the past 5 years is set as the cut-off rate, after referring to not only the Japanese aviation industry, but also the financial data of successful LCCs in foreign countries.

Probability to be less than the cut-off rate is calculated by the next EXCEL functions:
=NORMDIST (X, Average, Standard deviation, TRUE)
X = Cut-off Rate, TRUE = Cumulative Distribution

$$\text{Normal Distribution} \quad f(x,\mu,\sigma) = \frac{1}{\sigma\sqrt{2\pi}} exp^{\left(-\frac{(x-u)^2}{2\sigma^2}\right)}$$

$$\text{Cumulative Distribution Function} \quad F(c^*) = \int_{min}^{c^*} f(x,\mu,\sigma)\, dx$$

min: Minimum, C^*: Cut-off Rate, μ: Mean, σ: Standard Deviation

Table 4-30 shows the probability to be less than the cut-off rate by Monte Carlo simulation.

Chapter 4

Table 4-30 Results of risk analysis

Decision Index	Cut-off Rate	Case 1(%)	Case 2(%)
NPV(million JPY)	0	0.00	0.00
Cumulative EVA(million JPY)	0	0.00	0.00
Cumulative Ordinary Profit(million JPY)	0	0.00	0.00
Revenue Operating Profit Margin(%, average of 10 years)	4	0.00	0.52
ROA(%, average of 10 years)	3	0.00	0.00

According to Table 4-30, the probability that NPV becomes negative is 0.00% in both cases. As mentioned in the previous sections, this simulation model is set in a 10-year project period and from this perspective, it could be considered that evaluating NPV is difficult due to its short time duration. It is considered that the ordinary profit may be appropriate for executives, and cumulative EVA may be so for investors. Moreover, as shown in Figure 4-30, the probability that both cumulative ordinary profit and cumulative EVA become negative is 0.00% in Case 2.

On the other hand, there are some differences in the revenue operating profit margin between the two cases. Whilst the probability that the revenue operating profit margin in Case 1 would become less than 4% is 0.00%, the probability of Case 2 is 0.52%. Regarding ROA, the probability that ROA becomes less than 3% is 0.00% in both Case 1 and Case 2.

In Case 1, all indices fullfill the standard, and the project is feasible with minimum risks. Moreover, Case 1 is a significantly attractive business since the revenue can be stabilized. On the other hand, in Case 2, indices related to financial margins(i.e., revenue ordinary profit margin, revenue operating profit margin) show certain risks despite the indices of cumulative profit(i.e., NPV, cumulative EVA, and cumulative ordinary profit) being positive. It is considered that if the discount rate of the airfare can be kept in the lower level(ex. 30%), the LCC business can be carried out sustainably. On the other hand, if the discount rate of the airfare is forced to increase, the business profits will decrease whilst the uncertainty relevant to financial indices may increase.

Chapter 4

● 4.2 Parametric Study for the Cut-off Rate

To conduct further risk analysis by cut-off rate, a parametric study is implemented. In the previous subsection, the cut-off rate is set up with only one value for each management index. It is generally difficult to estimate cut-off rates and the estimation tends to be loose especially when one calculates for its own project.

Table 4-31 shows the results of various cut-off rate simulations summarized in the result. According to the result, Case 1 shows small risk against any cut-off rate conditions. On the other hand, Case 2 shows the possibility of risk increasing as each cut-off rate does. For instance, the VaR may be 0.32% under the condition that the cut-off rate of ROA is 6%. However, if it is under the condition that the cut-off rate of ROA is 9%, the VaR increases to 52.04%.

In this simulation, as shown in Table 4-30, the value of the cut-off rate is based on general numbers of typical industries including the aviation industry, whereas in

Table 4-31 Results of the cut-off rate and risk analysis

Decision Index	Cut-off Rate and Risk Analysis			
NPV(million JPY)	Case 2		Case 1	
Cut-off Rate	4,000	6,000	50,000	54,000
VaR	0.32%	3.29%	0.88%	31.49%
Cumulative EVA(million JPY)	Case 2		Case 1	
Cut-off Rate	4,000	6,000	48,000	52,000
VaR	0.53%	12.67%	0.49%	26.18%
Cumulative Ordinary Profit(million JPY)	Case 2		Case 1	
Cut-off Rate	8,000	12,000	87,000	93,000
VaR	0.00%	0.13%	1.25%	36.43%
Revenue Operating Profit Margin(%, average of 10 years)	Case 2		Case 1	
Cut-off Rate	4	5	21	23
VaR	0.52%	9.53%	0.16%	44.44%
ROA(%, average of 10 years)	Case 2		Case 1	
Cut-off Rate	6	9	20.7	21
VaR	0.32%	52.04%	1.20%	27.05%

terms of considering new LCC businesses, which is a relatively high-risk business, it may be necessary to simulate more cases and analyze the results further. Although a parametric study is conducted as a supplementary in this study, it may be essential to simulate cases with various cut-off rate conditions for multiple purposes in the future.

As shown in Table 4-31, the results are analyzed as follows:

(1) NPV

The cut-off rate for NPV is set from 0 to 6 billion JPY in the same way. The value of cumulative NPV is 55,930 million JPY in Case 1 by the corporate model in comparison, and 6 billion JPY is almost one-tenth of it.

According to the results of the cut-off rate analysis of NPV, the risk soars from when the cut-off rate is 50 billion with 0.88% of risk to 31.49% when the cut-off rate is 54 billion in Case 1. In Case 2, if the value of the cut-off rate is 4 billion JPY, the VaR is 0.32%. The VaR increases to 3.29% when the value of the cut-off rate is 6 billion JPY, and for the same reason as EVA, this index is used to evaluate whether the project is feasible or not. The only absolute condition for this index is that NPV is positive.

(2) Cumulative EVA

As mentioned in the previous section, EVA is an index indicating the returns to shareholders. There is no specific recommended value for this index other than that the value must be greater than 0. Therefore, in this parametric study, a value from 4 to 6 billion JPY has been adopted. In comparison, the value of cumulative EVA is 54,742 million JPY in Case 1 with 6 billion JPY being approximately one-tenth of it(as shown in Table 4-25).

According to these results, in Case 1, no risk emerges up until the cut-off rate of 48 billion JPY. On the other hand, in Case 2, the risk appears at a lower cut-off rate, as can be seen in Table 4-31, it is 0.53% when 4 billion JPY and 12.67% when 6 billion JPY, which are relatively large numbers. This means that if the stakeholders require 4 billion JPY as cumulative EVA, the credibility may decrease. Originally, however, this index is the cumulative value of undivided profits for shareholders and is therefore

Chapter 4

not a major problem if the value exceeds 0.

(3) Cumulative Ordinary Profit

The value of the cut-off rate of this index is changing depending on the type of the project and year of cumulative ordinary profit. In this calculation, the calculation results of cumulative ordinary profit by a corporate model, which is used for fixed data calculation, is almost 100 billion JPY. The maximum cut-off rate is set to 12 billion JPY for this management index. This is one-tenth of the cumulative ordinary profit, which is 100 billion JPY. It indicates that the amount of ordinary profit for 1 year is set up as the cut-off rate, and additionally, in Case 2, cumulative ordinary profit is almost 20 billion JPY (as shown in Table 4-22).

As a result, in Case 1, VaR is 0.00% against any cut-off rates. In other words, no risk emerges until 87 billion JPY, according to the risk analysis. On the other hand, in Case 2, the VaR of the cut-off rate for 12 billion JPY is 0.13%, whereas the VaR is 0.00% for 8 billion JPY. However, the rate of 0.13% is insignificant when comparing the cut-off rate. In short, it can be said that this project does not have high risks, such as by reviewing from a conservative viewpoint.

(4) Revenue Operating Profit Margin

The average revenue operating profit margin is almost 6% according to the research of the Japanese aviation industry. As a result, the risk drastically increases from when the cut-off rate is 21% with 0.16% of risk to 44.44% when the cut-off rate is 23% in Case 1. On the other hand, in Case 2, the risk for each cut-off rate of 4% and 5% are 0.52% and 9.53%. Since the cut-off rate of 5% with a 9.53% risk is close to the average revenue operating profit margin of the Japanese aviation industry, the numerical value is a tough decision to make for investors.

(5) ROA

The ROA of a typical Japanese airline company is almost 2.78%. It can be said that ROA may return to investors since it is equal to ROE in this study. In addition, this study focuses on new LCC business, and the risk exposure is not small. Therefore, in this cut-off rate analysis, 6% and 9% are adopted for cut-off rates as input parameters.

The results of Case 1 indicate that only 1.20% of risk arises until the cut-off rate of 20.70%, which implies the project to have low risks. However, a sharp increase can be seen when the cut-off rate is 21.00% with 27.05% of risk and continues to increase thereafter. In Case 2, VaR is 0.32% and 52.04% for cut-off rates of 6% and 9% respectively. Applying the value of 2.78%, which is the average of the Japanese aviation industry, it is estimated that VaR will be around 0.01%. It is said, however, that VaR of 0.01% is relatively low for new LCC businesses. In this research, in which ROA of 9% is assumed as a condition, VaR of 52.04% may seem relatively high risk to investors. In a further study, it may be worth conducting an analysis on cut-off rates of ROE and ROA by reviewing fund raising methods.

To summarize the results of the parametric study of Case 1 mentioned above, which is a good scenario for investors even with conservative cut-off rates, in other words, the business is rarely exposed to serious risks. It is important to confirm the results of VaR by setting up higher cut-off rates, in terms of evaluating the project's risks more accurately. It will show how the business is stable and that the strategy to be very effective. Moreover, it will indicate that a basic strategy of the business is fully justified. It can be said that it is highly possible to acquire a profit with a 38.3% discount of airfare (Case 1) with the possible change to a 50% discount of airfare (Case 2) depending on the situation.

The purpose of this simulation is to demonstrate the target value of management indices and the probability of each index that fails to achieve the target value for investors. The current discount rate for both LCs (Case 1) and LCCs (Case 2) are assumed based on the numerous simulations that have been conducted until now as a model case of LCs and LCCs. In Case 1, the discount rate is presumed to be 38.3%, which is estimated from the receiving rate performance of major carriers. On the other hand, in Case 2, the discount rate is assumed to be 50%, which enable LCCs to compete with other airlines. In Case 1, almost all target value of management indices are achieved without risks, when the receiving rate is the same as an LC. However, in Case 2, which is what the LCCs are aiming for, the risks increase rapidly due to various airfares. These results show that LCCs are struggling to succeed in the domestic aviation market. These simulation results indicate that one of the reasons for the success of Japanese LCs is because they seize control over LCCs,

Chapter 4

adopt the LCC's cost structure, and code-share with LCCs. Consequently, the results of the risk analysis in both cases revealed to be a clarified business model of the current Japanese aviation market.

5 Comprehensive Consideration of Results of Simulation

In this section, the simulation results of the financial statement in Section 3 and the simulation results of risk analysis are presented. The results of both will be analyzed in a comprehensive approach.

1. Examination of Each Simulation Case

Simulation results of risk analysis in the two case studies are shown in Table 4-32.

(1) Case 1 (Discount rate of airfare with 38.3%)
In this case, the LCC operates its business with a 38.3% discounted airfare rate. The decrease in maintenance cost, and the securing of stable demand may help to increase its business profits, and each number of the principal management index seems successful. If the shareholders are willing to invest 9.5 billion JPY at the initial stage, they might be interested in the project when the cumulative EVA is more than 54,700 million JPY. Yields are 12.9 JPY/km for domestic flights and 11.2 JPY/km for international flights. Major foreign LCCs' yields are lower by almost 9 JPY/km, and Case 1 is competitive. Meanwhile, the index of ASK in Case 1 is almost the same or higher than typical foreign LCCs'. If it is compared with other Japanese LCC cases, it can be considered to be competitive.

(2) Case 2 (Discount rate of airfare with 50%)
In Case 2, the LCC operates with a 50% discounted airfare rate. It tends to generally have less income compared to Case 1, which had 38.3%. Cumulative EVA of Case 2 had only 9,569 million JPY due to this, and the investors may think it is not as profitable and lose interest in this project. However, Case 2 indicates the worst scenario to maintain business in terms of discounted airfare rate. Yields are respectively

Chapter 4

Table 4-32 Case comparisons by each management index (redisplayed)

Principal Management Index	Case 1	Case 2
NPV(million JPY)	55,930	10,471
Cumulative EVA(million JPY)	54,742	9,569
Cumulative Ordinary Profit(million JPY)	96,137	22,157
Revenue Operating Profit Margin(%, average of 10 years)	23.35	6.64
ROA(%, average of 10 years)	21.2	9.1
ROE(%, average of 10 years)	21.2	9.1
Average Capital Ratio	1.00	1.00
Domestic Flight Yield(JPY/km)	12.9	10.4
International Flight Yield(JPY/km)	11.2	9.0
Domestic Flight Load Factor(%, average of 10 years)	76.0	76.0
International Flight Load Factor(%, average of 10 years)	76.8	76.8
Cost per Passenger Kilometer(JPY/km)	9.21	9.09
Cost per Seat Kilometer(JPY/km)	6.80	6.71
Single Year Deficit Cancellation Point(Year)	Year1	Year2
Cumulative Years Deficit Cancellation Point(Year)	Year1	Year4

10.4 JPY/km for domestic flights and 9.0 JPY/km for international flights, and these numbers are almost the same level as other receding LCCs. In contrast, the ASK of Case 2 is 6.71 JPY/km, which is lower than that of other typical Japanese LCCs. Therefore, even if the discount rate of airfare is increased, the business model of this study seems to be strongly effective.

◘ 2. Consideration by Management Factor

(1) Airfare

It is well known that the airfare of LCCs tends to be more economical than LC's. However, if both major airline companies and LCCs sell discounted tickets under the same condition of airfare, flight schedule, and grade of the seat, consumers tend to choose tickets from major airline companies, arising from their invisible goodwill of such and those which are cheaper in price. This phenomenon is most likely to occur in Japan. The marketing strategy for major companies in terms of online sales

Chapter 4

is that they will adopt the price fluctuation system, offer a wide range of airfares, and strive to increase more passengers who are capable of searching flights online by themselves.

The new LCC's airfare strategy is simple; the new LCC offers a discount rate of 38.3% to 50%. Compared to Skymark Airlines's fare, for instance, the new LCC can offer a better price for domestic operation routes such as Kobe Airport–Tokyo International Airport (the new LCC: 8,000JPY, Skymark Airlines: 12,000JPY, ANA: 12,000JPY) and Kobe Airport–New Chitose Airport (the new LCC: 9,430JPY, Skymark Airlines: 14,000JPY, ANA: 25,000JPY). As discussed in Section 2 of this chapter, the airfares of new LCCs are on a significantly lower level compared to other major airline companies including Skymark Airlines. In addition, regarding international routes, Skymark Airlines has not entered the market so far. Accordingly, it is estimated that the LCCs' share of major routes is 30% and the share of local routes is 40%. The share rate of the Tokyo route is estimated to be 10%. With regard to international operation, although Skymark Airlines has not started operation yet, considering the competition by the entry of other foreign companies and the two-existing major Japanese airline companies, it is expected that new LCCs can gain a share of 20%, at least.

Under such strategy, it is determined that airfare receiving rates of the route between Tokyo International Airport and New Chitose Airport, with Tokyo being the world's largest passenger arrival destination, is only 30% of the profitability rate. This means many of the passengers applied for the package tours, in which the profitability rate is lower. The occupancy of a round-trip airfare within a package tour is less than 60% of the price of a normal one-way trip airfare ticket, and the rest of the expenses, which is approximately 40%, is mainly for the accommodation. This determines that the cost of a normal one-way air ticket could be countervailed with the cost of round-trip air tickets and accommodations, and the airfare itself would be extremely low. According to the regulation of the CAB, the discount rate of airfare is 70% and most airline companies sell the tickets to the wholesalers or travel agencies with a 70% discount.

To sell air tickets at competitive prices, the following sales structure should be introduced. An LCC sells air tickets online, which means that the company is not required to pay any commission fee to the travel agencies. Some airline companies have even stopped cooperating with travel agencies and have focused more on online sales. CRS is being adopted with the Aeronautical Radio Incorporation (ARINC), the Society of International Telecommunications of Airline (SITA), and in destination marketing. The collaboration with LCCs, local governments, and economic organizations around the airport may induce further business for both sides.

(2) Operating route structure
LCCs usually gain profits from target segmentation of passengers. Therefore, it is necessary that the size of its market is significantly large. To achieve this goal, LCCs operate their flights on either high-demand routes between large cities or sub-routes near large cities, as a secondary option.

In this analysis, the routes with a large number of passengers from western Japan and the portion involving LCCs, which are able to maintain business profitability, were selected. Therefore, LCCs are not required to change the number of flights depending on the number of passengers, and these are only required to operate all services by using efficient route alignment and the fundamental demand from the passengers. For instance, if an LCC operates only 2 round-trips per day, the route should have a larger number of passengers. In this case, almost all load factors are fixed, and furthermore, LCCs have to make more efforts in selling tickets and asking for support from local communities.

(3) Maintenance cost
Many LCCs tend to spend a huge amount of money for aircraft maintenance, which is comparatively larger than estimated. This could mean that this high aircraft maintenance cost is an obstacle for LCCs to sustain their businesses. Therefore, it is required for LCCs to reduce their maintenance costs.

In this section, the following two conditions stated below were used to consider the possibility of a successful business while saving on the expense of aircraft maintenance:
 – Entrusting aircraft maintenance services to MRO
 – Introducing B737-800 and A320, which are heavily used in the world and parts being reasonably acquirable.

Chapter 4

According to this simulation, the LCC business would become prosperous if the maintenance cost is kept down by the strategies mentioned above.

In Japan, minor airline companies have to outsource their maintenance services since major airline companies monopolize the aircraft maintenance business, thereby having to maintain their aircraft by themselves. Nonetheless, minor airline companies petitioned for the CAB of MLIT to abolish the regulation. As a result, it became eligible to entrust services to providers outside of their company.

As a remarkable movement of deregulation, the CAB of MLIT announced an "Update Program", which reconsiders the aviation security standards for the purpose of enhancing competitiveness in the airline industry and emphasizing the social needs of airport renovations (i.e., expansion and renovation of Tokyo International Airport and Narita International Airport), the Asia Gateway Plan, and liberalizing entry into airports including locals for LCCs. The "Update Program" additionally includes the deregulations, which leads to a re-examination of in-flight inspection and an introduction of approving the joint airlines. Repealing the essential principles of the Aviation Act, it accelerated the trends of price competition without emphasizing safety such as leasing of aircraft, maintenance outsourcing, and hiring more temporary employees. Within the maintenance department in major airline companies, particularly, the plans of department separations and outsourcing were promoted, and entrusting to MRO companies has become significantly common since 2009. From an example of a major airline company, it has started to outsource heavy maintenance services mainly in developing countries for cheaper labor forces. At the same time, some airline companies, including those of which are popular, argued about the negative effects of advanced outsourcing as well.

Moreover, it will be less problematic for major airline companies to ship an aircraft, which takes more than two weeks via ferry flight, for maintenance. However, it will be a huge disadvantage for LCCs due to their limited number of aircraft, therefore it would be more likely to maintain their aircraft by themselves.

Although major airline companies entrust maintenance services to companies abroad, there are several problems remaining such as low quality of maintenance services, higher personnel expenses of technicians, and labor union issues. There is recently a growing movement in establishing MRO companies in Japan, even in Okinawa. This will lead to a significant reduction of aircraft maintenance costs for all the airline companies, and benefit the middle and small companies to help them create more jobs in Japan as well.

In conclusion, the establishment of domestic aircraft maintenance companies in Japan will contribute to the further development of the Japanese airline industry. It is important to cooperate with several airline companies, since these actions may break the monopoly of maintenance service business by the major airline companies, and result in the entire aviation market being far more competitive. What is more is that if MRO becomes an aircraft maintenance industry, it might boost the Japanese economy greatly by inducing relevant businesses, both domestically and internationally. This suggests that the establishment of domestic aircraft companies is a necessary step for the current Japanese airline industry to sustain its business and initiate further development.

(4) Type of aircraft
It is widely known that it is efficient for airline companies to use aircraft made by Airbus, since almost all Airbus's aircraft have the same style of cockpit and commonly used mechanical and electrical parts. In this simulation, a 150-seat B737-800 was selected same as many LCCs in other countries. The reason for using Boeing aircraft are as follows: (1) the Boeing aircraft are recommended by METI, and almost all airline companies in Japan operate their services with them, (2) if an airline company buys B737-800, part of its expense is defrayed by the Japanese government, (3) in terms of efficiency of maintenance services, it is advantageous and rational to introduce B737-800 so that airline companies can outsource such MRO services in developing countries. Therefore, it may significantly reduce the costs of flight equipment and training for technicians from LCCs' revenue.

In this simulation, the price of a B737-800 was set to 3.78 billion JPY (43 million USD) with a fixed depreciation of 17 years, which reflects the data of recent years. The residual value is 378 million JPY (10%), meaning that the annual cost is estimated at approximately 205 million JPY. If an airline company purchases an aircraft, it is able to borrow money from banks with a 3% interest rate and a total interest cost of 116 million JPY.

The leasing cost, which depends on the number of aircraft leased, is estimated to be in the range of 0.9% to 1.0% of the total amount per month. Thus, the leasing cost of the aircraft will be 417 million JPY per year, indicating that the leasing cost is more expensive than its purchasing cost.

In short, it would be more beneficial as a managerial option for LCCs to purchase aircraft if the MRO establishes in Japan, even if the maintenance cost is still high. In this simulation, the number of aircraft by lease and purchase would be a key factor for all airline companies to decide their management policy strategy. A total of 15 aircraft has been estimated under a lease from Year 1. In Year 8, 10 aircraft will still be leased and the rest will be fully paid, based on calculated results.

(5) Customer acquisition

In Japan, most airline companies have not focused on air ticket sales markets, and travel agencies have become one of the biggest sellers of tickets. By ITC, the cheap package tours attracted consumer's attention, and travel agencies were sending people to such airline companies automatically. These customers prefer to choose travel agent-organized tours, and it contributed to the sales of seats of the aircraft. The market of individual passengers had never been the main business target for airline companies. This is an unique characteristic of the Japanese market, which is not common among the western countries at all.

Since LCCs give priority to receiving reservations from individual customers, some experienced customers have bought air tickets through LCCs, especially those who are able to coordinate their own excursions, and have used services provided by LCCs. This led the load factor to increase. On the other hand, major airline companies have conducted seat up-grade services as one of their strategies to retain customers that moved on to LCCs. Although there are competitions between major airline companies, LCCs have been successful.

Chapter 4

(6) Fund raising

In a successful case of establishing an LCC, JetBlue Airways has secured 160 million USD at its launch and continued to shift itself towards early Initial Public Offering (IPO) for stable stream of funds. In contrast, Japanese LCCs struggled with limited available funds to launch their businesses. This indicates the importance of procuring the initial expenditure at an early stage for an successful LCC establishment.

It usually takes a long time for new LCCs to list their stocks in the market. Securing funds from investors has become a major task for many LCCs, as it is relatively difficult to convince investors to trust LCCs and in their success. Even though there is a restriction on foreign investments, direct foreign investments without going through stock markets could be a beneficial step. In addition, it is also very important to maintain stable and close relationships with the major banks for LCCs. Since starting up a new LCC requires a lot of funds, it is important to find ways to acquire money other than the initial fund. The early IPO is one option to secure additional funds for stability as well as for the growth of business operations.

There are other measures to raise money, such as the utilization of the public funds. Air Do, for example, started its operation with private funding, and since it faced shortage in funds, local governments within Hokkaido provided 5 billion JPY as loans and subsidy. However, Air Do eventually went out of business. Skynet Asia Airways considered Air Do's failure as a "lesson", and received 800 million JPY from Miyazaki Prefecture as a subsidy as well as investments from local citizens and companies before its launch. It is important to remember, though, that such easy dependence on local governments may cause problems regarding morals within management and thus failure in business.

AirAsia, a Malaysian LCC, took over the bankrupted airline company, including its debt, stocks, and other assets such as aircraft and pilots. Establishing its new business model as a cheap airline company, this LCC restructured operations and increased the company's stock values, expanding the scale of its business. The company also hired the former aviation director of Ryanair as an advisor and main stockholder, and captured the hearts of investors with an LCC business model of Ryanair.

According to this example, the method of starting a new LCC by taking over an existing airline company including its assets, and transforming it with a new business model, which may be the most appropriate approach. Instead of starting from scratch, the new LCC was able to operate with a number of available aircraft, and especially from a cost-effective point of view, making it the most effective approach.

In addition, the positioning of the experienced management team for the new LCC could bring large and positive effects. AirAsia placed the former executive of Ryanair in its management team. One of the reasons JetBlue Airways successfully secured ample funds was due to its excellent business model and management team with a proven track record of establishing LCCs.

In Japan, the reason for ANAHD's cooperation with several LCCs was said to be due to its available slots. Securing LCs' management rights may relate to the launch of LCCs by obtaining the slots at Tokyo International Airport and Osaka International Airport as well. The aviation industry is still dominated by large-sized LCs in Japan.

In many analyses up to now, the annual loss is typically complemented by a loan in financial simulations. LCCs tried to do the same in reality, but found that Japanese financial institutions do not accommodate such requests. Thus, LCCs failed to raise funds for continuing their businesses, eventually merging into large-sized LCs.

Airline companies hold large assets and have to maintain a high degree of safety. For that reason, a variety of preparation including training, maturity and inspections, are necessary along with a large cost until the start of operations. Furthermore, it takes a long time to retrieve the revenue. In Japan, such revenue retrieving activities, including adjustment with credit card companies and other business entities, may take up to five months. With such business background, the new LCC will require enough funds to cover the first year's expenses plus six more months worth of additional funds before receiving payments. Securing this much funds becomes a success factor of LCC startups. Therefore, an adequate amount of initial funds is required, and 9.5 billion JPY, as defined in this analysis, creates stable operations for LCCs.

Chapter 4

LCCs' failure in the past several years provides recognition that the key to success for a new LCC is to begin with securing sufficient funds prior to launching the business. Japanese LCCs struggle raising enough funds to start their businesses due to Japanese investor's reluctancy of taking risks. Even after the launch, LCCs often spend too much efforts securing loans that they cannot focus on managing their businesses. Evaluations of Japanese investors on such operations come up short, as they mainly look into management infrastructures and business execution conditions. As a result, LCCs are not able to gather additional funds, and face failure. All failure cases of LCCs have followed this pattern.

These unsuccessful LCCs launched their businesses with a capital amount of less than 2 billion JPY. As a result, they had difficulties convincing investors with bright outlooks. The difficulties of fund raising efforts worsened, and LCCs have relied on speculative investors. Eventually the management was taken over and sold to large-sized LCs.

FDA learned from the failure cases of Japanese LCCs. They secured 20 billion JPY at the beginning and have continued their operations. With enough funds in their account, the management could focus on operations, instead of raising money during their busiest times. FDA started their service at Shizuoka Airport where demand was not expected much, and without agonizing over operating funds, the management was able to shift its hub to Komaki Airport where a much larger demand existed. FDA's case demonstrates good and flexible judgment of its management team.

In Japan, not only the investors but also financial institutions have a tendency not to make their own investment decisions. If a large-sized financial institution is operating a business, other smaller institutions then have to follow and invest in the same business. With this trend, the investor's investing decision depends on the evaluation of large-sized financial institutions.

The mission of this analysis is to prove that the LCC business model is successful if there is an adequate initial capital. Since external risk factors are included in the simulation, the LCCs' success with sufficient funds has been proved.

Chapter 4

◘ 3. Desirable Management Policy of LCCs

Considering the simulation results regarding the current aviation industry including LCCs, the management policy of airlines needs to be reconsidered and reclaimed as follows:

(1) An LCC should obtain a certain amount of initial funds, which cover the necessary expenses for establishment.

(2) If local airports such as Kobe Airport become hub airports, it is preferable if airports operate both domestic and international flights.

(3) An LCC should utilize outsourced maintenance services carried out by MRO.

(4) B737-800 aircraft is the most suitable model in terms of maintenance efficiency in Japan.

(5) To improve their operation performances, LCCs ought to introduce same aircraft types and specification including mechanical parts, in order to simplify the training of pilots and flight attendants for both domestic and international routes.

(6) It is proper for LCCs to sell tickets with 40% to 50% discounts to customers who are willing to buy a ticket at the last minute.

(7) LCCs should not focus on the passengers of package tours. They ought to focus on passengers who are able to make their own travel itinerary, book tickets, and find accommodation by themselves.

(8) An LCC should make good use of electric devices, such as computers and mobile phones to promote ticketless services. This operation does not cost any commission fee to travel agencies.

(9) Destination marketing is one of the useful tools for LCCs to compete with the major airline companies. LCCs may gain more customers if they work with local governments and airports to promote their landing locations such as providing local information (i.e., restaurants, accommodations, things to do, etc.).

Chapter 4

✈ Conclusion: Meanings Behind the Analysis Results and Future Challenges of Methods

◆ 1. Suggestion for Successful Business Models

In conclusion, preferable conditions and requirements of establishing new LCCs were identified through various simulations. The following are key elements to establish a successful LCC:

(1) Developing its own training system for aircraft maintenance technicians and cabin crew, or to outsource maintenance services.
(2) Operating its business with a certain number of aircraft from the beginning, preferably more than 15 aircraft.
(3) Utilizing leased aircraft at the beginning and then increasing the ratio of owned aircraft gradually after acquiring profit.
(4) Setting up discounted airfare rate in the range of 50% for both domestic and international flights, thus enhancing the market to be more competitive.
(5) Combining both short and middle-distance flights, and initiating frequent use of 150-seat aircraft.
(6) Operating international routes.
(7) Preparing enough funds for operations from the time of establishment (minimum 9.5 billion JPY).
(8) Utilizing secondary airports including Kobe Airport as a hub.

First and foremost, (1) it is necessary for a new LCC to develop its own maintenance department and training system for employees, however, it will cost a significant amount for a new LCC. On the other hand, it is a much better option than outsourcing such services to LCs.

Secondly, "economies of scale" is applied until the business volume reaches a certain level. As a result of both simulations, it is more beneficial for a new LCC (2) to operate its business with more than 15 aircraft, and (3) to lease for a while and then begin to purchase aircraft as the company grows. Moreover, the simulation proves that the above effort of cost reduction enables (4) an LCC to compete against LCs with higher discount rates of around 40% to 50%.

Furthermore, a number of flights and combination of routes become extremely critical factors, in order to set up business conditions; higher rate of operations in reducing the cost and capturing higher yield by improving convenience. Due to the simulation, it has become obvious that (5) frequent use of smaller aircraft (150 seats) is profitable. In addition, (6) the combination of short and middle-distance flights show better performance only in domestic routes.

Lastly, the analytical results indicate that (7) preparing sufficient funds before operating stabilizes the financial footing and provides an advantage in financing for business expansion. Therefore, financing at an early stage is a critical and a successful factor for a new LCC.

Additionally, other advantages are revealed in the simulation such as (8) using a secondary airport as a hub. The first reason behind this advantage is the size of demand in the Kansai area, which is the second largest after Tokyo Metropolitan area. Kobe Airport is the secondary airport of the Kansai area, which is equally important. In this simulation, Kobe Airport is selected for the following reasons. Firstly, Tokyo Metropolitan area does not have an ideal secondary airport. Whereas, Osaka International Airport, a hub in the Kansai area, has tough restrictions for arrival and departure slot allocations and operation hours, and both Osaka International Airport and Kansai International Airport charge immensely for landing. The advantages of using Kobe Airport include cheaper landing fees and freedom of flight volume selections, and the simulation clearly reflects these advantages in the result. These advantages are also general characteristics of utilizing secondary airports, and thus these characteristics are proven through the simulation. Other than the simulation results above, the advantages in the utilization of Kobe Airport for LCCs are also indicated in previous analyses. Utilization of Kobe Airport as a secondary airport is expected to have the possibility of favorably contributing to new LCCs in terms of differentiation from LCs, and also in terms of the flexibility of setting the airport usage fee.

Chapter 4

2. Contribution of Analysis Methods and Future Challenges

One of the most important contributions of this study is providing risk analysis using the Monte Carlo simulation and profitability analysis using the corporate model simulation. This model is a profitable model that can not only offer limited analyses including profitability and risk, but also combine a wide variety of factors necessary to simulate complicated cases.

The reasons for Japanese LCCs having been in the red for a long time are due to domestic management policy issues and strict regulations. However, this could mean that such LCCs have not implemented enough risk management analyses for their businesses. As a result, it is difficult to predict factors that include costs, external factors, and demands on the establishment of a new business.

Uncertain factors, such as the currency exchange rate with a daily fluctuation of 10%, for example, have to be handled as random variables. The Monte Carlo method can be utilized on project decision-making, although there are still some modifications required for its structure. However, the model's effectiveness is relatively high since this is verifying the validity of investment using profitability and risk analyses.

One challenge that needs to be improved is data integrity. Cost data for the simulation is obtained from public data and interviews, and numbers close to the data were selected. However, some publically available information on the expenses does not represent the scale of the actual airline companies. Therefore, the result may vary for LCCs, making it difficult to reflect such factors in the models. However, a large number of improvements are required, and in addition, updates on the latest information depending on the operations and environmental changes are also necessary.

Lastly, there are still challenges for the corporate model. As repeatedly mentioned, this universal model can accommodate a wide range of factors and variables. If modifications, development, and improvement of the model can be achieved considering the following issues, it will become even more effective to come up with management policies.

Chapter 4

(1) To construct a corporate model that reflects the behaviors of multiple airline companies and simulates game theory including the conditions of competition with other companies.

(2) To develop and improve the model to include an "Inverse Calculation Program", which can calculate the input variables such as fare discount rates and ASK, as well as the principal desired values of output, such as NPV, and when operating profitability is set. It would also be beneficial for investors to indicate not only NPV but the "Internal Rate of Return (IRR)" that is recently attracting attention.

(3) In regard to future corporate model simulations, it is necessary to construct a model considering the recent LCC business conditions. In particular, examples of cost reduction measures exist as the one indicated below, shortening the turnaround time at the airport to increase operation efficiency. Countermeasures such as to install a pedestrian way by adopting an apron roof or a switchback style as mentioned in the previous chapter, and to inform passengers their boarding times directly through mobile devices, making use of the electronic ticket information, can be taken.

(4) As for an uniquely Japanese issue, the decreasing birth rate and aging population will have an great impact on the Japanese economy and the aviation industry. Therefore, it will be necessary to take both labor costs and recruitment expenses for professions such as pilots and mechanics into account, and have them included in the simulation model hence forward.

CHAPTER 5

Reforming Airport Management in Japan: Effective Methods and the Necessity of Privatization

The quality and quantity of the Japanese aviation industry has drastically changed due to the emergence and entry of the LCCs. It can be said that a new era has arrived, but the need for reform remains: the reform of inefficient airport management. The era of establishing a new airport has long passed, and now is not the time to take superficial measures to open and maintain new routes. Regions with airports, which are enormous public infrastructures, must break down the resistance of vested interests and promote airport management reforms that meet the needs of each region. To increase the number of appropriate secondary airports that will eventually become hub airports for LCCs, through airport privatization would also contribute to the growth of LCCs. This chapter will examine the current reality and the future expectations for airport privatization, one of the top priorities in the nation's growth strategy.
This chapter is especially written for this book.

Chapter 5

✈ Introduction

There is an increase in the concession method for local airports where central or local governments sell the rights to operate a local airport to a private business operator while keeping the ownership of the airport. The reason behind the positive attitude of local governments is because this would enable them to increase the number of airport users by utilizing the wisdom and know-how of the private sector for airport operation and increase the nonresident population in the region. In airports abroad, Bristol Airport and London Luton Airport in the U.K. and Gold Coast Airport in Australia utilized the concession method to lure LCCs, and succeeded in increasing the number of visitors and routes. They were able to increase the number of airport users, use the resulting profit to lower the landing fees, and acquire more flights and thus increase the number of airport users even more. Consequently, the airports that succeeded with concession created a virtuous cycle.

London Heathrow Airport is one of the largest gateway to Europe with the largest number of international flight users in the world. However, the airport is operated entirely by a private company. In addition to the commercial terminal buildings, it integrally operates air navigation facilities such as the runways, and furthermore the company is a foreign company based in Spain. Private companies operate most of the major airports in Europe and there are many airports operated by foreign companies other than London Heathrow Airport such as Copenhagen Airport, Brussels Airport, etc. This way, following not far behind from the liberalization of the aviation market, the waves of privatization and globalization are spreading throughout the world, starting with the airport privatization policy in the U.K. in mid 1980s. Based on numbers from 2016, there are more than 70 airports in the world that were privatized through listing or selling to a specific company.

These days, in addition to traditional airport management body, companies from various industries, such as the construction industry that presents know-how of international social capital construction, and investment funds that have methods to collect funds from a wide variety of sources, form consortiums to develop global airport businesses. It is difficult to develop airport businesses these days under public management with constraints by the national budget and borders between other countries. An airport as a public facility has become a thing of the past, and has entered an era where global private corporations are taking the central role in the aviation industry, just like the manufacturing industry.

1 Pioneers of Airport Privatization

1. Cases in the U.K. and Australia

Based on the Airport Act of the U.K. of 1986, the U.K. privatized the state-owned British Airports Authority (BAA) that owned the major airports in London and Scotland. At the same time, the 16 major airports owned by the local governments were formed into corporations owned by them, and a system was introduced that allowed it to be sold off to a private business if the local governments required to do so. As a result, most major public airports in the U.K. have been privatized, including London City Airport and George Best Belfast City Airport that were constructed initially as airports operated by private companies. The fact that airports of any size, from London Heathrow Airport to a small local airport that serves 6,000 passengers annually, could be sold to the other markets, had a great influence on other countries. Following this, Australia launched a large-scale plan to privatize airports, and as the candidates for the first privatization, three out of 20 airports owned by FAC (Federal Airports Corporation), Melbourne, Brisbane, and Perth were sold by June 1997 through competitive biddings. The second sale that targeted the remaining FAC airports was also completed in May 1998 through competitive biddings.

The number of passengers serviced by the airports that have gone through privatization in both the U.K. and Australia cover almost all categories of airports in Japan. Although it cannot be determined simply from the number of passengers, it is thought that many Japanese airports can secure passenger revenues equivalent to those of privatized airports in the U.K. and Australia if the maintenance system could be adjusted.

Chapter 5

What the U.K. and Australia have in common is the globalization of airport management. Although Australia limits the level of foreign capitals to no more than 49%, it does not deny their entries, but in fact actively invites them in. There are absolutely no restrictions on foreign capital participation in the U.K. and their airport management companies are actively finding their ways into other countries.

In contrast with this large worldwide trend of airport privatization that even includes the control of the airports, Japanese airports had been left behind completely, and competition between companies has largely declined. Japan seems to have followed the worldwide trend belatedly with the privatization of airports that started early on with the demutualization of Kansai International Airport, the privatization of Narita International Airport, and the opening of Chubu Centrair International Airport by a privately-operated organization. However, even with these three airports, the level of commercialism is inadequate compared to the major privatized and public airports of the world. It can also be said that airport policies have ignored the worldwide trend of privatization, and have forgotten the needs of the passengers, airlines, and the freight shippers for a long time.

2. Possibilities of Privatization in Local Airports

In the U.K., where they began airport privatizations at an early stage, most local airports are operated by private companies, and they have come up with ways to increase the number of passengers. Almost all of them, with a few exceptions, are profitable. Bristol Airport is a great example, and although it has the same conditions as Shizuoka Airport (no route connection to the capital city, similar surrounding population), the number of passengers have reached nearly 6 million, six times of the 1 million estimated for Shizuoka Airport, which was criticized for being too optimistic in their demand estimate number.

Bristol, a city with a population of about 500,000 people and a sphere of activity of surrounding with a total of only about 2 million people, cannot achieve profitability without domestic routes to London, which is the central city for just about everything. This is exactly like the case in Japan. Moreover, there are neither outstandingly large tourist sites nor resorts nearby, and an airport with such conditions is lucky to have even a million passengers. For example, Sendai, which is a city larger in scale than Bristol, has 3.3 million passengers, and Niigata, a city of a similar size, has 1.2 million passengers. It is therefore understandable that Shizuoka was criticized for its demand estimate of 1 million passengers.

However, after the privatization in 1997, Bristol Airport had served 2 million passengers in 2000 which has grown to 6 million currently. Most passengers using the airport are from intra-Europe regions or within the country. Although LCCs represented by easyJet and Ryanair are the central force in serving short-range routes, existing major airlines also provide frequent route networks between the capitals of their own countries and Bristol Airport. Bristol Airport's management power is lauded for luring such attractive airlines and making it attractive for passengers to use Bristol Airport, which was privatized in 1997. The foreign capital, Macquarie Group, then became the sole shareholder and took over control. It can be inferred that the growth to 2 million passengers was the power of privatization, and that the operation of the foreign capital grew it further to 6 million. It is certain that the privatization and the introduction of foreign capital somehow influenced the rapid growth of Bristol Airport. The primary incentive for foreign corporations is to turn a profit, and in order to do so, they must design airports that are easily accessible and attractive to passengers. They naturally put great efforts in marketing for such purpose.

Moreover, there are various foreign corporations located around Bristol Airport and this shows that not only the airport, but also the U.K. itself is open to foreign investments. This is an important factor in bringing about prosperity to the area and Bristol Airport. It can also be said that the overall national policy of openness brought about the prosperity to the airport and the surroundings through management by foreign capital linked to the effective operation of the airport. The local airports of Japan are forecasted to fight an uphill battle, but the likes of Ibaraki Airport can follow the example of Frankfurt-Hahn Airport, and there is sufficient potential for development through privatization. Although Frankfurt-Hahn Airport is further from the capital than Ibaraki Airport, it successfully collaborated with Ryanair with outstanding marketing power and grew the number of passengers from 70,000 to 4 million.

Chapter 5

In contrast, the local airports of Japan, where the custom of "petition marketing" is still firmly in place, and the creation and maintenance of routes depend on the political power, would lose their power of negotiation with airlines if the present situation were to continue. There is a high possibility of them being left behind amidst the trend of aviation industry.

2 Merit of Airport Privatization

1. Expected Benefits

In the case of Japan, the most important benefit to be expected from airport privatization is that an independent accounting system would be adopted through privatization. The relationship between beneficiary and burden would clarify, and sense for self-support of the airport would rise. Besides that, the following types of benefits are to be expected from privatization as proved in the examples of the foreign countries:
(1) high efficiency of employees through a privatization mindset, (2) clarification of management responsibility, (3) incentive for improvement based on the possibility of bankruptcy, (4) reduction of political intervention, (5) possibility of modernized investments not bound by the constraints of the government finance, (6) expanded freedom for diversified operation as the core airport operation, and (7) promotion of integral development with other social capital and peripheral developments.

By taking advantage of such various benefits, the airport privatization achieves the reduction of airport usage fee through cost reductions, increases the ease of use of the airport, brings about user benefit, increases the competitiveness of airlines, and gives profit on sales to the country and the local governments.

Among the benefits mentioned above, points (1) to (3) relate strongly to improve the cost side. Regardless of airports, the public management system is known to show low labor productivity, and in the case of East Midlands Airport, the number of airport employees have been reduced to half from the days when the local government operated it. Furthermore, the estimate of the reconstruction cost of

Chapter 5

London Heathrow Airport terminal after privatization was reduced to half of what was made before privatization.

● 1.1 Enforcement of Commercialism and Emphasis on Marketing

Privatization induces the management and employees to place importance on the market, to focus on the fee settings and marketing that corresponds to the passengers, and to bring about an increase on the revenue side in addition to the cost side. Successful airports worldwide share a common characteristic where they do not set their airport fees based on just the landing fees, but also considering the number of passengers, and setting it in detail according to airlines, flights and routes.

In addition, the airports strive for higher efficiency by adopting various measures corresponding to the local markets of the airports such as the development of a detailed enticement marketing method complying to the fee system, the airport development plan based on long term contracts with specific airlines, integral operation of the air navigation facilities and commercial facilities, efforts to emphasize the existence of demand by successfully launching charter flights with the airport itself acting as the promoter, frequent market surveys in order to effectively layout the commercial stores, marketing to set the proper tenant rent, installation of the facility inside the airport that can become the core of the local business, preparation of access transportation at its own expense, hiring a traffic controller for each airline, priority boarding system based on membership, introduction of biometrics authentication system, etc.

In this way, marketing activities are conducted as a means of winning against other airports globally amidst airport privatization. Although this is normal in other industries, there are many cases that have showcased the reality of Japanese local airports, in which under the ownership and management of the government, there was no movement in trying to make a profit or to reform the system in generating such awareness.

● 1.2 Increase in Investments and Self-Responsibility

Privatization brings about an increase in investments. Following its privatization, BAA made a large scale investment in London Stansted Airport, the third airport of

Chapter 5

London. East Midlands Airport has performed the renewal of the airport controller facility, and the extension and reconstruction of its terminal, further deciding on a plan to extend its runway.

Under a low growth subjected to deficit financing, the government budget cannot be increased only for a specific public investment even though the investment will yield a profit. An administration that aims for a small government believes that the growth areas of airports should be left to the private sector, and an administration that aims for a large government allocates a large budget to welfare and medical care but does not invest in the growth of industrial areas. Privatization is effective for removing such constraints, and detaching the growth areas from the government budget, which is the very thing that enables the increase in investment. Furthermore, the expansion in the level of freedom of sales by privatization, and growing awareness to turn a profit, promote the investment in the peripheral regions and transportation.

In the local airports of the U.K., even though it was legally possible during the days of ownership by the local governments, the peripheral development, which was overlooked due to government's poor understanding of the latent potential, has been actively set forward following privatization. For instance, after the privatization, East Midlands Airport Corporation constructed the business park and the airport station. It is natural that the incentive for an integral development is reduced under the public management system in which the profit from the peripheral development is not returned to the social capital developer. Since access transportation is installed for the benefit of the airport users, it is logical for the airport itself to do the same.

Moreover, the effectiveness of regional development of airports is quite indeterminate, and often optimistic numbers result when the local or the central government performs this estimation, and investments tend to be ineffective. However, when the peripheral development is to be performed by the privatized airport itself, investments will surely be limited to sound and recoverable ones, similar to when the Japanese private railways developed areas along their routes. Besides this, the benefits of privatization to the country are due to financial contribution made by the profit from sales, the possibility of it becoming an important export industry with the

Chapter 5

improvement of the know-how in the airport management, and so forth.

2. Airport Regulation Reform and Consistent Privatization

Airport privatization is executed with the goal of optimizing airport management and maintenance, and is not only for the sake of being a private corporation. Being consistent with this goal, it is simultaneously necessary to reform systems such as the abolition of internal subsidization by social infrastructure development business special account, and the reform of the system of subsidy to regional areas, as well as the abolition of aviation fuel tax, liberalization of airport use fee, and integration of non-aviation and aviation facilities. Furthermore, it is necessary to examine the sales of the airport and the regulation method appropriate for such goal.

2.1 Reform of Fiscal Resource Allocation to Regions

In Japan, one of the important purposes of privatization is the need to abolish the internal subsidization system, and reform the aviation development system to increase the independence of airports. As a matter of fact, in the U.K., the internal subsidy between airports was denied even before its privatization, and each airport was operated with independent budgets. The reason the U.K. was able to execute the privatization before others, was because the internal subsidy system was not a basic concept in the airport development. Furthermore, removing the airport development payment exclusively from the social infrastructure development special account would have no effect. The system in which the central government takes care of the principal and interest of the airport development through tax revenue allocated to local governments should also be abolished. On the other hand, since these systems aim to give aid to regional areas, it should be examined first whether the aid to the regional areas is appropriate or not. If the income distribution to the regional areas is politically unavoidable, the allocation to regional areas should be lumped only as a general grant tax, and a thorough decentralization should be simultaneously implemented so that the local governments can decide for themselves how much they want to disburse for the airport development.

● 2.2 Public Listing and Individual Sales

In general, privatizing through public listing or selling it off to an individual corporation, depends on the scale. A large airport that can attract funds widely from the world may be suited for public listing. The privatization of BAA in the U.K. that manages the group of airports in London can be done through the same way.

As for the privatization in Australia, the candidates that were interested in the purchase were invited to a bid, with future investment planning and regional coordination also taken into consideration. The bidder with the highest bid was selected. The organizations that purchased each Australian airport are all consortiums organized by international airport managements. The reason why the BAA method was not used is due to its privatization purpose to introduce world-class level of efficient management methodology in Australia. However, there are no restrictions on reselling after the purchase.

Furthermore, since local airports in the U.K. are small compared to BAA, raising funds from the public market is difficult, and most of the airports select a sales method through negotiation. The airport owners are investment companies, financial institutions, food companies, and even a bus company, and many foreign airport management entities participated in the purchase.

◘ 3. Integration of Aviation and Non-Aviation Business

If privatization is seen as an initiating reform for the airport development system, it should be understood that to divide the airport operation and maintenance, and sell only the management rights to a private business through the concession method, is not desirable.

However, MLIT executed a concession with Kansai International Airport and Osaka International Airport combined together as a solution for the problem regarding Kansai airport. It was explained that the reason for selecting the concession method was so that the government loses its right to intervene if the land was included in the asset sale.

Chapter 5

However, privatizing airports without government regulations is inconceivable. Security regulation is a matter of course, and economical regulations can be imposed on airports if necessary. Looking at privatization within developed countries, the typical practice is to sell off including facilities to a private business, but imposing the necessary regulations such as the suppression of monopolistic activities so no problems are generated. If the entire facility including the land cannot be sold as a whole, the same mistake would be made like the time when privatizing Japan Highway Public Corporation.

The concession method is used in all cases of developing nations except for London Luton Airport. In developing countries, the power to control the capital investment is poor, and from the perspective of developed nations that invest, it is not desirable to select a risky investment method. One of the reasons why the concession method for operation rights is considered mainstream is because in the U.S., where the privatization did not progress well to begin with, there were restrictions regarding local government finances that were unique to the country.

In the case of Australia, a sell-off is a long term exclusive use right, instead of a sell-off that includes the ownership of the asset, and that use right lasts for more than 50 years up to 99 years. It looks like a concession contract in form, but in reality it is the same as a sell-off. The division of aviation and non-aviation business is not desirable for a company that operates its business since it impairs management incentive. It is different when the right of full land use is sold like in the Australian privatization, but when only the operation concession is privatized, the level of freedom and the attractiveness of managing to achieve the goal of reducing the usage fee, by raising the benefits for the users through cost reduction, will be greatly constrained.

The current aviation business is making global progress similar to the conventional manufacturing industry. As in the case of East Midlands Airport, the company that owns the airport, with an increase in asset value due to large profit improvements, is planning to expand its business internationally by selling its airport and using the fund to purchase a foreign airport with a higher return on investment. However, such dynamic activity does not occur in a company that has only been approved for

Chapter 5

the operational rights of an airport.

Moreover, the social infrastructure development such as airports is only possible when it is managed integrally with the peripheral development, but those companies with operation businesses only, are not allowed to do so. When the "public" organization is still in charge of the development, the profit from the peripheral development is not returned to the main constituent of the development of social infrastructure. Furthermore, it is important to remember, although investment expansion is possible as a result of privatization, operation privatization without investment rights are not allowed to receive such benefit.

4. Integrated Management of Commercial Facilities and Aviation Facilities

In Japan, airports with the exception of the three—Narita International Airport, Kansai International Airport and Chubu Centrair International Airport—the airport's aviation (runways, traffic control, etc.) and the non-aviation (commercial) facilities are operated by separate organizations. This has caused various problems for the airport policy and management. Some airports that are said to be unprofitable in Japan can turn out to be profitable if both facility types are integrally managed. Many private terminal companies that operate commercial facilities easily bring about profit, and even though a large portion of this profit is due to the external effect of the aviation facility on the non-aviation ones, this effect is not internalized and does not contribute to the overall improvement of the airport budget. In airport management, commercial facilities are equally important to airport usage fees and marketing to airlines. Many private capitals would probably hesitate to participate in the airport management with only the aviation part. In privatized airports of foreign countries, serious and detailed market researches on the layout and concept of the commercial facilities are conducted, and their results are fed back. It would have been impossible to increase the commercial revenue and difficult to attract airlines to develop privatized airports without such private mindset and professional marketing power.

However, commercialism has been neglected in Japan. During the discussion of the issue regarding foreign capital regulations in airports in 2008, it has been criticized that airports managed by foreign capital are designed so that passengers must go through the commercial facilities. Moreover, since the two facilities are managed by different organizations, they are not interested in one another's management results, and therefore, are not interested in nurturing commercialism within the airport management. The profitable commercial side lacks the incentive to improve the management to further increase profit, and has become passive towards privatization.

On the other hand, in the case of integral management, the weight of the commercial revenue in the airport management will increase, as well as the marketing mindset and skills to attract airlines in the aviation facility. As long as the aviation facility is being operated, the top executive position for the airport operation is taken up from an executive from a technical field, and organization reform such as appointing the management professional to the top of management, a common practice in the privatized airports of foreign countries, is not done either. Therefore, it is necessary to reform regulations so that it becomes possible to publicly list terminal building companies, and have a private airport corporation or private investor purchase it, in order to integrally manage it with privatized aviation and non-aviation facilities.

5. Multiple Airports in the Same Metropolitan Area Should Compete with Each Other

5.1 To Separately Sell Multiple Airports in a Large Metropolitan Area

It is typical for the major cities in the world to have multiple airports. Moreover, in Japan, there are a few examples of Narita International Airport and Tokyo International Airport for the capital region, Kansai International Airport and Osaka International Airport for the Kansai region, Chubu Centrair International Airport and Nagoya Airport for the Nagoya region, New Chitose Airport and Sapporo Okadama Airport for the Sapporo region and Hiroshima Airport and Hiroshimanishi Airport for the Hiroshima region. In most of these large cities, where older airports try to expand their airport capacity, most of the newer ones are built away from central cities mainly due to environmental reasons. The relationship between Fukuoka Airport and Kitakyushu Airport, as well as Saga Airport, despite their background

Chapter 5

differences, is a case of multiple alternative airports existing in the same large metropolitan area.

When multiple airports exist in the same metropolitan area, the government tends to artificially decide the share of the two airports in order to control both of them. Due to the governmental deliberation council in 2010, in addressing problems of Kansai airports, they proposed an integral sell-off and management by founding an integral company for Osaka International Airport and Kansai International Airport, instead of creating two separate companies. Similarly, the government is considering unified operations for Narita International Airport and Tokyo International Airport in the capital region.

Furthermore, following the construction of Hiroshima Airport, the use of a commuter airline was allowed as an exception in Hiroshimanishi Airport, but even that was cancelled due to regulations consolidating flights to Hiroshima Airport, thereby closing down Hiroshimanishi Airport. It is considered typical in the world to centrally manage the operation of multiple airports by a single management. There were pros and cons during the privatization of the old BAA airports, but ultimately the sell-off was made integrally.

However, a change was seen in this traditional way of thinking. In the process of the maturing airport operation and advancing privatization, it has been recognized that the benefit from having multiple airports compete is greater than the benefit from the merit of scale by the integral management.

Besides impairing the power of competition, the negative views toward competition among multiple airports within the same metropolitan region are not desirable for the development of those airports. Independent management and competition between multiple airports should be approved and have the market decide their habitat segregation. Opinions advocating the unified management believe that multiple airports cannot coexist in the same metropolitan region, and such should be discarded. However, if both are privatized and allowed to compete with one another, then the "more desired airport" will remain as a result.

Chapter 5

This discussion would have been simpler if Osaka International Airport had been abandoned when Kansai International Airport opened. At the time, however, it would not have been desirable to artificially discard demands that existed in Osaka International Airport when the benefits of the passengers are taken into account. These days, at a time when aviation demand has increased and people's preferences have diversified, the demand to support multiple airports exist abundantly in the metropolitan region with a scale equal to or greater than an ordinance-designated city.

The door should be open to all air transportation, and multiple airports should be allowed to compete instead of artificially making one of them difficult to use. Regarding the benefit of integral management of multiple airports, although there are views that advocate the merit of scale and the effectiveness of management strategy, that may be true for the facilities within the same airport. However, the effectiveness is thought to be small for the integral management of different airports. When the case of creating two airports of the same scale is compared with the case of creating one airport with the capacity of two airports, the merit of scale is obviously greater for the latter.

However, it does not apply to the case when one management operates the airports located in two separate locations. Although some believe that the stock price will be higher if multiple airports are sold all at once. However, if it is an integral sale consisting of a profitable airport and an unprofitable airport, it would not only reduce the average price, but would also mean to acknowledge internal subsidization. Moreover, if sale consists of two superior airports that are in a competitive relationship with each other (for example, Kansai International Airport and Osaka International Airport, and Tokyo International Airport and Narita International Airport), it would lead to the strengthening of monopoly which is not desirable.

If market competition is left alone, division of functions may take longer compared to when a single airport management artificially decides the role of the multiple airports, but the division of functions that actually exist between multiple airports, considering the fact that the facilities invested by the airlines in each airport are sunk costs, change merely. There is practically no difference in the loss of time between the market and artificial decisions.

Therefore, Narita International Airport and Tokyo International Airport, Kansai International Airport and Osaka International Airport, and multiple airports in other metropolitan areas should all be privatized as independent management entities. In this way, there would be competitive incentives to mutually capture customers, providing better service, and cheaper fees will be realized, resulting in the airport competitiveness for the overall metropolitan area to improve. In order to improve airport marketing and motivate the airport to strive to capture passengers and airlines, it is necessary to place a competitor right in front of it. The prerequisite for this is that both airports need to be independent privatized airports.

- ### 5.2 Utilization of the Metropolitan Secondary Airport

An old airport in the hub of a city may struggle to expand, but has the advantage of having maximum convenience due to its location, which would allow it to compete with the new airports. Airports like Sapporo Okadama Airport and Nagoya Airport, with the improvement of marketing and efficiency supplemented by privatization, are thought to have sufficient room for activity even for their small scale. That is representatively shown in the case of London City Airport and George Best Belfast City Airport. Though the difference between the two is that the former is a new central city airport and the latter is an old central city airport, both grew to service 2.7 million passengers annually through a policy which approved the competition between multiple airports within the same metropolitan area, and through the efforts of the management due to privatization.

London City Airport has only the 1,200-meter runway, and George Best Belfast City Airport's runway is only 1,800-meter long, but each provide short-range international flights. London City Airport services flights even to New York. Moreover, there is room for activity for secondary airports in metropolitan suburbs. London Stansted Airport, London Luton Airport, Frankfurt-Hahn Airport and so forth are the representatives of secondary airports in the suburb, unlike the central city, that utilize the European LCCs. In the case of Frankfurt-Hahn Airport, it is located farther away from Frankfurt city than Ibaraki Airport is from the capital city.

From such perspective, there are means of usage for Ibaraki Airport. Many people think of Ibaraki Airport as the main "airport of Ibaraki" and the local government advertises it in such way. If the airport peripheral demand is considered, it becomes a mere "local airport without a route to the capital region". However, if it is regarded as a secondary airport, the room for its use will greatly expand, and marketing from that standpoint should be considered.

● 5.3 Creating Competition Between Local Airports

Competition is necessary between local airports as well. The spheres of influence overlap considerably for local airports, and they are in a reciprocally competitive relationship as a tourist site or an active business location even when they are far apart. If these airports are made independent and privatized, their awareness for competition will be generated and improvement of efficiency can be expected.

However, if they are integrated or grouped with a large airport, progression of the status of dependency on internal subsidization and funds from local governments cannot be expected. For example, if subsidy for airports within Hokkaido is eliminated, and they are made independent allowing for them to compete with one another, profitable privatization is possible with the exception of remote islands.

◘ 6. Prospective Development of the Aviation Service Industry in Airports

● 6.1 Securing Management Freedom and Independence

Altering the form of the management has little effect on enhancing the results of privatization and marketing. The most important aspect is securing independence and freedom of the management. If there is no freedom in the management, it is impossible to deploy policies for investment, pricing, and marketing for effective efficiency improvements.

Therefore, management independence from regulatory agencies is necessary. Even if it is privatized, as long as the organization still receives economical control as well as management and personnel restrictions from its agencies, positive results cannot be expected. Considerable deregulation is required in order to enable the independence of the management. For example, airports in the U.K., except the four major ones, do not receive price regulation. Australia also maintains price capping of 5 years after privatization. As for New Zealand, the fee setting is done freely and currently, when social capital is greatly exposed to the waves of international competition, it is thought that economic regulations such as price regulation and business regulation need to be drastically removed.

- **6.2 Abolishing the Restriction of Cabotage**

Approval of management freedom is necessary to gather superior investors and management staff from worldwide. It is necessary to wipe out the impression that the world has of Japan; when an investment is made in regulatory Japan the freedom of management activities will be obstructed. The flexible stance on regulations on foreign capital is required as well. With regard to the three company-managed airports (Narita International Airport, Kansai International Airport and Chubu Centrair International Airport), those which exist currently as a company organization in form, only are tentatively aiming to be "completely privatized".

What is the reason behind capital regulations for airports other than security reasons? It is not as if a large share of regulations are put in place for economic reasons. If price regulations and service regulations are necessary for problems related to monopoly, it can be dealt through such rules. The largest share regulation was introduced even when such regulations were in place, whilst there was still indescribable insecurity towards a foreign management acquiring a majority of stock to perform management. This insecurity that cannot be expressed in words is often described with the term "publicness". When each separate foreign capital purchases 20% of the stocks, the foreign capitals can invest up to two-thirds of the stock while the government has one-third. However, this means that ownership is for investment purpose only and a private business cannot operate Narita International Airport as the main constituent as in Copenhagen Airport and Bristol Airport. If asked to prove whether the prosperity of Bristol Airport is due to the privatization by a foreign capital, the analysis would be a very difficult one. However, there are effects that cannot be explained. The government has declined private managements that include foreign capital due to "publicness". Even when terrorist activities can be prevented through behavior regulations, unless the foreign capital regulation is in place, there may be a possibility that a "investment capital" of a foreign country that the public feel an inexpressible discomfort towards, may participate in the airport management.

The way to deal with the globalization of the economy is a matter of choice between focusing on the effect brought on by the foreign capital or focusing on the indescribable insecurity and to adopt a defensive stance. The globalization of the economy is inevitable. If we are to deal with it, the focus should be on the positive side of the foreign capital introduction, and the intangible "publicness" should be ignored so that it can be constructively dealt with.

3 Current Situation of Privatization in Japanese Airports

1. Case of Privatization

1.1 Sendai Airport: Repairing Facilities Without Losing Inbounds

In July, 2016, Tokyu Corporation Group took over the operation of Sendai Airport, the first government-managed airport that introduced the concession method. The Group paid the government 2.2 billion JPY at once for the management rights, and purchased the stocks of the two semi-public corporations that operate the passenger and cargo terminals from Miyagi Prefecture for approximately 5.7 billion JPY. Tokyu Corporation Group is planning a capital investment of a total of 34.2 billion JPY towards achieving the goal of increasing the number of passengers 1.7 times and cargo volume 4.2 times in 30 years, and it is important to implement the necessary investment at the earliest timing considering the depreciation effect. The Earnings Before Interest, Taxes, Depreciation, and Amortization (EBITDA) for Sendai Airport in 2014 experienced a loss of 449 million JPY for the aviation business, and a profit of 1.147 billion JPY for the non-aviation business.

Up to now, the former business was mainly handled by the government and the latter by the semi-public corporations, but Tokyu Corporation Group will henceforth handle both of them integrated together, and plans to conduct efficient operation through such measures as reducing the landing fees supported by the profit from

Chapter 5

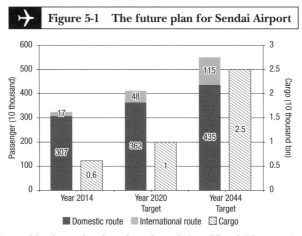

Figure 5-1 The future plan for Sendai Airport

Source: Created by the author based on the website of Sendai International Airport

the non-aviation business.

● 1.2 Kansai International Airport and Osaka International Airport: New Business Model for the Public Infrastructure

The two airports in Kansai area, which took over the operation of Kansai International Airport and Osaka International Airport from April 2016 for 44 years, pays 49 billion JPY for the operation rights annually. A simple calculation shows a total fee of 2.2 trillion JPY, but the operating revenue for the two airports in 2014 was 149.7 million JPY and the cost of the operation is one-third of that. Even so, Kansai Airports are considered to be "an infrastructure that can earn money". This is because the airports are usable 24 hours with two runways of 4,000-meter class in which long-range flights can land on and take off from, which is possible to increase the arrival and departure slots by 1.5 times. The number of passengers is expected to increase by 1.7 times during this period and the current EBITDA of less than 70 billion JPY will probably grow naturally to 74 billion JPY in 2017. By 2059, the goal is to double it to 120.9 billion JPY. The company that takes over the operation does not take on the debt of 1.2 trillion JPY. Without a deposit, the annual payment becomes 49 billion JPY for 45 years, but it can be paid from the revenue generated from the airport operation.

Chapter 5

Figure 5-2 The future plan for Kansai International Airport and Osaka International Airport

Source: Created by the author based on the website of Kansai Airports

The special characteristic of the concession business of Kansai International Airport is that the construction of the buildings on a certain range of unequal settlement, and the elevation of the land construction are to be performed at the expense of Kansai Airports itself. The concession that Kansai Airports is progressing in is, so to speak, equivalent to the growth strategy of Abe administration, and it is a case that must succeed, and a test case for airport concession businesses to follow.

● 1.3 Takamatsu Airport

MLIT is planning to introduce the concession method in Takamatsu Airport, and announced its introduction on July 8th, 2016. The business duration will be 15 years at first with an approval to extend to 35 years maximum at the request of the private company. The operation plans to start in April 2018, and according to MLIT, the reason behind the set of the business duration as short as to 15 years in the beginning, is to limit the risk of change in the number of passengers due to the opening of the Linear Chuo Shinkansen.

● 1.4 Fukuoka Airport

On July 22th, 2016, MLIT announced that the concession method will be introduced to Fukuoka Airport and that the business duration will be set to 30 years.

Chapter 5

The goal of the operation is to be taken over by a private company by April 2019. The private company will integrally operate the runway and the terminal buildings and so forth. Whilst it earns landing fees, commercial revenue, and cargo handling fees, etc., it will also pay the government for the operation rights. The government will use the revenue from the sell-off of the operation rights to advance the plan to build a runway in addition to the current single one. The new runway is to be completed in March 2025, and the private company will operate the runway after its completion together with the current one. According to MLIT, the number of passengers in 2014 at Fukuoka Airport was 16.33 million for domestic flights and 3.67 million for international flights, totaling of 20 million. Since the airport is closer to downtown Fukuoka, the airport operation needs to pay close attention to noise control for the surrounding residents. It is essential to gain understanding and cooperation from local residents when increasing the number of flights.

The government owns 2.29 million square meters out of 3.53 million square meters of Fukuoka Airport's site, and the remaining 1.24 million square meters is owned by private parties and by Fukuoka city. The government indicated that it plans to renew or continue the lease contract with the landowners and the city, and re-lease it to the private company that will take on the operation business.

◘ 2. Future Issues Concerning the Method for Selecting Airport Concessions in Japan

In July 2016, Sendai International Airport became the first national airport in Japan to be completely privatized through concession. However, Ministry of Finance (MOF) questioned the evaluation method used by MLIT that selected a private operator who bid a low-purchase price for Sendai Airport. According to MOF, by introducing a private operator, it would reduce maintenance and operating costs of runways and other facilities using the expertise of the private sector. Furthermore, it would attract new flights and lower the landing fees through the sales revenue of goods in the airport facilities.

However, MOF noted some problems in the method for selecting the buyer for Sendai Airport's operating rights. In September 2015, MLIT announced that the leading candidate for the purchase of the operating rights was a group led by Tokyu Corporation Group, followed by a group led by Mitsubishi Estate Co., Ltd. When MLIT announced the outcome of the review process in October 2015, the Ministry stated that the two candidates differed mainly in regard to programs for revitalizing the airport. The Tokyu Corporation Group bid 2.2 billion JPY for the operating rights, whereas the Mitsubishi Estate group bid 4 billion JPY.

MLIT stated that it was more interested in the bidders' proposals for revitalizing the airport than in the amount of the bid. However, MOF contended that it was irrational not to select a private sector operator that was willing to pay double the amount for the operating rights. It highlighted inconsistencies in the evaluation method since a plan that would have increased income through revitalization should have had a higher bid. Furthermore, it stated that the scoring methodology used in selecting the winning bid for the operating rights should be reexamined

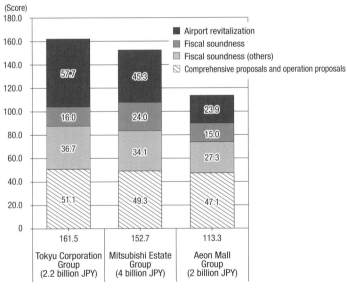

Figure 5-3 Outcome of selecting the bidder for the operating rights of Sendai Airport

Note: The amount that each group offered to pay for the operating rights is indicated in parentheses.
Source: Created by the author based on the website of Ministry of Finance

Chapter 5

going forward. MLIT responded that its scoring methodology always takes an objective view that considers the circumstances of each airport.

◘ 3. Initiatives to Link Infrastructure Privatization to Regional Revitalization

In 2015, the number of foreign visitors to Japan exceeded 20 million for the first time, reaching 21,359,000 people with an increase of 46% year-on-year. Many local governments are working to make improvements regarding airports—the doorway for the increasing number of visitors from overseas—including improving the airport functionality, and potentially changing the management systems. Particularly noteworthy is the use of public-private cooperative operations to resolve various issues that each region face.

In Wakayama Prefecture, for example, the local government has newly allocated a budget of 38.18 million JPY to allure international routes and streamline the airport operation in order to attract visitors from other parts of Asia. Nanki-Shirahama Airport of Wakayama Prefecture currently has only one boarding gate, and it has a limited time slot in which international routes can be serviced. In response, there are plans to construct a new terminal building, which includes the incorporation of the concession method as well as the altercation of the primary design.

Similarly, Shizuoka Prefecture has also allocated a new 72.4 million JPY budget whilst looking to implement a concession system at Shizuoka Airport. Furthermore, the prefecture intends to propose a plot with Central Japan Railway Company to establish a new station along the Tokaido Shinkansen, which runs directly underneath the airport. A budget of 1 billion JPY is to be allocated in order to expeditiously handle this new station development.

Initiatives are mounting in Japan to link infrastructure to regional revitalization as the battle begins to convert infrastructure from being an expense to becoming an income generator. Public work projects have large effects that cannot be measured only by objective cost-benefit analysis, such as improved scenic appeal, increased tourist satisfaction, and attracting companies and tourists to the region. The development of public work projects with a clearer strategic vision and stock effect in mind, is a critical factor in the success of regional revitalization.

Conclusion

When one mentions the privatization of social capital such as an airport, we hear counterarguments such as "it is wrong to give free rein on facilities with high public interest such as an airport to a private entity." Typically, people believe the simple scheme, "public management system for high public interest", but the high public interest does not mean that it must be publicly managed. "Private management + regulation or subsidy" is sufficient in most cases. Public interest means it is synonymous with the factor that it cannot be left to the market(=market's failure), where various issues of market failure are caused when it is left to the freedom of the private entity and the market mechanism. What needs to be confirmed here is that the privatization proponents are neither saying, "there is no public interest with regard to airports(=there is no market failure)" nor "no problems will occur if left to the hands of a private entity." No one believes, "everything will be alright if left to the hands of a private entity."

Organizations owned by the public such as airports and hospitals have their own reasons for being controlled by the public, and whether it is publicly or privately managed is a question of mere relative comparison. In regards to the airports of the 21st century, private organizations have more advantage than public organizations and it is easier to choose the former, if we were to make a choice between the two, since it is relatively more efficient. Therefore, the problems that occur due to privatization can be considered to be complemented by regulation and aid, whereas to leave it freely to the market would not be an option. For example, since minimum security and safety regulations are necessary, regulation for price and investment capital are sometimes considered as accurate.

This type of market intervention does not contradict in any way with the introduction of commercialism to airport management and the pursuit of efficiency through privatization. If this point is understood, then it can be said that "unprofitable airports cannot be privatized" is incorrect. By trying to privatize, the existence of unprofitable infrastructure becomes clear, and whether a subsidy is necessary may also become apparent. If self-support is not possible, consider the need for subsidy and choose the option of "private management + subsidy". Not choosing to privatize, since calculation shows that self-support cannot be achieved, is getting the priorities wrong. In order to escape from the infrastructure development through internal subsidization thus far, you should first "try to sell-off".

◘ 1. Privatization Is Liberalization for Business Management

Privatizing a management and setting it completely free is not synonymous. As explained before, in doing so, it is necessary to loosen regulations and raise the level of freedom of management. However, there are no alterations to the points of applying commercial law and general regulations of the Anti-Trust Law. When discussing "whether a regulation is necessary" for a certain property, it is natural to take into account the general regulations of the constitution, Criminal Law, Civil Law, Commercial Law, and the Anti-Trust Law as the premise.

On top of such regulations that exist, we also need to think about whether a special regulation is necessary or not for such an industry. These regulations are not set up in each industry, but target all corporate activities and commercial activities. In doing so, prohibited activities are indicated in advance, and regulative entity intervenes after a certain activity occurs in line with each individual case. Therefore, such general regulations are called "ex-post regulations". Ex-post regulation means, "when you break the Criminal Law or Anti-Trust Law, you will be punished later in such way."

Without limiting to a certain industry or group of companies, there are cases where "special additional rules" are added on top of generally applied rules for limited special groups or group of companies. For example, there are laws on the prevention of irregularities by gangsters that says, "because organized crime groups have high probability of committing crimes, their activities shall be restricted in advance" and rules such as "because taxi companies conduct illegal discounting, a lower limit is prescribed for the price in advance and charging a fare below the minimum is

Chapter 5

prohibited." Compared to the general rules that are ex-post regulations, these are "ex-ante regulations" that restrict activities for prevention.

In the discussion of airport privatization, when one thinks "whether a regulation is necessary or not," the existence of the general regulations is the prerequisite for thinking "whether additional regulations are necessary in advance." Regarding airport fees, even in the case of "no need for fee regulation", if the airport places monopolistic prices, Japan Fair Trade Commission will exercise its intervention rights. I have emphasized that Tokyo International Airport and Narita International Airport should compete with one another, and even though regulations are not necessary in advance, if Tokyo International Airport and Narita International Airport set a cartel pricing, naturally Japan Fair Trade Commission will intervene. The U.K., with an exception for three major airports, does not impose price regulation, but the airports other than the three have received commercial and anti-trust regulations. Locally owned small and medium airports are examined whether or not such regulations are sufficient, and thereupon, the additional "special price regulation" is imposed on the three major airports. Naturally, in regard to the ex-post general rules, examination of their validity is always necessary.

◇ 2. Privatization Without Regulations Is Impossible

A privatization that does nothing is not possible, but it is wrong to think that "optimum regulations are applied as long as it's under public management. There is no need for regulation standards or examination of regulation methods if managed by the public." The reason is, similar to a private company that does not act accordingly to the optimum social standard, the public organization also does not necessarily either, but in compliance with the activity standard that is optimum to the said organization. That is, whether owned by a public organization or privately managed, it is necessary to set a similar social optimum regulation standard, and establish transparency and disclosure.

For example, it is necessary for government-managed and privately-managed airports to examine the state of price regulation by discussing whether a general competition policy is sufficient, if additional pricing regulation is necessary in

Chapter 5

advance, and what kind of regulatory method is desirable. Inappropriate settings of airport fees by the discretion of a public organization must be avoided.

CHAPTER 6

Skymark Airlines' Bankruptcy and Recovery:
The Achievements and Misdeeds of Authoritarian
Management of an "Independent LCC"

Skymark Airlines, which went bankrupt on January 28th, 2015 went through civil rehabilitation proceedings, and completed the rehabilitation plan at the end of March 2016. In regards to that, the debtor's plan was adopted by the funds such as Integral Corporation and ANAHD (ANA Holdings Inc.) in the creditors' meeting in August 2015, and the company took a step towards rehabilitation. However, the impact of the bankruptcy still remains and it will be a long and difficult path for the company to get back on its feet again. There are numerous issues for reconstruction such as the code-sharing method with ANAHD, and the executive officer system that started in order to prepare for a capital injection and to protect its independence. Skymark Airlines was originally an innovative airline, but it required a change in the way of personnel thinking as well after a long period of authoritarian management. Even under such circumstances, the company ended up profitable in 2015. It is also currently necessary to increase the corporate value with the goal of relisting the company 5 years later. It is imperative to fix problems as soon as possible while there is benefit from lowered fuel cost. It examines how Skymark Airlines paved the way of solving such problems.

This chapter is especially written for this book.

Chapter 6

 Introduction

On September 29th, 2015, eight months after filing for the application of the Civil Rehabilitation Act, the new Skymark Airlines organization was established. In the frontline, freed from the reckless expansion policy, the employees are showing vitality toward rehabilitation by taking initiative to search for the path to redemption. The Japanese aviation industry is consolidated into only two companies for the domestic airline market, which kept the airfare at a high level due to insufficient competitive environment, and the system did not contribute to the benefit of the users.

On the other hand, the international aviation market faced fierce competition. The airfare had progressively decreased as well as the benefit returned to the users. Skymark Airlines started in September 1998 as the first LCC in the domestic airline market, and it is highly significant that it created a competitive environment as the third key player. Even in the management, there was ingenuity being exercised that had never been seen before, to provide low fares to the users and develop a new market. However, the new Skymark Airlines was stuck in between the two investors, Integral Corporation investment fund and ANAHD, who had different expectations and was left with multitude of issues to solve.

I wish to analyze how the company continues to maintain willingness toward reconstruction and indicates regrowth while maintaining motivation—the social significance of the third key player that the frontline employees had in mind—when there is difference between the ideal image of the corporation that the frontline employees have for the new Skymark Airlines and the reality of the new organization. Simultaneously, by verifying the circumstances leading up to the bankruptcy, to examine whether the path that Skymark Airlines should have chosen was to match what the LCs were doing, or to go back to basics when the company was a pioneer that breathed new life into the oligopolistic market of LCs, and developed attractive features that LCs and LCCs could not have done.

Chapter 6

✈ 1 The Pros and Cons of Authoritarian Management

In 2015, the background music stopped playing in the headquarters of Skymark Airlines, that was meant to relax the employees, but to them it represented the non-verbal pressure from the former president up until the bankruptcy. Before the incident, there were barely any conversations in the workplace, and the only sound people heard was the keystrokes on the keyboards and the flat sound of music. However, while the company was losing itself in the abyss of bankruptcy, the employees did not show any sense of despair.

After the company filed for the application of the Civil Rehabilitation Act on January 28th, investment funds, large creditors, and domestic and foreign airlines were fighting a fierce battle to gain control of the reconstruction. The chronological of events will be discussed later, but first, I would like to focus on the most important resource in an airline company, the personnel, in other words the transition in the conception of the employees at the frontline.

About 12 years ago, the former president came to rescue Skymark Airlines that was in a financial crisis, using his own fortunes gained from an IT venture, appointing himself as the president, and making a clear strategy to challenge the LCs, as a charismatic leader. However, when charisma shines that bright, it also casts a large and dark shadow. In addition to being an executive, the former president was also an investor who controlled more than 30% of the company stock, and ultimately the large shareholder's views were heard and agreed upon in the management conference over many other views.

The situation created the reckless expansion policy, introducing the midrange A330 and the wide-body A380, which led to its bankruptcy. Moreover, independent study groups, and the costly skill improvement trainings and so forth, were prohibited around the same time. Moreover, the former president took away the independence of the frontline employees as well. On the other hand, while raising the motivation of the employees by establishing a goal to compete with the LCs, there were cases where the employees were forced to work in a mechanical manner to realize a low-cost operation that LCs cannot match. The decision that had the worst external impact was the service policy presented to the passengers in 2012.[1] Not only did the passengers unfavorably receive the content of the proposal by the former president, but the employees also took it as a message that there is no need for them to think spontaneously. Due to this policy, the employees that were planning on acquiring repeat customers through excellent customer service, lost motivation and confidence to work.

1. Moving Forward with Motivated Employees

The resignation of the former president due to the bankruptcy meant freedom from suppression for the employees rather than losing a charismatic leader. The investment fund, Integral Corporation, which immediately became a sponsor, allocated financial support amounting to a maximum of 9 billion JPY, and simultaneously, did not execute workforce reduction which is the first thing that a fund usually does. This gave a sense of security to the frontline employees and served as a new guiding light in place of the former president.

After the bankruptcy, the management team allowed the employees to reinforce customer service and increase the number of personnel for safety, which was not possible before. They thought that they could appeal their smooth reconstruction externally by showing the vitality of the employees to the outside world. The representative example for this is the four cross-organizational committees established in March 2015, each of which is chaired by a company director. The four committees consist of the business improvement committee to reexamine business plans, the service improvement committee to reinforce customer service, the sales promotion committee to raise the recognition level and strengthen the sales, and the workplace environment improvement committee to improve the working environment. Active volunteers from all branches organize these committees, and many comments are made from employees regarding ideas on business improvements.

---

1 The content is such as (1) We will not assist with the storage of luggage (2) We do not require the flight attendants to use polite words.

Improvements were made through the service improvement committee, and services that were not written in the manual could be finally provided flexibly in order to help passengers who are in need. Since this quality of service was initially only possible for LCs, thus the company's service broke the stereotype of LCCs. A sense of crisis existed in the company that it could not repeat the same mistakes of prioritising innovative ideas and strategies without well thought-out plans. There was a concern that the passenger traffic would fall after the announcement of its bankruptcy, but in fact it rose.

Before the bankruptcy, the average daily passenger traffic fell to 11,456 in middle-January 2015, but it recovered to 14,783 in early March. The sales also fell below 900 million JPY per week in the latter half of January 2015, but exceeded 1.2 billion JPY per week in the three weeks from the latter half of February to early March. This was a result of taking the A330 out of service and reducing 152 flights to 128 flights, thereby increasing the passenger load factor and changing the operation to an efficient system. As a result, only 4.5 billion JPY out of the 9 billion JPY that was allocated by Integral Corporation, when announcing its support, has been used. The cash on hand also increased from 1.8 billion JPY in the end of January to 3.7 billion JPY in the end of February. When Skymark Airlines originally operated only using B737 in 2011, the operating margin was 19% and boasted profitability that was higher than other domestic competitors.

The bankruptcy of Skymark Airlines can be traced back to the shift of strategy towards large aircraft that did not match the company's operational needs, and the employees thought, "We can certainly make a profit if we changed the system back to how it was before." In this way, there is a sign of business recovery compared to the immediate aftermath of the bankruptcy, and a cheerful mood started to spread among the employees of the new Skymark Airlines. The momentum is also gaining to build the new Skymark Airlines. This corporate rehabilitation is a first of its kind for Integral Corporation, and hopes for a sponsor who can support the plan to maintain this situation. Integral Corporation believes that it is important to gain the support from the employees of the investment destination by taking care of them before trying to make money from the investment.

The motivation of the employees is inseparable from the fact that Skymark Airlines is an independent entity, and the employees of the new Skymark Airlines continue to believe as being the third key player, and are working towards the goal of becoming an airline equal to the scale of ANAHD and JAL.

◆ 2. The Conflict Between ANAHD Affecting the Process of Civil Rehabilitation

When Skymark Airlines' finances got worse in the middle of November 2014, the company was negotiating to code-share with JAL as a plan for reconstruction. The funding was necessary but a strong partnership with a Japanese LC might jeopardize the independence of the company. That is when code-sharing came up as an excellent plan.

Code-sharing is a system in which the seats of Skymark Airlines are sold using the name of other companies, and the seats are wholesaled to an LC relying on the sales power of the LC. However, JAL had received public funding during its business restructuring and was prohibited from making new investments until 2016. MLIT showed reluctance to code-share only with JAL. Since MLIT insisted that code-sharing should be with ANAHD in addition to JAL, Skymark Airlines started discussing code-sharing with ANAHD in the middle of December 2014 as well. If code-sharing became a reality, it would be an extraordinary partnership with the three domestic airlines that would gain momentum on airplane ticket sales, and Skymark Airlines' financing would improve. Skymark Airlines expected an increase of 1 billion JPY in revenue through code-sharing with LCs, and furthermore strengthen its financial base with support from the investment companies.

However, the negotiation with the main investment company broke down and a foreign LC offered the maintenance parts to be sold off as well. All plans failed to produce expected results. While finance was getting worse, Skymark Airlines started negotiating with ANAHD for code-sharing and the sell-off of the maintenance parts in the end of December 2014. This was a surprising decision by the former president. The company had kept its distance from ANAHD having seen that it invested in independent airlines that entered the airline business at the same time as Skymark

Chapter 6

Airlines one after another, and acquired them into its group as subsidiary companies.

When ANAHD officially started its audit on January 5th, 2015 and closely inspected the finance, they identified payment items that were not evident before. As a matter of fact, ANAHD had briefly audited Skymark Airlines' finance in the midst of December 2014 for the discussion of code-sharing, and at that time they were shown documents presenting cash flow of about 1 billion JPY with no problem regarding the operating funds up to the end of March. However, when a full-blown audit was executed, there were payment items that did not exist in the document shown in December, and it was discovered that the company would be short of funds immediately. Moreover, even during the three days of audit, the cash on hand decreased drastically. ANAHD was surprised at the situation. They notified Skymark Airlines on January 13th, 2015 that purchasing maintenance parts would not be possible, however, code-sharing could be considered even with JAL as a partner.

The notice was a devastating blow to the Skymark Airlines' management who worked through consecutive holidays from January 10th to the 12th to draft in the reconstruction plan with the expectation of aid from ANAHD, and hoped to make payments on 4 billion JPY in lease fees, airport usage fee, etc., at the end of the month. The inability to make payments in January due to the lack of cash on hand was what triggered the bankruptcy. On January 28th, the day of filing for bankruptcy, the cash the company had on hand was only 290 million JPY, and Skymark Airlines as the rebel of the industry at the helm, was at the end of its rope.

The only thing that was left to Skymark Airlines from the series of events was distrust towards ANAHD that triggered the bankruptcy, and since then, an impassable gulf has been created between the two companies. It was interpreted as ANAHD behaving in a way as if to give support, but in reality, tried to ruin Skymark Airlines for the arrival and departure slots at Tokyo International Airport, which emphasized betrayal loud and clear. When they could not get the support from ANAHD, the Skymark Airlines' management notified Integral Corporation who had offered support if the LC gave support as well that they had exhausted all the resources.

However, Integral Corporation conducted a close inspection on the finance again

Chapter 6

untill January 26th, and determined that the company can survive without support from the LCs and declared its support on the 28th of January, when filing for the application of the Civil Rehabilitation Act. Skymark Airlines thought that ANAHD was the last straw that broke Skymark Airlines altogether. Integral Corporation also has its doubts about the position that ANAHD took. As long as ANAHD does not show a strong gesture to recover their relationship, the employees of Skymark Airlines continue to have a strong dislike towards ANAHD. If Integral Corporation had not announced its support, Skymark Airlines would have terminated its service by February for the time being, and would not have maintained the employment of its personnel. For that reason, it would be difficult to resolve the friction between ANAHD, which wants to get actively involved in the business reconstruction, and the Skymark Airlines/Integral coalition. It would be interesting to see how ANAHD can join in to rehabilitate Skymark Airlines. I wish to analyze the reason why ANAHD is preoccupied with Skymark Airlines even under such circumstances, along with the series of events before and after the bankruptcy.

2   Series of Events that Led to the Bankruptcy of the Third-Force Airline

Skymark Airlines is an airline that had its mark in the Japanese aviation history from the beginning till the end. Following the airline deregulation, the chairman of HIS established the company in 1996, and the government supported it as a symbol of liberalization. However, the high-demand arrival and departure slots at Tokyo International Airport was limited, and LCs competed by discounting their fares drastically, since the deregulation of airfares in 2000. As a result, LCCs started to face business difficulties one after the other.

While LCCs such as Air Do, Solaseed Air, and Star Flyer received support from ANAHD, only Skymark Airlines survived through the reconstruction by itself and remained independent. Although the company suffered financial problems in the first half of 2000, since the former president took over in 2004, he advanced various optimizations with so-called basic LCC management strategies such as the standardization of aircraft and reassessment of the service. Though it is a common

Chapter 6

approach for LCCs now, it was innovative at the time. The company belonged to neither JAL nor ANAHD, and had a large presence as the third key airline. In addition to the efforts made by the management, the strength of the JPY helped reduce the cost of fuel and aircraft lease, which was paid in USD, and the company soon became highly profitable.

The reduction of fuel cost and aircraft lease costs, due to the extreme strength of the JPY(exchange rate of 1 USD = 80 JPY or so), helped give lustrous business results with peak sales of 80.2 billion JPY in 2012, with an operating profit of 15.2 billion JPY and cash on hand of 30.6 billion JPY, which ranked the company as the third most profitable airline in the world. However, 2012 was the first year for LCCs to start their services in Japan, which was then followed by Peach Aviation, Jetstar Japan, and AirAsia Japan. Skymark Airlines had the pride of having started the price war in the Japanese airline market but its originality began to fade. Even so, the company continued to pursue the expansion policy supported by the momentum of the profitable business results. It was around that time that the steps Skymark Airlines took backfired, such as the decision to introduce A330 and A380 and so forth. Following the monetary easing of Abenomics, the JPY lost value to a level of 1 USD = 100 JPY, causing the external environment to change completely. For example, the drastic rise in fuel cost and USD denominated aircraft lease fees.

Meanwhile, the A330 that Skymark Airlines began to introduce successively from June 2012 was beginning to have a large impact on the business foundation. The number of seats on A330 was reduced to increase the comfort of the passengers in order to differentiate itself from LCCs. However, the first year of LCCs brought a fierce competition, and the passenger load factor did not increase much as expected. The company tried promotional activities such as introducing flight attendants with miniskirts in March 2014, but the operational cost was double the amount for B737, which Skymark Airlines used to operate, and the more Skymark Airlines flew the more it lost its money.

Additionally, the decisive damage to the business was done by the purchase plan for A380 and its cancellation. At the time of good business results, the company failed to make a correct future ascertainment and planned to enter the international

Chapter 6

market with A380, signing the contract with Airbus to purchase six A380 in February 2011. The company planned to provide seats with a premium feel that are cheaper than LCs. However, the company had difficulty paying the advance payment due to poor business results in 2014. When the request was made to cancel the order, Airbus demanded the payment of 82 billion JPY as the penalty for contract breach, which ultimately put the company in financial difficulties. Other than that, the entry of other LCCs, and the rise in fuel cost due to cheaper JPY, affected the company and it entered the final stage of walking the tightrope of financing. Suffering from poor business performance, Skymark Airlines abandoned self-reconstruction and filed for the application of the Civil Rehabilitation Act on January 28th, 2015. Total liabilities amounted to around 71 billion JPY and the company stock was delisted on March 1st, 2015. The former president who acted as the president of Skymark Airlines for 11 years and built a highly profitable organization, took responsibility for the failure of the business and resigned on January 28th.

◻ 1. Financial Condition of Skymark Airlines Prior to the Bankruptcy

The details of the financial condition when filing for the application of the Civil Rehabilitation Act needs to be reviewed in order to analyze why Skymark Airlines made the mistake ascertaining the warning for bankruptcy at the time of investment decision. The total asset of Skymark Airlines at the end of September 2014 was 77.4 billion JPY and the capital-to-asset ratio, a number indicating the financial soundness, was 49.7%. The company with this ratio of more than 40%, is generally considered to have low risk of a bankruptcy, and although the performance, past the peak of March 2012, had worsened, the capital-to-asset ratio was trending at a relatively high level. In reality, however, drastic business expansion strategies such as the purchase plan for A380 steadily deteriorated the health of the financial strength. Skymark Airlines had no interest-bearing debts such as loans or corporate bonds, and it operated without bank borrowings, therefore had no main bank or financing credit facilities. As a result, the funds for investment basically had to be earned from its main business. When the business became unstable, the former president frequently used his own private funds to undertake capital increase. Skymark Airlines' business was having difficulties to the extent that it had to rely on the former president's own money.

Chapter 6

◘ 2. Cash on Hand Decreased Despite Good Business Results

The total investment for the introduction of A380 exceeded 100 billion JPY, an amount greater than double the annual revenue, with the plan to start the payment from March 2011 over several years. The exact purchase price for the A380 was not made clear, but even if it were 27 to 28 billion JPY per aircraft, an incredible bargain price, the total would have been over 70 billion JPY. Additionally, related parts worth about 5 billion JPY would be necessary. However, the operating profit, an indication of the cash income from the main business, has taken a downturn from the beginning of March 2012. This was due to an increase in long-term deposits paid to the aircraft lease company for the increased number of A330.

Moreover, the untimely and drastic devaluation of JPY put the pressure on the revenue of Skymark Airlines, and likewise the operating profit started to diminish instantly. The 9.6 billion JPY ending in March, 2012, became 1 billion JPY in the following year, 2013, and was reduced to 350 million JPY in the next year, and in the first half of 2014, the company was finally losing money. It was a critical situation where the dependable main business, which should be generating cash, was actually losing money.

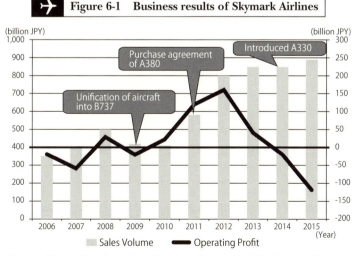

Figure 6-1 Business results of Skymark Airlines

Source: Created by the author based on Skymark Airlines' annual report

On the other hand, the cash outflow for investment continued to exceed 10 billion JPY from 2012, and 30.6 billion JPY cash on hand at the peak of March 2012 was reduced drastically to 7 billion JPY by the end of March 2014. In the aviation industry, it is normal to hold a reserve of 20 to 30 billion JPY to prepare for the transition in the external factors such as the fuel cost. Skymark Airlines had fallen to a level much less than that, and by the end of September 2014, the cash on hand had decreased to 4.5 billion JPY. The sell-off of the maintenance parts and leaseback was executed, and 1.8 billion JPY of cash was secured by the end of October 2014, at which point, all that can be sold were sold off. About 30% of the total asset of Skymark Airlines is in the construction-in-progress account, and almost all of it consists of the prepayment of 25.3 billion JPY for A380. There was a possibility that it can be confiscated by Airbus and could not be called an actual asset. Even from the finance perspective, the investment strategy by the former president was admittedly reckless.

This time, the source of fund for Integral Corporation's support for Skymark Airlines is a fund totaling 442 billion JPY formed in November 2014. Based on the agreement with the institutional investors, who provided the financing, the fund cannot invest more than a total of 20% to 30% in a single investment. For this reason, the amount of investment and loan is limited to about 13 billion JPY or less. The bridge loan executed in February is called DIP Finance,[2] and is a secure method with middle-level of risk. If there are USD denominated payments at an investment decision stage, it is natural to have currency hedging and risk-taking tolerance measures. An excuse cannot be made that a prepayment cannot be paid all of a sudden. The fund that was requested to make an investment asked for detailed business documents from Skymark Airlines but hardly nothing was provided.

---

2 This financing is for the bankrupt corporation to avoid failing due to shortage of operating funds before it receives approval for its reconstruction plan. Compared to the financing executed before the bankruptcy called "rehabilitation claim" which has a low repayment rate, DIP financing is paid back as "common benefit claims" preferentially. It has been used for the restructuring of JAL and Mycal Corp. previously. However, as an investment target, its return (profitability) is not that high. The main target for Integral Corporation is the investment scheduled after the rehabilitation plan approval in the latter part of June 2015. The success or failure of this depends largely on the selection of the cooperating business partner.

Moreover, at the time of filing for the application of the Civil Rehabilitation Act, though Skymark Airlines announced that the total amount of liabilities was 71 billion JPY, the aggregated sum from the creditors grew to 300 billion JPY. Skymark Airlines became a corporation ruled by an authoritarian former president, and the price it had to pay for misreading the winning financial investment strategy was enormous.

Table 6-1 Series of events that led to the bankruptcy of Skymark Airlines

	Activity involving Skymark Airlines	Financial condition
July 27, 2014	Airbus announced the cancellation of sell-off/purchase contract for the wide-body A380	700 million USD (82 billion JPY) as penalty for the breach of contract
July 31		5.7 billion JPY of loss for April-June accounting period / "serious doubt" for business continuity
September 30		4.5 billion JPY of cash on hand / fear of running out of cash by end of November
October 30		5.7 billion JPY of loss for April-September accounting period / expected loss of 13.6 billion JPY for full year
October 31		Over 3 billion JPY of cash on hand
November 21	Announce partnership negotiation with JAL / MLIT expresses disapproval	
November 30		Over 1 billion JPY of cash on hand
December 10	Requested support from ANAHD also / considering financing from external sources	
December 19	Airbus declared that it is preparing to file suit at English court	
December 31		600 million JPY of cash on hand
Early January, 2015		Former president loaned 700 million JPY of personal money to the company
January 9	News report of a request to invest to ANAHD	
January 13	Terminated negotiation with ANAHD / request financing to various investment funds	
January 15	ANAHD and JAL basically agreed to code-sharing	About 5 billion JPY of capital increased through private placement of new shares if the application for code-sharing is completed
January 21	Canceled the application for code-sharing	
January 28	Completed the application of the Civil Rehabilitation Act / charismatic former president resigned	4.5 billion JPY of bridge loan from Integral Corporation / 300 million JPY of cash on hand

Source: Created by the author based on Skymark Airlines' annual report and MLIT document

Chapter 6

⊞ 3 As a Result of the All-Out War After the Bankruptcy, "Skymark Airlines' Proposal" Passed

In July 2015, while Intrepid Aviation Partners, who objected to ANAHD's support, was negotiating with Delta Air Lines in the U.S. to join as a sponsor. ANAHD, who was to become a sponsor for Skymark Airlines, was conducting an all-out war by directly visiting the voters behind the scenes and requesting them to vote early so that they would not change their minds. The consolidated sales revenue of Delta Air Lines for 2014 was about 40.3 billion USD which is about three times the scale of ANAHD, and if Delta Air Lines used its size as an advantage to unsettle the large creditors, then ANAHD would be put in a disadvantage position.

On the Pacific routes, United Airlines is code-sharing with ANAHD, and American Airlines with JAL. Delta Air Lines has been using Narita International Airport thus far as a transit base for US–Asia routes. It is one of the powerful players in Narita International Airport along with ANAHD and JAL. Since Narita International Airport is a hub airport in Asia for Delta Air Lines, acquiring a partner in Japan was an essential business strategy. Therefore, it announced its support for business when JAL went bankrupt in 2010, but JAL decided to remain in the Oneworld Alliance and continued its partnership with American Airlines.

In this way, the big reason for Delta Air Lines to announce to be a sponsor for Skymark Airlines, which was under the protection of the Civil Rehabilitation Act, was the absence of a partner in Japan. The benefit of a partnership is being able to expand the network efficiently by utilizing the partner's routes. When it becomes a sponsor of Skymark Airlines, Delta Air Lines, not only could expect attracting passengers from various areas of Japan, but also make investments to have Skymark Airlines service Asian routes.

108 companies out of the 193 creditors of Skymark Airlines had business transactions with ANAHD, and the ANAHD management worked hard to collect the votes. Moreover, ANAHD approached and began negotiating with the large creditors holding the greater part of the vote before the small creditors in order to collect

majority of votes. Intrepid Aviation Partners, a rival of ANAHD, held 37.91% of votes, and in order for ANAHD to obtain more than half the votes for its support plan, it had to gain approval from all the remaining large creditors: Airbus, US aircraft leasing company CIT and UK Rolls-Royce.

However, Delta Air Lines is a lager customer of Airbus, Rolls-Royce and CIT than ANAHD. Moreover, the top executive at the U.S. headquarters was serious enough

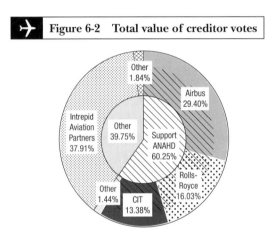

Figure 6-2　Total value of creditor votes

Source: Created by the author based on Skymark Airlines' annual report

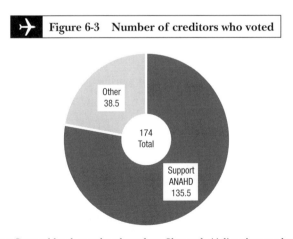

Figure 6-3　Number of creditors who voted

Source: Created by the author based on Skymark Airlines' annual report

to make direct contact with the large creditors. On the other hand, ANAHD had a deep business relationship with Rolls-Royce only for engine purchases, but the transactions with Airbus were for small and medium aircraft only. As for CIT, there were no business transactions at all. In the Skymark Airlines' creditors meeting on August 5th, 2015, two rehabilitation plans, the ANAHD plan and the Delta Air Lines plan were to be discussed, which was extraordinary in a civil rehabilitation proceeding.

In order to decide on a rehabilitation plan, two conditions must be met: more than half of the total creditor amount and a majority of the creditor's votes are necessary. As long as the large creditors show disapproval to ANAHD's support plan, the voting for this is not expected to proceed smoothly. However, 135.5 companies out of 174 creditors who voted, and in terms of value held by voters, all large creditors except Intrepid Aviation Partners approved the ANAHD's support plan.

◘ 1. The Key to Business Reconstruction Is the Negotiation to Reduce the Debt

Civil rehabilitation proceedings is business reconstruction in exchange for the pain of the creditors. Generally, the creditors are forced to cut their claim by 90%, and if the stockholder's rights are untouched, then only those of the creditors, which should naturally have priority over the stockholders, will be sacrificed. Therefore, the rehabilitation proceeding approves 100% capital reduction for the insolvent enterprise. Although Skymark Airlines was not insolvent in the accounting period of September 2014, if the damage claim by Airbus is recorded as a liability, then the 100% capital reduction will be possible. The purpose of this proceeding is to reduce the liabilities thus far and have the company continue to run business so that even a small amount of money can be returned to the creditors.

From the creditors' point of view, if the company goes bankrupt, the money that rightfully should be returned would be lost, and this proceeding will make it possible to return some of it, however small, back to them. Therefore, they would reluctantly agree to the reduction of liability amounts in order to restructure the company. In the case of the new Skymark Airlines, the court of justice decided in April 2016

Chapter 6

whether the 300 billion JPY that was claimed by the creditor side was appropriate or not, and the claim amount was fixed. The negotiation then began between the new Skymark Airlines and the creditors regarding how much the claim could be reduced. For creditors such as Airbus and the aircraft leasing company, they want to be paid back as much as possible. However, if they do not agree to make any reductions, then chain-reaction bankruptcy is a possibility, and is faced with a tough decision.

Whether the new Skymark Airlines can restructure its business smoothly depends on whether Airbus and the leasing company would agree on reducing their claim amount, and in order to do so, the support of the LCs is essential. Integral Corporation has offered not only a bridge loan but also an investment, and plans to purchase fuel and sell seats jointly with a business sponsor, with the premise of a business tie-up between the airline and the capital. If an LC becomes a sponsor, it is possible for Integral Corporation to propose a business expansion as well in exchange for the reduction of the claimed amount.

The most important point at this time is the corporate value of Skymark Airlines. If the total amount of liabilities is ultimately determined to be 300 billion JPY, and the sponsor estimates the value of Skymark Airlines as so, then the reduction in claim needs to be 270 billion JPY, which affects the foundation of the restructuring. In order to judge the corporate value, the current cash flow and the like need to be closely assessed, but there was a tug-of-war here as well. The corporation that announced its candidacy wanted to perform the asset assessment, but Integral Corporation, who had already provided funding and took the initiative, did not give approval easily. If Integral Corporation imagines that its support alone is insufficient, then it would allow ANAHD and other corporations to perform the assessment. However, Integral Corporation announced that the total amount of liabilities of 300 billion JPY is within the expected range and that it can proceed even without the support of an LC.

Skymark Airlines believes that it is not necessarily beneficial to have an LC infused capital. The financing relief by the loan from Integral Corporation and the support from the recovery of business, made its obsession as both the third key player and an independent airline come to the fore again. Integral Corporation thought that a

Chapter 6

solo rehabilitation method without a business sponsor would be a potential choice, and in that case, it will take the company to be listed. However, what the lawyers for the Skymark Airlines' restructuring focused on was the feasibility of the restructuring plan and the merit for the creditors, employees and passengers, and thought that being the third key player was secondary importance.

One point that was argued to the end was the investment ratio. The investment ratio of ANAHD alone would be 19.9%, but it was counting on acquiring a majority when combined with a closely associated financial institution. As the result of the negotiation, it was settled that Integral Corporation will invest 50.1%, but the new president will be selected by ANAHD, which indicated the powerful influence of the LC. It remains to be seen whether the new Skymark Airlines' independence can be maintained.

2. The Opportunity and Risk ANAHD Obtained in Exchange for Skymark Airlines

In late July 2015, a consensus was created in the new Skymark Airlines that the restoration is practically impossible without ANAHD, who has abundant track records in safety management and flight operation, knows about the airline industry inside out, and has the know-how of reconstruction and good relationship with Airbus. At the time, ANAHD obtained approval from Airbus, CIT, and Rolls-Royce, the largest customers of Airbus, which also announced support for ANAHD resulting in changing the tide. CIT, who did not have any business transactions in Japan yet, thought that a potential future business with ANAHD would give it a leg up to enter the Japanese market. Intrepid Aviation heard from Airbus in advance that if negotiations on A380 were completed with ANAHD, Airbus would support the ANAHD plan.

However, while A380 is an enormous aircraft with a catalog price of 430 million USD and a maximum of 853 seats capable of transporting double the number of passengers of a conventional aircraft, it cannot be effectively utilized by an airline without a network of routes and sales power to fulfill this demand. This is a troublesome aircraft that had no orders for the last 2 years, and whose purchase plan became the trigger for the bankruptcy of Skymark Airlines. The contract was

Chapter 6

Table 6-2 Details of Airbus A380

	Airbus	
A380	Price	432.6 million USD
	Seat number	544–853 seats
	Cruising distance	15,200 km

Source: Created by the author based on the website of Airbus

signed at an extraordinary price of 27 to 28 billion JPY per aircraft, since the JPY was strong at the time, and Airbus wanted to sell large aircraft into the Japanese market. At this point, ANAHD stated that it would take over the aircraft at an ever lower price of 20 billion JPY including the modification fee and so forth, and that it would consider purchasing the aircraft if the price of A380 was lower.

ANAHD's domestic share became overwhelming with Skymark Airlines as a subsidiary. However, in exchange, it had to purchase the wide-body A380. Investment after the purchase was necessary since it was a new aircraft to be introduced into Japan, and the construction of a new hanger for A380 and trainings for maintenance engineers and pilots were necessary. Moreover, since the A380 aircraft is large, there is a disadvantage that the current regulation does not allow it to fly to and from Tokyo International Airport. However, ANAHD promised to purchase three A380 in return for obtaining the approval from the large creditors. Moreover, the reason it is overly eager for the support, knowing that Skymark Airlines resents it, is because it will strengthen its price leadership for domestic flights. In the domestic market, the so-called third key player, Skymark Airlines, was the only one left that upset the market with a price war, and was an obstruction in ANAHD's side.

The 36 arrival and departure slots that Skymark Airlines had at Tokyo International Airport were attractive for the investment in Skymark Airlines this time, and were very precious rights that could not be given to another competitor. The arrival and departure slots at Tokyo International Airport was worth 2 to 3 billion JPY per slot per year, and ANAHD would use them through code-sharing and prevent them from being used by JAL and foreign airline competitors, thus creating a firm anti-JAL network. ANAHD has taken control of three failed LCCs so far and has created a win-win relationship through code-sharing and the like. Although regulations

Chapter 6

forbid an investment of more than 20% and thus cannot be called a group company, the management is filled with ANAHD people, and the management can practically be called an ANAHD management. Although the Anti-trust Law does not allow a full control over airfares and networks, ANAHD will have most of the share at Tokyo International Airport and this will establish a battle array against JAL.

There is a strong feeling to reinforce the anti-JAL network before the restriction on JAL to make any new investments is abolished in 2017. Moreover, MLIT has a strong wish to locate domestic airlines in Tokyo International Airport. As a result of becoming a sponsor of the new Skymark Airlines this time, 65% of the domestic airlines that have rights (such as the arrival and departure slots) in Tokyo International Airport have been collected in the ANA group. As a result, the low-priced routes are eliminated. For instance, Star Flyer which had been selling the Tokyo International Airport–Fukuoka Airport route for 10,000 JPY terminated the ticket sales right after ANA made an investment in it at the end of 2012 and substantially raised the airfare.

By acquiring Skymark Airlines, the domestic airlines that arrive and departure Tokyo International Airport are reduced to two major groups, ANAHD and JAL, and the brake is put on the price war, which means the airfare can be raised. There is a concern inside the new Skymark Airlines and Integral Corporation that when the influence of ANAHD on the new Skymark Airline becomes great and the Japanese aviation market is taken up by the two LCs, then there would not be any competition to create a distorted competitive environment in the domestic aviation industry resulting in the price of the airfare to soar.

Since starting its service in 1998, Skymark Airlines introduced competition into the oligopolistic market and survived as the third key player, neither belonging to ANAHD nor JAL for 17 years, during which the significance of the company's existence and its social mission was to compete with low-price as a weapon, and reduce the airfare for the benefit of the passengers. That sense of existence became especially significant from 2004 onward when the former president took over the business.

Chapter 6

Figure 6-4   Domestic airline shares of arrival and departure slots at Tokyo International Airport

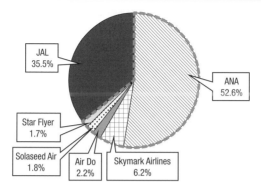

Source: Created by the author based on the website of MLIT

However, the new Skymark Airlines became an typical airline after the former president left. During the days of the former president, the low-price policy was firmly kept thereby even yield management was not done. Since then, however, the airfare was adjusted higher during the peak season, and as a result, the new Skymark Airlines' business became steady, and the cumulative operating profit turned positive for 2015. Concequently, the domestic aviation market has been conquered by ANAHD.

The now Skymark Airlines' initiative makes a positive contribution to ANAHD's business. In the last nine months, ANAHD's profit from the domestic route rose 3.5 billion JPY excluding the effects of low-priced fuel. Since the investment for the new Skymark Airlines is 3.5 billion JPY, it can be said that the investment is already recovered and a certain level of success has been achieved. However, it should not be forgotten that the investment is not limited to 3.5 billion JPY, and the additional large expenditure for the purchase of three A380 is taken on as a risk. Airbus demanded ANAHD to purchase not only the A380 but also other flight equipment required to operate, including maintenance was the total amount of the transaction. ANAHD and Delta Air Lines have negotiated repeatedly with Airbus regarding the possibility of expansion in future businesses. However, the proposal of the transaction size from ANAHD was incomparably bigger than that of Delta Air Lines.

Chapter 6

More than the rights and interests that Skymark Airlines held at Tokyo International Airport, the support for Skymark Airlines meant more economical rationality to ANAHD. There was a long-standing rivalry with JAL at the root. JAL declared bankruptcy in 2010 and rehabilitated with the support from the government, and now its financial strength is more solid than ANAHD. Although it is prohibited from making active investments until the end of March 2017. It is expected that it will change to the offensive thereafter. ANAHD believes that if it cannot acquire the new Skymark Airlines now, someday it will lose to competitive battle against JAL, and if Delta Air Lines, one of the world's largest foreign airlines, enters the Japanese market, it would become a greater threat than JAL. The ANAHD management team must have had such strong sense of this imminent crisis.

ANAHD must have thought that an investment after the bankruptcy, when the huge debt is drastically cut, would be more rational. Moreover, as long as the claims are well sorted out and the business is relieved of burden, the airline is a type of business that can rapidly recover. This is the reason ANAHD is actively giving it support.

Table 6-3 Major internal and external events after Skymark Airlines' bankruptcy

	Internal	External
January 28, 2015	Filed for the application of the Civil Rehabilitation Act	
January 30	Serious warning from MLIT for insufficient maintenance	
February 1	Middle-range A330 taken out of service	
February 5		Signed sponsor contract with the investment fund, Integral Corporation
Late March	Started training employees	
April 1	11 new employees joined	
April 22		ANAHD announced to participate as sponsor
May 29		Skymark Airlines submitted the creditors' rehabilitation plan. The largest creditor, Intrepid Aviation Partners, submitted its own rehabilitation plan
June 1	Invited proposal for business improvement	
July 15		Delta Air Lines announced it would participate in Intrepid's plan
August 5		Skymark Airlines' creditor's plan is approved overwhelmingly at the creditors meeting.
September 29	100% reduction of capital and capital increase by new sponsor. New organization started after the extraordinary meeting of stockholders	

Source: Created by author based on Skymark Airlines' annual reports and MLIT documents

The Japanese aviation market is structured as such that the competitive principle does not function, and the airlines that should be weeded out by competition are forcibly kept alive by the aviation policy. The reconstruction of JAL is a symbol of the warped aviation policy, and ANAHD was the reason and the source of power to strive as one for the acquisition of Skymark Airlines.

4 Major Issues of the Aviation Policy Regarding Skymark Airlines' Rehabilitation

Skymark Airlines is the key figure that spearheaded the new entry into the airline industry when the deregulation was active discussed in the latter part of 1990. At the time, various business models turned up in Europe and the U.S., but the business models of only three companies remained unchanged in Japan, and the nationwide latent demand for aviation could not be fully cultivated. Pressured by the public opinion that the aviation administration should approve new entries that have the capability and will, the decision was made to approve new entries. Although there were several important phases leading to Skymark Airlines' bankruptcy, at a certain time it tried to code-share flights arriving and departing from Tokyo International Airport with JAL in order to restructure the business. However, since MLIT disapproved this restructuring plan, Skymark Airlines had no choice but to explore a partnership with ANAHD.

The company had two problems, one being the private enterprise's bankruptcy and rehabilitation, and the other being an important event that questions the government policies regarding competition between airlines. Since the aviation industry is an industry based on permits and licenses, MLIT and the government need to watch the progress of Skymark Airlines' reconstruction carefully.

1. Fair Allocation Method for the Arrival and Departure Slots

There are two most important issues in the Japanese aviation policy. First topic is to achieve the goal to create an environment, where all airports in the nation can supply sufficient arrival and departure slots, and that users can freely utilize the

Chapter 6

airport. Since the number of arrival and departure slots have increased in a congested airport,[3] the way it is fairly allocated to the airlines, directly affects the business performance of an airline, making it the most delicate policy issue. As explained in Chapter 3, the slots of Tokyo International Airport are said to be essential facilities and it is not easy to increase them. Airline companies are constantly thinking of important management strategies in order to own such facilities.

Among them, the number of arrival and departure slots at Tokyo International Airport, which are highly valuable, is difficult to increase. In order to prepare for the 2020 Tokyo Olympics, MLIT is aiming to develop new flight routes[4] flying over Tokyo Metropolitan area, but is facing a difficult situation due to the resistance from the residents of Shinagawa area who are directly under the flight path. There will be a debate over the allocation of the arrival and departure slots by the government, and if there is a bidding for them, they will be sold at a high price, which will be reflected onto the airfare, resulting in heavy burden on the users and the airlines.

There is a limit to the number of arrival and departure slots, which are the most important producer goods at Tokyo International Airport, and how it is allocated determines the profits for the airlines. The question at hand is then how to fairly allocate the essential facilities such as the valuable arrival and departure slots at

---

3 An airport that requires an approval in advance from MLIT before starting service. It is prescribed by Aviation Law and currently four airports come under it: Narita International Airport, Tokyo International Airport, Kansai International Airport and Osaka International Airport. The approval period is set at 5 years and it is renewed upon application from the airline. Skymark Airlines has renewed its approval on December 2014, but it is conditioned that the airline reports the finance condition and business plan to MLIT until the time business improves.

4 New flight routes established by loosening the flight restriction over Tokyo Metropolitan area and Kanagawa Prefecture in order to extend the departure and arrival capacity of Tokyo International Airport in preparation for 2020 Tokyo Olympics. The expert committee of MLIT proposed it in the summer of 2014. As a general rule, flights are limited only over the Tokyo Bay currently, but take-offs and landings are possible from many directions if flights over the metropolis is possible and many flights can be accommodated. However, there is a strong concern from the local residents concerning the noise and such.

Tokyo International Airport. For these reasons, the actual aviation market is not structured in such that the airlines can completely and freely develop businesses. The airports in suburbs, the so-called secondary airports, have restrictions on their usage, and led to business limitation for the four LCC companies that entered the market after 1990. It is important for the LCCs to put forth their best features and cut their way into the market drastically. The successful LCCs such as Southwest Airlines in the U.S. purchases 50 to 100 of the same type of aircraft simultaneously, and are successful at reducing the airfare.

In order to do such, there needs to be a sufficient number of arrival and departure slots, but the number of arrival and departure slots at Tokyo International Airport are in short supply compared to the demand. In such a case, in overseas, the supply is increased or the arrival and departure slots are sold and bought between the airlines. Moreover, the idea of acquiring more arrival and departure slots by merging with another company is not common in Japan. The fact that MLIT initiated the three domestic airlines to code-share as part of Skymark Airlines' relief measure is a symbolic act of the Japanese aviation policy.

There are several methods[5] for the allocation internationally, but in Japan, MLIT decides it consistently. Skymark Airlines had 36 of these arrival and departure slots at Tokyo International Airport and it represented 6.2% of the essential facility rights at the airport, and ranked third in the domestic share after ANAHD(52.6%) and JAL(35.5%). As mentioned earlier, code-sharing with JAL would create a concern that it would, in effect, lead to the increase in share for JAL and this led MLIT to express disapproval. The restriction is based on a document created by MLIT on August 10th, 2012 describing the policy guidelines giving consideration to the competitive environment between JAL and ANAHD. On the other hand, if ANAHD made the investment in Skymark Airlines, the share of the arrival and departure slots at Tokyo International

---

5 How to efficiently and fairly utilize the arrival and departure slots at a congested airport has been the target of discussion for policymaking for a long time. Four methods were proposed in the 1998 Council for Transport Policy: (1) Evaluation method (MLIT Civil Aviation Bureau decides the number of distribution slots based on the comprehensive evaluation of airlines.) (2) Auction method (3) Lottery method, and (4) Equal distribution. Although many comments recognizing the effectiveness of the (2) Auction method was made by the experts, the (1) Evaluation method is still being used.

Chapter 6

Airport for the airline that receives the investment from ANAHD would exceed 60%. Then there is a fear that Japan Fair Trade Commission would cast doubt on this situation, and MLIT would need to be very careful how it deals with it. In other words, how Skymark Airlines rehabilitates is almost equivalent to how to allocate the arrival and departure slots at Tokyo International Airport, and it is an important issue that manifests the problem with the Japanese aviation policy.

2. Promoting the Market Competition Without the Government's Lead

The second issue is how to strengthen the competitiveness of Japanese airlines. The Japanese aviation industry continued with a "45/47 Structure" until the latter part of 1990s, and additionally, the business scope of each company was prescribed for a long time. As a result of the government strictly regulating the number of flights to be flown with which aircraft on which routes domestically and internationally, the airfare system of the three companies became exactly the same. In other words, there was absolutely no competition in the Japanese aviation industry. It was significant that Skymark Airlines entered the Japanese market under these conditions and consistently led the airfare war maintaining the position as the third key player. The company claims it is its social right to do such activities.

When these two issues are considered as a base, MLIT may support the rehabilitation of Skymark Airlines maintaining its position as an independent airline. It is thought that in the future, this trend may become a factor in changing the flow of Skymark Airlines' reconstruction. If the restriction on foreign investments are eliminated, there may be a foreign corporation that would want to effectively utilize Skymark Airlines. In addition, if no investments from Japanese LCs are made and the management policy of a foreign corporation is strictly executed 100%, it enables Skymark Airlines to restart without changing its business model of being the "third-force airline".

However, in Japan, it is customary to get an approval for even those parts requiring no approval from the aviation law such as discontinuance of a non-profitable route. Therefore, it is necessary for an airline management to have the know-how to negotiate and convince the politicians and government officials. The role of the third key player who brought the competition to the domestic airline industry is great and its future is being closely watched.

3. Impact of Skymark Airlines' Bankruptcy on Regional Airports

The future of Skymark Airlines' rehabilitation is extremely important to the regional airports. The impact was especially large to Kobe Airport, which relied on Skymark Airlines for 70% of its total number of routes. Skymark Airlines treated Kobe as the base for Western Japan and made investments such as maintaining hangers. Kobe Airport was used as a base for Western Japan even after filing for the application of the Civil Rehabilitation Act, and although the possibility is low for the airline to withdraw completely from the airport, the routes will all be scrutinized. Of the eight routes being serviced, the routes to Tokyo International Airport has a passenger load factor of about 63.1% and remaines strong, and therefore, there is a good chance that the service would continue in the future. However, when compared to Peach Aviation, which also has two routes in Kansai International Airport with a passenger load factor of over 80% consistently, Skymark Airlines is certainly under tough circumstances. Kobe Airport's existence is determined entirely by Skymark Airlines and there will be a focus on future activities to promote the utilization of Kobe City.

Moreover, the domestic routes to and from Ibaraki Airport are all serviced by Skymark Airlines and Ibaraki Prefecture, which operate the airport, has a strong sense of crisis, and is taking prompt measures to deal with the situation after the filing of the application for the Civil Rehabilitation Act. Ibaraki Prefecture is taking actual utilization promotion measures such as budgeting 600 million JPY for the promotional program fee in the supplementary budget bill for the 2014 general account budget, and has proven track record of contributing greatly to the passenger load factor. Ibaraki Prefecture said that Skymark Airlines' service increased the convenience of the locals in the prefecture and created new demand for flights.

This kind of visible local support is a factor that positively influences the decision to continue or eliminate routes. It is expected that each route will be closely reexamined in the future. Within Skymark Airlines' rehabilitation plan for profitability and

Chapter 6

future prospect, the routes with low passenger load factor will perhaps be abolished. Skymark Airlines itself has repeatedly appealed the importance of being the third key player for the past 17 years before the bankruptcy and many consumers have recognized it. This fact is clearly evident from the disappointment of the regional airports after its bankruptcy.

✈ 5 Start of a New Organization: Business Rehabilitation by the Three Forces

There was constant battle for the selection of a sponsor for Skymark Airlines' restructuring, and finally, the new organization has been launched. In the new Skymark Airlines with capital injection from Integral Corporation and ANAHD and so forth, Integral Corporation with 50.1% of the shares has appointed the chairman and two directors (a key figure from Integral Corporation and a proper employee from Skymark Airlines). Other than the directors, the important positions such as accounting, general affairs, human resources, and maintenance have been filled with Skymark Airlines' full-time employees.

On the other hand, ANAHD, with 49.9% of the shares, is participating in the management as the official business sponsor with the approval of the extraordinary meeting of shareholders on September 29th, 2015, and about ten ANAHD employees with experience in maintenance, including the president from Development Bank of Japan (DBJ) and two directors, have started working in the new Skymark Airlines. In fact, though it did not directly relate to a problem for safe flights, there were series of inadequacies in documentation from January 2015 such as the certificates of airworthiness that normally should have been prepared, which MLIT determined that the company did not adhere to the fundamentals of an airline operation, and including those scheduled for regular maintenances, four aircraft out of 26 B737 were not able to be utilized. In order to improve the situation, Skymark Airlines had no choice but to rely on the know-how of the maintenance specialists dispatched from ANAHD.

For the time being, the company is aiming for relisting after 5 years, and the three powers, the employees of the new Skymark Airlines, Integral Corporation, and ANAHD are in a delicate relationship, keeping an eye on one another. In preparation for this type of situation, when the organization drastically changed course from the authoritarian rule of the former president, the new Skymark Airlines had introduced the executive officer system[6] in secret after the bankruptcy, in February 2015. Even when a sponsor and its people are introduced into the new business organization, the frontline is operated by the new Skymark Airlines' proper employees and even when the executive board is at an equilibrium state, the young senior officers were being trained so that they can put forth their own uniqueness into their services.

The source of motivation of the new Skymark Airlines' employees for rehabilitation is in the future "growth". Before the bankruptcy, even when the company atmosphere was stifling, to challenge the LCs as the "third key player" and the expansion of service routes gave hope to many employees. If given the benefit of the doubt, the decision to introduce A330 and A380, which became the reason for the bankruptcy later on, may have been to give hope to the frontline people with an aircraft that even ANAHD or JAL were not using. The feeling of reality of catching up with the LCs may have been the real motivation power for the employees, but currently the growth scenario to pursue the LCs is not visible. The reason is that the reconstruction should get the company back to its state before changing direction towards expansion, when only the small B737 aircraft were flying.

The medium-term management plan in the contract signed by Integral Corporation and ANAHD with the stockholders, forecasted sales of 2017 to be about 83 billion JPY and the operating profit of 3 to 5 billion JPY, which is an extremely conservative plan when compared to 2012, when the record profit was 15.3 billion JPY. The performance of an airline is affected by the currency rate and the fuel oil market price, and depending on code-sharing and route strategy, there is a good chance for an uplift in performance. Even under such conditions, there was an operating profit in 2015. The passengers that left around the time of the bankruptcy have started to come back, and if all 26 of the B737 begin to fly and the code-share with

---

6   The executive officer system is an attempt to promote management efficiency through the activation of the boad directors and the expedition of the decesion-making process, or to reinforce supervisory function as a part of the reform of the boad of directors.

Chapter 6

ANAHD, then the performance of the business would improve even further. This is not an unachievable goal at all. However, the goal for Integral Corporation is to increase the corporate value by the time of relisting, and it does not have the control over the growth strategy after it sells its stake.

The proper employees of the new Skymark Airlines must keep in mind that the real battle starts from here. Up till now, the battle was fought outside the company, but they must realize that the battle has moved within the company, and they need to commit themselves to the rehabilitation of the company.

1. Multitude of Issues for the New Skymark Airlines' Independence

There are many issues regarding the decision-making of the new management team, being stuck between two sponsors with entirely different expectations. ANAHD believes that the investment is meaningless unless there is synergy with ANA group. This confrontation is conspicuously shown in the problem of ANAHD's ticket reservation and sales system in Skymark Airlines. ANAHD has so far implemented the original reservation system into the LCCs that were acquired and integrated into the system. They believe that by purchasing the seats from Skymark Airlines and selling them to the consumer, thereby taking on the seat inventory risk by ANAHD, the burden on Skymark Airlines will be reduced and would be effective for the reconstruction.

While ANAHD claims that the stabilization of revenue foundation through code-sharing is essential for rehabilitation and the implementation of the ANAHD system is necessary for that purpose, Integral Corporation insists on independence and refused stubbornly. The reason being that the strength of Skymark Airlines is the low airfare, and if the ANAHD system is implemented, there will be restrictions on the flexibility of pricing and detailed data such as the number of customer, customer gender information, the ratio of sales through travel agencies will fall into ANAHD's hands.

In contrast, ANAHD thinks that it is the trend of airlines globally to use highly flexible reservation systems to connect with other airlines, and though it normally costs 3% of expenditures to implement a highly flexible reservation system, ANAHD system is inexpensive, costing only 1%, and will contribute substantially to the reconstruction of the new Skymark Airlines. However, this type of battle regarding the ANAHD system implementation is already delaying the new Skymark Airlines' restructuring schedule. While the opinion of the new management team is divided, the prospect for realizing code-sharing that was initially expected is grim. There is a multitude of issues on management policies to decide regarding the restructuring of the new Skymark Airlines which are code-sharing, airfare, routes, etc. In any case, there are many instances for the new management team to make difficult decisions, being immovable between two sponsors with completely different views.

However, the ANAHD support plan has merit for both sides. The most important point is to restructure the new Skymark Airlines surely and quickly. The fact that ANAHD can cooperate as a sponsor by dispatching multiple maintenance specialists, and implement highly flexible ANAHD reservation system at a low cost is because ANAHD is an airline company. It is thought that since it is an airline, it is possible to identify the problems smoothly and to prepare a full-scale support immediately.

◘ 2. The Essence of the New Skymark Airlines' Support Is in Its Realization

While there is intermingling of expectations between the sponsors, the important thing is to actually rehabilitate Skymark Airlines in real life. The reason why Integral Corporation, an investment fund without the restructuring experience of an airline, took on the task of rehabilitating Skymark Airlines is because it believes that if it were to be successful with Skymark Airlines' rehabilitation, the reputation of it as a fund would be enormous. Not only is the fixed cost of an airline high, but also the change in the external factors such as the price of crude oil, the currency exchange rate, and change in the economy affects the airline greatly. Moreover, there is an argument that an airline has high public interest and therefore the management flexibility is limited. As can be seen in examples overseas, there is a tendency that the airline reconstruction is handled by a limited number of funds. In the process of selecting the sponsor for Skymark Airlines, Integral Corporation had no choice but to partner up with a fund that has experience in this area, or depend on the comprehensive support accompanying the investment from ANAHD. Although the investment ratio is lower, ANAHD's relief method is considered to be through dispatching the people to steadily improve the operation. Sandwiched between the two sponsors who have different expectations, ANAHD who wants to strengthen its influence on the Skymark Airlines, and Integral Corporation who wants to minimize such influences, the new Skymark Airlines is facing a rough path to business reconstruction.

3. Drastic Change of LCCs' Competitive Environment

Due to the differences in the sponsors' thoughts, the rehabilitation of the new Skymark Airlines is not as easy as the case of JAL. In the case of JAL, the president in charge of the restructuring made every employee understand the reason the business was allowed to continue, and under his direction solidary was formed between the management team and all the employees which became the motivating power for moving toward rehabilitation and the new growth thereafter. It is essential in corporate restructuring to part with the past, which caused the bankruptcy, and to impart a strong motivation to create a new future. Moreover, in the new Skymark Airlines, the positive enthusiasm of the employees has been maintained, thus far by parting with the former president.

However, in the restructuring of the new Skymark Airlines, there is not even a growth strategy that one can see to catch up to LCs. It should not be forgotten that the current Skymark Airlines is neither an LC such as ANAHD or JAL, that has the reputation for its service, nor an LCC, which has the advantage of cost competitiveness. Firstly, upon re-starting, it is necessary to re-establish the position in the market. The competitive environment of the aviation industry has changed greatly over the past 3 years. An LC, as an FSC, has refined the content of its service. Furthermore, LCCs such as Peach Aviation has expanded its routes, and it may be difficult for the new Skymark Airlines to survive in the drastically changing aviation market only using the conventional strategy of providing a somewhat lower price than LCs.

Chapter 6

🛬 Conclusion

It seems Skymark Airlines has lost sight of its raison d'être along the way. The image of the company that the consumers were hoping for, the one who brought on the competition to the oligopolistic market with lower airfares than the LCs, has receded. Striving to be on a par with LCs by acquiring various aircraft as the LCs has replaced the significance of being the third key player, and tried to become the likes of ANAHD and JAL by pressing forward the expansion policy at full speed. This may be due to the fear that an LCC will appear with overwhelmingly low prices as a weapon and threaten its own existence. The results might have differed if Skymark Airlines began with charter flights allowing the cabin crew to get used to the procedure, rather than flying regular flights without any preparation, if it desires to enter the long-distance international routes.

Skymark Airlines has corporate value that is more than just a monetary value as can be seen in the series of events concerning the restructuring framework where airlines representing Japan and the U.S. have competed for the sponsor position. Through the bankruptcy, we were able to understand the strengths and weaknesses of Skymark Airlines and the form of its success. By changing the awareness of the employees and the company culture, the company that was overpowered by the charisma of the former president ought to be able to return to the innovative airline that it once was.

Along with recovering the trust, the first step of rehabilitation is to take another good look at the reason for its existence. In order to maintain the motivation of the employees, it is necessary to describe to the employees, who have actively began to move forward, the restructuring vision as soon as possible. The employees at the frontline know by heart that the satisfaction of flying that customers enjoy is due to the low airfare that Skymark Airlines came up with, and is the precious asset for Skymark Airlines.

In order to have the employees find the brightness they once had, the new Skymark Airlines must find the path to reconstruction taking into account every possibility,

Chapter 6

and persist as the third key player. Moreover, it is necessary to come up with services and a business model that others do not have, and incorporate them into the rehabilitation plan. Attention will be focused on the business restructuring movement to see whether the new Skymark Airlines persists as the third key player, and whether it recovers or ends up being controlled by ANAHD.

CHAPTER 7
Japan Airlines: The Bankruptcy and Management Re-Establishment of a "Domesticated LC"

Up to this chapter, the problems of airline management and the aviation policy have been discussed taking the new entry and developments of LCCs into account. However, the Japanese aviation policy has affected even JAL, the largest domestic LC, resulting in problems such as bankruptcy, restructuring and relisting of the company. Based on the fact that JAL established a strong financial structure by being allowed to reduce the amount of tax liability after the bankruptcy, the rival ANAHD protested for the continuation of management surveillance because "the competitive environment had not been corrected." However, MLIT did not acknowledge the protest because the monitoring was "an exceptional measure taken for a limited time." Therefore, from April 2017, the Japanese aviation industry will enter a new era of competition. There are complex reasons why the government had to support a company to rehabilitate. The economic conditions and simple management failures were not the only factors for the bankruptcy of JAL. It has become evident that the fundamental factors are the regulations and protective policies of the longstanding aviation policy. Therefore, the reconstruction measures should be taken with a full understanding of the path to reconstruction. Chapter 7 will examine the process from the failure of JAL to its rebirth, and analyze what process Japanese aviation policies should and should not undergo.

This chapter is especially written for this book.

Chapter 7

Introduction: From the Bankruptcy to the Public Relisting

There were already several attempts to endure the managerial crisis at JAL a few years before the bankruptcy, but each time, the government took measures to prolong the management of the company. However, in the interim results in September of 2009, the company reported a dismal number of 130 billion JPY of consolidated net loss, and furthermore, the increasing accumulation of loss led to insolvency by the end of 2009. The situation could no longer be handled with stopgap measures used previously, and the company finally went bankrupt in January 2010.

The administrationin in those days, similar to the previous ones, did not leave JAL to become extinct and injected funds from the Corporate Restructuring Assistance Organization assigning the organization as the custodian for the restructuring of JAL. The company was able to make a profit by March 2011 and got out from the rehabilitation company. By the end of the same year, the company recovered to the extent that it made an operating profit of 200 billion JPY, nearly 30% more than planned and was relisted on the stock market by September 2012. However, MLIT's management supervision restricted JAL to operate new businesses until March 2017.

JAL was an airline that represented Japan for over half a century including the period as the National Flag Carrier. It is understandable that the fact that such an airline went bankrupt created more publicity than any other large company in any other industry. However, even though the impact of the bankruptcy was quite small compared to the Lehman Brothers bankruptcy and the subsequent "Lehman Shock", the media coverage was much greater. The reason for such high interest was because many Japanese people thought that a bankruptcy of an airline was an unusual occurrence, which is not in the global aviation market. In modern times, the aviation industry is facing a fierce competition and its current profitability is at the same level as the food service industry. Therefore, it is common knowledge in overseas that an airline can go bankrupt as well. A famous food service company went out of business at the same time as JAL, but the media coverage did not last long. The reason is because Japanese people are well aware that a company can freely enter the food service industry and confront a fierce competition, and the bankruptcy of such a company does not deserve much publicity.

However, the aviation industry is highly regulated and protected in Japan, thereby bankruptcy in such an industry is rare. The public especially was overwhelmed that a-half-century-old JAL with established reputation could go bankrupt. The reaction was filled with both "surprise" and "excitement". Excitement is possibly due to the jealousy towards an elite airline and because of the company's high public interest. The bankruptcies of airlines such as Air Do, Skynet Asia Airways, and Skymark Airlines grabbed much publicity in Japan, and the case of JAL attracted even more.

Yet, in the European market where liberalization and competition are highly advanced, even bankruptcy of an LC is common. The reason for the high public interest was because the public misunderstood the aviation industry as being an important industry that required overprotection from the government. In fact, Japanese airlines have been regulated by the government for a long time. The fact that bureaucrats and politicians could not take measures without paying attention to this point, and that the government ended up intervening heavily into the reconstruction of JAL was the problem. The management and the employees of JAL, on the other hand, were slow to take measures to improve the business since they also did not understand, albeit not as badly as the public, that the aviation industry was in a global competitive environment, and thus a company can go bankrupt instantly if the management failed. When the bankruptcy occurred, the change in awareness spread expectedly and considerably to the employees in the frontline.

Nevertheless, the fact that there were employees who rejected the layoff indicates the relative lack in the sense of crisis of the company. ANA is in the exact same competitive environment as well. There was public opinion on the reason behind the success of ANA business while JAL went bankrupt. Indeed, ANA started as a completely private company whereas JAL was protected as a semi-governmental company, resulting in a difference in the awareness of the employees and thus impacting the business results. However, there is no difference between the two companies as both were incapable of conducting businesses under the regulatory constraints. This indicates that it is not a problem exclusively for JAL, but ANA could also fall into the same footsteps as JAL in the future, if the aviation policy is steered the wrong way.

1 Overview of the Business Restructuring Plan of JAL

In the management support of JAL this time, Development Bank of Japan (DBJ) and the Enterprise Turnaround Initiative Corporation of Japan (ETIC) infused capital into JAL in order to avoid insolvency and the BS improved temporarily. The BS shows the assets and liabilities side by side. The restoration of the BS means getting out of insolvency and taking measures to raise the assets until it reaches an equilibrium with the already-existing liabilities. The fund for the improvement of the BS is not necessarily defrayed directly from tax revenue. However, it does not change the fact that the money, based on the tax revenue source, is a loan from the public. Fortunately, the reconstruction went well this time and the fund was paid back without any problems, but if liquidation had taken place and the money could not have been paid back, then the general taxpayer would have borne the burden. Therefore, the company is required to make an operating profit and return the investment back to the people.

Generally, the stakeholders of the company are required to take measures before receiving such support from the public. First, 100% reduction of capital was executed and the value of the stock of JAL was reduced to zero. In other words, the stockholders lost all of their investments. Moreover, the creditors, the financial institutions, were asked to waive the debts and were forced to abandon 521.5 billion JPY. The pension for the former employees was reformed and the benefit payment was reduced, which decreased the company's burden by 30%.

These measures taken by the stakeholders and the support from the public prevented insolvency. However, avoiding insolvency would be meaningless if the business loses money again. It is important to create a business plan to properly reconstruct the business to be profitable. The management measures to achieve such goal was, in a nutshell, downsizing. This downsizing resulted in JAL exceeding its target value in 2012 and returned to profitability.

1. Evaluation of the Business Restructuring Plan

JAL should be highly evaluated for implementing the management restruction and returning the company to profitability. However, the question remains whether the management restruction was good the way it was. In March 2017, the management supervision by MLIT will end. Examination once again from various perspectives is necessary for the future of the airline's management restructuring, and I would like to analyze in detail as much as possible for the future.

1.1 Whether JAL's Choice to Downsize was Correct or Not

JAL and the government's investigation team announced that factors for the bankruptcy were: the large number of old flight equipment, the burden of corporate pension, a large number of unprofitable routes, and excessive number of employees. They explained that the expenditure increased due to these factors and exceeded the level that the revenue could cover.

However, these factors can not explain JAL's bankruptcy. Renewing the aircraft, reducing the pension, withdrawing from the unprofitable routes, and reducing the number of employees, then could have solved the problem. The managerial crisis did not happen all of a sudden. If the aging and diversity of the aircraft were problems, then the question at hand is why it had not been addressed before. Moreover, unprofitable routes means that the revenue does not cover the expenses. If the revenue and expenditures of the unprofitable routes can be balanced, then the company can be profitable. Why was the service withdrawn without trying to make the unprofitable routes profitable again? Furthermore, the number of employees may be large compared to the scale of the company itself, but if so, why were no measures taken to make the company scale bigger (increase the production volume) so that it could accommodate the number of employees?

When the company showed a loss without solving these fundamental problems, the stereotypical plan was adopted for its corporate reconstruction; downsizing. The

Chapter 7

downsizing, judging by the outcome, was the proper direction, but it was not explained in the management-reconstruction plan at all. It is necessary to explain clearly to the public and the stakeholders, "why such a measure was taken."

This relates to the original business model of JAL, which decides which market segment the company will focus on, and in what form the company will survive. In other words, the grand design was not mentioned in the reconstruction plan at all. Since the grand design was not shown, the targets were not mentioned in detail either. Although it was mentioned that the company should be profitable in 3 years, detailed targets such as how much yield is to be secured on which routes, and how much employee productivity is to be improved and so forth were not indicated. Only the target of certain percentage reduction in personnel expenses was mentioned.

- **1.2 Aged Aircraft: How They Have Affected the Restructuring Plan**

In the case of JAL, the aged aircraft were worth less than the financial statement value, and if they were re-evaluated, the value of the asset would be reduced to about one-third. This point was not clear in the books, and when the asset value of the aircraft was properly estimated for this managerial crisis, the seriousness of the insolvency was accidently made public.

However, even though the aging flight equipment indicated the need for reassessing the asset value, and the liabilities exceeding the assets was greater than what is indicated on the book, they do not explain why constant profit cannot be made. Though the aircraft may be old, it would not be a problem if the aircraft can make a profit. In the case of JAL, the replacement and standardization of aircraft was the correct decision, but the utilization of old flight equipment is not necessarily a bad management decision.

To an airline, the aircraft plays an important role in the quality of airline service and cost. The latest aircraft is fuel-efficient, has little trouble once past the initial break-in period, is low on maintenance costs, and contributes to establishing the important on-time performance. Due to the advance of computerization, the training cost has become relatively low. From a marketing perspective, the introduction of the latest aircraft would promote the safety and comfort of the aircraft to the general passengers. In fact, if the interior of an aircraft is frequently upholstered, it would lead to an increase in cost. On the other hand, a new aircraft does not necessarily mean that it is safe; needless to say, it is more expensive. In the case of an LCC that mainly flies charter flights, which are not concerned much with on-time performance, it is more reasonable to fly a used aircraft safely. However, in the case of an airline that promotes high-quality airline services with reliability and comfort, utilizing the latest aircraft even with a higher price would be right for the business.

Evidently, a newer aircraft is not necessarily better for the business, and it depends on what concept the airline is based on. In other words, it depends on the management strategy and attitude on what type of company they want JAL to be reconstructed into. Moreover, it would be against reason to make a request to the government to "fund the purchase of a new aircraft". As in the cases of companies renovating a factory or a shop, the management should be making its own decisions to do so and not depend on the government.

As for the diversity of aircraft, there are two points: (1) variety of aircraft for the diversified market, and (2) variety of aircraft for the same market. Implementing the two points simultaneously should be avoided as much as possible in the management of an airline. As described in Chapter 4, if different aircraft types are used for the same route with a demand of about 150 seats per flight, the maintenance and training costs would increase considerably. Therefore, it is strategically correct for JAL's management to standardize the aircraft. However, in regard to point (1), it all depends on the age of the aircraft and the concept of similar companies. As described in chapters thus far, LCCs serve only the short-distance routes with a certain demand and target economy class passengers as their main customers, and thereby can standardize the aircraft and compete in the aviation market with low airfares.

In contrast, LCs, as they are called the FSCs or NCs, compete with networks that combine routes of various transport density and distance including international routes and regional routes. The regional or commuter routes can be separately owned as a subsidiary, but the variety of aircraft must correspond to the diversity of the market. Although point (2) must be avoided as much as possible because a simple standardization of aircraft leads to a breakdown of a concept. In order for JAL to remain as an NC, it is unavoidable to have a certain level of aircraft diversity. Although JAL was well aware of this point, the aircraft were old up until its bankruptcy, which got them into a situation similar to (2). The most inefficient situation was created, where different types of same size aircraft for routes of similar demand level were used. The cause was the merger with JAS in 2004, where JAS and JAL used completely different aircraft for the routes of similar scale.

● 1.3 Problems Regarding Low Labor Productivity

As can be seen when JAL, which started out as semi-governmental corporation, became completely privatized in 1987, with the CS strategy being established for the first time,[1] the awareness of management improvement was relatively low. The merger with JAS allowed JAL to acquire the arrival and departure slots at Tokyo International Airport and was content with being the "No.1 rights holder of arrival and departure slots at Tokyo International Airport", and the immediate expansion of its market share. However, it neglected to put efforts into reducing unnecessary management resources from the merger, namely, the necessary improvements in labor measures, fund problems, aircraft renewal, route reconstruction, etc.

Aside from the problem of the merger with JAS, the low-level labor productivity is basically due to the protection by the Japanese aviation policy. Frequently it is pointed out that there are seven labor unions for JAL, and they have a negative effect on the business in terms of negotiation costs compared to ANA, which has fewer labor unions. It can be said that the labor strategy to divide and rule has worked against JAL. It is important to reflect on the fact that losing its international competitive power was due to the low labor productivity of Japanese airlines. It is the same for the case of ANA, and in that respect, reducing the corporate scale or the number of employees cannot solve the problem. A personnel adjustment system that incorporates the system of promoting employees based on competence should have been considered. Reducing only the labor cost would demotivate employees in the long term, who strived together for the reconstruction. The pension problem has similar issues as well. It may have been possible to make high benefit payments when there was no competition, but that is impossible today. It should not be criticized as the "pension

---

1 Shiotani(2003a; 2007b; 2010b; 2010d).

benefit payment is too high," but instead the value of the work performed at the time of employment should be criticized for not deserving the pension payment amount.

● 1.4 Correlation Between Unprofitable Routes and the Bankruptcy

The existence of unprofitable routes is pointed out as the cause of deterioration of business, but that is an overly simplified explanation of the problem. Airlines should freely enter and withdraw from routes, and political power should not intervene in route management of airlines. As discussed in previous chapters, although the aviation law prescribes that an airline can establish or abolish a route freely, there is a history of decision-making on domestic routes and part of international routes that differ from the airline management decisions. As mentioned above for the case of JAL, the fact that JAL could not dispose the unprofitable regional routes due to political reasons was part of the cause for the deterioration of business, and that is also true for ANA—"Failure of Japanese aviation policy(politics)".

Additionally, as explained in Chapter 5, the existence of airports that were maintained and supported by the tax revenue allocated to local governments, though unprofitable, has put the pressure on airlines to maintain the routes. In addition to providing service to airports that are excessively maintained due to political reasons, the airlines have been carrying the double burden of providing funds for the maintenance of unnecessary investments at airports on the unprofitable regional routes.

It is against reason to entrust an airline, which is a private company with the responsibility of maintaining regional routes. The route situation is related to the grand design of an airline, and it is necessary to clearly establish it after careful consideration. Firstly, the revenue and expenditure for each route should have been made clear from the beginning, but this was not done in the management improvement plan. Secondly, it was necessary to consider the requirements to make unprofitable routes profitable before withdrawing them from the unprofitable routes. It is natural for JAL to withdraw from unprofitable routes that cannot make profit no matter how hard it tries. However, such routes were only a small part of the main business of JAL. Out of the entire network of JAL, the unprofitable routes that were related to JAL were only a few former JAS routes. This is because most of such

Chapter 7

unprofitable routes were already incorporated into the subsidiary networks such as JAC. Since the profitability of each route is dependent on the productivity of overall labor, cost of flight equipment, ability to attract customers, etc., the cost factors that are common to the whole should be improved first, and those routes that are still unprofitable should be examined for innovative ideas and methods to improve the earning power (increase customers, save costs, etc.), and if still unsuccessful, then a withdrawal may be the reasonable solution for its improvement.

Although the problem of unprofitable regional routes demonstrate the typical aspect of politics having influence on the airlines, in terms of the magnitude of money involved, the major main routes that became unprofitable due to losing to competition were the principle cause of the bankruptcy of JAL. Therefore, with such routes that were lost to competition, even if service is withdrawn from the current unprofitable routes, the present profitable routes may also lose to the competition someday unless the overall productivity and the ability to attract customers are raised. In this regard, it was important to decide which routes to keep and which market to target, and was necessary to improve the current balance by raising the overall labor productivity.

- **1.5 "Rehabilitated JAL": Having a Clear Vision Before the Relisting**

As discussed above, there was insufficient explanation in the reconstruction plan such as where did JAL have problems, what kind of airline it should become, and what should be done to achieve that. There were practically no indications as to what kind of market it will survive in, to what level it will try to contain the expenditures such as personnel costs, and what kind of marketing it will execute in such market. Without such information, it would not be possible to establish a detailed business plan or even forecast the revenue. In the business recovery scenario of JAL, a revenue and expenditure plan with an operating profit of 115.7 billion JPY was announced for 2012, but there is no explanation of how the numbers were calculated or how they will be achieved.

The reconstruction plan simply sets a mechanically calculated target amount. For example, "an operating profit of such an amount is needed to avoid insolvency, therefore, this level is what we need," and it indicates only the withdrawal from unprofitable routes and the disposal of old aircraft and provision of new ones regarding how to achieve this target amount. The reconstruction plan should be composed of a vision of an airline and policy indicating what kind of company it will become, and the kind of market it is to compete and survive in. The management policy of an airline is to be decided by the airline itself and not to be discussed in terms of policy or be intervened by others.

If I were to make comments as a former employee, JAL should leverage the JAL brand and target a customer segment or market with a large number of customers who request high-quality airline services even if the price is high. These high-price-paying customers exist sufficiently in the market, mainly in the older generation and business customers of Japan. Therefore, it is important to regulate the corporate concept, pricing strategy, and the air routes to such scope. It should not try to become a global company in the first place. This should be considered after the labor productivity has improved.

Firstly, the routes limited to Japan's first Japanese-centred market should be constructed. Secondly, the customer target definitely should not be set on customers paying low fares. This customer segment should be limited to when there are empty seats available since it is impossible to win against LCCs in a price war. Thirdly, efforts should be made to save costs even with the focus on a market winnable by JAL, the "high fare and high-quality service market of Japan". It is difficult for JAL to expect a high level of loyalty from its employees as seen in the successful LCCs, therefore it is impossible to raise the labor productivity to the level of LCCs.

However, in order to win against the rival LCs in this market, it is necessary to improve the labor productivity to their level. For instance, only after securing labor productivity equal to that of the rivals in the Pacific routes, the airlines of the U.S. and Southeast Asia, can JAL provide higher quality services than theirs with airfare equal to theirs. Indeed, it can be definitely concluded that the primary reason of JAL's steady recovery after the relisting is due to the improvement of the labor productivity. These are merely my personal viewpoints, but it is important for JAL to establish a management strategy based on its own responsibility, and only after this kind of basic policy is established, can the details of the reconstruction plan be presented. They then should investigate what is obstructing the reconstruction plan, and if necessary, a

Chapter 7

reform of the past stagnating elements such as clearing away or resetting the labor agreement and labor union system should be executed. The business does not improve simply by reducing the routes, the number of employees, and renewing the facilities.

In all likelihood, JAL and the trustee have sufficiently examined what kind of reconstruction plan and management strategy are required. However, it would be disadvantageous to unveil the management strategy to the competition, and therefore, it could have been withheld from the presentation of the reconstruction plan. Indeed, as the confidence in the reform began to appear, the subsequent explanations included such points little by little. If not so, it would have been impossible to deliver such good results being able to relist after 2 years. It would also be difficult to maintain the high efficiency in the future however, unless a more detailed reconstruction plan is presented. Although it did not experience a bankruptcy, this is also a big issue for ANAHD which serves the same market under a similar policy.

◘ 2. Assessment of the Rehabilitation Method

With the controversial points of the reconstruction plan thus far in mind, this section will explain and evaluate the corporate rehabilitation method actually used in the reconstruction of JAL. The choices of social measures for JAL, which fell into insolvency, are grouped into the following four categories depending on the method of company reorganization.

(1) Genuine bankruptcy
The insolvency continues for a certain period and if left as it is, the assets are divided among the creditors and the airline ceases to exist.
(2) Rehabilitation through private reorganization without the use of public funds
Find a supporter before the bankruptcy to take over the liabilities, and obtain postponement or waiver of payments from the creditors, and readjust the liabilities to avoid bankruptcy. The airline can exist as it is, and make a fresh start.
(3) Rehabilitation through private reorganization using public funds
This is a private reorganization supported by a public fund. The major part of the private reorganization takes on the form of (2) mentioned above. However,

Chapter 7

sometimes a business that is judged to have a "high publicness" is given financial aid from a public institution such as the government.

(4) Rehabilitation through legal reorganization

This method relies on the court to decide the processing of liabilities by applying for the Corporate Reorganization Act and not through the discussion with the interested parties such as the creditors. Different from a private reorganization, the airline superficially ceases to exist and abandons various obligations and restarts as a new airline.

In this case, method (4) was chosen.

In contrast, JAL had been rescued previously in the conventional way of (3). However, this relief method will end up repeating the same mistakes as before, and the government and the financial institutions did not approve it. On the other hand, the methods (1) and (2) are approaches that basically leave it up to the market. If the market assumes that JAL should continue to exist, then a rescuer will voluntarily appear and the method (2) can be selected. If a rescuer does not appear, then the method (1) will be taken. Even in the case of (1), there still will be aviation demand, and even without JAL, another airline or a new JAL will provide the supplies. However, the service would be interrupted for a certain period of time. Nowadays, it would be difficult to think about the economic logic of rescuing an airline. Since the government should not intervene in the aviation market, fundamentally the method (1) or (2) should be selected.

In order to have the government not to intervene in JAL and have JAL rehabilitate by reforming various regulations inside and outside the company, the method (2) should have been selected. In that case, a sponsor to give relief for the insolvency is necessary. At this point, the expectation is directed towards the foreign capital for its rehabilitation. There was a fear of JAL's management crisis from a few years before, and there were a few foreign capital corporations that showed interest. If it takes control of the management, a new management and its know-how will be introduced in addition to the supply of funds, and the past restraints that Japanese people could not abandon can be severed, and a drastic reform could be possible. However, the cabotage restriction exists for airlines and the foreign capital cannot own more than one-third

Chapter 7

of the asset.

In the chapters thus far, it has been described that the abolishment of the cabotage restriction is necessary for the development of LCCs, and it is also an important aviation policy issue for the reconstruction of an LC in Japan. If JAL goes bankrupt again, there is no more funds available from the government. However, during the JAL crisis this time, there was no time to investigate the abolishment of the cabotage restriction, and the government did not have that intention either. "The government should rescue JAL," was the intention of the government and did not want to create confusion by stopping the JAL flights. On the other hand, the public opinion did not allow an easy rescue. Accordingly, the method (4) was selected as a compromise.

In fact, a guarantee by the government and an investment by Industrial Revitalization Corporation (IRC) were added to the method (4) so that it would be easier for the court of justice to enforce the preservation of claims in order to continue the service. This type of rehabilitation processing method is called "pre-packaged insolvency". When an airline goes bankrupt and its claims are processed, the court of justice processes the claims specifically according to the Corporate Reorganization Act, and if the assets are distributed to the creditors without assuming that the aircraft are being used in service, then the operation cannot be continued. Therefore, in order to avoid this situation, it is necessary to have the court of justice preserve the necessary assets to continue operating the aircraft. In order to get an approval for the preservation of the assets, the government has to make a guarantee and the like before a decision by the court of justice is made to show the involvement by the government, and to guide the decision of the court of justice toward "the government is also taking steps necessary to continue the operation and the court of justice should consider that point and preserve the assets necessary to continue the operation." In the case of JAL, the content of prepackaging included the guarantee by the government, the investment by IRC, the acknowledgement of postponement or waiver of the claims by the financial institutions and so forth.

Many LCs in the U.S. have experienced this type of planned bankruptcy freaquently and continued to operate aircraft while they were bankrupt. In Chapter 11 of the

Bankruptcy Act in the U.S., there is a special provision, which states that the claims necessary to operate the aircraft in order to avoid the termination of operation must be preserved. On the other hand, the Corporate Reorganization Act of Japan did not take into any consideration that an airline could go bankrupt, and does not include this type of provision. Therefore, since the bankruptcy processing cannot be done while continuing business in Japan as allowed in Chapter 11, it is thought that a prepackage is necessary so that the airline operation does not stop, and therefore, such measures were taken this time. This method can be considered, so to speak, as the "second best".

The "first best" choice is that the government does nothing and the airline operation continues through its reconstruction by foreign capital and if that is not possible, the airline simply goes out of business. However, since there is no breakthrough currently about removing the cabotage restriction, the prepackage was the only solution that allowed the thorough execution of the reform without ceasing the operation of the aircraft. If the government had sentenced that "this is the last time" when the government made the guarantee, it could be appreciated that it was an unavoidable measure in order not to stop the operation of the aircraft.

The problem, first of all, is the fact that the government did not declare, "this is the last time." Not only that, the government failed to learn from the background of JAL's bankruptcy. Secondly, the cabotage restriction has not been alleviated as of yet. If the cabotage restriction was lifted, it would have been possible to expect foreign airlines with superior management capability and white knights from all over the world to appear at the time of its bankruptcy, and the aviation industry would have been revitalized. Thirdly, the lesson learned from the case of JAL should be used to reform the Corporate Reorganization Act to the likes of Chapter 11 of the U.S., but no improvement is seen at all. If a provision is provided to approve the continuation of businesses even under a bankrupted condition, an airline can continue its operation even without the pre-packaged guarantee while it reorganizes the company to change it to an efficient structure. The fourth point is the re-examination of preferential treatment of the bankrupted company. The preferential treatment of such company is not a problem unheard of for JAL, and the company does not deserve to be treated severely or leniently because it is an airline. However, it may be necessary to discuss

Chapter 7

the need to re-examine the preferential treatment by comparing the impact to the morale of the companies that survived the weeding out process, the impact to activate the industry, the chance to restart and so forth.

2 Protective Aviation Policies Indirectly Affecting Japanese Airlines

The aviation policy of the deregulation age should place importance on the promotion of competition and not on the aid for new airlines. The measures for JAL should focus on reinforcing its independent competitive power, and not on the prolonging of its life. The policy that places importance on relief measures ultimately increases the reliance of LCCs and LCs on the government, and causes the degradation of competitiveness in the aviation market, which can also be said for other markets.

Japan has fallen behind the worldwide trend by ten-odd years and finally introduced competition to the domestic aviation market in 2000. Since then, however, the government continued to intervene substantially by distributing arrival and departure slots and so on. Even in the 21st century, in the international aviation market, the government continued its policy of protecting its own country's airlines through the protectionist aviation agreements. During this time, the aviation markets were liberalized in the regions handling two-thirds of the world's air transport volume, and the airlines took measures to correspond to intensifying competition and improved their management in order to endure. Many airlines, regardless of LCs or LCCs, have retired from the market. In other words, the current airlines today have endured 20 years of fierce market competition and natural selection. In this environment of degrading productivity due to the protectionist policy, it is natural for the Japanese airlines, in which various mediocre tasks have been forced as compensation, to lose their competitiveness.

The aviation policy in a developed country must consider the benefit of the user. The Japanese aviation policy has neglected this point, and the user benefit was not considered in the aviation negotiations up to the end of 1980s. It resulted in preserving the policy of denying competition between airlines until the end of the 20th century. Due to the aviation policy that does not consider user benefit, the airlines were late to switch their stance from "putting importance on the government over the market" and lost competitive power. This problem was not limited to only JAL. In the case of JAL, the relative cost it received from the aviation policy was simply too much due to the fact that it started out as a semi-governmental and a national flag company, and it merged with JAS for political reasons and so forth. ANAHD was a private-sector corporation from the beginning, switched the whole company in the 1990s to the management direction that anticipated market competition, and was active in the internationalization of Tokyo International Airport, and the competitive bidding system for the arrival and departure slots. However, even though it was in marked contrast to JAL, which followed the government policy, it can be said that it had similar problems organizationally as well. The major reason that brought about the management crisis in JAL was the burden put on it ranging from such things as the provision of unprofitable services to the engendering of lack of self-reliance of the company due to overprotection by working close with the government.

The aviation market is a market that adapts very well to competition, and a particular company or an industry is not to be given preferential treatment, protection, or restriction in there. JAL or any other LCCs should be treated the same. Therefore, the measures for JAL's bankruptcy, even though the infusion of the public fund that unavoidably happened for the relief this time may be the last one, needs to sever the relationship with the government once and for all, and execute a planned bankruptcy by legal reorganization to clear out all the in-house restraints and restart from the beginning. Moreover, the government needs to announce such changes and make free corporate activities possible to correspond to the competitive market by abolishing the government's economic restrictions.

1. Consequences of Government and Citizens' Intervention

Since about the time of the bankruptcy, JAL has faced the reality of the bankruptcy, and has strived to improve the labor productivity. The labor agreement was not reformed, but the change in awareness of the employees, and the improvement of the labor productivity was achieved to a certain extent, and the results appeared in

Chapter 7

the form of surplus.

It could be said that the company recovered by the efforts of the employees without the reform of the aviation policy that has been emphasized previously. While JAL is trying to change in this manner, the issue is with the forces that do not want to change, such as part of the management, awareness of the public, politicians, etc. Even though it was essential to secure the independence of the management and become fully self-responsible for the reconstruction after being released from government control, these points were not fully recognized and they continue to be so even now.

- ## 1.1 Allowing the Market to Determine the Number of Airlines and Routes

The volume of domestic air traffic in Japan is ranked third in the world. In other words, Japan is not a country with small aviation demand. The U.K., with smaller land area and population than Japan, not only has British Airways, a leading global airline, Virgin Atlantic Airways, known for its unique management, and easyJet, an LCC ranked consistently high on the number of international passengers carried, but also has many other LCCs competing fiercely. As mentioned before, the market should decide the number of airlines, and who flies which routes instead of the government. It is the same case for the unprofitable regional routes as well. If aviation service is needed for regional areas, such as remote islands and rural areas, funds for such purpose should be provided by the local allocation tax, and the municipalities themselves should consult among themselves regarding the consistency with the regional plan and other transportation, and then establish a route maintenance plan and select the airline through a competitive bidding. The support of the unprofitable routes should not be included in the relief measures of JAL due to the possibility that it could be restored to its former state.

- ## 1.2 The Importance of Protecting a Company's Independence

There was an asymmetric regulation on the airfare of JAL until 2012. Although airfare was deregulated, there was a lower limit regulation prohibiting the LCs to set their airfare lower than those of LCCs, which inhibited competition. Furthermore, there was a regulation prohibiting JAL from setting their airfares lower than that of ANAHD as well. This is based on the notion that JAL that is reviving using the

Chapter 7

government support should not undercut others.

Indeed, the government funds is used in the aid for JAL's reconstruction to restore the BS to eliminate insolvency, and such funds should not be included in the revenue as an assistance or support measure that affects the PL. The support measure should be limited to the restoration of the BS only. However, government funds provided for the restoration of the BS is not used as a source of fund for an airfare war unless the management makes a mistake. For instance, if it is used for airfare wars instead of updating aircraft, then the aircraft remains as they are and the BS gets worse, and finally the reconstruction fails. There is no problem if JAL were to fight an airfare war as long as it is to make a profit.

Moreover, the government pointed out that JAL's advertisements are excessive and that the new lounge at Tokyo International Airport is too extravagant. With reconstruction at stake, JAL's strategy is to attract the customer segment that pays high airfares, and being told in such a critical time that the advertisements are excessive and the lounge is too extravagant, defeats the purpose. Even if it is an economically correct indication, the government should not be the one to do so.

There are various interventions by the government that hold back the efforts of JAL from relisting. Under this circumstance, there is a fear that no matter how hard JAL tries, ultimately, the government policy will crush it and may go bankrupt again. Unnecessary intervention only delays the reform, and unless the company stands on its own as a completely privatized company, the consumer will not select it in the market. It would only make JAL into a semi-governmental company shaped like a private company on the outside again, after going through great pains to improve the management with a privatized mindset. The government should recognize that its market intervention or the remnants of the past aviation policy were the reasons for putting JAL in jeopardy, and to declare that it would support JAL one last time. It will watch over JAL until it is relisted, but it will not support nor obstruct JAL thereafter.

It should also be pointed out that there is pressure from the "public opinion" created by the traditional regulation that causes this type of excessive intervention by the government, and neither the government agencies nor JAL can take firm measures against it. For instance, JAL temporarily abolished the employee discount system and other preferential treatments, in consideration of the external pressure. Unlike the intracompany sales in other industries, the marginal cost of the privilege measures for the employees of an airline is small. In a time when the personnel cost has to be reduced as much as possible, it is an extremely valuable and reasonable way to keep the employees. The reason behind the abolishment of this system was due to the incorrect interpretation of, "airlines have high publicness therefore the government and the public have the right to give an opinion" that the public traditionally held toward the airline.

It is most important for JAL to repay the favor of utilizing the fund from government aid by reconstructing the management and securing a profit. In order to do so, it was important to raise the morale of the employees and focus fully on the market. The government authorities and the news media should not let the erroneous public opinion distort the resource distribution.

◘ 2. Let JAL Keep Its Own Sovereignty

From the point when the company was relisted, the tendency of politicians to intervene in the management, such as demanding the opening of unprofitable routes and imposing penalty on JAL through the distribution of arrival and departure slots, has realistically grown stronger than before. The behavior of the public and the government forcing JAL to perform activities that are no different from voluntary social service as if they had forgotten their activities were partially the cause of the bankruptcy, seems to have revealed that, "it was actually the public and the politicians rather than the employees of JAL who did not have any sense of crisis."

The government should declare even at this point that the relief measure of 2010 was for one time only and final, and once the reconstructed JAL enters the competitive environment, the government would not intervene in the future at all. Otherwise, other companies that survived the weeding out process, and the stockholders who were weeded out will not accept it. At the same time, it is natural to "recognize the rehabilitation of the airline as a full-fledged airline when it completes its reconstruction since the public has committed to support it." It would defeat the purpose of the relief if greater demands are made in addition to "paying back the principal and interest of the money for the rescue" and forcing the company to go bankrupt again.

In this way, while the reconstructed JAL is treated as an independent company, a thoroughly competitive environment needs to be established in the aviation market including the abolition of the cabotage restriction. Moreover, in order to eliminate the custom of politically intervening in the management of an airline to maintain an air-route, the misunderstanding of airlines by the locals needs to be re-examined. Simultaneously, a reform is necessary to include the subsidy from the government in the allocation tax, which is not limited in its use, and thus raise the awareness for self-responsibility by the locals.

3 Increasing the Effective Use of Assets and Breaking Through the "Slowdown"

In more than 3 and half years since the relisting of JAL, the operating profit in 2016 has recorded the highest level in its history with 209.1 billion JPY(year-on-year increase of 16.4%). However, it seems to have hit the "wall of growth" according to the evaluation by the international aviation market, and its stock price remains relatively cheap compared to the LCs of the world. It is important to refrain from a large-scale aircraft investment and focus more on efficient asset management.

JAL introduced 45 B787 on May 27th 2016. It is evident that the management of JAL has transitioned from "reconstruction" to "growth" looking at the smooth introduction of B787 since filing for the application of the Corporate Reorganization Act and relisting in September 2012. ROE, an indicator of earning efficiency, was about 20% and the profitability far outperformed ANAHD, which owns ANA(operating profit of 136.4 billion JPY, 49.1% increase year-on-year, ROE 8%). It seems the reduction of the financial statement value of the aircraft and the exemption of corporate tax during the management-restructuring period had a large positive effect.

However, the financial market is concerned with the "EV/EBITDA ratio" indicator.

Chapter 7

This indicates how much investors evaluate the Enterprise Value (EV) with respect to the airline's earning power EBITDA. The higher the ratio, the higher the investor's expectation for the growth of the company. Even though JAL has an outstanding high profit constitution, it is ranked low in the industry based on this indicator. When the EV/EBITDA ratios of the LCs worldwide are examined, mostly the ratios of the LCs in Asia are higher than those of the LCs in Europe and the U.S. According to Figure 7-1, the ratio for JAL is 4.1, whereas that of Cathay Pacific is 6.7 which means that the airline expects the company to continue earning power for 6 to 7 years in the future. The ratio is 6.3 for ANAHD and 4.4 for Singapore Airlines.

The financial market believes that "a company with higher profit level causes the company to fall into a dilemma in which the company withholds more than enough earnings without returning it to the shareholders sufficiently, and the ROE tends to decline in the future." JAL seems to have entered a phase where it is being questioned on its strategy to break through the slowdown. Moreover, since JAL was able to reconstruct with the help of public funds, it is restricted by the "government shackles" from making new investments and opening new air routes until the end of March

Figure 7-1   EV/EBITDA ratio of major and global airlines

$$\text{EV/EBITDA ratio} = \frac{\text{Market Capitalization} + \text{Debt} + \text{Preferred Share Capital} + \text{Minority Interest} - \text{Cash and Cash Equivalents}}{\text{Operating Profit} + \text{Amortization Expense} + \text{Depreciation Expense}}$$

- **Asian airlines are highly evaluated in the market**

  The EV/EBITDA ratio compares enterprise value such as earnings of interest, taxes, depreciation and amortization. This is a very commonly used as a metric for estimating business valuation and compares the value of a company, its debt inclusive and liabilities, to exclusive cash earnings of non-cash expenses. A lower enterprise multiple can indicate under devaluation of the company.

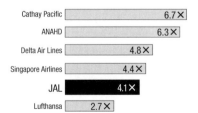

Source: Created by the author based on annual reports of each company

Chapter 7

Figure 7-2 Profitability and market capitalization of major Asian airlines

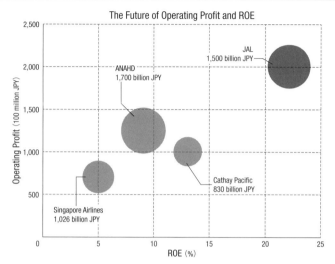

Note: The size and value of each circle shows the total market capitalization (the average value of 2015).
Source: Created by the author based on annual reports of each company

2017. JAL is planning to announce an aggressive strategy in the new medium-term management plan starting in April 2017. We wonder what secret measures JAL has planned in order to raise the EV/EBITDA ratio.

Normally, it is a royal road to increase the EBITDA equivalent earning power, the denominator, and then investigate the capital structure that influences EV, the numerator, while maintaining the financial soundness. Specifically, (1) improve EBITDA by raising the effectiveness of aircraft asset by refining the profitability of routes and sectors. One example is the utilization of aircraft. The Tokyo–New York route is serviced by seven flights with two aircraft, but when it was increased to 14 flights at the end of March 2014, three aircraft were used instead of the normally required quantity of four. Combining them with the Paris route raised the utilization per aircraft. (2) Switching the aircraft that was obtained through an expensive lease contract around the time of the bankruptcy to ownership leads to improvement of the asset effectiveness. JAL sets up daily flight services using 223 aircraft (as of September 2015). The company owns 186 (83%) of the aircraft and the rest are leased. The overall scale of operation is about the same compared to right after the relisting at the end of September 2012, but the number of aircraft owned by the company has steadily increased from 159 aircraft (72%) at the time. When the aircraft are switched to being purchased, the depreciation cost can be recorded and the cash flow improves.

In the case of EV, the numerator, the "smart way to use capital" is the issue. The capital-to-asset ratio is expected to increase to about 60% by the end of 2017 due to the accumulation of profit. Although it is at a level equivalent to other Japanese corporations that have good financial reputations, an excessive amount of capital causes many investors to demand increased dividends or stock repurchase and contains the side effect of decreasing the ROE as well. JAL will continue investing in aircraft even after 2017 and will have to keep an eye on fund raisings.

The company plans to introduce a maximum of 56 A350 as the successor to B777, and the cost would be nearly 1 trillion JPY if calculated using the list price. Prepayments are being made already to prepare for the operation in 2019. JAL plans to cover the necessary cash for the investment with the profit from the main business, but the corporation's fund-raising expense is declining due to the negative interest introduced by the Bank of Japan. JAL is considering to reissue corporate bonds that was stopped since 2003. Interest-bearing debts such as corporate bonds have an effect on raising EV as well. It is also necessary to keep a large capital in preparation for an event risk (sudden decline in passengers due to disaster, economy, terrorism, etc.), and diversified financing options is an important management issue. It seems like the company is considering to issue company bonds worth 50 billion JPY mainly with 5 year bonds that has much demand with investors. The coexistence of growth and restoration from a financial perspective is also at stake for the purpose of "managing without self-conceit", a lesson from an honorary advisor.

Conclusion: A New Era of Competition in the Global Aviation Market

6 years have passed since filing for the application of the Corporate Reorganization Act and JAL's profit has dramatically improved. As a result of executing various management improvements as mentioned above, the company excels in the amount of profit in Asia though the sales have been scaled down.

Although JAL is an LC, it has climbed its way to the world's top class, equal to European and the U.S. LCCs such as Ryanair known for high profitability constitution. The capital-to-asset ratio is expected to be 60%, far exceeding the other airline companies' average of 30%. Of course, there was a large benefit from the waiver of 521.5 billion JPY of debt and an investment of 350 billion JPY from IRC. In addition to the large increase in the operating profit due to the reduction of depreciation costs (until 2015), the net profit also expanded due to the exemption of the corporate tax and thus the capital was easily accumulated.

1. The Proper Form of Corporate Reorganization

However, the self-help efforts by the employees of JAL for the reform of awareness should be appraised the most. The honorary advisor who took on the job of rehabilitating JAL in 2010 said, during the management reconstruction process to, "set the goal high at a level where you can barely reach," and introduced performance reporting sessions for each division. The failure to achieve a goal itself is not to be reprimanded but to require an answer for how to achieve the goal in the future. The reform that the honorary advisor wanted to achieve was to have all of the 32,000 employees of JAL to feel like they are entrepreneurs. There were only a handful of employees who were interested in the financial results of their company before the bankruptcy. Today, every employee is interested in the financial results of the company and they constantly think of what they could do to improve them. The transformation of the employees' awareness was the most important asset for JAL after the legal reorganization.

Chapter 7

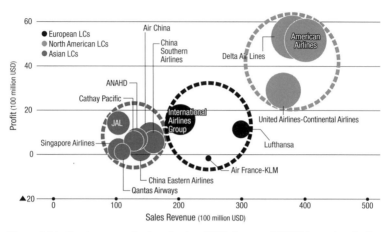

Figure 7-3 Overcrowded Asian aviation markets

Note: Financial indicators are calculated using LTM data, and EBIT is used to indicate the profits. The size of each circle shows the total market value of December 2014. (The three Chinese companies show September 2014.)
Source: Created by the author using Capital IQ data based on AlixPartners as a reference

Meanwhile, the so-called 8.10 paper that MLIT issued in August 2012 when JAL relisted, which was a burden on growth, will come to an end soon. However, not all new investments were blocked up until now, but the necessary investments were steadily executed. The number of seats did not suddenly increase, for instance, but an innovative measure to reduce the unit price of a seat was taken. JAL has introduced the new seat, SKY SUITE, in the business class of B777 used in international flights from 2013, and the economy class reduced the 10-seat row common in other airlines to 9 seats and increased the seat pitch by 7 centimeters more than the industry's average. The number of seats was reduced by 5% compared to the conventional specification due to this change. This design strategy baffled even Boeing, the manufacturer, and there were arguments for and against the measure within JAL.

In order to increase revenue with this number of seats, it was necessary to raise the unit price per seat as well as increase the load factor. These days, the revenue has increased compared to previous aircraft mainly on Tokyo–London and Tokyo–New York routes. The yield has definitely increased due to this strategy. JAL's future depends not only on attracting the wealthy Japanese, but also on the wealthy class of overseas in order to continue this type of high-unit-price routes. The strategy is to focus on the upper class of the tourists to Japan and the transit passengers.

2. JAL's Future in the Aviation Market

The old JAL ran small profits and quick returns, high-turnover business, and there were routes that were not profitable even with a load factor of 100%. After the bankruptcy, the company focused on profitability index of "10% operating profit", and not on the volume as discipline. Singapore Airlines, Delta Air Lines, and United Airlines are more advanced in their management improvements than JAL for the future target of Southeast Asia–North America routes, and they should be taken as benchmarks. Many LCs worldwide have experienced to expand the air-route scale when the business is going well and downsize in times of economic stagnation due to event risk. JAL should adopt a new strategy to change its corporate culture not to make a loss in times of economic downturn instead of trying to increase revenue in the good times.

As mentioned above, this premium strategy is the correct direction for corporate rehabilitation. It would be a good choice to build an airline that continues to grow in realistic terms and shine even if it is small in scale. The future of JAL depends on whether the wealthy class from overseas select JAL as their choice or not.

CHAPTER 8

Peach Aviation: ANAHD's Successful Affiliated Japanized LCC

Peach Aviation is an LCC established with ANA as its parent company. Peach Aviation, a pioneer of Japanese-style LCCs, started its service in March 2012 with two domestic routes based in Kansai International Airport. It is striving to steadily acquire customers, focusing around the local Kansai area, providing a series of new services that are not restricted to the conventional LCC business model. Even though people tend to link LCCs with simple services and low prices, Peach Aviation has also established the concept—a "flying train", to achieve its on-time operation, high-quality service, and safety like a typical Japanese railroad. In order to realize this motto, innovation that breaks the mold as well as thorough understanding and knowledge about the industry is required. In that respect, it is particularly meaningful for Peach Aviation to be established through corporate venturing of ANA. In this chapter, the relationship between Peach Aviation as the airline baby and ANAHD, the parent company, and its success factors will be examined.

This chapter is especially written for this book.

Chapter 8

✈ Introduction

ANA and JAL, two major LCs, hold a large share of the Japanese domestic aviation market. Therefore, it was important for ANAHD to protect and increase the domestic market share, which is the core of its sales. Moreover, ANAHD feared that LCCs could take over the market share of LCs in Asia, questioning the necessity to deliberately create a competitive environment in the domestic Japanese aviation market. Peach Aviation was created under such circumstances with ANAHD as its parent company. There were fundamental doubts concerning the establishment of an LC such as (1) To establish an LCC that is the opposite of an LC, will lead to the cannibalization of the parent company. (2) Will there be any potential risk of damaging the reputation as well as the brand image of ANAHD. (3) Will LCCs be able to adapt to the Japanese aviation market. Ultimately, ANAHD decided that the establishment of an LCC was not a threat neither Japan nor ANAHD, and that ANAHD should be the first mover if an LCC was to be established. Peach Aviation's establishment seemed to go smoothly, but in fact there were various management and aviation policy issues. This chapter will examine the founding process of Peach Aviation and its success factors as a successful and rare case of corporate venturing[1] in Japan, where an LC (ANA) established an LCC that were generally competitors.

✈ 1 Overview of Peach Aviation

◻ 1. Peach Aviation's Performance Review and Success Factors

Peach Aviation was established in February 2011 as an affiliate LCC of ANA. The capital is about 7.5 billion JPY and the number of employees has reached about 800 people as of April 2016. According to the results in March 2016, the operating profit reached 12.9%, average load factor 86.7%, and the number of revenue passengers 4.54 million; increased revenue and profit were achieved for three consecutive years

---

1 The word "corporate venturing" can refer to an activity, where a large company creates a new business within its own company. Though it can also refer to a large company's investment in a smaller company, this chapter mostly uses the former definition.

Chapter 8

 Figure 8-1 Business results of first 5 years: Peach Aviation's rapid growth

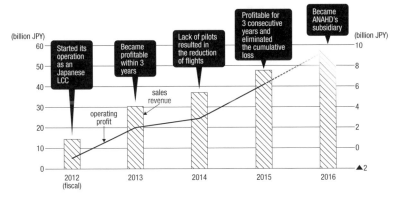

Note: Sales and profits are both expected to increase in 2016.
Source: Created by the author based on Peach Aviation's *annual reports*

and the cumulative loss was eliminated.

2. Sharp Route Expansion

Peach Aviation is aiming to develop demand in the Asian aviation market by providing low airfare and high-quality service through a mechanism that LCs do not have, and create new value and alternatives. It began with Kansai International Airport–New Chitose Airport/Fukuoka Airport domestic routes in March 2012 and its service network has expanded to the current 14 domestic routes and 12 international routes. The airline currently operates cost-effective 18 A320 (180 seats) and is looking to operate the service with 20 aircraft by the end of 2017. It has established routes using Kansai International Airport as the hub, and has also set up Naha Airport as a base to expand into other Asian countries besides Japan in July 2014. It also plans to set up Sendai International Airport as a base by the summer of 2017 and New Chitose Airport by 2018, aiming to increase its business by rapidly expanding the domestic bases. The centralization of Sendai International Airport was Peach Aviation's long-cherished desire. Since the population of the six prefectures of Tohoku region is approximately the same size as Seoul, there is a large latent demand for flights in and out of Sendai International Airport that would be a gateway for such routes.

Chapter 8

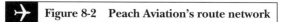

Figure 8-2 Peach Aviation's route network

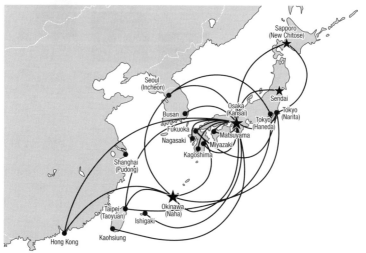

Note: ★ = indicates a hub airport. In addition, New Chitose Airport and Sendai International Airport are planned to be hub airports in the future.
Source: Created by the author based on Peach Aviation's internal documents

Furthermore, Tohoku region is very popular among tourists from other Asian countries and it would be easy to actively establish routes to various parts in Asia. The issue of flight network for Peach Aviation is its insufficient approach to the Tokyo Metropolitan area. There is a very large demand for service to the metropolitan area, and despite the fact that the aviation market and the latent demand are large, the competition has not grown fierce enough to the level of scrambling for customers between LCCs. It is currently servicing the Kansai International Airport–Narita International Airport route, but it is constantly pursuing an opportunity to establish a route to Tokyo International Airport.

◘ 3. The Acquisition of Knowledgeable and Superior Employees

Peach Aviation's swift establishment was due to having ANA as its parent company, thereby the four senior executives, including the CEO, were from ANA. The management centrally run by these experts of the aviation industry, has greatly contributed to the establishment of Peach Aviation. In January 2008, the CEO of Peach Aviation was ordered by the then president of ANA to establish an LCC within

Chapter 8

3 years that would bring in increasing demand of the Asian aviation market to Japan. Specifically, the responsibilities included collecting information regarding LCCs, building connections, and researching the possibility of establishing an LCC in Japan.

With ANA heavily relying on domestic routes for nearly 90% of its profit, expansion to overseas was unavoidable in order to grow its business. It is currently especially necessary to take in passengers from Asian countries nearby. In addition, there were movements in the LCCs all over the world, executing strict control over costs, utilizing IT for efficiency, and thereby decreasing the regular airfare to half its conventional amount to cultivate customers. To reduce the airfare by 20% to 30% can be achieved somehow by improvements in business flows, but the new LCC is aiming for the airfare to be less than half of that of the regular airfare for LCs. It was necessary to rebuild the entire company's cost structure fundamentally from the structure itself.

Establishment of a new LCC involves numerous difficulties such as the hiring of personnel, an acquisition or the purchasing of aircraft, selection of air routes, sourcing of funds, etc. It would be more efficient to act as a division of ANA where the abundant human networks and in-house resources can be utilized. However, that would create a lack of self-reliance and lead to relying on the brand value of ANA, an LC. To actualize a company with a cheap cost structure offering half the price of the regular airfare is impossible, unless Peach Aviation abandons its ideologies and perspectives as ANA, an LC.

On the other hand, the personnel policy to hand one-way tickets to those who retired ANA, including the four executives, who were to become employees of the new airline, Peach Aviation, which started as an in-house venture, was the first of its kind in the history of ANA. However, in order to express the commitment to achieve the goal of being profitable in 3 years, erasing the accumulated loss in 5 years, many of the employees believed that they should cut ties with ANA.

For instance, even though employees participated in LCC related conferences, it was difficult to gather information from LC employees. During that time, they received advice from people who worked at the frontline of LCC businesses, and began to give the employees the confidence to establish Peach Aviation.

Mr. Murphy, the former chairman of Ryanair[2] who successfully established the first LCC in Europe, instructed the importance of cost management and hospitality as the key factors for the success of LCCs. He explained that the success of an LCC depends on the region, and how hard it is to find domestic latent demand until you actually can start the business, and indicated the need for an original LCC unique to Japan. The CEO also began to feel that the LCC business model that made great strides mainly in Europe may not fit well in Japan, and asked Mr. Murphy who shared similar ideas to become an adviser of Peach Aviation. He contributed much towards the establishment of the airline. Mr. Branson, the chairman of Virgin Group, emphasized the importance of differentiation and providing outstanding experience like no other to customers. His advice, based on his experience as a latecomer to the aviation industry who outclassed others, was significant. Moreover, the importance of innovation was explained: the accumulation of unusual things creates innovation and triggers to uncover the latent needs of the customers. They explained the key points of LCC businesses including the mistakes and the successes unsparingly to the CEO who might one day become a rival in the business. The reason for this is because as entrepreneurs of LCCs having the same aspiration, they had an executive mindset of a business venture that creates services as never before that contributes to the benefit of the consumer. What makes an LCC an LCC is its liberal and easy-going environment, and this notion did not exist in LCs like ANA. By retiring from ANA, the determination to commit to the establishment of a new airline is freshly made. Moreover, nobody would follow a leader if the leader does not enjoy the job the most—a lesson to success taught by the elder entrepreneurs of LCCs.

In addition to the management team from ANA, other regular employees were required to be hired to start and deploy the new LCC, Peach Aviation. The factor that enabled the launching within a short period of about 1 year after the establishment,

---

2 Ryanair is the largest airline in Europe that transformed from an LC to an LCC, and it currently operates services to 86 destinations with 1,800 flights daily (33 countries, 200 routes) and boasts 31 years of no accidents and No. 1 in Europe for on-time performance.

was the personnel hiring standard that had been firmly established, and professional personnel who shared the same policy could be hired. It was important to share the "sense of values" for the vision of establishing the company which is based on Peach Aviation Spirit: "Safety first", "Understanding and respect", "Inventive ideas while caring about costs", and "Enjoy working".

In terms of the hiring process of professionals such as pilots, JAL went bankrupt right around when Peach Aviation was recruiting. Therefore, the airline acquired many of their excellent and seasoned former JAL pilots and engineers who support the current growth of Peach Aviation. The pilots who were hired evaluated Peach Aviation as an airline where they are expected to do more than what they are told to do, unlike the LCs they used to work for, and contributed much to its growth. In the hiring of the flight attendants, there was practically no budget for advertisements, but the in-house idea of creating round paper fans, and for the employees to distribute them caught mass media's attention, and the company was able to attract more than 4,000 applicants, greatly exceeding expectations.

Through these cases, the company noticed that creativity was the only way for an LCC in Japan to survive. The employees are comprised of a variety of people: one-third from ANA, one-third are foreigners from other LCCs, and one-third from other industries. There are various nationalities, ages, careers, and many different opinions among them, but such diversity is considered good for the company. While Peach Aviation is a group with diverse backgrounds, the same sense of values and aspirations are shared by all, and this leads to strength in unity. Unity is thought to link to smooth operation of services.

It is important during the start-up of a venture to have ideas to do something interesting or something never done before. People who want to be protected by a renowned brand such as ANA are not suitable for a business like LCCs. Based on experience thus far, the CEO decided to find the best way to establish the company with employees who are not afraid to fail and are fully committed to make innovations. The company was filled with motivated employees, the experienced personnel who regarded the future entry of foreign LCCs in the Japanese aviation market as a business opportunity, ready to create new aviation services with their

Chapter 8

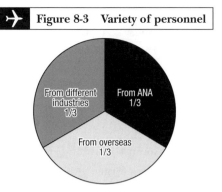

Figure 8-3 Variety of personnel

Note: Demographics of Peach Aviation's employees
Source: Created by the author based on Peach Aviation's internal documents

own hands.

4. Raising Funds for the Establishment

The initial preparation for the establishment of the LCC involved creating a 5-year business plan necessary to present to investors, when seeking for external investors. Until now, ANA has experienced establishing aviation related subsidiary companies and giving technical support during the establishment of LCCs such as Skymark Airlines. However, it was the first time to start up an LCC on its own.

ANA decided on September 9th, 2010 to invest in a joint business regarding an LCC with First Eastern Investment Group (FE), an investment fund based in Hong Kong led by Mr. Chu. The environment surrounding the Japanese aviation industry at the time was drastically changing, including the promotion of liberalization and deregulation in the aviation market. In Asia, where the economic growth is pronounced, ANA has been seeking to be "Asia's No. 1 Airline", and has felt the need for the creation of new demand contrasting from the past ANA brand. FE was established in 1988 and has made various investments mainly inside China such as infrastructure businesses and real estate developments. It was looking for a business partner to work together on developing a business as an opportunity with the increasing number of Chinese travelers visiting Japan. Furthermore, the promotion of LCC's entry was included in the growth strategy[3] of MLIT, and the two companies agreed to conduct the LCC business in Japan together.

The following three conditions are adopted for the direction of the LCC that ANA and FE are aiming for together: (1) independent management, (2) business structure to promote low-cost operation, and (3) provision of low airfare that breaks the norm. Of these three points, "independent management" indicated clearly the thinking of ANA towards the entry of LCCs, and clearly showed its view of how crucial it is to guarantee the independence of the LCC management even if there may be some cannibalization, since too much involvement by the parent company during the establishment led to failures in many cases in the past. In this way, the predecessor of Peach Aviation was established in February 2011, raising funds of up to 15 billion JPY from the domestic investors before the start of its service.

A320 was selected as the aircraft and the company planned to introduce 10 aircraft through an operating lease. Innovation Network Corporation of Japan (INCJ) acquired 33.3% of the stock (10 million JPY) of the predecessor airline of Peach Aviation in March 2011. As a result, the ratio of capital contribution became ANA 33.4%, FE 33.3%, INCJ 33.3%, and by applying the equity method to the original goal of guaranteeing independence from ANAHD was achieved. The investment of these two companies not only enriched the funding, but also resulted in the secondary effect of creating a realistic business plan through the board meeting.

5. Establishing and Spreading the Brand Concept of Peach Aviation

Peach Aviation's airfare is, when operating on the same routes, one-third between Osaka–Sapporo, and a half between Osaka–Okinawa routes. The lowest fare is set to less than one-third compared to the other airlines.

Nevertheless, the in-service rate[4] of Peach Aviation for 2015 was 99.3% and the on-

---

3 The expansion of merit to the users by promoting LCCs' entry is adopted as a strategy in MLIT's policy investigation of each field.
4 The probability of an aircraft to arrive at the destination on schedule. It is a big thing that passengers expect.

Chapter 8

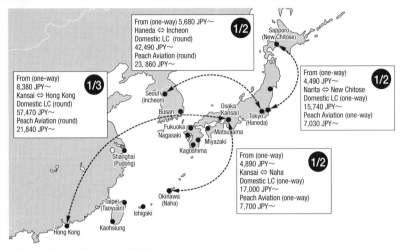

Figure 8-4 Comparison of airfares between Peach Aviation and LCs

Note: Data of Summer 2016
Source: Created by the author based on Peach Aviation's internal documents

time departure rate was about 80%. In other words, the high-quality service model of inflight service rate and consistent low airfares is actualizing the concept a "flying train". The flights leave on time, leaving behind the late passengers. Just as passengers buy tickets by themselves for trains, the flight tickets are mainly sold through a website, and 97% of reservations are made through the website. Machines were developed to process the check-in as fast as 5 seconds, and the airline computer arbitrarily chooses the seats just like the non-reserved seats on a train. The check-in process can also be completed by just scanning a barcode on the passenger's contactless smart card like the Suica in Japan. The ticket is issued in a receipt format, and advertisements of its destinations are inserted as well. The advertising revenue covers the cost of the check-in machine terminals. These ideas are implemented to simplify the workload of the customers and to save costs. Additionally, in recent years, the check-in machines are manufactured with corrugated material to save cost and weight. Furthermore, the in-flight sales are provided just like the cart service on the Shinkansen; passengers can purchase food, beverages, and in-flight meals with local delicacies of various regions. These meals are popular among foreign passengers and they sell out constantly despite the short flight time.

Chapter 8

Moreover, Peach Aviation has customized the LCC business model to accommodate the Japanese people. As a general rule, refund is unavailable on an LCC, but insurance can be added by paying an additional 10% of the airfare, so that a full refund can be possible under certain circumstances. The flight tickets are sold directly through the airlines' website as well as through the partnership with other travel agencies. In addition, the flight tickets can be purchased in convenience stores, and this customization of the business model for the Japanese market seems to be contributing to the increase in number of users. However, on March 1st, 2012, the first day of service, numerous Internet accesses brought down the website server, and it showed the risks caused by network direct sales unique to LCCs. In other developed countries, the LCC image of "you get what you pay for" is obsolete and an LCC such as Ryanair which renewed its website recently has changed it to a sophisticated design like that of an LC. Peach Aviation follows the conventional LCC model for the basic platform such as the aircraft management but realizes a change in the expectation of the customers worldwide, and tries to provide services that can help differentiate itself from competitors.

The customers of Peach Aviation are 48.2% male and 51.8% female. In terms of age group, 50% of the passengers are comprised of people in their twenties and thirties who do not have much flight experiences. In international flights, 70% of the passengers are foreigners.

When the international flights were operated with low airfares, customers in Osaka began to visit South Korea and Taipei, and return on the same day. Additionally, women from Taipei were coming to Okinawa to go to beauty salons. As you can see, it has become convenient to visit Japan. For instance, the lowest round-trip airfare for the Kansai International Airport–Incheon International Airport route is on a 7,000 JPY level, and there are a lot of people who fly for the first time. Idyllic scenery of flowers blooming in the peach groves of Wakayama Prefecture has become a popular topic on social media, and tourists from Taipei and Hong Kong are rushing to these locations. The flower sightseeing period is short, but friends of the customers who visited last week are coming for a visit the following week based on word-of-mouth information. Foreign tourists are discovering new ways to travel by themselves finding many attractive regions, where Japanese people never expected

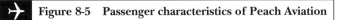

Figure 8-5 Passenger characteristics of Peach Aviation

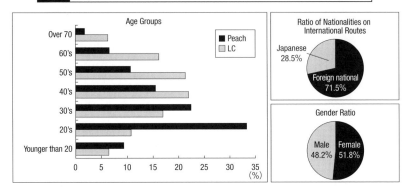

Note: Data of 2015
Source: Created by the author based on Peach Aviation's internal documents

them to be a tourist destination, and spread the word through social media. Since Peach Aviation's airfares are cheap, travelers can afford to visit Japan frequently and visit not only the famous tourist sites, but also the unvarnished locations with "traditional Japan" intact that have not been developed into tourist attractions yet. Peach Aviation has correctly guessed that "a movement searching for the Real Japan" will start from hereafter. The purposes of travel using Peach Aviation are "spur-of-the-moment tour", "event participation", "nursing", "commuting to hospital", and so forth, and over 90% of them are for personal travels.[5] Like this, the purposes of trips are mainly for leisure with very few business passengers, resulting in the cabin atmosphere to be friendly and casual.

Peach Aviation has focused on women in their twenties and thirties having created a brand concept of "Cute & Cool" (inspired by the Akihabara subculture) from the beginning of its service, and has continued to disseminate modern Japanese culture. In order to spread this concept, pink and purple were chosen as the predominant colors for the aircraft and the uniform of the flight attendants. The company is striving to establish a stylish and individual image. The cabin design is integrated with the color highly popular among women, and the aircraft is painted to make it

---

5 Peach Aviation's internal documents.

glittery and shiny. These efforts aroused people's interest, and when the aircraft lands at Kansai International Airport, there is an increasing number of female passengers taking pictures of it. The company succeeded in gaining recognition with little cost by working with social media. Eliminating boarding bridges and making customers walk to the aircraft to board was a style chosen to cut costs, but it uncovered an unexpected need of the passengers wanting to take pictures in front of the aircraft to upload to social media and spread it.

The name of the company also reflects the influence received from the top executives of other preceding LCCs. Peach is a fruit that has its origin in Asia, and Japanese peaches are very popular in other Asian countries. Hence, the word "peach" has a positive image. "Peach" written in English will be easily recognized by people globally. The company received and respected the advice from others that both "air" and "sky" in the company name would make it sound like any other airline.

Thus, Peach Aviation succeeded in establishing an original image as an innovative airline, staying away from the low-cost airline image of "you get what you pay for" without incurring advertisement costs. They express the feature of the ease of flying at any time as a "flying train" and succeeded in its branding strategy that differentiates the brand from others. They created new passenger needs, developed latent demand, and contributed to acquiring repeat customers.

Peach Aviation's brand image is low airfares supported by low costs, but also offers high quality aviation services. Unlike Southeast Asia, the LCCs in Northeast Asia are all lined up on the start line with no company outstanding others. By establishing an innovative brand concept differentiating from others, and building cost competitive power, the company believes it can gain and maintain a certain level of market share.

✈ 2   Development and Innovation of Peach Aviation

Thus, the headquarters was moved from Tokyo to within Kansai International Airport. It was the birth of the first airline based in Osaka servicing both domestic and international routes. Although it was thought to be difficult for a Kansai-based LCC to succeed, contrary to expectations, the passengers in the Kansai area seemed to be gladly accepting the efficient service model. Accordingly, the airline revitalized Kansai International Airport which traditionally had an annual utilization of about 14 million passengers, and aroused the latent demand of travelers who had not yet traveled before. As a result, it can be appraised that the airline increased the size of the pie of the overall transport mode.

Since then, Peach Aviation obtained the Air Operator's Certificate (AOC) in July 2011 and the approval for flight operation using congested airports in October 2011.[6] When reflecting back on the situation at the time, the number of foreign LCCs providing service to Japan in July 2011 point in time was nine airlines with 21 routes and 200 flights (100 roundtrips per week), moreover the LCC share of international flights in Japan was merely 3%. Furthermore, AirAsia Japan and Jetstar Japan were established around the same period in August and September 2012 respectively, through the mergers with ANA, and 2012 was called the "first year of LCCs in Japan".

1. Coexistence of Low-Cost and High-Quality

The low cost of its flight tickets is not the only reason for the popularity of Peach Aviation. There were existing issues at the time of entering service due to utilizing Japanese airports: (1) the capacity limit of the airport parking aprons, where aircraft park for their operations, and an increase in the number of flights, (2) the need for expansion of the check-in counters, and the time lag between acquisition of aircraft and the start of service, and (3) maintaining low fares despite the high airport fees, and so on.
These issues were possibly hindering LCCs to maintain low airfares.

2. Installation of the Terminal for the Exclusive Use of LCCs

When an LCC is pursuing low costs by all means, there is a limit to how much an

---

6 Peach Aviation's internal documents.

Chapter 8

LCC can handle by itself. With the cooperation of Kansai Airports, a terminal exclusively for LCCs was finally established (established in April, 2012). In addition to focusing on functionality, economy, safety, and minimalistic interior design, there are various arrangements implemented to save the costs. For instance, by parking the aircraft diagonally at the parking apron, there is no need for a tow tractor for push-back at the time of departure, and it can lead to saving costs for an LCC.

Moreover, the passengers do not use the boarding bridge but head to the aircraft on foot. These arrangements reduce the terminal usage fees, and have a large cost-saving effect to an LCC. Additionally, until the LCC terminal is completed, instead of using the expensive existing terminal, the headquarters will use the adjacent building, where a department store had previously conducted business with escalators and other facilities still left as it was, as a terminal to reduce costs and enable flight service.

3. Aircraft Procurement Method and Establishment of Operation System

In order to make sure that the profitability can be raised by definitely acquiring a new aircraft, the "operating lease method" was selected thus far as the aircraft procurement method. However, it has been changed to a method called "sales and leaseback" for the recent contract for three aircraft, in which they were purchased from Airbus and were immediately resold to a company from which they were then leased. In this way, corporate strength and the negotiation power with the aircraft manufacturer are examined depending on the situation, to keep the cost down for the procurement of high-cost aircraft.

Furthermore, as for the operation system, a combination of a centralized control system and a completely entrusted system is utilized to aim for an efficient operation. By consolidating all functions to the center with the centralized control system, it became possible to provide stable high-quality service and make quick decisions. In addition, the experts of the aviation industry and qualified people were gathered in the headquarters to simultaneously attempt the clarification of the responsibility-taking system and the reinforcement of the entrustment management system. Through these efforts, the shortening of the training period for related works, and prevention of misoperations were possible. At the same time, the resources at the entrusted company were able to be fully utilized which resulted in the preparation period to be shortened, and flexible correspondence was executed according to the number of service flights.

◆ 4. Securing Punctuality and Safety with Innovative Technologies

Peach Aviation attaches importance to the improvement of key quality indicated by "punctuality". The in-service rate for 2015 was 99.3% and the on-time departure rate was about 80%, exceeding those of the LCs, and almost at the highest level of the airlines in Japan. They have been supported by the construction of a thorough safety promotion system from the day of its establishment and by the existence of technological strength. As an example of the two factors mentioned above, the company held 64 in-house conferences related to safety from the AOC issue in July 2011 to October 2016. Furthermore, in order to acquire the skills and the know-how regarding flight safety, the company pays for technical support from ANAHD. Although ANAHD does not interfere in the business operation of Peach Aviation, it cooperates in regard to safety which is the largest mission of public transportation. The new aircraft, A320, is used as the operational and maintenance aircraft, and aircraft that are older than 8 years are not to be used as a policy. This policy contributes to the effort to suppress aircraft malfunctions. All of the aircraft it owns have obtained the continuous airworthiness certification for an indefinite period, in 3 years and seven months from the day of launch, confirming its high technical capabilities. Simultaneously, the tasks involved in the maintenance of A320 are the same for an LCC or an LC, and in order to implement low costs, the organization is promoting multi-skilled workers, who can perform work done by several people at an LC by oneself, and providing IT support to achieve that. In addition, the periodic process of aircraft inspection is included in the daily maintenance for the leveling of work so that cost-savings can be achieved.

The technical power and innovations are supporting such stable high-quality service and safety systems, and have high-cost-saving efforts that are linked to the increase in revenue. The design for the new company was carefully planned at its establishment and that is why the business established smoothly. It can be said that this is the result of the efforts made by everyone in the company, and the full preparation and research based on a precise plan.

3 Analyzing the Factors of Rapid Growth and Successful Performance

This section will analyze the success factors for the appraised performance of Peach Aviation whilst the other LCCs in Japan were found in a slump. Although Peach Aviation is an LCC, the LCC business model itself started with Southwest Airlines in the 1970s. Peach Aviation was late in entering the aviation industry as an LCC. This LCC in the late starters group would have difficulties even if it followed the business model of successful predecessors. In order to differentiate itself from other LCCs, the strategies in the following seven points, the so-called "LCC that suits the Japanese aviation market(Japanized)", were necessary.

(1) While many LCCs were based in Narita International Airport, only Peach Aviation was based in Kansai International Airport. It succeeded in attracting customers with the Kansai model that became established in the local area as the "Kansai Local LCC". As a result, the average load factor exceeded 86.7% throughout the year. This number is miraculous in the Japanese aviation market where the difference between the peak and low season is great. The numbers for the other companies flying domestic routes are 66% for JAL and 75% for Jetstar Japan.

(2) It started out as the first LCC in Japan with already an economy of scale, and the utilization rate of the aircraft was high as well. The 18 aircraft currently in possession are being fully utilized. Since merely retaining the aircraft cost large expenditures such as parking fees and maintenance fees, the service plan for new routes and aircraft procurement timing were carefully adjusted beforehand so that there was no deviation.

(3) Peach Aviation has chosen to have a large portion of international routes compared to other LCCs, establishing nine international routes within two months after the beginning of service to balance the route plan. In addition, the international routes would comprise half of the total routes in the future. Compared to other LCCs that have around 20% of international routes, Peach Aviation's overwhelming

Chapter 8

routes are money-generating, since they are long-range, great value, and the aircraft utilization is better.

(4) It has followed the example of Ryanair implementing safe operations and high quality simultaneously, gaining customer trust.

(5) It has thoroughly implemented innovative cost management in various places to raise productivity.

(6) It has presented strong brand concept towards women and made it immediately clear to which customer segment it is targeting.

(7) It is necessary to constantly create innovations to provide new customer values in order to continue growing as a corporation. For example, the check-in machines are made of cheap corrugated boxes and cost a few tenths compared to that of an LC. The machine has two large monitors, and display two different types of information—the lower display shows the customer check-in process while the upper display shows information for the next customer. The multilingual display helps the foreign tourists to understand the operation, and the customers in line can prepare in advance which contributes to shortening the check-in time.

The company succeeds in constantly creating new customer value through various innovative efforts as shown above.

◘ 1. Room for Improvement and Growth in the Mature Aviation Market

The growth strategy of the Abe administration is to increase the number of foreign visitors to Japan to 40 million by 2020, and the government is seriously organizing its support structure. The aviation industry believes that although there are many regulations, many opportunities to create innovations exsist. There is also an issue of shortage of facilities for immigration of passengers at the airport.

Airlines themselves cannot solve these types of problems but the airports as well as, the transport facilities responsible for the access to airports, and the municipalities at the service destinations need to all work together as one, and try to acquire foreign visitors to Japan. When the ASEAN Economic Community(AEC) inaugurates, the traffic will increase compared to before and the demand for aviation is expected to explode. The foreign LCCs mainly from Asia are expected to enter the Japanese market increasingly in the future, and there are still many places to make improvements and challenges to face even in this aviation industry with many regulations. In addition, the LCCs in Japan need to make efforts and be creative in their activities to acquire foreign visitors to Japan. Thereby, there are many elements that must be improved in the aviation policy. Due to foreign capital restrictions, the difficulty of procuring funds for launching business, and the lack of training facilities for foreign pilots are becoming an issue.

2. Sustainable Growth and Evolution of Peach Aviation

Peach Aviation was founded from the corporate venturing of ANA and began its service as an LCC in March 2012. It has grown quickly through various efforts that were well received by the Japanese passengers which were not available in other conventional LCCs, such as the naming, the design of the cabin interior, in-flight meals, check-in machines made of corrugated boxes, etc. The shares of Peach Aviation stock were held by three companies, ANAHD, IRC, and FE, the investment fund, since its establishment in 2011, and now, ANAHD is to buy nearly half the shares held by each of the other companies. Most of the LCCs of the world have succeeded as independent companies, and though ANA held back to be a company under the application of the equity method at its establishment, on February 24th, 2017, the leading stockholder invested an additional 30.4 billion JPY and increased its share from 38.7% to 67%, and announced its plan to make Peach Aviation a subsidiary by April 2017.

Peach Aviation was fighting alone from the beginning of its service, but it had trouble in continuing such battle independently throughout intense competition in its growth phase. The airline believes that it could receive the support from ANAHD to accelerate its strategies even further. It also wants to have more passengers to benefit from the increased corporate value of Peach Aviation. It can receive support from ANAHD for the operation and maintenance, joint purchase of aircraft and fuel, and so forth. ANAHD will respect the independence of Peach Aviation in its personnel, airfare and service, and will not send in executives intentionally from the parent company. However, it is undecided in regard to mileage partnerships, sharing of the reservation system with ANAHD, membership in an alliance, and code-sharing.

Chapter 8

There is an apprehension in Peach Aviation that the traditional independence will be lost by becoming a subsidiary. However, the company has no authority to decide in this matter and the decision will be made among only the three investing companies. The stockholders, however, have promised that the independence of the company will continue to be assured in the future. It is uncertain, however, that ANAHD will respect the independence of Peach Aviation, since ANAHD has invested in various domestic LCCs, taking control, and code-sharing with them in the past.

Vanilla Air operates as a subsidiary of ANAHD already, and in contrast to Peach Aviation that steadily produces profits, Vanilla Air faced fierce competition on the Taipei route and reported a loss in the period of April to December 2016. There are some routes from the two companies that overlap one another, and although ANAHD said it will leave them to compete freely, there is a demand to streamline the internal operation. Thus, it is possible that the two companies will integrate in the future. Moreover, Vanilla Air is looking to enter the middle and long-range international routes, and if that plan materializes, ANAHD may consolidate the short-range routes to Peach Aviation in order to optimize routes and aircraft.

ANAHD is the major shareholder in many of the middle-class airlines in Japan. As

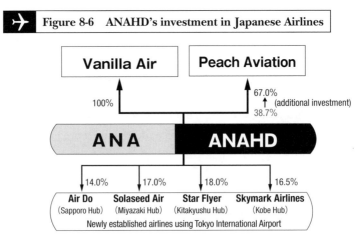

Figure 8-6 ANAHD's investment in Japanese Airlines

Note: Numbers are investment contribution ratio.
Source: Created by the author based on Peach Aviation's internal documents

shown in Figure 8-6, it invested 16.5% in Skymark Airlines that went bankrupt in January 2015 and became its rehabilitation sponsor. Similarly, some LCCs that newly entered the market since the deregulation in the latter part of 1990 such as Air Do, Solaseed Air, and Star Flyer were in financial difficulties and became subsidiaries of ANA. Skymark Airlines is refusing to code-share with ANAHD in order to maintain its independence, but the remaining three companies are already using ANAHD's CRS and code-sharing.

ANAHD has currently estimated the corporate value of Peach Aviation at a little less than 110 billion JPY and executed additional stock purchase. The price of the purchase is 40 times more than the recent net profit, and many insist that the price is too high, when considering the Price Earnings Ratio (PER) of the listed airlines worldwide and the growth potential. It may be correct to think that ANAHD intended to go that far to make Peach Aviation its subsidiary, to increase its business before the government restriction ends for JAL in March 2017.

As mentioned in Chapter 6, ANAHD hoped to avoid letting the limited number of arrival and departure slots to fall into the hands of JAL as much as possible. JAL, which happened to gain a profitable structure with the support of the Japanese government, is only making ANAHD more impatient. Our attention is focused on the skills of Peach Aviation and ANA group to see whether Peach Aviation can continue to grow without losing its most attractive feature of independence while it leverages the scale of merit with ANA group.

Conclusion: The Succesful Japanization of an LCC

The total number of passengers of Peach Aviation has exceeded 10 million in August 2015. Moreover, the results for 2015 were: in-service rate 99.3%, annual number of passengers 4.54 million, load factor 86.7%—all at a high level. Such results were also shown in the financial results. Peach Aviation gained a profit in only 25 months after starting its service in March 2012, grew into an innovative company that established the LCC concept in Japan, and accelerated the construction of the LCC business model that did not exist in the past, proving that

Peach Aviation changed the sky of Asia entirely. Furthermore, by March 2016, it achieved three consecutive years of increasing revenue and profit as well as eliminating its cumulative loss as originally planned (Figure 8-1). Furthermore, it can be seen from its presence in Kansai International Airport, its base airport, that Peach Aviation is established in Japan as an LCC. In addition, Peach Aviation has surpassed the domestic LCs such as ANA and JAL to be ranked No. 1 in the number of domestic and international flights serviced in the last week of September 2016 at Kansai International Airport.

On the other hand, it is important to consider the value of Peach Aviation's establishment to its parent company, ANAHD. The consolidated accounts as of current March 2016 are: revenue of 1,791.1 billion JPY and a record net profit of 78.1 billion JPY. As for the airline business, the revenue for the domestic passenger revenue was 685.6 billion JPY, and the international passenger revenue was 515.6 billion JPY, an increase year-on-year.[7] It is assumed that the cannibalization by Peach Aviation's revenue of less than 50 billion JPY by March 2016 has minimal impact. As mentioned previously, the major customer segments of Peach Aviation are the young generation in their twenties and thirties who use the airline for personal travel, and foreigners, which are different from the customer segments of an LC. This fact implies that Peach Aviation has uncovered a new and different demand. It can be said that Peach Aviation's service entry has changed the "lifestyle" of many foreigners. Due to such circumstances, ANAHD has recognized that Peach Aviation's service entry has developed a new demand and has given a certain appreciation to the LCC's service entry.

Subsequently, the question at hand is then what kind of role did Peach Aviation play in terms of blocking the entry of foreign LCCs into the domestic aviation market. Jetstar Japan, established mainly by Qantas Group, and JAL, is ranked top in terms of number of aircraft, passengers, and operating revenue, but Peach Aviation is on the same level with them and far exceeds in terms of profit. AirAsia Japan, subsequently, restarted as Vanilla Air and is ranked third as a 100% subsidiary of ANAHD. From this perspective, the existence of Peach Aviation, an LCC born in Japan, is assumed to

---

7 According to ANA Group's *Annual Report 2016* and *Fact Book 2016*.

have contained the entry of foreign LCCs, including Qantas Group, into the Japanese market up to a certain extent.

Although Peach Aviation started its service smoothly as the Japanese LCC, it also has some issues to solve. Currently, the LCC share of the Japanese domestic routes is about 8% and there is much room to grow in comparison to the LCC share in oversea markets. To support this type of growth, it is necessary to prepare for the increase in aircraft procurement, securing of human resources and so forth along with the increase of routes. On the other hand, a change is still required for Peach Aviation that has grown to over 800 employees. Future issues are examined below.

(1) It is believed that the development-stage has ended. In order to accelerate growth in the next growth phase, Peach Aviation needs not only to make use of its company culture and brand while respecting originality, but also to receive the necessary support from ANA group. Peach Aviation will further promote the expansion of domestic and overseas bases, taking lead in the aviation market as the representative of Japanese LCCs, and will contribute to the development of tourism and the Japanese economy through the creation of aviation demand and regional revitalization. Moreover, the company should continue to have the mindset to keep making innovations in order not to fall into defensive mode, which will be the key to success.
(2) Even if the company were to grow large enough to own 300 aircraft, it is highly possible for it to suffer along other LCCs in the battle for survival amongst fierce competition. When there are many competing factors with other candidates then ultimately a price war will ensue. Therefore, Peach Aviation will become an LC for Japan, differentiating itself from other LCCs.
(3) Since Peach Aviation started its operation, Taiwan and Korea have become day-trip destinations. It made traveling affordable and accessible for everyone who seeks to enrich their lives with traveling. Peach Aviation is more than just an alternative to LCs, and it influences customers' lifestyles. Peach Aviation's remarkable progress has already exceeded the role of an LCC supplementing an LC.

There is a need to consider what direction Peach Aviation will move towards in the future. Although it has been said that LCCs can never succeed in Japan, Peach Aviation, a Japanized LCC has succeeded. Hereafter, Peach Aviation should continue to expand and develop its business, in virtue of synergy with a strong stockholder, ANAHD, whilst seeking the uniquely constructed sense of Peach Aviation. As the leading LCC symbolizing Japan, Peach Aviation will aim to become a bridge for Asia, taking on the role of a "flying train" globally, making air travel more familiar to everyone.

CHAPTER 9
Conclusion and Future Challenges

Chapter 9

✈ Introduction

In this study, after analyzing success factors of international LCCs, the reasons behind the unsuccessful business models of Japanese LCCs were studied in Chapter 3. Based on the study results, a new successful business model was constructed and verified through profitability analysis by financing simulation using a corporate model as well as risk analysis according to the Monte Carlo method in Chapter 4.

This chapter, based on various analyses conducted in previous chapters, will discuss successful management factors for establishing LCCs as well as proposals of reform in instructional and market structural restrictions and aviation policies, which are to be related to successful management factors.

✈ 1 Conclusion of Management Policy

◆ 1. Building Low-Cost Structures

Cost reduction is a key element for LCCs in competing against LCs. From such aspect, cost analysis in Chapter 3 has revealed that Japanese LCCs are not operating under a low-cost effort.

The first reason for this is LCs' uneven distribution of management resources in the Japanese aviation market. While LCCs in Europe and North America operate at a low cost by outsourcing aircraft maintenance since they have a rich variety of outsourcing destinations, the training system for crew members and aircraft maintenance, sales as well as related operations in Japanese LCCs must face a peculiar situation in that they must outsource such resources to the rivaling LCs. The outsourcing cost will be high for new LCCs due to the limited number of outsourcing choices and little negotiation power. To avoid high-cost outsourcing, LCCs must establish their own self-management systems. However, self-management of such resources will be expensive until the company grows into a certain business scale. It must pay high outsourcing fees until it establishes a self-management

Chapter 9

system, but now it has become possible for LCCs to put resources together to establish a co-founded maintenance facility to serve all of their aircraft at a much lower cost. This new choice is reflected in the simulation. For the first time in this simulation, the maintenance outsourcing cost is included. The simulation results show that a new LCC can be established even by executing in-house training for mechanics and crew members if other management factors are in fine condition. Therefore, new LCCs must aim at establishing a self-management system for management resources.

The second reason is due to the restriction of arrival and departure slots. Japanese LCCs had to start operation with only one aircraft, which meant there was little to no effect in terms of economies of scale in the airline industry. At the time of launch, however, a reasonable size of fleet benefitted from economies of scale, and therefore was able to lower the average cost. As indicated, in the simulation results in Chapter 4, thus a new LCC must start with a business model utilizing a fleet of 15 aircraft. Prior to the start of business, the freedom in route selection and number of flights has to be guaranteed, and the funding issues have to be solved.

Thirdly, the simulation results demonstrated its effectiveness in launching an LCC with leased aircraft and then purchasing them as more funds become available. Still, leased aircraft are relatively expensive, and shifting to one's own aircraft at an early stage is required to lower the middle and long-term costs.

Fourthly, new LCCs need to put even more effort into lowering costs even though institutional barriers are recently becoming less of a problem. However, institutional issues may still prevent the airline companies from lowering costs to some extent. In order to achieve such objectives, LCCs must learn from efforts of successful foreign LCCs such as using a single type of aircraft, implementing simpler operations, selecting the most efficient route structure to maximize the operation rate, and enforcing no-frills services.

Finally, as LCs still control management resources relative to sales such as the CRS system, LCCs need to focus on building an online-based sales network in order to simplify the sales process and lower sales costs, by referring to successful examples of LCCs in North America, Europe, and Asia.

◘ 2. Setting up Appropriate Fare Levels and Fare Structures

The results of the detailed analysis on competitive relationship between LCCs and LCs in Chapter 3, as well as the simulation results in Chapter 4, demonstrate that a new LCC in Japan must set its airfare at around a discount level of 40% to 50% compared to the normal fare of LCs.

The simulation analysis presented in Chapter 4, demonstrated the target value of management indices and the probability of each index that fails to achieve the target value, for investors. It examined each case of when the discount rate is 38.3% based on the receiving rate performance of LCs, and 50% for LCCs to compete with LCs which is their aim, applying the simulation that was carried out repeatedly as a reference. In Case 1(LCs), nearly all target values were achieved without risks, since the receiving rate was applied to that of LCs using the cost structure of LCCs. On the other hand, in Case 2(LCCs), the risks increase rapidly. These two cases clearly show the domestic aviation market in Japan. Moreover, it concludes that the current Japanese LCs have a profitable and sustainable management because of its control over LCCs, their incorporation of LCCs' cost structure, and their code-sharing with LCCs.

The pricing, however, is affected by the competition position of other markets as well. As analyzed in Chapter 3, competition has become more active in the Japanese aviation industry compared to the time when the LCCs first entered the industry. It has become less likely for LCs to offer predatory prices, however a competition by only offering low fares has a limit, as shown by the failures of cheap airlines that initially entered the market in the U.S.

To not repeat the same failures, LCCs must specify and clarify their own customer targets. Southwest Airlines, for example, is focusing on passengers who are sensitive to fare levels. JetBlue Airways is focusing on business class passengers. AirAsia is focusing on middle to low-income passengers who do not regularly travel by plane.

Chapter 9

In addition, LCCs must compete against railways and bus transportation. LCCs in Europe and North America compete mainly against road transportation. Whereas Japanese LCCs must compete against both road transportation and the Shinkansen, by offering relatively low fares to compete with fares offered by highway buses and the Shinkansen for the competitive routes due to increasing general demand.

Furthermore, LCCs need to target a certain class among existing passengers whose price elasticity is relatively low, in case the airline cannot offer low fares on a constant basis. In this sense, Star Flyer, a new LCC that had just entered the Japanese aviation market, at the time, is getting attention for its strategy similar to that of JetBlue Airways. Star Flyer strongly focuses on business travelers as its target, in order to differentiate itself from its competitors.

◘ 3. Setting of Route Structure and Number of Flights

The route structure plays a critical role in the productivity of airline companies. Analyses and simulations in Chapter 4 indicate that a combination of middle-distance routes and short-distance routes with high-demand contribute to the operation rate of aircraft.

In addition, the simulation adopted 100 to 150 seat small aircraft on such middle-distance routes with high-frequency operations under the conditions that the business passengers find more value on middle-distance flights, and that successful LCCs commonly operate on high-frequency flights with smaller aircraft than low-frequency flights with larger aircraft. The simulation has obtained an excellent result.

LCCs in principle operate high-frequency flights with small aircraft. However, the first-generation of LCCs in Japan had to operate according to a route structure and flight frequency determined by a restrictive and uneven institutional framework, including restriction on the number of arrival and departure slots. This was in contrast to situations in Europe and North America, where LCCs were able to choose their own routes and operate their own flight frequencies. Airline companies, which have recently entered the market, have more freedom in selecting routes compared to before, and LCCs such as Skymark Airlines have began operating. The degree of freedom in selecting routes, however, still remains as an aviation policy issue to be resolved, which will be discussed further.

Based on the results of the simulation, it is also clear that Japanese LCCs need to expand into the international market to obtain more profitable routes, as European LCCs and AirAsia have already done. This is beneficial to LCCs if they can choose a large number of potential routes with relatively high demand from a wider number of options. In that case, considering not only domestic but international routes results in more opportunities. The international aviation policy certainly has to be deregulated to make such changes possible.

4. Proactive Use of Secondary Airports

As described in Chapter 3, the use of secondary airports is the key for LCCs to succeed with low airfares. Leading LCCs in North America and Europe, such as Ryanair and Southwest Airlines, are known for their utilization of secondary airports. This is a clear contrast to new Japanese LCCs that use Tokyo International Airport, an existing hub airport as their launching location. The simulation in Chapter 4 utilizes Kobe Airport, a secondary airport with lower usage fees and less restriction on operations and slots, which became one of the key reasons in drawing a favorable result.

In the past, there were not many secondary airports in Japan, but nowadays older existing airports are being made into secondary airports as new airports are being built. In addition, new airports have been built with the function of secondary airports, such as those in Kobe Airport and Kitakyushu Airport. Newer LCCs, therefore, should consider more active use of secondary airports. Although the number of secondary airports is increasing, their use is still restricted by regulations. Recommendation for regulation changes is explained later in this chapter.

… Chapter 9

◻ 5. Securing Sufficient Funds to Prepare for Launch and Early Stages of Operations

As discussed in the first section of this chapter, "Building Low-Cost Structures", considering commonly required costs, there is a minimum economic scale for an LCC to start operating, including costs for maintenance facilities, airport-related expenses, and investment costs in IT systems for sales. As stated in the simulation in Chapter 4, it is desirable for an LCC to start operating with at least 15 aircraft.

In order to start at a certain scale of operation, by securing the number of aircraft mentioned above, new LCCs must plan a financial base to prepare for survival during its initial years, when it is bound to accumulate deficit. One key success factor for an LCC is obtaining sufficient funds at the launch of business. This is obvious as JetBlue Airways started with 160 million USD, whilst Skynet Asia Airways struggled with a fund shortage. In this study, the simulation indicates that the required cost for a new LCC to launch with 15 aircraft is approximately 9.5 billion JPY, and is four times as much as the sum that Skymark Airlines needed at the beginning of its operation. Therefore, the challenge for newer LCCs is how to secure such initial funding.

There are three scenarios for raising funds effectively. The first is the acquisition of an existing company. Referring to the case of AirAsia, the company acquired a controlling interest of a bankrupt company to start its business. For a new LCC, this is the most attractive scenario, since all existing assets such as aircraft and pilots can easily be reused for the new business model. This enables the newer LCCs to launch their services with a larger number of aircraft from the beginning.

The second scenario is the most standard method of raising funds: by presenting business plans to investors, and receiving funds from them. Since it takes quite a long time for any airline to be publicly traded, a key issue is how to convince the investors that the business will be profitable.

It is not an easy task to convince investors in Japan, who have witnessed past experiences of LCCs, and are not ready to take risks. It may be more promising to seek funds in other Asian countries where LCCs in the area receive funding mostly from local sources, and where investors are risk-takers, due to the development in the Asian airline market. There is quite a gap between the 95% and 99.99% scopes of management indices as shown in Chapter 4. For example, the difference in the bottom limit of the accumulated operating profit has risen up to 4 billion JPY. Cautious Japanese investors may not make a move unless it falls in the scope of 99.99%, whilst aggressive risk-taking foreign investors may feel comfortable at the 95% scope. Therefore, laws and regulations must be amended in order to accommodate foreign investments.

The third scenario is to seek subsidies from public sources as Air Do in Hokkaido Prefecture and Skynet Asia Airways in Miyazaki Prefecture did. Although this is an easy option, it might cause moral hazard and result in the impairment of the management.

6. The Key Factors for a Successful LCC Management Policy

The management policy requirements mentioned above are needed in order for LCCs to succeed in Japan. In other words, a successful LCC in the Japanese market consists of a business model which incorporates the following changes:

(1) Improving efficiency and lowering costs by the use of a single type of aircraft, emphasizing no-frills services, utilizing an IT-enabled sales structure, operating frequently with smaller aircraft (100 to 150 seats), self-managing maintenance and training for crew members, and constructing appropriate route structures with potential deployment of international routes

(2) Differentiation by utilizing secondary airports in metropolitan areas and targeting specific customer segments while maintaining a competitive edge against LCs by offering at least 50% discount from normal fares of LCs

(3) Ability to launch business with an operation size of 15 aircraft with 9.5 billion JPY in capital

(4) An airline with a strong innovative mind which aggressively advances into the field of air cargo services

Chapter 9

⊕ 2 The New LCC Business Model Suitable for LCCs' Endurance in Japan

◊ 1. Similarities and Differences in Strategy Between Skymark Airlines and the New LCC Business Model

● 1.1 Strategies During the Flourishing Period of Skymark Airlines

The Skymark Airlines case study will be featured one last time, to make a comparison between the empirical analysis and the harsh reality of the Japanese aviation market in order to analyze the potentiality of independent LCCs in Japan hereafter.

Although Skymark Airlines went into bankruptcy in 2015, the strategies of the company are worth mentioning, since its plans on routes, airfares, aircraft, etc., were somewhat similar to those of the simulation. Skymark Airlines had been actively expanding its domestic routes, with Kobe Airport and Tokyo International Airport as hub airports, mentioned in Chapter 6. As of December 2012, the company possessed 29 B737 aircraft, and operated 80 daily round-trip flights on 26 routes.

Skymark Airlines began service on the Tokyo International Airport–New Chitose Airport and Tokyo International Airport–Fukuoka Airport routes as its hub, and targeted high-demand routes. However, the company could not be assigned a sufficient number of arrival and departure slots, and as a result, failed to increase sales. They were able to secure passengers on the Osaka International Airport–New Chitose Airport or Osaka International Airport–Fukuoka Airport routes, but its sales issue was not solved since it had to compete against the Shinkansen, and the cost per unit was low due to touristic routes.

They were planning on beginning service on international routes in 2014 with A380 on the Narita International Airport–New York route. The existing flights have one class only, but the New York route will be operated with two classes: Premium Economy and Business class.

The winning formula of Skymark Airlines was to attract customers away from major airlines by offering lower fare on the routes operated by major airlines. Skymark Airlines did not want to get involved in a grueling campaign, such as a low price competition, with other LCCs any longer. Therefore, with regard to entering into the international market, Skymark Airlines targeted operations not on short-distance Asian routes operated by LCCs, but on long-distance international routes, which are the stronghold of LCs.

Skymark Airlines was changing its strategy on not only international routes, but also domestic routes as well. The company was initially planning to introduce larger A330 aircraft (300 seats for two classes in total) in 2014 to major routes including Tokyo International Airport–New Chitose Airport and Tokyo International Airport–Fukuoka Airport, which have the largest demand. Skymark Airlines operated the Tokyo International Airport route with an incredibly high load factor of 94% on average in 2011. Although it decreased in the spring of 2012, it recovered to 90% in October and November. This shows that every flight on this route was almost full. Originally, Skymark Airlines was operating on a small type of aircraft, B737, with only 177 seats. As no airlines are expected to secure more arrival and departure slots at Tokyo International Airport, Skymark Airlines replaced B737 with a larger aircraft (A330) to increase its capacity.

- **1.2 The Premature Expansion Process of Skymark Airlines and Its Consequences**

However, there were some flaws in Skymark Airlines' strategy, anticipating expansion by introducing two types of Airbus aircraft. The first factor was the company's ability to attract more customers to international flights, for which the company planned to use A380. It is difficult to fill up 228 seats of business and economy class to exceed the break-even point with a load factor of 60%. JAL or ANA can provide only 77 seats in business class and 46 seats in premium economy class at maximum on the New York route. Although Skymark Airlines could attract customers utilizing contracts with more than 1,000 industrial clients and travel agencies, it is expected to face an uphill battle especially in the U.S. due to its low profile. Thus, partnerships in the U.S. were necessary.

Secondly, regarding domestic routes operated by A330, Skymark Airlines had 10%

of share on the Tokyo International Airport–New Chitose Airport route and 15% on the Tokyo International Airport–Fukuoka Airport route. JAL and ANA have ignored smaller portions of shares since they can earn sufficient profit by providing seats at an expensive price. However, if Skymark Airlines had achieved a level of 20%–30%, the major airlines had to offer a counteractive discount price.

The former CEO of Skymark Airlines, was open-minded and an important figure, similar to CEOs of successful foreign LCCs. He utilized his experience in the IT industry, and insisted that the most important mission for the company is to maximize profits with lower costs. Major airlines in the world are still competitive despite LCC's attack, due to the diversity of their businesses. They have long-distance international routes, charter flight services, with first and business classes. It is necessary for LCs to improve the diversity of businesses to avoid cost competition. Thus, Skymark Airlines did not follow the existing LCC's strategies such as the use of a single type of aircraft, short-distance flights, and having only one class type.

◘ 2. The Comparison Between the Simulation and Skymark Airlines

Despite similarities between the simulation and Skymark Airlines, some strategies were completely different. Skymark Airlines began to target high-demand routes from Tokyo International Airport, however, failed when the company was not able to acquire enough arrival and departure slots. Although Skymark Airlines still secured high-demand routes from the Kansai area, including some touristic routes, they were not able to compete with the Shinkansen and cost per unit was relatively low. Correspondingly, the load factor did not increase, as it did not acquire enough passengers.

The new LCC model will use Kobe Airport as a hub, and will operate only on high-demand routes. Moreover, by providing service on international routes, it will obtain customers at the final destinations other than Kobe by maintaining same demand, increasing the profitability. It will also conduct web-based destination marketing, which had not been used by Skymark Airlines. For the middle and long-term goals of the new LCC model, it is important to attract original target customers of LCCs, the individual tourists. Skymark Airlines did not create any strategy regarding this point. The new model concentrates on routes with high-demands, and constantly continues its operation without expansion for 10 years. Its fare structure is simple, being set to only 40% or 50% of the normal fare. The fare for the Kobe Airport–Tokyo International Airport and Kobe Airport–Nagasaki Airport routes will be cheaper than that of Skymark Airlines this way, and with the price setting, tickets can be sold directly via the website and not through travel agents. On the other hand, Skymark Airlines occasionally attracted customers by setting an unreasonably low price. The new business model, as a business cost reduction measure, will use only a single type of aircraft, B737, to cope with the problem of maintenance costs. This is a issue that has been commonly shared by many LCCs. The model will minimize parts procurement costs as well, and will minimize maintenance costs by outsourcing the maintenance to MRO, a co-founded maintenance company. As a result, the new model can maintain cost per ASK at a low level. Indeed, ASK is an important management index for an airline company, but as for the initial funds, Skymark Airlines was established with 150 million JPY, and increased its capital every few years. The new business model for this study procures the 9.5 billion JPY of funds required prior to the start of business. This is necessary as an operating fund for establishing a business and surviving its initial stage. With no funding, the business cannot be established. Many LCCs failed in Japan, but the new business model, as was seen in this study, is targeted to an appropriate size, so it should be highly profitable. Therefore, I believe investors who support the LCC business model suggested by this study, who fully understand the LCC business, can procure the initial funding.

Under these conditions, deregulation and European LCCs were analyzed and the results were incorporated into the business model to construct a corporate model. The conditions used in the simulation reflected the current aviation situation in 2017, and profitability and risks considering such were analyzed as well. As a result, a 10-year NPV totaled 56 billion JPY and VaR was also within an allowable range as a new business company. For example, cost per ASK of Skymark Airlines was 9.4 JPY, while it was 6.8 JPY for the new LCC. The profit and cost structure was individually reviewed, and these factors influence the simulation for improving the business' high validity.

3 Conclusion of Aviation Policy

As was discussed previously, institutional barriers in Japan restrict a significant part of the management policy. The results of the simulation analysis in Chapter 4 were compared to analyses in Chapter 3 and were eventually combined. This was to develop suggestions from the perspective of both competition and aviation policies, as shown below, and for reforming institutional and market structural factors, which hinder the degree of freedom in the management of LCCs.

1. Abolishment of Restrictions on Market Structures and Measures to Be Taken

As was discussed in Chapter 3, uneven distribution of management resources and possibility of predatory pricing by the LCs were critical factors in the late 1990s, when LCCs first entered the market. Now, these factors are no longer critical.

To solve the uneven distribution of management resources in the currently improved institutional environment of new airlines, an action taken by an LC to hinder fair competition must be individually dealt with in principle by after-the-fact regulation policy.

It is now also becoming more difficult to set a predatory price, as was noted in Chapter 3. When considering conditions of predatory pricing, it is not easy for an LC to set a price for a monopolistic route that is more than double the fare of the competitive route.

Though the monopolistic power of large airline companies is decreasing, there are still a considerable number of monopolized routes. In addition, there is a sizable disparity in the financial strength needed to survive the price competition between LCCs and LCs. As was analyzed in Chapters 3 and 4, new Japanese airline companies are vulnerable until they grow to a certain size. They are also weak in securing funds, and would be a loss for the market in the long run if some new airlines quit before establishing their management base, considering the effect of long-term competition. Furthermore, as mentioned previously in Chapter 3, the fact that the aviation market is not necessarily contestable must be taken into consideration.

In principle, the situation must be dealt with, not by the before-the-fact regulation, but by the after-the-fact regulation. Until a new and small airline company with low funds grows, regulations for restricting counteractive fares, however, must be implemented for obtaining a positive effect of long-term competition.

◘ 2. Complete Abolishment of Control over Supply and Demand Adjustment and Foreign Capital Restrictions

With the revisions made to the Aviation Act in 2000, it has been made legally possible for airline companies to choose routes on their own. However, now there are many traces of past regulating policies that work as institutional obstacles to free operations of newly participating airlines, as was discussed in Chapter 3. In reality, control over supply and demand is still performed by regulatory authority.

Therefore, as mentioned in Chapter 7, the following measures, which will affect both LCs and LCCs, must be taken into account for a completely free selection of routes and number of flights:

Firstly, it is vital that substantial supply and demand adjustments for arrival and departure slots in crowded airports are to be abolished. New airline companies now receive prioritized essential facility, so they do not have to encounter serious problems at the time of new entry. Essential facilities, however, are restricted in most hub airports. Regulatory authority can arbitrarily control the market through the distribution of arrival and departure slots, and such circumstances results in lessening the freedom of the management of the airline companies. This will have a negative effect on the healthy development of the aviation market.

Secondly, in conjunction with the liberalization of selecting routes and number of flights, the international aviation market itself must be liberalized. The results of the simulation analysis in Chapter 4 demonstrated that expansion of service to international routes would improve business profits. On the other hand, as was

Chapter 9

previously discussed in Chapter 3, Japan's international aviation policy can be characterized as protectionist in compliance with traditional bilateral agreements. This policy is restricting the free expansion of service to international flights for LCCs. Such a system has adverse effects on the development of LCCs in Japan and other Asian countries.

Thirdly, it is important for LCCs to start at a certain scale by utilizing funds from foreign risk-taking investors, including Asian nations. This is an important method for LCCs to procure funds, and to vitalize the Japanese aviation market.

In Asian countries other than Japan, LCCs occupy about one-third of the total share of the aviation market, mostly by Asian capital. Abolishment of foreign capital restrictions is expected to lead to proactive utilization of Asian capital with active investors. Moreover, abolishment of foreign capital restrictions means approving cabotage (domestic flight operations of foreign airline companies). Therefore, with the abolishment of foreign capital restrictions, the current cabotage prohibition policy will lose its purpose, in order words, the policy itself must be abolished as well. In addition, the contents of bilateral agreements must be liberalized.

Some might disagree, asserting that such measures might contribute to the development of foreign LCCs, and not to the development of Japan's LCCs. Abolishment of foreign capital restrictions, however, will lead the entry of foreign airline companies into the Japanese market. Management improvements in the airline companies, vitalization of the entire aviation market, and improvement of consumer profits stimulated by the measure will maximize public welfare. Introducing foreign capital means not only the introduction of funds, but also the introduction of new business approaches and management policies. Business know-hows and strategies developed in such a manner will stimulate Japanese businesses for regrowth, and examples for this can be seen in the manufacturing (Nissan Motor Co., Ltd, etc.) and other service industries.

Chapter 9

◻ 3. Promoting Proactive Use of Secondary Airports and Privatization of Airports

As shown in Chapter 3 and in the simulation results in Chapter 4, proactive use of secondary airports is a critical factor in the development of the LCCs. In addition, as mentioned in Chapter 5, privatization of airports, which started in 2016 in Japan, is equally significant. Nowadays, airports in Tokyo Metropolitan area, other than Tokyo International Airport and Narita International Airport, include Okegawa Airport and Chofu Airport for commercial aircraft, and Yokota, Atsugi, Iruma and Hyakuri for military use. Airports in other areas that are expected to play a role as secondary airports include Sapporo Okadama Airport in Sapporo, Komaki Airport in Nagoya, Hiroshimanishi Airport in Hiroshima, Kobe Airport in Kansai, and Kitakyushu Airport in Kitakyushu.

Utilizing secondary airports, as discussed previously in Chapter 3, is an advantageous measure for LCCs, since the airports are operating at lower costs. New companies can differentiate themselves from the LCs in the use of airports, and this also results in a wider selection of routes for users. Competition between LCCs and LCs as well as competition between airports will contribute to the expansion of public welfare.

Among the airports mentioned above, Kobe Airport, Kitakyushu Airport, Sapporo Okadama Airport, Komaki Airport and Hiroshimanishi Airport are operating for scheduled flights. The current regulation restricts the use of the airports to particular aviation services including commuter flights. With the abolishment of regulations for completely free entry to the market, these airports will function effectively as secondary airports.

As for the use of the military airports, discussion between the U.S. military and Japan's self-defense forces is required. With the end of the Cold War era, with no more urgent need for air defense in Tokyo Metropolitan area by neighboring military bases, the possibility of joint military and civilian use of airports must not be eliminated. There are already a large number of such airports in Japan.

In conjunction with the development of secondary airports, low-cost airport facilities and promotion of competition between airports are required. One of the reasons why worldwide LCCs utilize secondary airports is that the airport has low usage fees with simpler facilities, rather than high-level facilities seen in large airports with expensive usage fees. Moreover, standards of usage fees are set to promote competition between airports. Some larger airports such as Changi Airport in Singapore and Kuala Lumpur International Airport in Malaysia have implemented a policy to attract low-cost airline companies by offering simple facilities for LCCs.

Such circumstances demonstrate that competition between airports plays an important role in the development of LCCs. To promote such competition, it is necessary to allow airline companies to freely set the number of flights and routes, and have unrestricted use of airports. Furthermore, airport management entities must improve customer-oriented policies by privatizing airports.

◘ 4. Significance of Skymark Airlines' Entry in the Market

The reason behind the vague growth of LCCs was due to the bitter legacy of the industry. Skymark Airlines, which failed in the end, tried to overcome the problem. It can be said that Skymark Airlines changed the market, according to the three following reasons:

Firstly, Skymark Airlines challenged the Japanese regulations. Japan had not seen a deregulation trend nor a competition promotion, and instead, had been under strict regulations. In 1996, the scope of fare system was implemented, however, competition was inactive, and there was no drastic management strategy. Long-term studies said that the airline industry needed a company that would stir the market in order to vitalize the Japanese airline industry. Skymark Airlines did, to some extent.

There was a misunderstanding when LCCs entered the market due to deregulation. It was actually the other way round with Skymark Airlines challenging the regulations, and successfully changing them. Provoked by Skymark Airlines' establishment, MLIT began to study on authorizing the entry of LCCs, thus resulting in the abolishment of the lower limit of the fare. Initially, the ministry was against new entries due to restriction on the arrival and departure slots, but it altered its stance on the policy, due to a great deal of public attention and expectation.

Secondly, Skymark Airlines demonstrated performances on the deregulation process. Skymark Airlines' social role was that the airline market became competitive by its entry, and brought about improvements of consumer benefit and recovery of competition in the industry. In fact, when Skymark Airlines entered the market, the discount fare was introduced even on routes with no new entries. From this point, it provoked competitiveness of the three LCs and costs were reduced.

Thirdly, Skymark Airlines continues to fight against social climate and customs that are unique to Japan. The reason why new entrants do not perform well in Japan is due to Japanese social climates. The society tends to work against new challenges, and focuses on remedies, and in fact, Japan's domestic air traffic volume is ranked third in the world. There are a limited number of challengers, due to the delay in the deregulation process, failure of the new entrants, and the Japanese social climate itself that does not welcome new comers. Under such structure, capitalists would not be willing to invest, and new entrants need fund procurement capacity to survive the airfare competition until they are established in the market. However, there are currently no angelic investors in Japan, and it is therefore difficult to procure funds from the market. On the other hand, the irrational way of both parties, namely the new airline and public sectors, use the subsidy system which is an issue. New airline companies have a strong sense of dependence on the public sectors for assistance, and the public sectors are willing to assist them with subsidies. This trend in policy for all industries including the aviation industry, which allows an irrational way of using the remedy system, will encourage new entrants to depend on subsidies with no rational reason. Development of LCCs was hindered by the fact that the deregulation process was delayed; a long-term policy for the benefit of the three scheduled airline companies had lasted for a long period; no drastic measures to improve essential facility had been taken even though LCCs entered the market; and the government underwent an outdated policy of protecting LCs and rescuing LCCs. Skymark Airlines initially survived since they were standing against regulations and continued to operate its business with an independent spirit.

The problems of the aviation industry in Japan, as was discussed above, are not simply problems of deregulation. The Japanese cultural background and social structure are woven in a complicated manner to have an impact on the problem. The deregulation process was successful to a certain extent by Skymark Airlines's entry. However, in Japanese culture, people tend not to welcome newcomers and do not appreciate one with an innovative and out-of-the-box mind. Diversity like in the aviation industry in the U.S. is necessary in Japan. For a healthier market, both deregulation by the authorities and raising awareness of the people who will be involved in the aviation industry, including consumers, are required.

To conclude, Skymark Airlines contributed considerably to the market environment by the three aspects mentioned above: challenging regulations, promoting deregulation processes, and battling against old-fashioned social climate.

◘ 5. The Requirements for a Suitable Aviation Policy for LCCs

Therefore, the significance of this study is a new business model suitable for 2017 that is constructed by considering these points as well as the circumstance in which a couple of years have passed after deregulation, and by incorporating analysis results of the LCCs in North America and Europe.

In conclusion of this chapter, the following points from the perspective of both the competition and aviation policy are presented as key establishment elements of LCCs:

(1) It is necessary to prevent unfair competition. The market should shift, however, from before-the-fact regulation to after-the-fact regulation in conjunction with the development of competition in the aviation market, and for the purpose of encouraging LCCs to be independent from public financial support (regulations on counteractive fares must remain in effect).

(2) It is necessary to abolish supply and demand adjustments at crowded airports, liberalize protectionist international aviation agreements, and abolish foreign capital restrictions for free setting of routes and number of flights. Abolishment of foreign capital restrictions is expected to contribute to the procurement of initial funds and the vitalization of competition.

Chapter 9

(3) It is necessary to review the airport policy in order to promote the proactive utilization of secondary airports that is essential for LCCs. Airports must be privatized so that their functions will be simplified to fit the needs of low-cost airline companies, and that competition will be promoted between airports, which will contribute to the implementation of such measures.

4 Recommendation for Future Challenges

Firstly, this book focused on the simulation analysis and its results. Therefore, the main portion of the study is about management policies of LCCs including cost issues and pricing strategies. The study does include other management issues that are not appropriate for analysis. In particular, other important factors in the airline industry, such as service, corporate identity setting, management quality, and customer-targeting are not fully examined.

For instance, it is said that JetBlue Airways was successful in raising their initial investment due to the management personnel that had previous career experiences. Funding is only a partial reason for a company's successful business model and a visionary business leader with expertise, a clear management policy, and corporate identity play critical roles in the management of airline companies. Japanese LCCs tend to be more focused on emphasizing low fares as selling points, and this marketing strategy is likely to relate to their sluggishness. Japanese LCCs must develop their outstanding characteristics and strive to make their own company stand out from others, by referring to the examples of corporate identities such as "like-a-family" style by Southwest Airlines and "Now Everyone Can Fly" by AirAsia.

Secondly, some aspects of changes in the aviation market must be studied. Analyses in this research are based on business growth of new LCCs outside of Japan and international aviation regulations. The aviation industry, however, seems very unpredictable due to its fluctuating industrial nature. Making strategies based on trends and experiences are not sufficient resources, and additional considerations described below, are essential to adjust to these changes and make continuous improvements.

Chapter 9

The market shares of LCCs in North America and Europe have already become very large. This means that they are not able to further increase their market shares by implementing the same measures based on past trends and experiences. LCCs took advantage of the management and operation struggles of LCs and were able to conduct crew employment and ground handling, lease and purchase aircraft, and catering at a low cost. As newer entries come in, however, LCCs will face difficulties in maintaining lower costs, and therefore, increase capital charges.

In the near future, newer LCCs in North America and Europe will face other cost-related obstacles. Sluggishness of development is noticeable in the entire airline industry in North America and Europe, so the newer LCCs will face employment cost and labor union issues as their business expands, as well as system-related cost issues as their networks grow larger. LCCs' business transition to the long-distance flight services will require the use of hub airports instead of secondary airports, and entering the long-distance flight markets will further require a wider variety in the types of aircraft. The business transition of LCCs to the long-distance flight services will require the hub-and-spoke model, instead of secondary airport utilization. Furthermore, entering the long-distance flight markets require a wider variety of fleets, and by mixing and maintaining a variety of aircraft types, the fleet will cost LCCs even more.

Furthermore, LCs are utilizing the same strategies and implementing lower-cost models, competing against rivaling LCCs. For example, LCs are implementing effective allocation of human resources and route networks to enhance their productivity and reduce costs, and eventually have some affiliated LCCs, even though success has not been achieved yet. In the near future, LCs will accelerate their strategy in discontinuing touristic routes and focus on business routes, as seen in the example of JAL which discontinued its route to Saipan in 2005. LCs will prioritize high-yield business passengers by offering them advantages in transit and long-distance routes. As a result, LCCs should consider new business strategies, which correspond to future trends and expect more acceleration in this industry.

Thirdly, this book discussed the suitability of utilizing Kobe Airport, a secondary airport, as a main hub airport, but has not analyzed and compared the possibility of presenting military airports as hub airports. This comparison requires a considerable amount of additional analytical calculation, however it will be an additional resource that strongly and accurately supports the benefit of using secondary airports.

Lastly, there are many more issues to discuss regarding competition and the aviation policy. In particular, further studies are necessary on market contestability and side effects related to asymmetric regulations. These challenges are upcoming topics to be explored and discussed further with the development and growth of new Japanese airline companies.

It will be such a privilege if this book would somehow contribute to the vitalization of the Japanese aviation industry.

List of Abbreviation and Acronyms

AD	Airworthiness Directive
AEC	ASEAN Economic Community
ANA	All Nippon Airways
ANAHD	ANA Holdings
AOC	Air Operator's Certificate
ARING	Aeronautical Radio Incorporation
ASK	Available Seat Kilometer
ASM	Available Seat Mile
BAA	British Airports Authority
BS	Balance Sheet
CAA	Civil Aeronautics Act
CAAS	Civil Aviation Authority of Singapore
CAB	Civil Aviation Bureau
CAPA	Center for Aviation
CD	Certificate of Deposition
CEO	Chief Executive Officer
CF	Cash Flow Statement
CI	Corporate Identity
CRS	Computer Reservation System
CS	Customer Satisfaction
DBJ	Development Bank of Japan
DOT	Department of Transportation
EBIT	Earnings Before Interests and Taxes
EBITDA	Earnings Before Interest, Taxes, Depreciation, and Amortization
ES	Employee Satisfaction
ETIC	Enterprise Turnaround Initiative Corporation of Japan
EV	Enterprise Value
EVA	Economic Value Added
FAA	Federal Aviation Administration
FAC	Federal Airports Corporation
FDA	Fuji Dream Airlines
FE	First Eastern Investment Group
FFP	Frequent Flyer Program

List of Abbreviation and Acronyms

GSE	Ground Support Equipment
INCJ	Innovation Network Corporation of Japan
IPO	Initial Public Offering
IRC	Industrial Revitalization Corporation
IRR	Internal Rate of Return
ITC	Inclusive Tour Charter
JAL	Japan Airlines
JAS	Japan Air System
KLIA	Kuala Lumpur International Airport
LC	Legacy Carrier
LCC	Low-Cost Carrier
MAX	Maximum
METI	Ministry of Economy, Trade and Industry
MLIT	Ministry of Land, Infrastructure, Transport and Tourism
MIN	Minimum
MIT	Massachusetts Institute of Technology
MOF	Ministry of Finance
MOT	Management of Technology
MRO	Maintenance Repair and Overhaul facility
NPV	Net Present Value
PL	Profit and Loss Statement
PMA	Parts Manufacturer Approval
ROA	Return On Asset
ROE	Return On Equity
RPK	Revenue Passenger Kilometer
SITA	Society of International Telecommunications of Airline
SOC	Single Operating Certificate
ULD	Unit Load Device
VaR	Value at Risk
VoIP	Voice over-IP
WACC	Weighted Average Cost of Capital
WWII	World War II

The Structure of the Book and Relationship with Past Research

The starting point of this book is based on the results of nearly 20 years of research by the author and the initial works:

· Nippon ni okeru shinki kokugaisha seiritsuyoken no hokatsuteki kenkyu: Corporate model to real options ho wo mochiite [A comprehensive study of key aspects for a successful low-cost carrier in Japan: Using the corporate model and real options analysis]. Doctoral dissertation, Waseda University, 2007.

· *Shinki kokugaisha jigyoseiritsu no kenkyu: Nippon ni okeru business model to koku seisaku no kakushin* [*Key factors for the success of a low-cost carriers in Japan: Innovation in business models & aviation policy*]. (Chuokeizai-sha, 2008), which is the updated published version of the doctoral dissertation.

In order to publish this book, the author has conducted thorough research to update and revise her initial works, while keeping the fundamental viewpoints of her study. In addition, four new chapters, which is the culmination of such long period of research, have added newly updated information and data to explain the trend of recent years. The details are as follows. (Please see the references for more papers written by the author on aviation industry.)

Chapter 1 Objective and Contribution
Although the purpose of this research, problem awareness, and the significance of this book are in common with the following published works, the trend of the recent years and current situation are reflected and updated in this chapter.
· *Shinki kokugaisha jigyoseiritsu no kenkyu: Nippon ni okeru business model to koku seisaku no kakushin* [*Key factors for the success of a low-cost carriers in Japan: Innovation in business models & aviation policy*]. (Chuokeizai-sha, 2008).

Chapter 2 Recent Low-Cost Carriers (LCCs) of the World and Growth Factor Analysis
The following published work is updated with the growing LCCs worldwide as of 2017 and the key factors for the growth are analyzed.
· *Shinki kokugaisha jigyoseiritsu no kenkyu: Nippon ni okeru business model to koku seisaku no kakushin* [*Key factors for the success of a low-cost carriers in Japan: Innovation in business models & aviation policy*]. (Chuokeizai-sha, 2008).

Chapter 3 Current Japanese Low-Cost Carriers (LCCs) and Stagnancy Factor Analysis
The following published work is updated with the economic growth situation of LCCs within the Japanese aviation industry as of 2017 and the key factors for such growth are analyzed.
· *Shinki kokugaisha jigyoseiritsu no kenkyu: Nippon ni okeru business model to koku seisaku no kakushin* [*Key factors for the success of a low-cost carriers in Japan: Innovation in business models & aviation policy*]. (Chuokeizai-sha, 2008).

The Structure of the Book and Relationship with Past Research

Chapter 4 Identifying the Success Factors Through Simulations for New LCCs
The following published work was rewritten using the simulation methodology as a reference, updating the prerequisite data to that of 2017, along with the business model. Correspondingly, the conclusion is re-interpreted.
・ *Shinki kokugaisha jigyoseiritsu no kenkyu: Nippon ni okeru business model to koku seisaku no kakushin* [*Key factors for the success of a low-cost carriers in Japan: Innovation in business models & aviation policy*]. (Chuokeizai-sha, 2008).

Chapter 5 Reforming Airport Management in Japan: Effective Methods and the Necessity of Privatization
This chapter is especially written for this book. The basic viewpoint is based on the following two works. Additionally, the direction for the system reform regarding the future management of airports is presented.
・ Additional personal reviews and analysis. In A. Graham, *Managing airports: An international perspective* [*Kuko keiei: Mineika to kokusaika*]. (Chuokeizai-sha, 2010), (U. Chujo & S. Shiotani, translated into Japanese with a concise summary, additional personal reviews, and analysis inserted.)
・ Nippon no kuko keiei ni okeru kokusaika, mineika no hitsuyosei [A comparison of Japanese airport management with global trends]. *Journal of Japan Foundation for International Tourism, 21,* 2014.

The following three case studies are newly written to clarify the current status of the airline management and the aviation policy that surfaced due to the changing trends of the aviation market in Japan where LCCs have recently emerged.

Chapter 6 Skymark Airlines' Bankruptcy and Recovery: The Achievements and Misdeeds of Authoritarian Management of an "Independent LCC"
This chapter is especially written for this book.

Chapter 7 Japan Airlines: The Bankruptcy and Management Re-Establishment of a "Domesticated LC"
This chapter is especially written for this book.

Chapter 8 Peach Aviation: ANAHD's Successful Affiliated Japanized LCC
This chapter is especially written for this book.

Chapter 9 Conclusion and Future Challenges
Suggestions for the outdated aviation policy and aviation management are presented.

References

Books and Articles

Amram, M. (2002). *Value sweep: Mapping corporate growth opportunities*. Boston, MA: Harvard Business School Press.

Amram, M., & Kulatilaka, N. (1999). *Real options: Managing strategic investment in an uncertain world*. Boston, MA: Harvard Business School Press.

Arthur, W. B. (1996). Increasing returns and the new world of business. *Harvard Business Review, 74*(4), 100–109.

Baba, N. (2001). Optimal timing in banks' write-off decisions under the possible implementation of a subsidy scheme: A real options approach. *Monetary and Economic Studies, Bank of Japan, 19*(3), 113–141.

Bailey, E. E., & Panzar, J.C. (1981). The contestability of airline markets during the transition to deregulation. *Law & Contemporary Problems, 44*(1), 125–145.

Barrett, S. D. (2001). Market entry to the full-service airline market: A case study from the deregulated European aviation sector. *Journal of Air Transport Management, 7*(3), 189-193.

Barzagan, M. (2004). *Airline operations and scheduling*. Farnham, UK: Ashgate Publishing.

Beder, T. S. (1995). VAR: Senductive but dangerous. *Financial Analysts Journal*, September-October, 12–24.

Bennett, R. D., & Craun, J. M. (1993). The airline deregulation evolution continues: The southwest effect. Washington D.C.: Office of Aviation Analysis, U. S. Department of Transportation.

Berger, P. G., Ofek, E., & Swary, I. (1996). Investor valuation of the abandonment option. *The Journal of Financial Economics, 42*(2), 257–287.

Bernstein, P. L. (1992). *Capital ideas: The improbable origins of modern Wall Street*. New York, NY: Free Press.

Bernstein, P. L. (1996). *Against the gods: The remarkable story of risk*. New York, NY: John Wiley & Sons.

Black, F., & Scholes, M. (1973). The pricing of options and corporate liabilities. *The Journal of Political Economy, 81*(3), 637–654.

Bookstaber, R. M. (1987). *Option pricing and investment strategies*. Chicago, IL: Probus Publishing.

Boyle, P. P. (1977). Options: A Monte Carlo approach. *The Journal of Financial Economics, 4*, 323–338.

Brennan, M. J., & Schwartz, E. S. (1985). Evaluating natural resource investments. *The Journal of Business, 58*(2), 135–157.

Brennan, M. J., & Trigeorgis, L. (Eds.) (1998). *Flexibility, natural, resources and strategic options*. New York, NY: Oxford University Press.

Brian, S. S. (1997). Profitability, transactional alignment, and organizational mortality in the U. S. trucking industry. *Strategic Management Journal, 18*, 31–52.

Brown, J.S.(Ed.) (1997). *Seeing differently: Insights on innovation*. Boston, MA: Harvard Business School Press.

Brueckner, J. K. (2003). The benefits of codesharing and antitrust immunity for international passengers, with an application to the Star Alliance. *Journal of Air Transport Management, 9*, 83–89.

Campbell, J. Y, Lo, A. W., & MacKinlay, A. C. (1997). *The econometrics of financial markets*. Princeton, NJ: Princeton University Press.

Chang, Z. Y., Young, W. Y., & Loh, L. (1996). *The quest for global quality: A manifestation of total quality management by Singapore Airlines*. Singapore: Addison Wesley Longman Singapore Pte. Ltd.

Chin, A. T. H., & Tay, H. J. (2001). Developments in air transport: Implications on investment decisions, profitability and survival of Asian airlines. *Journal of Airline Transport Management, 7*, 319–330.

References

Christensen, C. M. (2000). *The innovator's dilemma: When new technologies cause great firms to fail.* New York, NY: Harper Business.

Chujo, U. (2005). Shinki sannyu kokugaisha wo meguru seisaku kadai [Policy issue of low-cost carriers]. *Journal of Airline Transport Management, 1,* 12–19.

Chujo, U., & Shiotani, S. (2010). Additional personal reviews and analysis. In A. Graham, *Managing airports: An international perspective* [*Kuko keiei: Mineika to kokusaika*]. (U. Chujo & S. Shiotani, translated into Japanese with a concise summary, additional personal reviews, and analysis inserted). Tokyo, Japan: Chuokeizai-sha (Original work published 2008).

Copeland, T. E., & Antikarov, V. (2001). *Real options: A practitioner's guide.* New York, NY: Texere LLC.

Copeland, T. E., Koller, T., & Murrin, J. (1990). *Valuation: Measuring and managing the value of companies.* New York, NY: John Wiley & Sons.

Cox, J. C., Ross, S. A., & Rubinstein, M. (1979). Option pricing: A simplified approach. *The Journal of Financial Economics, 7*(3), 229–263.

Dixit, A. K. (1989). Hysteresis, import penetration, and exchange rate pass-through. *The Quarterly Journal of Economics, 104*(2), 205–228.

Dixit, A. K., & Avinash, K. (1989). Entry and exit decisions under uncertainty. *The Journal of Political Economy, 97*(3), 620–638.

Dixit, A. K., & Pindyck, R. S. (1994). *Investment under uncertainty.* Princeton, NJ: Princeton University Press.

Dixit, A. K., & Pindyck, R. S. (1995). The options approach to capital investment. *Harvard Business Review,* May-June, 105–115.

Doganis, R. (2001). *The airline business in the 21st century.* London, UK: Routledge.

Edwards, F. R., & Ma, C. W. (1992). *Futures and options.* New York, NY: McGraw-Hill.

Evans, J. R., & Olson, D. L. (1998). *Introduction to simulation and risk analysis.* Upper Saddle River, NJ: Prentice-Hall.

Faulkner, T. (1996). Applying options thinking to R&D valuation. *Research Technology Management,* May-June, 50–56.

Foster, R. N., & Kaplan, S. (2001). *Creative destruction: Why companies that are built to last underperform the market—and how to successfully transform them.* New York, NY: Currency.

Francis, G., Fidato, A., & Humphreys, I. (2003). Airport-airline interaction: The impact of low-cost carriers on two European airports. *Journal of Air Transport Management, 9,* 267–273.

Francis, L., & Perrett, B. (2010). JAL's future. *Aviation Week & Space Technology, 172*(33), 42.

Freiberg, K., & Freiberg, J. (1998). *Nuts!: Southwest airlines' crazy recipe for business and personal success.* New York, NY: Crown Business.

Froot, K. A., Scharfstein, D. S., & Stein, J. C. (1994). A framework for risk management. *Harvard Business Review,* November-December, 91–102.

Fujimura, S. (2005). Nichi-Bei ni okeru ote to shinki no kyoso to ANA no senryaku [Competition of Japanese and US LCCs and business strategy of All Nippon Airways]. *Journal of Transportation and Economy, 65*(5), 35–41.

Gillen, D., & Morrison, W. (2003). Bundling, integration and the delivered price of air travel: Are low cost carriers full service competitors? *Journal of Air Transport Management, 9*(1), 15–23.

Gomez, E. T., & Jomo, K. S. (1997). *Malaysia's political economy: Politics, patronage and Profits.* Cambridge University Press.

Grabowski, H. G., & Vernon, J. M. (1994). Returns to R&D on new drug introductions in the 1980s. *Journal of Health Economics, 13,* 383–406.

References

Graham, A. (2010). *Managing airports: An international perspective* [Kuko keiei: Mineika to kokusaika]. (U. Chujo & S. Shiotani, Trans.). Tokyo, Japan: Chuokeizai-sha. (Original work published 2008).

Graham J. R., & Harvey, C. R. (2001). The theory and practice of corporate finance: Evidence from the field. *Journal of Financial Economics, 60*, 187–243.

Grenadier, S. R. (Ed.) (2000). *Game choices: The intersection of real options and game theory*. London, UK: Risk Books.

Grenadier, S. R., & Weiss, A. M. (1997). Investment in technological innovations: An option pricing approach. *The Journal of Financial Economics, 44*(3), 397–416.

Grenadier, S. R. (1996). The strategic exercise of options: Development cascades and overbuilding in real estate markets. *Journal of Finance, 51*, 1653–1679.

Grenadier, S. R. (1999). Information revelation through option exercise. *Review of Financial Studies, 12*, 95–129.

Grinblatt, M., & Titman, S. (1998) *Financial markets and corporate strategy*. New York, NY: McGraw-Hill.

Gudmundsson, S. V. (1998). *Flying too close to the sun: The success and failure of the new-entrant airlines*. Farnham, UK: Ashgate Publishing.

Gudmundsson, S. V., & van Kranenburg, H. L. (2002). New airline entry rates in deregulated air transport markets. *Transportation Research* (Part E), *38*, 205–219.

Hamel, G. (1997a). Strategy as revolution. *Harvard Business Review*, July-August, 69–82.

Hamel, G. (1997b). Killer strategies that make shareholders rich. *Fortune*, June 23, 70–84.

Hanaoka, S. (2005). Low cost carrier ga koku shijyo ni ataeru eikyo: Southeast Asia wo jirei to shite [Influence of low cost carrier in the aviation industry: Example of Southeast Asia]. *Series of Aviation Policy Research Association, 451*, 13–38.

Harbison, P. et al. (2002). *Low cost airlines in the Asia Pacific region*. Center for Asia Pacific Aviation.

Harvard Business Review (1999). *Harvard Business Review on financial engineering*. Boston, MA: Harvard Business School Press.

Hufbauer, G. C., & Findlay C. (Eds.) (1996). *Flying high: Liberalizing civil aviation in the Asia Pacific*. Washington, D.C.: US Institute for International Economics.

Hull, J. C. (1996). *Options, futures, and other derivatives securities* (3rd ed.). Englewood Cliffs, NJ: Prentice Hall Business Publishing.

Hull, J. C. (1997). *Introduction to futures and options markets* (3rd ed.). Englewood Cliffs, NJ: Prentice Hall Business Publishing.

Jamieson, B. (2007). More flights: Is discount biz class catching on? *ABC NEWS*, April 15, 2007.

Joaquin, D. C., & Khanna, N. (2001). Investment timing decisions under threat of potential competition. *The Quarterly Review of Economics and Finance, 41*(1), 1–17.

Joo, S.-J., & Fowler, K. L. (2014). Exploring comparative efficiency and determinants of efficiency for major world airlines. *Benchmarking: An International Journal, 21*(4), 675–687.

Jorion, P. (1997). *Value at risk: The new benchmark for managing financial risk*. New York, NY: McGraw-Hill.

Jorion, P. (1997). *Value at risk: The new benchmark for continuous market risk*. Burr Ridge, IL: Irwin Professional Publishing.

Kagawa, M. (Ed.) (2007). *Kankogaku dai jiten* [Dictionary of tourism]. Tokyo, Japan: Kirakusha.

Kogut, B., & Kulatilaka, N. (1994). Options thinking and platform investments: Investing in opportunity. *California Management Review, 36*(2), 52–71.

Kole, S. R., & Lehn, K. M. (1999). Deregulation and the adaptation of governance structure: The case of the U.S. airline industry. *Journal of Financial Economics, 52*(1), 79–117.

References

Konishi, A., & Dattatreya, R. E. (Eds.) (1996). *The handbook of derivative instruments* (2nd ed.). Burr Ridge, IL: Irwin Professional Publishing.

Kulatilaka, N. (1995). Operating flexibilities in capital budgeting: Substitutability and complementarity in real options. In L. Trigeorgis (Ed.), *Real options in capital investments: Models, strategies, and applications* (pp.121–132). Westport, CT: Praeger Publishers.

Kulatilaka, N., & Lessard, D. (1998). Total risk management. Working Paper, Sloan School of Management, MIT.

Kulatilaka, N., & Marcus, A. J. (1992). Project valuation under uncertainty: When does DCF fail? *Journal of Applied Corporate Finance*, 5(3), 92–100.

Kulatilaka, N., & Perotti, E. C. (1998). Strategic growth options. *Management Science*, 44(8), 1021–1031.

Kupiec, P. H. (1995). Techniques for verifying the accuracy of risk measurement models. *Journal of Derivative*, 3(2), 73–84.

Kwoka, J., Hearle, K., & Alepin, P. (2016). From the fringe to the forefront: Low cost carriers and airline price determination. *Review of Industrial Organization*, 48(3), 247–268.

Lawton, T. C. (2002). *Cleared for take-off: Structure and strategy in the low fare airline business*. Farnham, UK: Ashgate Publishing.

Litterman, R. (1996). Hot spots and hedges. *Journal of Portfolio Management*, Special issue, 23(5), 52–75.

Majd, S., & Pindyck, R. S. (1987). Time to build, option value, and investment decisions. *Journal of Financial Economics*, 18(1), 7–27.

Mason, K. J. (2001). Marketing low-cost airline services to business travelers. *Journal of Air Transport Management*, 7(2), 103–109.

Mauer, D. C., & Ott, S. H. (1995). Investment under uncertainty: The case of replacement investment decisions. *Journal of Financial and Quantitative Analysis*, 30(4), 581–605.

McDonald, R. L., & Seigel, D. R. (1985). Investment and the valuation of firms when there is an option to shut down. *International Economic Review*, 26, 331–349.

McMillan, J. (1992). *Games, strategies, and managers*. New York, NY: Oxford University Press.

Merton, R. C. (1997). Applications of option-pricing theory: Twenty-five years later. *Nobel Lecture*, December 9.

Milgrom, P., & Roberts, J. (1992), *Economics, organization and management*. Englewood Cliffs, NJ: Prentice-Hall.

Miller, K. D. (2003). Knowledge inventories and managerial myopia. *Strategic Management Journal*, 23(8), 689–706.

Miller, K. D., & Waller, H. G. (2003). Scenarios, real options and integrated risk management. *Long Range Planning*, 36(1), 93–107.

Miyoshi, C. (2015). Airport privatisation in Japan: Unleashing air transport liberalisation? *Journal of Airport Management*, 9(3), 210–222.

Morrison, S. A. (2001). Actual, adjacent and potential competition: Estimating the full effect of southwest airlines. *Journal of Transport Economics and Policy*, 35(2), 239–256.

Mun, J. (2002). *Real options analysis: Tools and techniques for valuing strategic investments and decisions*. New York, NY: John Wiley & Sons Inc.

Mun, J. (2004). *Applied risk analysis: Moving beyond uncertainty in business*. New York, NY: John Wiley & Sons Inc.

Murakami, H. (2005a). America kokunai shijo ni okeru tei hiyo kokugaisha ga shijo ni ataeta eikyo no jissho bunseki: 3 sha kasen koku shijo no case [Empirical analysis of low cost carrier's influence in the U. S. aviation market: Case of monopolized aviation market]. *Journal of Transportation and Economy*, 65(5), 53–61.

References

Murakami, H. (2005b). Nippon no LCC shijo ni okeru kyoso bunseki: Beikoku LCC no jirei wo sanko ni [Sustainability and market effect of the new LCCs: The case of the U. S. duopoly market]. *Journal of Economics & Business Administration*, 191(4), 85–95.

Murakami, H., Kato, K., Takahashi, N., & Sakakibara, Y.(Eds.) (2006). *Koku no keizaigaku* [*Economics of aviation*](pp.84–85). Kyoto, Japan: Minerva-shobo.

Murakami, H. (2011). Empirical analysis of inter-firm rivalry between Japanese full-service and low-cost carriers. *Pacific Economic Review*, 16(1), 103–119.

Myers, S. C, & Majd, S. (1990). Abandonment value and project life. *Advances in Futures and Options Research*, 4, 1–21.

Nichols, N. A. (1994). Scientific management at Merck: An interview with CFO Judy Lewent. *Harvard Business Review*, January-February, 89–99.

Nippon Academy of Management. (2006). *Keiei kyoiku jiten* [*Educational dictionary of business management*]. Tokyo, Japan: Gakubunsha.

O'Connell, J. F., & Williams, G. (2005). Passengers' perceptions of low cost airlines and full service carriers: A case study involving Ryanair, Aer Lingus, Air Asia and Malaysia Airlines. *Journal of Air Transport Management*, 11, 259–272.

Ohta, M. (1979). *Feasibility study of the new Tegucigalpa Airport Project*. JICA.

Ohta, M. (1981). *Koku yuso no keizaigaku* [The Economics of air transport]. Tokyo, Japan: Waseda University Press.

Ohta, M. (1983). *Feasibility study of international Lesotho Airport project*. JICA.

Ohta, M. (1986). *The feasibility study on the development project of Jorge Chavez Lima-Callao international airport in the Republic of Peru*. JICA.

Oliver Wyman (n.d.). *Airline economic analysis: For the Raymond James global airline book 2015–2016*. New York, NY: Marsh & Mclennan Companies.

O'Toole, K. (1999). Reworking the model. *Airline Business*, November, 78–83.

Pawlina, G., & Kort, P. M. (1999). Real options in an asymmetric duopoly: Who benefits from your competitive disadvantage? Working Paper, Tilburg University.

Pindyck, R. S. (1993). Investments of uncertain cost. *Journal of Financial Economics*, 34(1), 53–76.

Pindyck, R. S. (2000). Irreversibilities and the timing of environmental policy. *Resource and Energy Economics*, 22, 233–259.

Pindyck, R. S., & Rubinfeld, D. L. (1998) *Econometric models and economic forecasts* (4th ed.). New York, NY: McGraw-Hill.

Quigg, L. (1993). Empirical testing of real options: Pricing models. *Journal of Finance*, 48(2), 621–640.

Reynolds-Feighan, A. J. (2001). Traffic distribution in low-cost and full-service carrier networks in the US Air transportation market. *Journal of Air Transport Management*, 7(5), 265–275.

Ross, S. A. (1995). Uses, abuses, and alternatives to the net-present-value rule. *Financial Management*, 24(3), 96–102.

Sabbagh, K. (1996). *Twenty-first-century jet: The making and the marketing of the Boeing 777*. New York, NY: Scribner.

Sahlman, W. A. (1997). How to write a great business plan. *Harvard Business Review*, July–August, 98–109.

Sarkar, S. (2003). The effect of mean reversion on investment under uncertainty. *Journal of Economic Dynamics and Control*, 28, 377–396.

Sawada, H. (2005). *H.I.S.: Tsukue futatsu, denwa ippon kara no boken* [*HIS: Adventure from two desks and one telephone*]. Tokyo, Japan: Nikkei Publishing.

References

Schatzki, T. (2003). Options, uncertainty and sunk cost: An empirical analysis of land use change. *Journal of Environmental Economics and Management, 46*(1), 86–105.

Scholes, M. S. (1997). Derivatives in a dynamic environment. *Nobel Lecture*, December 9.

Schwartz, E. S., & Trigeorgis, L. (Eds.) (2001). *Real options and investment under uncertainty: Classical readings and recent contributions*. Cambridge, MA: The MIT Press.

Schwartz, E. S., & Moon, M. (1999). Evaluating research and development investments. In M. J. Brennan & L. Trigeorgis (Eds.), *Project flexibility, agency, and competition: New developments in the theory and applications of real options*. New York, NY: Oxford University Press.

Sheehan, J. J. (2013). *Business and corporate aviation management* (2nd ed.). New York, NY: McGraw-Hill.

Shibata, I. (2015). How Narita airport stakeholders came together to unleash low-cost carrier service. *The Air & Space Lawyer, 28*(4), 10–14.

Shiotani, S. (2002). *21 seiki no koku sangyo no kadai to tenbo: Global alliance wo chushin to shite* [*Tasks and prospects for the 21st century airline industry: Focusing on global alliance*]. Master's thesis, Waseda University.

Shiotani, S. (2003a). Kokugaisha no kokyaku manzoku(CS) senryaku: Japan Airlines no taio wo chushin to shite [Customer satisfaction strategy of the airline industry: The case of Japan Airlines]. *Journal of Japan Foundation for International Tourism, 10*, 49–55.

Shiotani, S. (2003b). Nippon ni okeru shinki kokugaisha no sannyu kanosei ni kansuru jissho bunseki: Corporate model simulation wo mochiita jigyo seiritsu kanosei wo fukumete [A case study of a new entrant airline into the Japanese airline market]. *Journal of Japan Society of Public Utility Economics, 55*(1), 79–91.

Shiotani, S. (2003c). Malaysia ni okeru " AirAsia" no keiei senryaku to jigyo tenkai: Asia no shinki kakuyasu kokugaisha no tenbo to wagakuni heno kyokun [AirAsia's market strategy and development in Malaysia: AirAsia's implications of Asia's budget airlines and its lessons for Japan]. *Journal of Japan Society of Logistics and Shipping Economics, 37*, 131–142.

Shiotani, S. (2004a). Koku jiyuka jidai ni okeru "national flag carrier" no senryaku to jigyo tenkai: Malaysia koku no case ga shisa suru mono [The strategy and business plan of "national flag carrier" of developing countries in the era of airline liberalization: A case study of Malaysia Airlines]. *Journal of Japan Foundation for International Tourism, 11*, 59–65.

Shiotani, S. (2004b). Kokugaisha no keiei senryaku to shite no global alliance no saikento: Wagakuni no kokugaisha ni okeru igi [The review of global alliance as airlines' management strategy: Its significance for Japan's airlines]. *Journal of the Graduate School of Asia-Pacific Studies, 6*, 151–169.

Shiotani, S. (2004c). Kokuki saiteki hacchu model ni okeru real option hyoka no tekiyo [Discussing methods of purchasing aircraft using the real option approach: Modeling the most appropriate number of aircraft]. *Aviation Policy Research Association, 436*, 23–44.

Shiotani, S. (2005a). Real option ho ni yoru shinki kokurosen kaisetsu koka no hyoka: Tei juyo, ko risk rosen kaisetsu model no kochiku [Evaluating an investment decision to expand new air routes for an airline company based on the real option approach]. *Journal of Public Utility Economics, 56*(4), 15–25.

Shiotani, S. (2005b). East Asia no kankokyaku yuchi ni mukete no hosaku: Yori miryokuteki na Nippon no sozo wo mezashite [Ways to increase tourists from East Asia: Toward an more attractive tourists-friendly Japan]. *Tokyo Seitoku Tanki Daigaku Kiyo, 38*, 1–10.

Shiotani, S. (2005c). Fundamental challenges for inbound tourism promotion: Toward creating a more attractive country with more openness and through deregulation? *Journal of Japan Foundation for International Tourism, 12*, 44–53.

Shiotani, S. (2005d). Mineika ni mukete no kuko kigyokachi suikei to kaikaku subeki seidoteki yoin: EV/

References

EBITDA ho ni yoru shisan to kigyokachi jitsugenka no tameno gutaiteki joken [Methods for estimating the value of airports toward privatization and several aspects for structural reform: The assessment based on EV/EBITDA method and specific conditions for realizing the company value]. *Journal of Japan Society of Logistics and Shipping Economics, 39,* 110–119.

Shiotani, S. (2006). Corporate Model ni yoru shinki kamotsu kokugaisha no seiritsu yoken no kenkyu: Monte Carlo ho ni yoru risk bunseki wo fukumete [Feasibility study on a newly entrant freight airline by a corporate-model simulation: With its risk assessment based on the Monte Carlo approach]. *Journal of Japan Logistics Society, 14,* 181–188.

Shiotani, S. (2007a). Nippon ni okeru shinki kokugaisha seiritsuyoken no hokatsuteki kenkyu: Corporate model to real option ho wo mochiite [A comprehensive study of key aspects for a successful low-cost carrier in Japan: Using the corporate model and real options analysis]. Doctoral dissertation, Waseda University.

Shiotani, S. (2007b). Koku yusojigyo ni okeru CS senryaku [Customer satisfaction strategy in the air transport industry], In Y. Mita, S. Shiotani & H. Nakatani, *Gendai no koku yusojigyo [Contemporary air transportation business]* (pp. 95–124). Tokyo, Japan: Doyukan.

Shiotani, S. (2008). *Shinki kokugaisha jigyoseiritsu no kenkyu: Nippon ni okeru business model to koku seisaku no kakushin [Key factors for the success of a low-cost carriers in Japan: Innovation in business models & aviation policy]*.Tokyo, Japan: Chuokeizai-sha.

Shiotani, S. (2009). Ajian Open-Sky koso no mondaiten to shutoken kuko seisaku no arikata [Issues on Asian Open-Sky initiatives and aviation policy related to Tokyo metropolitan airports]. *Annual bulletin of the Institute for Industrial Research of J.F Oberlin University, 76,* 10–13.

Shiotani, S. (2010a). Nippon no koku seisaku to kukoseisaku no mondaiten: "Asian Gateway Vision" wo chushin ni [Issues regarding Japan's aviation and airport policies: With a focus on its "Asian Gateway Vision" initiative]. *Annual bulletin of the Institute for Industrial Research of J. F. Oberlin University, 28,* 107–118.

Shiotani, S. (2010b). Gekika suru kyoka ni okeru kokugaisha no kokyaku (CS) senryaku: Japan Airlines no case [Airlines' customer satisfaction (CS) strategy in an increasingly competitive environment: The case of Japan Airlines]. *Hospitarity, 17,* 40–50.

Shiotani, S. (2010c). LCC (tei cost shinki kokugaisha) no keiei senryaku [Management strategy of low-cost carriers]. In Y. Mita, S. Shiotani, Y. Sakamaki & H. Nakatani, *Kanko rikkoku wo sasaeru koku yusojigyo [The Air transportation business that supports the tourism nation industry]* (pp. 57–80). Tokyo, Japan: Doyukan.

Shiotani, S. (2010d). Koku yusojigyo ni okeru CS senryaku [Customer satisfaction strategy in the air transport industry]. In Y. Mita, S. Shiotani, Y. Sakamaki & H. Nakatani, *Kanko rikkoku wo sasaeru koku yusojigyo [Air transportation business that supports the tourism industry]* (pp. 141–180). Tokyo, Japan: Doyukan.

Shiotani, S. (2011a). Koku yusojigyo no kikohendo taisaku to global sector approach: Post Kyoto giteisho he muketa jishuteki torikumi no kanosei [Air transportation industries' efforts to address climate change issues and the global sector approach: Possible voluntary measures toward a Post-Kyoto protocol era]. *Journal of Japan Foundation for International Tourism, 18,* 41–47.

Shiotani, S. (2011b). Sekai de major, Nippon de minor: Wasei LCC no senryaku to kongo no tenbo [LCC is popular in the world but not in Japan: Japanese LCC strategy and its prospects]. *KokuJoho, 61,* 42–45.

Shiotani, S. (2014). Nippon no kuko keiei ni okeru kokusaika, mineika no hitsuyosei [A comparison of Japanese airport management with global trends]. *Journal of Japan Foundation for International Tourism, 21,* 41–46.

Shiotani, S. (2015). Lead user methodology for innovation: A case study of Nissin Foods' Cup Noodles.

References

International Journal of Japan Academic Society of Hospitality Management, 3(1), 23–29.

Shiotani, S. (2017a). Customized business model for regional revitalization support: Innovative banking strategy for sustainable entrepreneurship. *International Journal of Japan Academic Society of Hospitality Management, 4*(1), 19–29.

Shiotani, S. (2017b). Targeting high end clients in international business expansion: Hospitality management as a part of foreign private banking strategy in domestic markets. *International Journal of Japan Academic Society of Hospitality Management, 4*(1), 31–40.

Shiotani, S. (2017c). Sharing economy: Shinrai kankei ni yoru atarashii platform no sokushin [Sharing economy: Platform advancement for trust systemization]. *Journal of Japan Foundation for International Tourism, 24*, 145–154.

Shiotani, S., & Chujo, U. (2005)."Kanko rikkoku" heno gimon: Inbound kanko seisaku to kanren kotsu seisaku ni okeru open ka no hitsuyosei [Is the "Visit Japan" campaign relevant?: Openness and deregulation are needed to promote Japan's inbound tourism]. *The Japan Society of Transportation Economics, 49*, 31–40.

Shiraishi, Y., & Hirata, T. (2015). Analysis of the impact of abandoned direct air routes on inter-regional passenger travel flows in Japan. *Journal of the Eastern Asia Society for Transportation Studies, 11*, 2333–2346.

Silverman, B. S., Nickerson, J. A., & Freeman, J. (1997). Profitability, transactional alignment, and organizational mortality in the U.S. trucking industry. *Strategic Management Journal, 18*, 31–52.

Sinclair, R. A. (1995). An empirical model of entry and exit in airline markets. *Review of Industrial Organization, 10*(5), 541–557.

Smith, J. E., & Nau, R. F. (1995). Valuing risky projects: Option pricing theory and decision analysis. *Management Science, 41*(5), 795–816.

Sparaco, P. (2010). JAL trauma triggers bad memories of other downfall. *Aviation Week & Space Technology, 172*(5).

The Aircraft Value Analysis Company Limited (AVAC). (2001–2005). *Aircraft Value Reference, Commercial Jet*, AVAC.

The Center for Asia Pacific Aviation (CAPA). (2003). Asia pacific aviation outlook, post-sars 2003.

The Japan Port Economics Association. (2011). *Umi to sora no minato dai jiten* [*Dictionary of ports and airports*]. Tokyo, Japan: Seizando-shoten.

The Japan Society of Transportation Economics. (2011). *Kotsu keizai handbook* [*The handbook of transportation economics*]. Tokyo, Japan: Hakuto-shobo.

Titman, S. (1985). Urban land prices under uncertainty. *American Economic Review, 75*(3), 505–514.

Tretheway, M. (2011). Comment on "legacy carriers fight back". *Journal of Air Transport Management, 17*(1), 40–43.

Triantis, A. J., & Hodder, J. E. (1990). Valuing flexibility as a complex option. *The Journal of Finance, 45*(2), 549–565.

Tufano, P. (1996). How financial engineering can advance corporate strategy. *Harvard Business Review*, January-February, 136–146.

Tufano, P., & Bhatnager. S. (1994). Enron gas services. *Harvard Business School Case, No.294–076*.

Tufano, P., & Moel, A. (2000). Bidding for antamina: Incentives in a real option context. In S. Grenadier (Ed.), *Game choices: The intersection of real options and game theory* (pp.197–220). London, UK: Risk Books.

Williams, G. (2000). *The airline industry and the impact of deregulation*, Farnham, UK: Ashgate Publishing.

Williams, G. (2002). *Airline competition: Deregulation's mixed legacy*. Farnham, UK: Ashgate Publishing.

Windle, R., & Dresner, M. (1999). Competitive responses to low cost carrier entry. *Transportation Research,*

References

35E(1), 59–74.

Yabe, R., & Honma, Y. (2014). Optimal airline networks, flight volumes, and the number of crafts for new low-cost carrier in Japan. Selected papers of the annual international conference of the German Operations Research Society (GOR), RWTH Aachen University, Germany.

Yamaguchi, K. (2011). Cross-border integration in Northeast Asian air transport market. *Pacific Economic Review, 16*(1), 47–63.

Yi, C. (1997). Real and contractual hedging in the refinery industry. *DBA Dissertation.* School of Management, Boston University.

Corporate Publications (Annual Report, Press Release, etc.)

Administrative Reform Committee (1997). *New Japan creating by imagination*, Institute of Administrative Management.

AirAsia, *AirAsia press release*, n. d. Web. 11 April 2013.

Airbus S.A.S., *Document for in-house education for All Nippon Airways Co., Ltd. employees*, August. 1989. Web. 10 April 2013.

Air Canada, *Annual report*, n. d. Web. 1 January 2017.

Aircraft Value Analysis (AVAC) (2001–2005). *Aircraft value reference, commercial jet*, AVAC.

American Airlines, *Operating analysis*, n. d. Web. 1 January 2017.

ANA Group, *Annual report*, n. d. Web. 1 January 2017.

ANA Group, *Fact book*, n. d. Web. 1 January 2017.

British Airways, *Annual report*, n. d. Web. 1 January 2017.

British Airways, *British Airways fact book*, n. d. Web. 1 January 2017.

easyJet, *easyJet annual report and accounts*, n. d. Web. 1 January 2017.

Frontier Airlines, *Annual report*, n. d. Web. 1 January 2017.

IATA (2000–2005). *Airport & air navigation charges manual*, IATA.

ICAO (2000–2005). *Financial data: Commercial air carriers / Cargo tariff*, ICAO.

Japan Airlines, *Aviation statistics handbook 2000–2005*, Japan Aeronautic Association, n. d. Web. 1 January 2017.

Japan Airlines, *Community@JALStockholder communication*, n. d. Web. 1 January 2017.

Japan Airlines, *Currents 1999–2016*, n. d. Web. 1 January 2017.

Japan Airlines, *Public relations department*, n. d. Web. 1 January 2017.

Japan Airlines, *Recollection and the prospects*, n. d. Web. 1 January 2017.

Japan Airlines, *Japan Airlines annual report*, Japan Airlines Company and Consolidated Subsidiaries, n. d. Web. 1 January 2017.

Japan Airlines, *Securities report,* n. d. Web. 1 January 2017.

Japan Airlines, *SKYWARD*, n. d. Web. 1 January 2017.

JetBlue Airways, *JetBlue's 2016 annual report*, n. d. Web. 1 January 2017.

JetBlue Airways, *Prospects*, n. d. Web. 1 January 2017.

Skymark Airlines, *Business report*, n. d. Web. 1 January 2017.

Skymark Airlines, *Securities report*, n. d. Web. 1 January 2017.

Skymark Airlines, *Statement of accounts*, n. d. Web. 1 January 2017.

United Airlines, *Corporation annual report*, n. d. Web. 1 January 2017.

WestJet, *Annual information*, n. d. Web. 1 January 2017.

References

Website

AirAsia ⟨http://www.airasia.com/⟩ (Accessed January 1, 2017)
AirAsia, AirAsia Corporate Information (Investors information) ⟨http://www.airasia.com/site/en/home.jsp/⟩ (Accessed January 1, 2017)
Air Do ⟨http://www.airdo21.com/⟩ (Accessed January 1, 2017)
Air Do ⟨http://www.airdo21.com/company/info.html/⟩ (Accessed January 1, 2017)
All Nippon Airways ⟨http://www.ana.co.jp/⟩ (Accessed January 1, 2017)
All Nippon Airways, All Nippon Airways Corporate Information (Investors information) ⟨http://www.ana.co.jp/group/investors/⟩ (Accessed January 1, 2017)
American Airlines ⟨http://www.aa.com/⟩ (Accessed January 1, 2017)
An airport, airline-affiliated Web site Airbus ⟨http://www.airbus.com/en/⟩ (Accessed January 1, 2017)
ANA Group ⟨http://www.ana.co.jp/group/company/⟩ (Accessed January 1, 2017)
Aviation Wire ⟨http://www.aviationwire.jp/archives/tag/sky⟩ (Accessed January 1, 2017)
Center for Asia Pacific Aviation ⟨https://centreforaviation.com⟩ (Accessed January 1, 2017)
Continental Airlines ⟨http://www.continental.com/⟩ (Accessed January 1, 2017)
Chubu Centrair International Airport ⟨http://www.centrair.jp/⟩ (Accessed January 1, 2017)
Delta Air Lines ⟨http://www.delta.com/⟩ (Accessed January 1, 2017)
EasyJet ⟨http://www.easyjet.com/⟩ (Accessed January 1, 2017)
Fukuoka Airport ⟨http://www.fuk-ab.co.jp/⟩ (Accessed January 1, 2017)
Haneda Airport (Tokyo International Airport) ⟨http://www.tokyo-airport-bldg.co.jp/⟩ (Accessed January 1, 2017)
IATA ⟨http://www.iata.org/⟩ (Accessed January 1, 2017)
Ibaraki Airport ⟨http://www.ibaraki-airport.net/⟩ (Accessed January 1, 2017)
Japan Aeronautic Association ⟨http://www.aero.or.jp/⟩ (Accessed January 1, 2017)
Japan Airlines ⟨http://www.jal.co.jp/⟩ (Accessed January 1, 2017)
Japan Airlines, Japan Airlines Corporate Information (Investors information) ⟨http://www.jal.com/ja/ir/⟩ (Accessed January 1, 2017)
Japanese Prime Minister's Office ⟨http://www.kantei.go.jp/⟩ (Accessed January 1, 2017)
Japan Tourism Agency ⟨http://www.mlit.go.jp/kankocho/en/index.html⟩ (Accessed January 1, 2017)
JetBlue Airways, JetBlue Airways Corporate Information (Investors information) ⟨http://investor.jetblue.com/ireye/ir_site.zhtml?ticker=jblu&script=2100/⟩ (Accessed January 1, 2017)
Kansai Airports ⟨http://www.kansai-airports.co.jp/en/index.html⟩ (Accessed January 1, 2017)
Kansai International Airport ⟨http://www.kansai-airport.or.jp/⟩ (Accessed January 1, 2017)
Kobe Airport ⟨http://www.kairport.co.jp/⟩ (Accessed January 1, 2017)
Malaysian Airlines ⟨http://www.malaysianairlines.com.my/⟩ (Accessed January 1, 2017)
Ministry of Economy, Trade and Industry ⟨http://www.meti.go.jp/⟩ (Accessed January 1, 2017)
Ministry of Finance ⟨http://www.mof.go.jp/⟩ (Accessed January 1, 2017)
Ministry of Land, Infrastructure, Transport and Tourism ⟨http://www.mlit.go.jp/⟩ (Accessed January 1, 2017)
MRO Japan ⟨https://www.mrojpn.co.jp/en/about/⟩ (Accessed January 1, 2017)
Narita International Airport ⟨http://www.narita-airport.jp/⟩ (Accessed January 1, 2017)
Northwest Airlines ⟨http://www.nwa.com/⟩ (Accessed January 1, 2017)
One World ⟨http://www.oneworld.net/⟩ (Accessed January 1, 2017)
Osaka International Airport ⟨https://www.osaka-airport.co.jp/en/⟩ (Accessed January 1, 2017)
Peach Aviation ⟨http://www.flypeach.com/pc/jp/⟩ (Accessed January 1, 2017)

References

Ryan Air 〈http://www.ryanair.com/〉 (Accessed January 1, 2017)
Ryan Air, Ryan Air Corporate Information (Investors information) 〈http://www.ryanair.com/site/EN/about.php?page=Invest&sec=reports/〉 (Accessed January 1, 2017)
Sendai International Airport 〈https://www.sendai-airport.co.jp/〉 (Accessed January 1, 2017)
Skymark Airlines 〈http://www.skymark.co.jp/〉 (Accessed January 1, 2017)
Skymark Airlines, Skymark Airlines Corporate Information (Investors information) 〈http://www.skymark.co.jp/company/index.html〉 (Accessed January 1, 2017)
Skynet Asia Airways 〈http://pc.skynetasia.co.jp/〉 (Accessed January 1, 2017)
Skynet Asia Airways Corporate Information (Investors information) 〈http://www.skynetasia.co.jp/company/group.html〉 (Accessed January 1, 2017)
SkyTeam Airline Alliance 〈http://www.skyteam.com/〉 (Accessed January 1, 2017)
Southwest Airlines 〈http://www.southwest.com/〉 (Accessed January 1, 2017)
Southwest Airlines, Southwest Airlines Corporate Information (Investor information) 〈http://www.southwest.com/about_swa/financials/investor_relations_index.html/〉 (Accessed January 1, 2017)
Spirit Airlines 〈https://www.spirit.com/Default.aspx〉 (Accessed January 1, 2017)
Star Alliance 〈http://www.staralliance.com/〉 (Accessed January 1, 2017)
Star Flyer 〈http://www.starflyer.jp/mothercomet/mothercomet.html/〉 (Accessed January 1, 2017)
The Center for Asia Pacific Aviation 〈http://www.centreforaviation.com/〉 (Accessed January 1, 2017)
United Airlines 〈http://www.united.com/〉 (Accessed January 1, 2017)
Value Alliance 〈http://www.valuealliance.com/〉 (Accessed January 1, 2017)
Vanilla Air 〈http://www.vanilla-air.com/jp/〉 (Accessed January 1, 2017)
World Tourism Organization (UNWTO) 〈http://www2.unwto.org/〉 (Accessed January 1, 2017)

Other Websites Concerned

Airline Comparison Site 〈http://www.airlinequality.com/〉 (Accessed January 1, 2017)
Central Japan Railway Company 〈http://www.jr-central.co.jp/〉 (Accessed January 1, 2017)
Federal Reserve System 〈http://www.ny.frb.org/〉 (Accessed January 1, 2017)
Flying Cheap! European Bargain Aviation 〈http://europe.s9.xrea.com/〉 (Accessed January 1, 2017)
Government Accountability Office 〈http://www.ntl.bts.gov/DOCS/rc9599.htm/〉 (Accessed January 1, 2017)
Japan Fair Trade Commission 〈http://www.jftc.go.jp/〉 (Accessed January 1, 2017)
Kobe-city, Japan 〈http://www.city.kobe.jp〉 (Accessed January 1, 2017)
Nippon Express 〈http://www.nittsu.co.jp/〉 (Accessed January 1, 2017)
Stern Value Management 〈https://sternvaluemanagement.com/〉 (Accessed January 1, 2017)
Tax Navigator 〈http://www.tax-navi.com/kokuzei/koukukinenryo/〉 (Accessed January 1, 2017)
The Hokkaido Shimbun Press 〈http://www.hokkaido-np.co.jp/〉 (Accessed January 1, 2017)
United Parcel Service (UPS) 〈http://www.ups.com/〉 (Accessed January 1, 2017)
Yamato Transport 〈http://www.kuronekoyamato.co.jp/〉 (Accessed January 1, 2017)

Flying Smart with Low-Cost Carriers in Japan:
A Numerical Analysis of Innovative
Business Strategies in the Aviation Industry　　KGU叢書

■発行日──2017年3月31日　初版発行　　　　　〈検印省略〉

■著　者──塩谷さやか

■発行者──大矢栄一郎

■発行所──株式会社　白桃書房
　　　　　〒101-0021　東京都千代田区外神田5-1-15
　　　　　☎03-3836-4781　📠03-3836-9370　振替00100-4-20192
　　　　　　http://www.hakutou.co.jp/

■印刷・製本──藤原印刷

Ⓒ Sayaka Shiotani 2017　Printed in Japan　ISBN978-4-561-76217-1 C3365

|JCOPY| 〈(社)出版者著作権管理機構　委託出版物〉
本書の無断複写は著作権法上での例外を除き禁じられています。複写される場合は，そのつど事前に，(社)出版者著作権管理機構（電話03-3513-6969，FAX03-3513-6979，e-mail: info@jcopy.or.jp）の許諾を得てください。

落丁本・乱丁本はおとりかえいたします。

関東学院大学経済学会叢書（KGU叢書）発刊にあたって

大学をとりまく社会的、経済的環境が変化する中で、大学が果たすべき役割も、それに対応して変化していく。本叢書はこのような現状認識のもとに発刊される。

高等教育の実施機関としての大学の役割は、これまでのように、理論研究とその教育の場といったアカデミズムから、現実に生起する具体的な問題への応用研究と、その成果の教育へのフィードバックという新しい局面への適応も求められるようになってきている。

多様な社会的経済的現象の観察からの仮説設定、仮説の実証に向けた理論的再構築、意識に対する有効性の視点から評価されるべきものであり、その評価が大学における研究と教育に反映されることで「開かれた大学」としての新しい役割を担うことが可能になると考えている。

関東学院大学は源流を溯れば百年以上の歴史をもち、旧制高商部を拡充した経済学部としても半世紀にならんとしている。本経済学会は、経済学部の教員・学生を構成員とするものである。本学における研究が、この情報発信を契機として社会的評価を受けることで「机上の空論」の回避を期待している。また、高学歴社会における大学の役割として、単に学部学生だけでなく、社会人に対するリカレント教育にも十分対応できる情報発信でありたいとも考えている。これも「開かれた大学」の重要な要素であろう。

本叢書はここに産声を上げるが、その成長は学部スタッフの努力と精進、そしてその社会的評価にかかっていることを銘記しておきたい。

一九九三年十一月十六日

関東学院大学経済学会　会長　石崎悦史